CONTESTING RACE
AND CITIZENSHIP

CONTESTING RACE AND CITIZENSHIP

Youth Politics in the Black Mediterranean

Camilla Hawthorne

CORNELL UNIVERSITY PRESS   ITHACA AND LONDON

Thanks to generous funding from the University of California Santa Cruz, the Hellman Fellowship, and the Social Sciences Research Council, the ebook editions of this book are available as open access volumes through the Cornell Open initiative.

First published 2022 by Cornell University Press

Library of Congress Cataloging-in-Publication Data

Names: Hawthorne, Camilla A., author.
Title: Contesting race and citizenship: youth politics in the black Mediterranean / Camilla Hawthorne.
Description: Ithaca [New York]: Cornell University Press, 2022. | Includes bibliographical references and index.
Identifiers: LCCN 2021056142 (print) | LCCN 2021056143 (ebook) | ISBN 9781501762284 (hardcover) | ISBN 9781501762291 (paperback) | ISBN 9781501762307 (pdf) | ISBN 9781501762314 (epub)
Subjects: LCSH: Blacks—Political activity—Italy. | Citizenship—Political aspects—Italy. | Blacks—Italy—Social conditions. | Racism—Political aspects—Italy. | Italians—Race identity. | Italy—Race relations—Political aspects. | Italy—Emigration and immigration—Social aspects.
Classification: LCC JN5593 .H38 2022 (print) | LCC JN5593 (ebook) | DDC 323/.0420945—dc23/eng/20211129
LC record available at https://lccn.loc.gov/2021056142
LC ebook record available at https://lccn.loc.gov/2021056143

CONTESTING RACE AND CITIZENSHIP

Youth Politics in the Black Mediterranean

Camilla Hawthorne

CORNELL UNIVERSITY PRESS   ITHACA AND LONDON

Thanks to generous funding from the University of California Santa Cruz, the Hellman Fellowship, and the Social Sciences Research Council, the ebook editions of this book are available as open access volumes through the Cornell Open initiative.

First published 2022 by Cornell University Press

Library of Congress Cataloging-in-Publication Data

Names: Hawthorne, Camilla A., author.
Title: Contesting race and citizenship: youth politics in the black Mediterranean / Camilla Hawthorne.
Description: Ithaca [New York]: Cornell University Press, 2022. | Includes bibliographical references and index.
Identifiers: LCCN 2021056142 (print) | LCCN 2021056143 (ebook) | ISBN 9781501762284 (hardcover) | ISBN 9781501762291 (paperback) | ISBN 9781501762307 (pdf) | ISBN 9781501762314 (epub)
Subjects: LCSH: Blacks—Political activity—Italy. | Citizenship—Political aspects—Italy. | Blacks—Italy—Social conditions. | Racism—Political aspects—Italy. | Italians—Race identity. | Italy—Race relations—Political aspects. | Italy—Emigration and immigration—Social aspects.
Classification: LCC JN5593 .H38 2022 (print) | LCC JN5593 (ebook) | DDC 323/.0420945—dc23/eng/20211129
LC record available at https://lccn.loc.gov/2021056142
LC ebook record available at https://lccn.loc.gov/2021056143

For Dorothy and Nathaniel

Oh eh oh, quando mi dicon "va' a casa"
Oh eh oh, rispondo "sono già qua"
— Ghali, "Cara Italia"

"Saldi, saldi, saldi!"
teniamoci saldi
nell'interregno
tra le sindromi morbose
sindoni irradiate
antropogenici cambiamenti
antropologici mutamenti
e ammutinamenti
costituzionali scrostamenti
e crollo di nazioni.
Negli interstizi
vaga la voce,
fluisce la nota
che la bussola resetta
e come arca
spera e aspetta.
— Pina Piccolo, "Interregno"

Contents

Acknowledgments

It should go without saying that a book is always a collective effort, rather than a singularly individual one. At the time of writing, this project has been with me for over a quarter of my life; as a result, it has been profoundly shaped by innumerable people, communities, and institutions. My editor at Cornell University Press, Jim Lance, and my developmental editor, Steve Hiatt, have shepherded this book through its many stages with immense care and attention, and cartographer Mike Bechthold created two beautiful illustrations for the manuscript. At UC Berkeley, I am deeply indebted to my dissertation committee—Jake Kosek, Michael Watts, Donald Moore, and Stephen Small—for their unwavering support and guidance over the years. I am also grateful for the way that our mentoring relationships have evolved into deep and meaningful friendships. It is not an exaggeration to say that I would not have finished my PhD if it were not for my powerhouse of a graduate cohort in the geography department, and especially the sisterhood that we still to this day lovingly refer to as the "Geogrababes"—Andrea Marson, Meredith Palmer, Erin Torkelson, and Mollie Van Gordon. Beyond my cohort, Ilaria Giglioli was and continues to be a trusted interlocutor on questions of racial boundary drawing in the Mediterranean. In addition, my many stimulating discussions with Angelo Matteo Caglioti about racial science in Liberal and Fascist Italy through the Center for Science, Technology, Medicine, and Society at UC Berkeley Italy influenced this book in profound ways.

I feel incredibly lucky to have found several amazing "homes" at my current institution of UC Santa Cruz. My colleagues in the sociology department—Hillary Angelo, Julie Bettie, Lindsey Dillon, James Doucet-Battle, Hiroshi Fukurai, Debbie Gould, Miriam Greenberg, Naya Jones, Juhee Kang, Rebecca London, Christie McCullen, Steve McKay, Megan McNamara, Jaimie Morse, Jenny Reardon, and Veronica Terriquez—have given me hope about the future of academia. Together, they have worked to model a rare kind of departmental culture founded on respect for rigorous, interdisciplinary research; support for the career success of all colleagues; care for each other's well-being; and a dedication to research oriented toward social justice. I am also grateful to the community that is the Critical Race and Ethnic Studies Program at UCSC. Neda Atanasoski, Christine Hong, Jennifer Kelly, and Nick Mitchell in particular have provided immeasurable intellectual, political, and emotional comradeship over the years as I navigate junior faculty life. Finally, the Theorizing Race after Race research group at the Science and Justice Research Center has been a fruitful site of transdisciplinary engagement with questions of scientific knowledge production and the reproduction of racisms in the twenty-first century.

All along the way, my community at UC Santa Cruz has continued to grow and expand, even in the midst of the COVID-19 pandemic during which I am currently writing. Whether through (prepandemic) dumpling parties with Amy Mihyang Ginther, A. M. Darke, Muriam Davis, and Nidhi Mahajan, epic Dungeons & Dragons campaigns with micha cárdenas, Michael Chemers, Marcia Ochoa, and Elizabeth Swensen, or socially distanced Seabright walks with Lily Balloffet, I have found myself consistently surrounded by brilliant, caring, and politically fierce friends.

This book has been touched by more friends, comrades, and interlocutors in Italy than I could possibly list here—including Stephanie Adams, Angela Haisha Adamou, Evelyne Afaawua, Aida Bodian, Marilena Delli, Kwanza Musi Dos Santos, Gail Milissa Grant, Tommy Kuti, Fred Kuwornu, Ruth Maccarthy, Theophilus Marboah, Ark Joseph Ndulue, Medhin Paolos, Tamara Pizzoli, Adama Sanneh, Kibra Sebhat, Rahel Sereke, Ariam Tekle, Selam Tesfai, and Veronica Costanza Ward. I am also grateful for the community of academics and researchers I met over the course of my research in Italy who are dedicated to antiracism and anticolonialism, including Sandra Kyremeh, Barbara Ofosu-Somuah, Igiaba Scego, Mackda Ghebremariam Tesfau', Candice Whitney, Annalisa Frisina, Gaia Giuliani, Valentina Migliarini, and Pina Piccolo. I am especially proud to be a member of the Black Mediterranean Research Collective, alongside Ida Danewid, Vivian Gerrand, Giulia Grechi, Giuseppe Grimaldi, Christina Lombardi-Diop, Angelica Pesarini, Gabriele Proglio, Timothy Raeymakers, and P. Khalil Saucier. I have also benefited from the mentorship, support, and guidance of many other scholars of Italy and Black Europe, including Jacqueline Nassy Brown, John Gennari, Cristiana Giordano, Stephanie Malia Hom, Heather Merrill, Ann Morning, Olivette Otele, Lorgia García Peña, Laura Ruberto, and Angeline Young. And I could not have carried out the archival portion of my research without Cristina Cilli, head archivist at the Archivio Lombroso at the University of Turin's Museo di Antropologia Criminale "Cesare Lombroso"; Giacomo Giacobini, scientific director of the Archivio Carlo Giacomini at the Museo di Anatomia Umana "Luigi Ronaldo"; Gianluigi Mangiapane, researcher at the Museum of Anthropology and Ethnography at the University of Turin; and Giorgio Manzi and Giovanni Destro Bisol of the Istituto Italiano di Antropologia.

Two other scholarly communities have left an indelible imprint on this work. Over the eight years of my involvement in the program, the Black Europe Summer School has become something of a family to me. Kwame Nimako, Mano Delea,

Philomena Essed, Jennifer Tosch, and Melissa Weiner in particular have supported and nurtured my growth as a scholar of Black Europe. And the growing field of Black geographies has become my intellectual home—a source of theoretical insight, mutual support, and political inspiration. The Berkeley Black Geographies Project (Jovan Scott Lewis and Brandi Summers); the UC Santa Cruz Black Geographies Lab (Naya Jones, Savannah Shange, Breanna Bryd, Elsa Calderon, Xafsa Ciise, shah noor hussein, Theresa Hice Johnson, Christopher Lang, Ki'Amber Thompson, Andrea del Carmen Vásquez, and Axelle Tousaint); and the Black Geographies Specialty Group of the American Association of Geographers (especially the group's founder LaToya Eaves) have all profoundly shaped my thinking about the entanglements of racism, spatiality, and liberation.

Words cannot express the love and gratitude I hold for my parents Gigliola and Edward, who have been a rock of support throughout this entire project. They have read every word of this book (or listened to me read it) multiple times; they have been a sounding board for my ideas; and they have buoyed me with encouragement when I was feeling most discouraged and insecure. My partner Ali Esmaili was a source of infinite love, care, and empathy (not to mention, some deliciously decadent Saturday morning breakfasts) throughout the final stages of this book project, and for that I appreciate him immensely. I am also fortunate to have amazingly compassionate friends—including Melissa Henry, Ash Inglenook, Sarah Jimenez, Janina Larenas, Costanza Rampini, and Barbara Snyder—who have been willing to drop everything and swoop in with food, a stiff drink, a long phone call, new music, silly animal GIFs, or a walk when I need them most. And those who know me well would be shocked if I did not mention Claude Debris, my beloved dumpster gremlin. I never could have imagined that a fuzzy little stray kitten found in a compost bin at a marina would become my most fiercely loyal (though stubbornly bitey) comrade.

I also want to thank all of those who have helped me tend to my mental and physical well-being. My therapist Lara Lenington has worked with me to cultivate a practice of mindfulness and self-acceptance that enabled me to see this book project through. The mind is not separate from the body, and so I am also grateful to my trainer Jason Lenington and my aerial hoop instructor Kelsey Keitges. Not only have they gotten me out from behind the computer screen, they have helped me become more confident and learn to embrace my strength.

I would like to extend an additional thanks to the many institutions that have invited me to present pieces of this book when it was still a work in progress, including the Canadian Association for Italian Studies, the University of Arizona, UC Santa Barbara, UC San Diego, UC Irvine, the Ohio State University, UNC Greensboro, the Freie Universität Berlin, UC Berkeley, Stanford University, UC Merced, the University of Michigan, the University of Minnesota, New

College of Florida, Ohlone College, and the Center for Cultural Studies at UC Santa Cruz.

The research undergirding this book was supported by a UC Berkeley Cota-Robles Graduate Fellowship, a Ford Foundation Predoctoral Fellowship, UC Berkeley geography department travel grants, UC Berkeley Graduate Division travel grants, an Associated Students of the University of California Academic Opportunity Fund Grant, a UC Berkeley Center for Science, Technology, Medicine, and Society fieldwork grant, and a UC Santa Cruz Committee on Research New Faculty Research Grant. I also received funding from the UC Santa Cruz Institute for Social Transformation to hold a book manuscript accelerator workshop with scholars including Chris Benner, David Theo Goldberg, Fatima El-Tayeb, and Claudio Fogu. Their careful, incredibly generous feedback helped to make this book into the best version of itself.

Some notes on the text you are about to read: I have used pseudonyms for most names; these instances are marked in endnotes. I used real names (with permission) when writing about individuals who were speaking or acting in their capacity as prominent figures in the public eye. In addition, some of the material in this book has been previously published elsewhere. The introduction and chapter 4 draw from my article "In Search of Black Italia: Notes on Race, Belonging, and Activism in the Black Mediterranean," which was published in *Transition* 123 in 2017. Chapter 2 draws from my article "Making Italy: Afro-Italian Entrepreneurs and the Racial Boundaries of Citizenship," published in *Social and Cultural Geography* in 2019.

In 2019, the award-winning Nigerian author Chimamanda Ngozi Adichie was awarded the Premio Speciale Afriche (Special Africa Prize) at the BookCity Milano festival. During a question-and-answer session, she turned to the subject of Black Italian representation:

> The story of not just Afro-Italians, but of Afro-Europeans, is invisible. We don't hear those stories. They exist, right? And by Afro-Europeans I mean people of African descent who were born in European countries, whose lives have been here, who speak the languages. The same people who, I am told, today in this country are not allowed to be citizens until they are 18. I find that ridiculous. . . . Those stories, even I don't know them; I want to hear them, because I think they haven't been heard; they're invisible. We need to hear them.[1]

Her comments were met with raucous applause, including shouts of "Thank you!" from Black Italians in the audience. But the next day, the Italian-Somali writer Igiaba Scego responded to Adichie's remarks by pushing back against the notion that Black Italian stories are hidden:

> The story of Afro-Italians is not silent, and this is important to reiterate. . . . There is a history of literature, a plural story, that has not been silent; a story made by immigrants and the children of immigrants, who have fought against the color line that was imposed upon them by an Italian system that is deaf to plurality. What we have to tell Chimamanda and everyone else is that there is an Afro-Italian story and, more broadly, that there is a plural story here of people with immigrant backgrounds. A story that has been forged in trade union struggles against labor exploitation, in the struggles in the *piazze* for citizenship, in the taking of stands against racist murders (Fermo, Florence, Macerata), in the struggle against colonial amnesia, in the demands by asylum-seekers against an Italian state that does not even remember colonizing those countries. . . . It is our duty to tell our stories, and above all to build bridges with their struggles, because even if it comes in different shades, ultimately we all experience the same discrimination.[2]

I hope that the stories, accounts, and analyses I share in this book can contribute to the ever-growing chorus of voices helping to narrate the past, present, and future of Black Italy and the struggle for substantive racial justice across Italy, Black Europe, and the Black Mediterranean.

Note on Language, Terminology, and Translation

What are the terms by which one's political claims can become recognizable?[3] Or, to echo Tina Campt's provocation in *Other Germans*, what labels should be used to describe a "group of people for whom there existed no positive term of reference as individuals of both Black and [Italian] heritage"?[4] For Black Italians, language is a key terrain on which debates about identity and belonging are currently staged.[5] Unlike in the United States, where there is at least some general consensus around the use of terms such as "African American" and "Black," in Italy the language of self-identification is vast, varied, and highly contested—a testament to the relative newness of these conversations. Some of the terms used by my interlocutors included "second generation," "new generation," "new Italian," "Italian-plus," "Black Italian," "Afro-Italian," and hyphenated terms that identify specific countries of family origin (such as "Italian-Ghanaian" and "Italian-Eritrean"). Each term marks a different set of commitments and has certain political implications.

For the purpose of consistency, I use "Black Italian" throughout *Contesting Race and Citizenship* to refer to the children of Black African or Afro-Latinx immigrants who were born and/or raised in Italy, as well as the "mixed-race" children of unions between Black Africans / Afro-Latinxs and white Italians, or between Black Americans and white Italians.[6] While my interlocutors span these categories, I found that they most frequently used the terms "Afro-Italian" or "Black Italian" to refer to themselves individually and collectively (though not necessarily to the exclusion of other labels). Appellations such as "Afro-Italian" or "Black Italian" are intended both by myself and by my interlocutors to designate similarities not in terms of biological descent, but in terms of lived experience—they work to establish a form of kinship based on shared (but not identical) struggles. On the occasions when I use the term "Afrodescendant," this is a deliberate choice to emphasize the political activation of a sense of shared connection to the African continent among Black people who were born and raised in Italy and Black migrants from the African continent. In the chapters that follow, and particularly in chapter 4, I will address the ways that contestations over the language of collective identification are also tied to a larger set of political negotiations about Black solidarity, alliance, and diaspora—negotiations that are always imbricated with ideas related to race, nation, gender, color, class, and kinship. It should also be noted that any references to Black Italians in this book are not intended to generalize across the experiences of *all* Black Italians—and indeed, part of my intellectual and political project in these pages is to challenge the notion of a unified, collective Black subject in Italy or elsewhere.

In this book, I also write about Black or sub-Saharan African immigrants, refugees, and asylum seekers. In those instances, I use "migrant" or "immigrant" to refer generally to people who have crossed a geopolitical border to arrive in Italy, and "refugee" or "asylum seeker" in specific reference to those who are migrating in search of humanitarian protection.[7] Nonetheless, while I recognize the juridical power of these categories to profoundly shape the experiences of migration, I am not interested in drawing ethical or moral distinctions between "economic migrants" and "humanitarian refugees."[8] Finally, in cases when I refer to sub-Saharan African (as opposed to Black) migrants or refugees, this is a deliberate decision to denote the places from which these groups arrived in Europe—not to suggest that the category of Black is inapplicable to them. The reason I employ these sorts of geographic descriptors is to signal the very distinct political and social responses in Italy to the presence of immigrants and refugees arriving from sub-Saharan Africa, as opposed to places such as Syria. Finally, I also use "African migrants/refugees" as shorthand for sub-Saharan African migrants/refugees—this is for the sake of textual brevity, not to collapse the experiences of North and Sub-Saharan Africans.

Of course, questions of terminology are not only relevant to Black folk in Italy. As Alessandro Portelli notes, Italians do not typically perceive themselves as "white," but rather as simply "normal."[9] Building on Portelli's observation, Angelica Pesarini argues: "Such a structural colour-blindness . . . is problematic because it associates Whiteness with normality and, consequently, with Italianness. Simply put, to be Italian is to be White. Within this discourse, those who do not fit the alleged (White) Italian type are deemed outside the Nation on a number of levels."[10] For this reason, throughout *Contesting Race and Citizenship* I have made a point to mark what is typically left unmarked by specifying white Italian (as opposed to simply Italian) where appropriate. This choice is intended to challenge the taken-for-granted conflation of Italianness and the Italian national body with both whiteness and normality in the popular racial imaginary.

CONTESTING RACE
AND CITIZENSHIP

INTRODUCTION

Contested Borders in the Time of Monsters

The crisis consists precisely in the fact that the old is dying and the new cannot be born; in this interregnum a great variety of morbid symptoms appear.

—Antonio Gramsci, *Selections from the Prison Notebooks*

Changes will occur that we cannot even begin to imagine, and the next generation will be both utterly familiar and wholly alien to their parents.

—Walidah Imarisha, *Octavia's Brood*

On October 7, 2013, Italian prime minister Enrico Letta declared a national day of mourning. Just four days earlier, a twenty-meter fishing boat carrying over five hundred Eritrean, Somali, Ghanaian, and Syrian asylum seekers from Libya caught fire and capsized just one kilometer off the coast of the Italian island of Lampedusa. While the bodies of all the victims were never recovered, by October 11 it was estimated that the death toll had reached at least 359—making this shipwreck the deadliest disaster in the Mediterranean since World War II.[1] The spectacle of hundreds of coffins lined up in seemingly endless rows inside a spartan Lampedusa airplane hangar (the coffins for children, one journalist observed, were adorned with stuffed animals)[2] came to symbolize the incalculable scale of violence reproduced daily as migrants were attempting to traverse the maritime borders of Europe in the Mediterranean Sea—or, as commentators increasingly began to call it, the "Mediterranean graveyard." In response to the tragedy, Letta publicly declared during the October 7 commemoration that all those who had perished in the shipwreck while attempting to reach Italy were "Italian citizens as of today."[3]

Yet, while the dead were awarded posthumous citizenship, what of the 155 asylum seekers who were rescued? They were investigated for illegal entry, which under the 2009 "Security Set" immigration law is regarded as a criminal offense. These survivors were shunted into overcrowded detention centers and faced deportation to their countries of origin, while the European Union unveiled plans for a new high-tech surveillance system that would track migrant boats

1

attempting to cross the Mediterranean.[4] And, in cities and towns across Italy, the children of immigrants who were born and raised in Italy were also being legally barred from Italian citizenship due to a restrictive nationality law that links citizenship to blood descent.

These contrasts represented in dramatic fashion the coming together of the many forces that characterize our current conjuncture: explicit racial nationalisms, heightened border securitization, and restrictions on certain forms of transnational mobility. Indeed, we are now firmly entrenched within what the Sardinian-Italian Marxist philosopher Antonio Gramsci infamously called the "time of monsters."[5] All around us swirl the morbid symptoms of late neoliberal capitalism and ever more widespread economic precarity and dispossession. Alongside these rapidly intensifying political economic crises, our current moment is also characterized by some of the largest-scale mass movements of people across borders in recent history. The global population of people displaced by economic instability, environmental degradation, the disintegration of authoritarian regimes, and long-term insurgencies has reached its highest levels since World War II, and these transborder movements have been met with a proliferation of new technologies for the surveillance and fortification of national borders.[6] And across the globe—from the United States, to Brazil, to the United Kingdom, to India, to Myanmar—there has been a frightening resurgence of explicitly racist, xenophobic nationalisms that seem to mark a break from the liberal "color blindness" that characterized the post–World War II era.

Southern Europe, and Italy in particular, stands at the forefront of these global transformations. Still ravaged by the 2008 to 2009 Eurozone economic collapse, Italy has faced a series of national government failures along with long-brewing right-wing backlashes to migration, the transnational forces of globalization, and the European project itself.[7] In addition, Italy is an important port of arrival in the context of European refugee emergency, with both a relatively accessible Mediterranean geography and deep colonial ties to four of the primary African countries from which people have been so violently displaced en masse—Libya, Eritrea, Ethiopia, and Somalia.[8] Migrants who arrive in Italy face varying degrees of neglect, marginalization, and outright violence. And, paradoxically (as a relatively young country with a tenuous nation-building project and long history of being marginalized as "racially inferior" to a supposedly "Aryan" northern Europe), Italy has also emerged as a key node in the global far-right, neofascist, and white nationalist / Eurocentric political resurgence.[9]

In recognition of Italy's geopolitical and analytical significance for understanding the current conjuncture, critical scholars of migration have responded by investigating the securitization of the Mediterranean border, the politics and limitations of migrant solidarity movements, and even the lived experiences of refugees. But comparatively understudied are the many concurrent contestations unfolding around *national citizenship*—mobilizations that have been disproportionately propelled by the activism of Black people in Europe who are not necessarily migrants or otherwise recent arrivals in these countries. Yet, as the seemingly contradictory conferral of honorary Italian citizenship on deceased migrants and the criminalization of those who survived reveals, citizenship—and its profound historical entanglement with questions of racism and the politics of difference—remains an important part of the analytical puzzle if we wish to understand just how the boundaries of Europe (and in a broader sense, the liberal nation-state itself) are being remade, negotiated, and undone today.

One of the most prominent citizenship mobilizations unfolding in Europe today is the movement to reform Italian nationality law. Italy has among the most restrictive citizenship laws in Europe.[10] Italian nationality is conferred on the basis of jus sanguinis (right of blood), which has left unrecognized and disenfranchised as many as nine hundred thousand children of immigrants who were born and raised in Italy.[11] This is therefore the place from which my story begins. *Contesting Race and Citizenship* asks why and how so many Black Italians have adopted national citizenship as a privileged terrain of struggle over racial justice, inclusion, and belonging in Italy. In this book, I argue that citizenship—and specifically, the long-standing debate about the legal inclusion of Black subjects within European polities—is key to understanding the connection between subtler, late-twentieth-century "color-blind" or "cultural" racisms and the resurgence of overt racial nationalisms during the last decade. After all, in the wake of World War II—after the horrors of Fascism and subsequent international campaigns challenging the "myth" of race—racism and racial nationalism did not simply disappear. Instead, they were re-embedded within the seemingly race-neutral apparatus of national citizenship.

But rather than asking whether citizenship is inherently "good" and "just" (i.e., as the highest legal principle or a path to rights and inclusion) or "bad" and "unjust" (i.e., as an apparatus of racial exclusion or a form of liberal accommodationism), in this book I am more interested in the political work that citizenship *does*. National citizenship is a powerful yet often overlooked crucible within which racisms are being reproduced and reconfigured, new racial distinctions are articulated, and the constitutive exclusions of liberalism are laid bare.[12] And, as generations of women of color, transnational, and postcolonial feminist theorists have argued, this process is in turn inextricable from the power-laden dynamics of gender and sexuality.[13] Italy, as a post-Fascist country currently embroiled in the global resurgence of racial nationalisms, undoubtedly offers valuable historical insights about fascist entanglements of race, citizenship, and nation. But at the same time, a closer engagement with the *linkages* between liberal and fascist racisms in the Italian historical record—and their reverberations in the present—also encourages us to acknowledge racial nationalism not merely as an extremist, fascist aberration, but rather as foundational to the liberal nation-state itself.

On an empirical level, this book represents one of the first full-length accounts of Black politics in Italy. I attend to the incredible proliferation of Black Italian movements, projects that address the Italian nation-state and the wider Black diaspora, the "unspoken whiteness" of Italian identity, and the interlocking racist violence of Fortress Europe (the hardened external borders *around* Europe established in relation to the dissolution of borders *between* individual European countries as part of the supranational vision of the European Union).[14] What are the possibilities and limitations of these emergent mobilizations? What new formations are possible, and what older ones are resuscitated in this attempt to challenge the racial borders of Italy and of Europe? I am interested in opening up discussions of the migrant "crisis" by focusing on a largely invisiblized generation of Black people who were born or raised in Europe but have been thrust into the same racist, xenophobic political climate as the immigrants and refugees who are arriving in Europe across the Mediterranean Sea from the African continent. How are these Black Italians now actively remaking what it means to be Italian and to be European today?

But this is not only a descriptive story of social movements and Black identities.[15] The point of *Contesting Race and Citizenship* is not to problematize and surveil Black Italians—by asking questions such as whether they feel "more *Italian* or more *African*." Instead, I endeavor to show how their mobilizations exhume long-buried links between the bureaucratic apparatus of liberal citizenship and racism, a connection that has effectively paved the way for the explosion of far-right, neofascist, populist politics across Europe and much of the rest of the world. The new Black Italian politics point to the many contradictions at the heart of the liberal project, and of citizenship itself: Is it possible to mobilize for rights and recognition without reproducing the racial state? If, as Engin Isin writes, citizenship represents "how relentlessly the idea of inclusion produces exclusion"—namely, through the distinction between "citizen" and "alien"—then what new forms of differentiation and exclusion are emerging through efforts to expand Italian citizenship?[16] Does activism that engages with the racial state's language of citizenship have the potential to radically reformulate that category from within—and to what extent can it inadvertently preclude the articulation of alternative solidarities between Black Italian citizens-in-waiting, migrants, and refugees?[17] To answer these questions, in this book I trace not only mobilizations for national citizenship, but also the more capacious, transnational Black diasporic possibilities that emerge when activists confront the ethical and political limits of citizenship as a means for securing meaningful, lasting racial justice—formations that are centered on shared critiques of the racial state, as well as shared histories of racial capitalism and colonialism.

In Italy and beyond, citizenship has become a container for debates about the relationship between race and nation. In the United Kingdom, supporters of Brexit (the UK's departure from the European Union) have explicitly contrasted the figure of the suffering white British citizen with the figure of the immigrant "undeserving poor."[18] And in the United States, former president Donald Trump repeatedly expressed his desire to abolish birthright citizenship because it creates a "magnet for illegal migration."[19] DREAMers (undocumented individuals who arrived in the United States as young children) continue to mobilize in a tenuous state of legal liminality, held hostage by politicians who are using them as pawns to fund the further militarization of the US–Mexico border.[20] And in response to political criticism from the so-called "squad" of progressive Democratic congresswomen of color—Alexandria Ocasio-Cortez of New York, Rashida Tlaib of Michigan, Ilhan Omar of Minnesota, and Ayanna Pressley of Massachusetts—Trump and his supporters responded with vitriolic tweets and chants of "Send them back!"[21] The fact that three of these four women were born in the United States, and all four are American citizens, alludes to the ways that the question of *who* constitutes a legitimate national citizen is repeatedly made intelligible through an overlaid grid of racial difference. To paraphrase a formulation coined by abolitionist geographer Ruth Wilson Gilmore, race and citizenship together constitute a powerful, "fatal coupling" in our modern world.[22]

Entanglements of Race and Citizenship

How did citizenship become such an important terrain of contestation over racism in Italy? While a range of fields has attempted to comprehend the social, political, and cultural dynamics of national citizenship, the answer to this question remains surprisingly elusive. Indeed, the strategic importance of national citizenship for Black Italians seeking to challenge biologically determined notions of Italianness points to some limitations in contemporary citizenship theory.

The liberal sociology of citizenship has focused on citizenship primarily as a legal contract between the state and the individual that produces access to formal rights. Scholars working in this tradition have examined the various paths by which migrants become citizens, as well as the political, cultural, and historical reasons for differences among countries' nationality laws.[23] As Bloemraad and colleagues observe, these analyses often use distinctions between ethnic and civic conceptions of citizenship, or assimilationist and multiculturalist approaches to incorporation.[24] In response to these liberal understandings of citizenship as *access to formal rights*, critical citizenship studies instead considers national citizenship in relation to dynamics of *inclusion, exclusion*, and *differentiation*.[25] While sociologists of citizenship have also recognized the exclusions inherent to the apparatus of national citizenship, critical citizenship studies tends to emphasize the various forms of insurgent citizenship "from below" (urban citizenship, global citizenship, etc.) that have emerged as a counterpoint to the state's exclusionary practices.[26] But while these interventions represent a powerful reimagining of citizenship, race is often peripheral to these analyses, and the ongoing sovereignty of the state is downplayed in favor of these transgressive, nonnational acts of citizenship.[27]

The field of Black studies has taken on the relationship between citizenship and racism through an analysis of Blackness's position within liberal understandings of rights, subjectivity, and political agency. As Orlando Patterson argues, racialized chattel slavery represented "social death," predicated on the preclusion of the right of natality; for this reason, newly emancipated Black Americans mobilized for US citizenship through claims to birthright citizenship that culminated in the passage of the Fourteenth Amendment.[28] In contemporary accounts—particularly those focused on the United States—scholars emphasize the persistent condition of second-class citizenship for Black folk in the afterlife of slavery.[29] But in a different geographical context, Black European studies has instead emphasized the normative claim that Black people in Europe *should* be recognized as national citizens rather than migrants.[30] This is an intellectual and political project meant to contest the idea that Black people are eternally Europe's outsiders—that they are perpetual migrants and newcomers, regardless of how long (and for how many generations) their communities have been firmly established in Europe.[31] Indeed, as Barnor Hesse has observed, "[Black Europe] is located at the intersections of *non-Europe / Europe, outside / inside, other / same, immigrant / citizen, coloniality / postcoloniality.*"[32]

When these North American and Black Europe studies approaches to citizenship are put into direct conversation with each other, what can inadvertently emerge is a teleology of Black politics across the diaspora that goes something like this: first, we should focus on achieving national citizenship; only then can we begin to question how the very categories of the liberal state are shot through with racism (and anti-Black racism specifically), in ways that ultimately preclude the realization of *substantive* citizenship. But this linear story did not square neatly with my experiences in Italy. I found that Black politics had taken on a range of divergent (rather than cumulative) forms, in which Black immigrants, refugees, and second-generation Black Italians were articulating distinct political goals and different relationships to citizenship. For Black people born and raised in Italy, citizenship was a means of obtaining rights; for newly arrived refugees, it functioned as a strategy of racial filtering and exclusion on behalf of the Italian state.

In a 2019 Instagram post, the Italian-Ghanaian writer, curator, and medical student Theophilus Marboah highlighted what is at stake in Black Italian struggles for recognition, through this clever "remixing" of a James Baldwin quote from *Notes of a Native Son*:

> For the history of the American Negro is unique also in this: that the question of his humanity, and of his rights therefore as a human being, became a burning one for several generations of Americans, so burning a question that it ultimately became one of those used to divide the nation.[33]
>
> For the history of the *Black Italian* is unique also in this: that the question of his *citizenship*, and of his rights therefore as a *citizen*, became a burning one for several *legislatures*, so burning a question that it ultimately became one of those used to divide the nation.[34]

Marboah's reformulation is especially poignant because the original text is, in fact, an excerpt from "Stranger in the Village"—an essay Baldwin wrote about his experiences in Leukerbad, Switzerland (just about four hours from Milan, Italy). Baldwin describes a snowbound alpine village where "no black man had ever set foot," on a continent where "the black man, *as a man*, did not exist," except as an abstraction geographically bounded to Europe's colonies. For Baldwin, this observation is what distinguishes Europe from the United States, where "even as a slave, [the black man] was an inescapable part of the general social fabric and no American could escape having an attitude toward him."[35] Marboah's engagement with Baldwin thus provides a subtle, yet loving, disruption of the comparison at the heart of "Stranger in the Village." Marboah suggests that Blackness has long been central to Italian understandings of citizenship—and indeed, that it is precisely the *invisibilization* of the Black man [*sic*] in Europe that has systematically externalized Black communities as foreign to European nation-states.[36] By linking Baldwin's analysis of rights, humanness, and Blackness to the Italian context, Marboah also helps us to see how "citizen" in Italy effectively functions as a racial proxy for the category of the "human."

In these ongoing struggles for citizenship, Black Italian activists have made use of shifting alliances and tactical engagements with the state for purposes that may include, but also extend beyond, the objective of nation-state recognition. Their relationship to citizenship is continually in motion—Black Italians alternatively accept the terms of nation-state citizenship and sometimes reject them outright; they also "stretch" the discourses and practices of citizenship in the sense of Fanon's famous stretching of Marxist analysis to the colonial context;

and they swerve citizenship, engaging strategically with it on the terrains of law, cultural politics, and political economy but simultaneously decentering it as the apex of anti-racist struggle.[37] Indeed, as Charles T. Lee argues, "social movements adopt a more variable use of political strategies, creatively negotiating with complicitous logics and antidemocratic powers to recraft spaces of social change in varied locations and social contexts."[38]

Black Mediterranean Geographies of Citizenship

Why look at the racial politics of citizenship via Blackness—and specifically, Blackness in Italy? A significant proportion of the refugees landing on the shores of southern Europe from the Mediterranean are from sub-Saharan Africa, and the threat of a supposed "African invasion" figures prominently in far-right political messaging. But even beyond this current moment, the idea of Blackness has long served as a foil against which the boundaries of liberal categories (citizen, natural rights, sovereignty, freedom) were constructed. In the context of Italy, for instance, Heather Merrill notes that Blackness *specifically* works as a symbol of nonbelonging: "African bodies are (re-)marked as iconic signifiers of illegitimate belonging, represented for instance in media images of packed fishing vessels entering the country clandestinely through southern maritime borders, and in tropes of itinerant street peddlers and prostitutes, suggesting that their very being in an Italian place threatens the moral purity of the nation state."[39]

Yet the empirical context of Italy also demands that we move away from any generalized notion of Blackness (and its relationship to citizenship). After all, the Black diaspora in Italy includes refugees, asylum seekers, first-generation migrants, and foreign university students; it spans multiple generations, some with direct ties to Italy's former colonies, and some who have been in Italy since the 1960s; it includes people who were born in Italy, and individuals with a range of citizenship and immigration statuses. For this reason, scholars have increasingly turned toward the "Black Mediterranean" as an analytical framework for understanding the historical and geographical specificities of Blackness in Italy and the wider Mediterranean region. This work explicitly draws on and extends Paul Gilroy's powerful theorizations of the Black Atlantic by asking how Blackness is constructed, lived, and transformed in a region that has been alternatively understood as a "cultural crossroads" at the heart of European civilization, a source of dangerous racial contamination, and—more recently—as the deadliest border crossing in the world.[40] My emphasis on this sort of "racial regionalization" points to the importance of geography and spatiality in understanding the politics of

Blackness—indeed, as recent work in the field of Black geographies has argued, Blackness is neither singular, fixed, nor ontologically predetermined.[41]

Since the origins of the Italian nation-state itself, the process of constructing the ever-shifting racial boundaries of Italian citizenship has been bound up with notions of Blackness, Mediterraneanness, and the production of space.[42] Following the Risorgimento project of Italian national unification, which lasted from 1848 until the incorporation of Rome as Italy's capital in 1871, citizenship was defined in relation to both southern Italians and Africans. The consolidation of the geobody of Italy out of a patchwork collection of city-states and empires into a nation-state was intertwined with processes of internal colonialism.[43] Southern Italy was understood by northern Italian elites through an Orientalist lens of cultural and civilizational inferiority due to its perceived geographical and racial proximity to the African continent (i.e., the so-called Southern Question). This racial mapping must also be understood as a response to northern European racial theorists' dismissal of the Italian peninsula as a site of racially impure, degenerated Mediterraneans.[44] And, in a foreshadowing of the ways that Black Italians today draw on diasporic resources from Black Americans, these debates about southernness and Mediterraneanness in Italy also unfolded in relation to struggles over racism, nationalism, and citizenship in the United States. Giuseppe Mazzini, a politician, journalist, and leader of the Italian unification movement, once declared that Italians were the "the negroes of Europe"—a metaphor intended to highlight the subjugation of Italians and rally support for the nationalist cause.[45] Across the Atlantic, in the United States, southern Italian immigrants were systematically classified as racially proximate to Black Americans (due to the transnational influence of the same racial theories that orientalized southern Italy during and after the Risorgimento), and were only fully incorporated into the category of whiteness around the mid-twentieth century.

Italy's precarious national-racial identity was also shaped in relation to its trans-Mediterranean empire building on the African continent, which was unfolding alongside national unification.[46] And multiple, spatially extended diasporas—from the mass exodus of Italian emigrants after the Risorgimento to the large-scale arrival of African migrants in the 1980s and 1990s—have contributed to both the redefinitions of Italianness and the legal frameworks governing citizenship. These observations about the geographies of Italian racial formation are very much in keeping with Etienne Balibar's influential observation that racism develops via both (super)nationalism *and* supranationalism.[47] In other words, the particular conflation of race and citizenship in Italy was formed not only in relation to the consolidation of the new country's national identity, but also through Italy's participation in broader, transnational trajectories of Euro-Mediterranean race-thinking and imperialism. Contemporary

Black Italian struggles over citizenship today are therefore shaped by a long, global history of spatial contestation over the racial boundaries of Italianness in relation to Europe, Africa, and the Mediterranean.

While the framework of the Black Mediterranean helps us to ground Black Italian politics in historical and geographical specificity, the Black Mediterranean is also not simply a claim to an incommensurable difference or exceptionalism that sets the region apart from the rest of the world. Rather, drawing again on insights from Black geographies, supposedly "marginal" sites are actually relational spaces that offer profound insights about the workings of power and the organization of the modern world.[48] In this sense, then, Italy also becomes a powerful site from which to theorize about race, citizenship, and Blackness on a *global* (rather than purely regional) scale. After all, if we take Cedric Robinson at his word, the origins of racial capitalism actually lie in the Mediterranean, which served as a laboratory of sorts for the technologies of dispossession and exploitation that were then exported to the Atlantic.[49] And today, some of the most powerful mobilizations against border fortification, state racism, and coloniality are taking place across the Mediterranean. The duality of the Black Mediterranean as a site of both racist subordination and of innovative resistance reflects the many contradictions at the heart of the Mediterranean itself as a symbolic and material space. On the one hand, the Mediterranean has been a locus of engagement, exchange, and cultural florescence for thousands of years. On the other hand, it has long been a center of economic extraction, racist violence, and imperial ambition—indeed, today, the Mediterranean is immediately recognizable as the symbol of Fortress Europe's brutal border regimes.

The Black Mediterranean is thus a site where many different historical forces and subjectivities have converged, in ways that complicate linear understandings of politics and solidarity. It is a place where racism, xenophobia, and (post)colonialism cannot easily be separated into discrete political and analytical silos. For this reason, the Black Mediterranean is also a political demand—one that calls for radical and transgressive forms of solidarity that can actively subvert state categories such as "migrant," "citizen," and "refugee." As Ida Danewid contends, this is an ethical demand based not on abstract humanisms (like so many white European–led "migrant solidarity" movements), nor on biological or "blood" kinship ties, but rather on the shared histories of racist injustice and Black struggle across the Mediterranean, from colonialism to Fortress Europe.[50] These Black Mediterranean struggles with, for, and against citizenship provide glimpses into what Katherine McKittrick in *Demonic Grounds* describes as "alternative spatial practices and more humanly workable geographies."[51]

Here, it is worth noting that Italy does not exhaust the geography of the Black Mediterranean. While this book is focused specifically on Italy, there are still many other stories to be told. Spain, Portugal, and Greece, for instance, are notable as emerging sites of inquiry in the burgeoning field of Black Mediterranean studies. And beyond Europe, the broader Mediterranean region has long been a site of anti-Black racism, from the "slave markets" for sub-Saharan African migrant labor in Libya to the surveillance and violence enacted against sub-Saharan African migrants traveling through Algeria.[52] In addition, North Africa has also played a central role in the racial capitalist political economy of the Black Mediterranean, as a site of European aspiration for the establishment of new economic footholds on the African continent in the wake of post–World War II decolonization.[53] For this reason, Italy is not a stand-in for the Black Mediterranean as a whole; rather, I am interested in what the framework of the Black Mediterranean can disclose about struggles over race, nation, and citizenship in Italy today.

The Black Diaspora in Italy

Despite systematic denials and obfuscations, Italy was deeply entangled with both the Mediterranean slave trade (which, many historians argue, helped to establish the commercial foundations for the transatlantic slave trade) and African colonialism, in ways that continue to shape current contestations over the boundaries of Italianness and national citizenship.[54] As Cedric Robinson notes in *Black Marxism*, Italy was a major hub in the networks of trade, intellectual dialogue, and cultural production linking what would come to be known as the European, African, Arab, and Asian worlds.[55] In particular, between the thirteenth and sixteenth centuries, the merchants and financiers of the Italian maritime republics established extensive Mediterranean trade networks. The use of enslaved labor (which, in this context, was not limited to Black Africans but also encompassed European Christians, Muslims, Jews, and Slavs) was central to agricultural production in the Italian outposts of the Mediterranean.[56] This economic system ultimately served as a template for the use of enslaved Africans in the Atlantic colonies during the transatlantic slave trade.[57] The Genoese in particular were key players in the lucrative trade that expanded rapidly from the Maghreb and the Mediterranean basin across the Atlantic Ocean.[58] Genoese merchant capitalists served as influential creditors and provided capital that ultimately "determined the direction and pace" of Spanish and Portuguese expansion across the Mediterranean and Atlantic, and the emergence of the transatlantic slave trade itself.[59] I've directed my attention to the writings of Cedric Robinson here because his work explicitly rearticulates the Mediterranean with the transatlantic slave trade, pointing to the deep historical ties that connected the Italian peninsula to the transnational circuits of racial capitalism and Blackness.

Italy was also a "strident imperialist" and significant colonial power, even before the rise of fascism in the twentieth century.[60] In the approximately seven decades from 1869 (when an Italian company purchased the Bay of Assab) to 1943, Italy's colonial footprint gradually spread over Eritrea, Somalia, Libya, Ethiopia, Albania, the Dodecanese Islands (in what is now Greece), and a forty-six-hectare territorial concession in Tientsin, China.[61] The Italian Empire came to an end with the 1947 Treaty of Peace with Italy (part of the Paris Peace Treaty), through which Italy was forced to relinquish control of its colonies and occupied territories. Still, as Cristina Lombardi-Diop and Caterina Romeo note, Italian geopolitical and economic ties persisted in many of the former colonies, even after formal political decolonization was complete—most notably in the trusteeship of Somalia from 1950 to 1960 granted to Italy by the United Nations.[62] In addition, the kinship ties, social networks, economic relations, and material infrastructure established through Italian colonialism laid the groundwork for the first waves of migration from North and sub-Saharan Africa to Italy during the second half of the twentieth century.

From the time of Italian national unification at the end of the nineteenth century up until the mid-twentieth century, Italy was primarily a country of *emigration*. During this period, millions of Italians abandoned rural poverty in search of economic opportunity abroad—not only in the Americas, northern Europe, and Australia, as widely recounted in popular culture, but also in the Italian colonies of Africa. By the mid-1970s, however, Italy finally achieved a "net positive" immigration balance (i.e., more arrivals than departures). This shift resulted from both the enactment of restrictive entry or "guest worker" policies in countries that had previously been receiving Italian immigrants, such as Switzerland and Germany, as well as an increase in transnational labor migration into Italy spurred by the decline of Fordism (a system of industrial production characterized by, among other features, standardized assembly-line production, higher wages to support mass consumption, and state intervention to stabilize periodic crises through the promotion of full employment and the institution of welfare programs).[63]

According to Heather Merrill and Donald Carter, the first major generation of immigrants in Italy comprised mainly foreign contract workers and university students.[64] During the 1970s, Wendy Pojmann explains, the largest groups of non-European immigrants living in Italy were men from Africa and the Middle East working in either unskilled manufacturing in northern Italy or agriculture in southern Italy, and women from the Philippines, Cape Verde, and the former Italian colonies in the Horn of Africa who were recruited by Catholic charities to provide domestic services for white Italian mothers who were increasingly working outside of the home.[65] Toward the end of the 1980s, Italy's immigrant population began to represent a new plurality of national groups, most of which had no apparent connection to Italy or Italian colonialism.[66] This fact distinguished immigration to Italy from the patterns that characterized earlier sites of immigration to Europe such as Britain, France, and the Netherlands. By 1991, North and sub-Saharan Africans constituted the second-largest immigrant population in Italy, surpassed only by Italian return migrants.[67] But while fears of a supposed "African invasion" continue to suffuse political discourse and mainstream media narratives in Italy, today the African immigrant population is actually far surpassed by the number of Romanians and Albanians living in Italy.

Italy does not collect official ethnoracial statistics (with the exception of data on certain historical linguistic minorities)—a legacy of post-Fascist reconstruction after World War II.[68] This absence of ethnoracial statistics in Italy makes it especially challenging to estimate the number of people of African descent living in Italy today. Still, it is possible to triangulate the numerical significance of this group from the various official "proxy" numbers that are readily available. The Istituto Nazionale di Statistica (or Istat, the country's national statistics body) estimates that there are over one million Africans with non-Italian citizenship living in Italy, and that they make up roughly 20 percent of Italy's immigrant population. About 360,000 hail from sub-Saharan Africa (primarily Senegal, Nigeria, and Ghana).[69] In addition, approximately 20 percent of children in Italy today have at least one immigrant parent, a number that demographers predict could grow in the coming years as white Italian birth rates decline.[70]

Notably, Italy does not have banlieue-style peri-urban residential segregation on the same scale as countries such as France. This means that African immigrants and their children are comparatively dispersed across many different neighborhoods, cities, and regions of Italy.[71] Historically, however, the Black presence in Italy has been largely concentrated in the wealthier, industrial northern half of the country, particularly around the cities of the Industrial Triangle economic powerhouse (Milan, Turin, and Genoa). As immigration patterns continue to change, however, the demographic balance of Black Italy has gradually begun to shift to the South, leading to rapidly expanding African communities in cities such as Naples and Palermo.

From "African Immigrants" to "Black Italians"

While scholars have devoted ample attention to the circumstances of first-generation African immigrants and refugees in Italy, the experiences of Black people born and raised in Italy remain comparatively understudied.[72] This constitutes a significant lacuna in the existing literature on race, immigration, and citizenship in Italy. Indeed, the centrality of the refugee crisis in Italy raises the question of what can be learned by studying Black people who grew up in Italy in particular, as opposed to those who arrived as migrants. I believe, however, that the mobilizations of Black Italians (and the discursive repertoires that have cohered around citizenship reform activism) will also shape the terrain of struggle for newly arrived refugees. In other words, while Black Italians and Black refugees did not come to Italy at the same time, their stories are now profoundly intertwined even as they are positioned differently in relation to the possibilities, promises, and perils of Italian citizenship.

One of the most notable characteristics of this generation of Black Italians is their hesitant transition toward a collective sense of Black identity and away from the category of "immigrant." Heather Merrill and Donald Carter note that during the early years of migrant settlement in Italy in the 1980s and 1990s, newcomers from across Africa, Latin America, the Middle East, and Southeast Asia banded together in interethnic activist and labor organizations.[73] For these groups, "immigrant" as a form of collective identity performed important political and coalitional work. Increasingly, however, Black Italians are rejecting the intergenerational imposition of the category "immigrant" (as seen, for instance, in the ubiquitous label "second-generation immigrant"). They are also turning away from an exclusive identification with specific African countries of origin, arguing that these national distinctions mattered more to their parents than to their own everyday lived experiences. Instead, they are moving toward new forms of self-identification that can capture the experience of racialization that stems from being born or raised in Italy. This shared condition is akin to what W. E. B. Du Bois called "double consciousness," or what Frantz Fanon alternatively described as dealing with "two systems of reference"—the lived experience of fracture and alienation generated by daily engagement with racialized social and economic structures.[74] This doubleness, for both Du Bois and Fanon, occurs when Black people must view themselves simultaneously through the distorting veil of white prejudice and through their own modes of self-understanding. Yet, this experience also generates what Du Bois in *The Souls of Black Folk* referred to as "second sight," a "privileged epistemological standpoint" that allows Black folk to see the world as it is, laden with racist hypocrisy.[75]

Over the course of interviews with Black Italians across Italy about their lives and preferred forms of self-identification in 2016, I was regularly told some version of the following after a moment of surprise, followed by careful reflection: "You know, I didn't even begin to *think* of the term 'Afro-Italian' [or 'Black Italian'] until three, maybe two years ago." This is confirmed in a 2002 article by Jacqueline Andall, "Second-Generation Attitude? African-Italians in Milan," one of the earliest studies focusing on the children of African immigrants in Italy.[76] Andall observed that the young people she interviewed saw Blackness and Italianness as mutually exclusive categories. Indeed, many of her interlocutors found it easier to identify with a general sense of Europeanness, African identity, or a wider Black diasporic consciousness than with Italianness specifically. Yet she also predicted that the up-and-coming "younger second generation" of African Italians might not necessarily dismiss the possibility of being both Black and Italian as many of the older, "involuntary pioneers" had done previously.[77] When she wrote this almost twenty years ago, Andall's hunch was absolutely correct: the children of African immigrants today are increasingly organizing themselves under the collective terms "Afro-Italian" and "Black Italian."

Many of my friends in Italy have related to me some iteration of a story in which they grew up understanding themselves as Italian, but then experienced an episode around high school that brought into sharp relief the reality that this recognition did not run in both directions. One of the founders of the popular blog *Afroitalian Souls* told me the following one overcast afternoon in Milan in 2016, as we sipped coffees in the trendy canal neighborhood of Navigli:

> For me, I grew up seeing myself only as Italian. I knew that I was African, but I was Italian, period. Because the few Africans I saw outside of my family were not regarded well, so I grew up saying, "I am Italian, you are African; we are not the same." Then I went to Uganda, I fell in love with my country, and I thought, wow, I didn't realize that I was always missing something! . . . When I came back here, I thought to myself, geez, I am also Italian! Then when I had trouble getting Italian citizenship, I said, "Well, who cares about those Italians, I am also African." And so I decided from that day, I was only African. I went from one extreme to another. Because I thought to myself, I was born and raised here. Why don't they consider me to be Italian? Why do I have to go through this whole hassle with citizenship? . . . Now, however, I'm finding a balance. The fact that Italians don't accept me doesn't mean that I have to stop seeing myself as Italian.[78]

Changing demographics certainly play a part in this story: Italy became an important country of immigration in the 1980s and 1990s, so the children of the immigrants who arrived during those decades and settled primarily in the industrial cities of northern Italy and around Rome are now well into their twenties and even their thirties. In other words, they have lived through humiliating episodes of discrimination at the hands of their high school teachers; they have struggled, and often failed, to successfully petition for Italian naturalization on their eighteenth birthdays; they have dealt with racism when applying for jobs or apartment hunting; and they are old enough to vividly remember the racist and misogynistic attacks in 2013 that were directed by right-wing politicians against Italy's first Black cabinet member, the Italian-Congolese former minister of integration and member of the European Parliament Cécile Kashetu Kyenge.[79]

Yet demographic momentum alone cannot explain the growing visibility of activism under the banners of "Black" or "Afro-Italianness." It is also a deeply uncertain and precarious time in Italy, one in which Black Italians have been forced to publicly demonstrate their worthiness as citizens-in-waiting as a direct response to the scapegoating of Blackness as a drain on scarce state resources and a threat to national integrity. In the context of such racialized refusal of recognition, Black Italians have marshalled practices like entrepreneurship and ideas such as the sedentarist logics of birthplace to legitimate their presence in Italy.[80] They are actively reworking the boundaries of Italianness, displacing blood and biological descent in favor of attributes such as cosmopolitan hybridity, economic productivity, and local cultural fluency. Increasingly, however, Black Italians are also questioning the normative "script" of citizenship activism for the ways that it generates new and pernicious forms of racial distinction between "assimilable" Black citizens-in-waiting and "nonassimilable" Black migrants. And from these challenging conversations about the meanings of national citizenship and its relationship to racial justice, exciting new political horizons have begun to emerge—ones that look beyond the Italian nation-state to imagine much more capacious diasporic and Black Mediterranean solidarities.

Methodological Approaches

An investigation of race, nationalism, citizenship, and Blackness in contemporary Italy poses a number of methodological challenges.[81] The persistence and intensification of regionalism in Italy—often glossed as "fragmentation"—means that one cannot easily generalize from one part of Italy to the entire country. The sites of Black Italian organizing in Italy are also geographically dispersed. The centrality of the Internet and social media to the circulation of diasporic resources, creation of alternative media, and enactment of visibility politics among Black Italians poses a further challenge to a spatially bounded analysis. The Internet has become a haven for emerging conversations (and arguments) among a spatially dispersed generation of Black Italians. Through an ever-growing number of Facebook pages, YouTube channels, and blogs, Black Italians have been able to connect, achieve new levels of visibility, and create relatively autonomous spaces for discussion, political organizing, and cultural production.

For these reasons, the multiplicity of practices by which Black Italians are articulating Blackness and Italianness, and attempting to challenge Italian ethnic absolutism, cannot be adequately contained within one community center, neighborhood, or city.[82] This emergent Black Italia does not have a singular geographical referent, but rather emerges from the interstices of everyday life, in what Heather Merrill calls "Black spaces."[83] It spans photo shoots in Milan's Piazza del Duomo about respecting the bodily integrity of Black women; Afrobeat-influenced DJ sets in Rome attended by Black Italian youth and their white Italian schoolmates; efforts to decolonize high school curricula in Bologna; international sporting events during which racist outbursts incite conversations about whether Black players can be representatives of Italy; a growing community of writers remapping Italian colonial history in relation to the present; and online spaces for sharing news from across the African diaspora. Capturing the density and complexity of these networks therefore requires a different sort of methodological approach that does not take for granted places and subjectivities as bounded. As McKittrick observes, the "nowhere of black life . . . provides a template to imagine the production of space not through patriarchal and colonial project trappings . . . but instead as a project that . . . engenders relations of uncertainty."[84] In this sense, then, the simultaneous "nowhere" and "everywhere" of Black Italy represents less of a methodological *challenge* to overcome than a conceptual and political *opportunity* to contest the idea of the Italian nation-state as a discrete and homogenous unit, and of Black subjects as hopelessly contained within naturalized and pathological spaces.[85]

Contesting Race and Citizenship is based on multisited, mixed-methods research carried out between 2013 and 2019 with Black activists, artists, and entrepreneurs from across Italy. I conducted in-depth interviews and participant observation at activist meetings, cultural festivals, workshops, protests, and other events. I undertook virtual ethnography of social media communities oriented on citizenship and Black cultural politics across platforms such as Facebook, YouTube, and Instagram. I engaged in content analysis of reporting on migration and citizenship issues in Italy from the 1980s to the present. I drew on a range of cultural texts as alternative forms of Black knowledge production, including novels, memoirs, poetry, films, and music by Black Italian artists. I delved into the archives of nineteenth-century Italian positivist scientists to study the relationship between race, geography, and Italian national identity. And I engaged in critical public policy analysis of Italian immigration and citizenship laws.

Because most African immigrants in Italy reside in the country's northern and central regions, and the major cities in those regions are important hubs of Black political organizing, most of my fieldwork was carried out in the northern half of Italy.[86] In particular, Milan, Brescia, Verona, Padua, Turin, Bologna, and Rome were key sites of research for participant observation, interviews, and archival research over the course of this study. I did, however, also spend time in southern Italy and had the opportunity to interview Black activists from Naples and Sicily—experiences I describe in this book's conclusion. I even traveled beyond Italy, going to sites such as Amsterdam to see how the emergent Black Italian diasporic politics I was studying engaged and linked up with Black European mobilizations in other countries.

A focus on *everyday* negotiations of citizenship constituted an important part of both my research praxis and my conceptualization of citizenship struggles. There has been a tendency among some scholars of migration to hail the abstracted figure of the refugee, whom they portray as embodying a fugitive form of "citizenship from the margins," and who in turn is recruited as a polyvalent analytical vehicle for unpacking the violence of the state and its borders. On the other hand, there is a vast literature on the relationship between race, nation, and citizenship from the interrelated fields of cultural studies and American studies—but this work has been largely conceptual, and less geographical in scope.[87] Ultimately, these various approaches, for all of their radical and deeply consequential theoretical insights about sovereignty, marginality, and the racial state, have not been able to fully contend with the fact that national citizenship still *matters* for so many marginalized groups. Indeed, this paradox only becomes evident through a close engagement with the ways different groups engage with citizenship (and its limits) in the realm of the everyday.

In this sense, then, my orientation on national citizenship in *Contesting Race and Citizenship* is not an arbitrary conceptual choice, but rather is guided by the empirical demands of my research. I must admit that I did not set out to study citizenship when I first arrived in Italy to work on this project in 2013—in fact, I had assumed that to focus primarily on citizenship was to take for granted the exclusionary categories of liberal statecraft. Instead, I was interested in the ways the Italian-born children of African and Afro-Latinx immigrants were increasingly collectively identifying as "Black" or "Afro" Italian, as opposed to the "Ghanaian-" or "Nigerian-Italian" labels favored by the generation of their parents. But I soon found that I could not avoid encountering citizenship: almost every discussion about Blackness I had during my years of fieldwork inevitably circled back to questions of Italian citizenship, nation-state (non)recognition, and the racial dimensions of jus sanguinis and jus soli (right of blood) as legal frameworks for the concession of citizenship. Whether or not activists agreed on the extent to which struggles for racial justice should focus on national citizenship, it invariably constituted the backdrop to most discussions about the past, present, and future of Black Italian politics.

While I came to these discussions about citizenship equipped with a theoretical framework that emphasized national citizenship's constitutive and racialized exclusions, I was also not comfortable arguing that my activist friends had been duped—that, as victims of false consciousness, they were naively putting their hopes for racial liberation in the hands of the racial state. Indeed, I have no interest in presenting a sort of "gotcha" story, in which the punch line of the book is that my interlocutors were actually wrong about the point of citizenship all along. My commitment, instead, is to understand *how* activists came to their particular understandings of citizenship in relation to the project of racial justice—with all of its possibilities and limitations.[88] After all, as profound theorists of their own conditions, they were always acutely aware of these contradictions, and their entanglements consistently pushed me to complicate my own sometimes overly narrow and binaristic understandings of citizenship.

In the spirit of Frantz Fanon's phenomenological approach, then, this book privileges the analytical, political, and ethical significance of lived experience for understanding the dimensions of a particular conceptual problem-space.[89] Indeed, I am interested in how Black Italian racial subjectivity is constituted, experienced, contested, and mobilized in relation to the many everyday sites and processes of racist violence Fanon described—including the gaze, epidermalization (the "fixing" of racial difference in the body), and language. The fact that the lived experience of Black Italianness was, for so many of my interlocutors, so intimately mediated by citizenship, in turn directed my analytical focus to the co-constitutive relationship between race and citizenship in the construction of the Italian nation-state. And because I could not easily brush aside citizenship, I then became interested in what political lessons the entanglements of race and citizenship could offer for Black struggles in other contexts.

As a self-identified Black Italian, I structured my engagement with these questions in a way that was necessarily reflexive, but also attentive to differences of power. I came to this research because the entanglements of race and citizenship in Italy have intimately shaped my own life. My mother is a white Italian who grew up in the small town of Trescore (about one hour from Milan); my father is a Black American who was born in rural Virginia and grew up in Oakland. They met when my father was drafted into the US Army and stationed in Italy; they married in Italy in 1976, and several years later returned to California, where I was born. Our household was bilingual, and I actually spoke Italian before I started speaking English. And since my mother was the youngest of thirteen siblings, I grew up spending every summer (and often winter) with her family in Italy. This is all to say that my life has been shaped by a deep connection to both diasporic Blackness *and* Italianness. I was struck by the profound resonances between the stories of Black Italians in Italy and my own lived experiences, and their insights ultimately helped me understand myself and my family in powerful new ways.

But at the same time, I have the privileges of relatively unfettered transnational mobility that come with an American passport and an elite US academic institutional affiliation.[90] In addition, I have Italian citizenship thanks to the same descent-based jus sanguinis framework that has simultaneously disenfranchised so many of my Black Italian comrades. In other words, despite the fact that I was born in California and they were born or raised in Italy, I am an Italian citizen simply because my mother was also born an Italian citizen. Yet it is also undeniable that I lived my research intimately, on the surface of my skin. I regularly endured the same types of questions that implicitly mapped race onto citizenship—"But where are you *really* from?" and "Where did you learn to speak Italian so well?"—that my interlocutors so frequently cited.

Ultimately, by grounding my analysis in these kinds of everyday negotiations and lived experiences (including those of my interlocutors *and* my own), I came to understand citizenship not simply as the highest goal of liberal politics, but rather as a complex, ambiguous, and deeply fraught terrain of struggle that can nonetheless become a platform for the articulation of other sorts of radical political solidarities. For that reason, this book is structured to trace a still-unfolding narrative and historical arc—as activists organize around citizenship, navigate the limits of liberal categories, and begin articulating other kinds of political visions and formations.

Overview of the Book

Contesting Race and Citizenship is organized into two parts. Part I, "Citizenship," explores the challenges and contradictions that can arise when Black anti-racism advocacy is yoked to the goal of national citizenship. Chapter 1, "Italian Ethnonationalism and the Limits of Citizenship," follows the emergence of the movement to reform Italian citizenship law from jus sanguinis to jus soli. While some scholars have been quick to dismiss these mobilizations as insufficiently radical because they are oriented on a politics of state recognition, I argue that they can actually reveal the complex ways that the boundaries of Italianness are being redrawn in the midst of interlocking economic, demographic, and migration "crises." I show that as Black Italians become entangled in the ambiguous process of redefining Italianness away from racialized notions of blood descent and toward the supposedly "race-neutral" categories of culture and birthplace, they are in turn shaping the terrain of political struggle in Italy for newly arrived refugees from the African continent.

Chapter 2, "Black Entrepreneurs and the '(Re)Making' of Italy," focuses on one surprising branch of these citizenship struggles: entrepreneurship. During the last half decade, there has been a veritable explosion of Black Italian women's entrepreneurship oriented on natural hair care, cosmetics, and African fashion. Drawing on interviews and participant observation with a group of young Black entrepreneurs, I show that these "Made in Italy" Afro-businesses are important—yet politically ambiguous—sites of struggle over access to Italian citizenship. In particular, Black women entrepreneurs are leveraging their businesses to advance glamorous and cosmopolitan images of Black life in Italy. Invoking older notions of Italo-Mediterranean *meticciato* (mixedness), these entrepreneurs also assert their worthiness as potential citizens by claiming that their diasporic networks can resolve Italy's economic stagnation and restore the country's status as a vibrant cultural and economic crossroads. Yet such claims only become legible in *contrast* to the figure of the refugee. Rather than a deracialization of Italianness, we instead witness the production of new distinctions between "productive" Black citizens (or citizens-in-waiting) and "unproductive" Black refugees—distinctions that invoke a much older liberal history of the racialized "undeserving poor."

Chapter 3, "Mediterraneanism, Africa, and the Racial Borders of Italianness," takes a step back in time. I situate contemporary debates in Italy about race and citizenship within a much longer trajectory of racial formation in the Mediterranean region, focusing on four key moments: national unification and colonial expansion, fascism, postwar reconstruction, and Italy's transformation into a country of immigration. Drawing on research conducted in the archives of nineteenth-century Italian racial scientists, I show that (in contrast to what happened in northern Europe), *meticciato* was not necessarily seen as a threat to racial purity in the fledgling Italian nation-state. In fact, at times it was also understood as a source of racial and cultural invigoration—a potential solution to the challenges of modernity. Italy's geographical proximity to Africa generated a range of efforts by scientists, politicians, and intellectuals to clarify the relationship between Italianness and Blackness. I argue that this historic precariousness of Italian "whiteness" in relation to northern Europe ultimately created a unique opening for Black activists to mobilize for a widening of the racial boundaries of Italian citizenship. At the same time, however, claims about Mediterranean racial fluidity can also (sometimes inadvertently) work to subsume and invisibilize Blackness within the overarching category of "mixedness."

Part II of the book, "Diasporic Politics," explores the new political horizons that emerge when activists confront the limits of citizenship. While Black Italians continue to mobilize for access to Italian citizenship, they are also increasingly engaged in forms of community that subtly challenge or undermine the exclusionary functions of liberal citizenship. Chapter 4, "Translation and the Lived Geographies of the Black Mediterranean," tracks the emergent politics of Black Italy in the aftermath of the 2016 murder of Nigerian asylum seeker Emmanuel Chidi Nnamdi. Drawing on participant observation and multiyear collaborations with several Black Italian organizations, I narrate the various ways Black activists attempt to craft a language that can attend to the specific contours of racism and exclusion in Italy. In this chapter, I also reintroduce the concept of the "Black Mediterranean," a framework that characterizes the dense relations of cultural contact and racist violence linking southern Europe and Africa. The Black Mediterranean, I argue, provides an antidote to the whitewashed vision of Mediterranean mixing critiqued in chapter 3—while also allowing for historically and geographically situated engagements with the dense material and symbolic networks of Italian Blackness. While Black people born or raised in Italy have only relatively recently begun to refer to themselves collectively as "Black Italian" or "Afro-Italian," I argue that these exciting new conversations draw on resources from across the global Black diaspora to contend with the possibilities of Black life in Italy today.

Chapter 5, "Refugees and Citizens-in-Waiting," explores alternative forms of Black Italian political organizing that do not necessarily regard citizenship as a primary goal. Drawing on anthropologist Yarimar Bonilla's notion of "strategic entanglement," I argue that Italy's continued descent into far-right ethnonationalism has sparked an important shift in Black Italian politics.[91] Specifically, Black Italian activists are increasingly using shifting alliances and tactical engagements with the Italian state apparatus for purposes that include, but also extend beyond, the objective of formal nation-state recognition. I focus on the work of a group of Italian-born Eritreans in Milan who self-organized in response to the arrival of large numbers of Eritrean refugees and asylum seekers to the Porta Venezia neighborhood in 2015. Rather than draw distinctions based on birthplace or legal status, they instead sought to craft new and transgressive sorts of political alliances—based on what I call *Black Mediterranean diasporic politics*—oriented on the shared ties of anti-racist and anticolonial diasporic struggle.

Finally, the conclusion considers the broader implications of this Italian story. Southern Europe has become a hothouse for the many, seemingly apocalyptic forces shaping our present, from economic precarity and austerity to ethnonationalism and fascism to global mass migrations met by deadly border regimes and walls. I travel to southern Italy and speak to Black activists in Naples to consider how this conjuncture has taken shape in a "marginal" region of a "marginal" European country in a "marginal" corner of the Black diaspora. Through these engagements, I conclude that the Black Mediterranean actually represents an instructive limit case wherein colonial legacies, neoliberal practices of migration management, and historically sedimented forms of anti-Black racism have all come together to produce not only new dynamics of racist violence and exclusion, but also inspiring new practices of border-transgressing, diasporic solidarity.

Part 1
CITIZENSHIP

ITALIAN ETHNONATIONALISM
AND THE LIMITS OF CITIZENSHIP

Until the middle of the 1980s, when Italian society was homogenous, defining citizenship was automatic; today, instead, being a society composed of diverse people, languages, religions, cultures, and ethnicities, the system is more complex.

—Francesco Occhetta, "La cittadinanza in Italia"

For the *extracomunitario* [non-EU citizen], the condition of being a foreigner becomes like a biological fact from which it is impossible to escape.

—Clelia Bartoli, *Razzisti per legge*

On a bright sunny morning in March 2016, a group of thirteen activists from across Italy converged outside a stately palazzo near the central Termini train station of Rome. We buzzed our way through the formidable wooden doors of the building and proceeded together up the stairs. As we headed through an office into its main conference room, we passed a poster of the Italian-Eritrean activist Medhin Paolos. Her arms were folded across her chest, a confident smile on her face, all above the bolded words "L'Italia sono anch'io" (I am Italy, too). We eventually took our seats in red chairs surrounding a translucent conference table. The tinny hum of cars and scooters zooming along the busy Roman street below filtered through the windows.

This meeting had been organized by Rete G2 (2G Network), a national advocacy organization comprising "second-generation" Italians who had been mobilizing for over a decade to reform Italy's nationality laws and make it easier for the Italian-born children of immigrants to become Italian citizens. The original founders of Rete G2 were now in their late thirties and forties, and many were raising young children. As such, they were eager to reach out to a younger generation of activists to invigorate the movement with new ideas and mobilization strategies. Two months earlier, they had sent personal invitations to individuals who had been active on Rete G2's Facebook page but were not formally part of the group's organizational core—these were people who themselves had large online presences and, in many cases, were also actively engaged in projects around anti-racism, Black Italian representation, youth empowerment, and women's employment. I had been invited to come down from Milan to observe and participate in this meeting by a friend and research participant, herself one of Rete G2's original members.

The conditions that had prompted this meeting were dire, to say the least. The lower house of the Italian parliament had approved an attenuated version of a citizenship reform proposal in October of the previous year, but the bill remained stalled in the Italian Senate. Despite months of backroom lobbying meetings with legislators and staffers working in the Chamber of Deputies offices of Montecitorio in Rome, Rete G2 organizers did not have a clear sense of when, if ever, the proposal would reach the Senate floor for formal consideration.

The broader political climate did not help the situation, either. The effects of the 2015 Mediterranean refugee crisis continued to reverberate across the country, prompting wildly xenophobic predictions that an expansion of citizenship rights to the children of immigrants born and raised in Italy would precipitate an unstoppable "invasion" of foreigners on Italian soil. A terrorist attack in Paris in November 2015, for which the Islamic State of Iraq and the Levant (ISIL) claimed responsibility, subsequently reignited fears about the establishment of a radical Islamic "foothold" in Italy—a country where Catholicism has come to stand in as an uneasy proxy for whiteness and national identity.[1] And last but not least, the upcoming Italian municipal elections meant that politicians were unwilling to take a decisive stance on citizenship reform—not only to avoid alienating voters, but also because of their uncertainty over how an expanded electorate that included the children of immigrants could shift the balance of political power.

Back in the conference room, we proceeded to go around the table and take turns introducing ourselves. The "old guard" of Rete G2 was clustered at one end of the table, while the newer participants had assembled at the other end. The group ranged in age from early twenties to mid-forties, with a wide swath of national backgrounds represented: Ethiopia, Morocco, Nigeria, Ghana, China, Albania, Eritrea, Chile, Argentina. Some had come to Italy as small children with their parents, while others were born in Italy; some were born with Italian citizenship, others had finally become naturalized after battling for years with the Italian immigration bureaucracy, and yet others were still waiting to become citizens of the country they had called "home" for their entire lives. Their individual stories of legal nonrecognition revealed the affective or emotional significance of citizenship, which is too often reduced in political discourse and political theory to a dry matter of bureaucracy and physical papers. A lack of Italian citizenship had cost many of these activists potential jobs and educational opportunities; they could not vote, nor could they travel easily to other countries. Yet beyond these more concrete or "material" concerns, restricted access to citizenship had also set into motion paralyzing identity crises and feelings of inferiority for many.

But despite this deep and abiding sense that citizenship was more than just a bureaucratic formality, the activists gathered expressed a range of differing opinions about *why* citizenship mattered so much. Indeed, as the conversation unfolded over an eight-hour day, some consequential differences began to emerge in the ways that people made sense of the purpose of citizenship, its limits, and how to organize effectively *and* ethically for the right of citizenship in a profoundly hostile political climate. These questions might, at first glance, seem painfully obvious and self-evident; after all, liberal social theory usually takes for granted the idea that national citizenship should be the ultimate goal for immigrants and their children. But for the activists who had gathered in Rome that day—whose lives had been so intimately shaped by their limited access to Italian citizenship—things were not so simple and clear-cut. Indeed, the nuances of the activists' lengthy conversation about citizenship suggested that *any* discussion of the politics of citizenship must start from the complex and sometimes contradictory lived experiences of those whose lives are most intimately shaped by restrictive citizenship laws.

"How does it feel to be a problem?," W. E. B. Du Bois famously asked in *The Souls of Black Folk*.[2] According to Du Bois, *being a problem* was both a psychological burden and a window onto the racist hypocrisy that constituted American democracy. In other words, the double consciousness that Black folk in the United States experienced—the result of being forced to measure themselves according to a set of standards that were never truly meant to include them—actually afforded them the unique ability to identify patterns of inequality and injustice.[3] But what does Du Boisian double consciousness look like in contemporary Italy? After all, given the particularly contested history of whiteness and nation building in Italy, is it accurate to describe this consciousness as merely *double*, or is it actually *multiple*?

In the case of the children of immigrants who had gathered in Rome for the Rete G2 meeting, their unique "multiple consciousness" was the product of a lifelong negotiation of Italy's ever-shifting (and increasingly exclusionary) standards of membership—standards that could at different moments entail assessments of their language and dialect abilities, cultural competency, birthplace, length of residence, bodily habitus, and phenotype. It was additionally shaped by their own everyday experiences as part of the Italian social fabric, as well as their negotiations of a form of social liminality wherein they could be interpellated neither as Italian "natives" nor as immigrants or refugees. As such, their discussion about how best to mobilize for citizenship rights also shed light directly onto the ways that normative understandings of Italianness and Italian citizenship were shot through with unspoken ideas about race and the racial characteristics of "true" Italians.

The debates that day hinged on two interrelated issues. First, *who* should have access to citizenship, and why? Was there a real difference between *birth* on Italian soil versus long-term residency in Italy from childhood? Should one's eligibility for citizenship be determined by the number of years she or he had spent in Italian schools, or by their parents' possession of a long-term residency permit? And what about the parents themselves? Could advocating for a law that expanded citizenship rights for the children of immigrants born and raised in Italy drive a painful wedge between generations, pitting the *seconda generazione* against their first-generation immigrant parents in a battle for legitimacy and recognition as authentically "Italian"?

And second, what form should their ongoing mobilizations for citizenship reform take? Did it make sense to march in the streets, making themselves visible to the Italian public as "invisible citizens," or would they only attract public scrutiny and endanger the larger cause? This question was linked to a broader philosophical matter—namely, what citizenship actually *means*. For some, it was urgent to stage mass demonstrations in which the children of immigrants could display themselves as culturally Italian "through and through." But for others, this question of cultural performance was a red herring—the *real* question was one of rights. If white Italians were not forced to endure tests of cultural authenticity in order to be recognized as full citizens, then why should this be required (informally or otherwise) of the children of immigrants who had grown up in Italy? In fact, our group introductions at the beginning of the day had been momentarily interrupted by a telling exchange between Angela, one of the newcomers, and Almaz, one of the founding members of Rete G2, about precisely this matter:[4]

> Angela: I was not able to get citizenship when I turned eighteen. Citizenship is an important component of life, and at first, I felt like I needed that paper to prove that I was Italian.
>
> Almaz: You know, as *seconda generazione* we are forced to "carry the flag,"[5] to be extra Italian, but we should also have the right to critique the country. The document is something else.
>
> Angela: Before, I felt like I had to be the *most* Italian. But now I want citizenship as a right. I have worked, contributed, gone to school.
>
> Almaz: But citizenship is not given based on merit.
>
> Angela: Citizenship blocks opportunities. When a job requires Italian citizenship, you have to create other opportunities for yourself. It was important for me to realize that other people didn't have citizenship; I felt like I was alone, like this was a reflection of my character.[6]

This dialogue, and others like it throughout the day, suggested that important shifts were underway. One was, of course, temporal—a generation had aged through the movement, and a younger cohort was beginning to explore diverse tactics and modes of engagement. But there was also an expanding plurality of philosophies at play about the politics of citizenship itself. Many of the young people who were invited to the meeting that day had been occupied with questions of racism and Blackness primarily—not necessarily citizenship. And the ongoing refugee crisis meant that many activists found themselves in the uncomfortable position of having to distinguish themselves publicly not only from their parents, but also from newly arrived African refugees—a stance that often contradicted their own deeply held kinship obligations and political commitments. Indeed, many activists expressed concern that the notion of a teleological, intergenerational transformation from "immigrant" into "Italian" was leaving people behind.

The meeting that day complicated the celebratory narratives that are often recounted in popular media about immigration and citizenship, in which migrants or their children slowly progress from being outsiders to insiders—a narrative that also presumes the boundaries of citizenship to be stable, immutable social facts. But how did citizenship become one of the primary means of advocating for racial inclusion in Italy in the first place, and what work does this conflation do? How have citizenship reform activists become entangled with the process of redefining Italy's legal, racial, cultural, and economic boundaries? And what are the consequences of these reconsolidations of Italianness? To be clear, this is not a story of citizenship per se, nor is it a story of what happens when people become citizens. Instead, it is a story of how different groups make sense of citizenship, and how the *possibility* of becoming a citizen produces subjects in different ways.

In this chapter, therefore, I seek to understand *why* and *how* citizenship emerged as a privileged terrain of struggle over institutional racism and racial inclusion in Italy. Is it indeed possible to "de-racialize" Italian citizenship, or does any engagement with the apparatus of citizenship beyond outright refusal inevitably reproduce the exclusionary dynamics of the racial state? The citizenship mobilizations of the children of immigrants in Italy reveal the complex ways that Italianness is currently being reconfigured in the midst of interlocking economic, demographic, and migration "crises," generating newer forms of differentiation and exclusion.

To capture these shifts, I trace a brief history of Italian citizenship law, as well as the movement launched in 2005 to reform the country's citizenship law toward a moderate form of jus soli, or right of birthplace. These mobilizations have recently opened up a series of powerful conversations among activists about the actual meaning and purpose of citizenship, as well as the relationship between access to citizenship and other political projects such as refugee rights and the inclusion of Black Italians within the material and symbolic boundaries of Italianness. Notably, in 2017 the Italian philosopher and public intellectual Giorgio Agamben openly announced his opposition to jus soli citizenship reform in Italy on the grounds that national citizenship is the problem, not the solution, to the violent regimes of exclusion and differential incorporation plaguing totalitarian regimes and liberal democracies alike in the modern world.[7]

Using Agamben's controversial provocation as an incitement to discourse, I look back to the prehistory of the Italian citizenship reform movement to demonstrate that the turn to *citizenship* in Italian anti-racism activism was not inevitable—and that citizenship reform activists are not simply naïve and misguided in their efforts.[8] I argue that the 1990s were a key moment when racial nationalism became structurally embedded within the apparatus of citizenship, a process that was also entangled with ideas about the market and productivity. While the standard narrative is that Italian racial nationalism disappeared along with state fascism after World War II, this relationship merely took on a new form as Italy underwent a dramatic transition from being a country of *emigration* to becoming a country of *immigration*. Ultimately, this development had the effect of establishing nation-state citizenship as the dominant terrain of struggle for racial justice and inclusion in Italy. But at the same time, this development has also created a troubling dilemma for activists, one in which their legal efforts to expand the boundaries of Italianness can also be co-opted by the state to perpetually reproduce citizenship's racialized "outside"—this time, in the figure of the sub-Saharan African refugee.

A Fragmented Nation: Different Diasporas and the Contours of Italian Citizenship

As I noted earlier, Italy has among the most restrictive nationality laws in Europe.[9] This is true even considering that after several decades of heated debate about the "integration" of migrants and their children, jus sanguinis (right of blood or descent) is still the dominant principle governing the acquisition of citizenship in Europe, and no European country has absolute jus soli citizenship like the United States.[10] Currently, the children of immigrants in Italy compose approximately 15 percent of new births in Italy, or 10 percent of the country's total youth population.[11] Yet, because Italian citizenship is conferred on the basis of jus sanguinis, the children of noncitizen immigrants who were born and raised in

Italy are not automatically granted Italian citizenship at birth. In fact, Italy is one of eight countries that signed but never ratified the 1997 European Convention on Nationality, an agreement stipulating that member states should facilitate the acquisition of citizenship for all people born in the country.[12] While minors born to naturalized immigrant parents are granted Italian citizenship at birth, Italy's restrictive citizenship laws have made it a very difficult and labyrinthine process for first-generation immigrants in Italy to naturalize in the first place.

The nationality law currently in force in Italy, Law No. 91 of 1992, specifies that the children of immigrants automatically inherit the nationality of their parents at birth.[13] On reaching the age of majority, or eighteen years old, they subsequently have a one-year window during which they can apply for Italian citizenship.[14] Technically, this means that children born in Italy to immigrants have a longer wait than immigrants themselves before they are eligible for citizenship in Italy—eighteen years, versus the ten years of legal residency required for immigrants to naturalize. To apply for naturalization, applicants must provide proof of continuous Italian residency and pay an application fee of 250 euros, among other application requirements.

Even for those who have lived in Italy from birth, proving continuous residence is not always a straightforward matter. As Jacqueline Andall has observed, many children of immigrants who would have been technically eligible for citizenship on turning eighteen have been unable to trace proof of continuous residence because their parents did not register their births with the local *anagrafe* (civil registry).[15] For instance, the children of Eritrean immigrants who arrived in Italy in the 1970s and took up residence in "occupied" or squatted homes due to housing shortages did not always have their births officially registered. When they applied for Italian citizenship on turning eighteen, they found themselves lacking official documentation to prove that they had been resident in the country from birth, and were thus ineligible to petition for Italian citizenship.[16] In another more recent case, a young man had his citizenship application rejected because there was a short period of his childhood when his parents were unemployed and between homes. Although he attempted to make up for the gap in his residency with school records, this was insufficient—the apparent assumption was that he could have been flying back and forth from his parents' home country in West Africa daily to attend school in Italy!

For applicants who *are* able to meet these requirements, the Italian naturalization process still has no guarantees. Many applicants find themselves languishing in interminable bureaucratic limbo, since the processing time for naturalization requests varies dramatically across the regions of Italy. For instance, in Modena—which has seen citizenship requests double over the course of the last four years—not a single one of the three thousand requests filed through the province's online system in 2015 had been processed as of the beginning of 2016.[17] Finally, for those whose requests are approved, their citizenship is formally a *concession*, not a right (unlike citizenship via marriage), granted based on "the interests of the State and the national community."[18]

Italian census estimates suggest that Law 91/1992 has left between six hundred thousand and nine hundred thousand children of immigrants without citizenship.[19] The impacts of Italy's restrictive citizenship laws are thus profound and far-reaching. Children without Italian citizenship cannot easily go on school-sponsored field trips outside of Italy with their classmates; often, they must request a visa first, and on return they must re-enter Italy through the customs line for non-EU citizens.[20] Without Italian citizenship, the children of immigrants cannot apply for jobs through the state system of *concorsi pubblici*, which encompasses career fields ranging from policing and law to medicine and teaching. They cannot vote in local or national elections. Perhaps the greatest source of fear for the children of immigrants who are unable to successfully petition for Italian citizenship is that they must live in Italy on the equivalent of a work permit (which requires a formal contract with an employer), a student visa (which requires enrollment in higher education), or a long-term residency permit (which, among other stipulations, requires the maintenance of a minimum income level). The loss of legal residency thus carries with it the statistically small but nonetheless real possibility of deportation to a parental home country that they might have never visited, and whose language they might not speak comfortably.[21] In sum, Italy's citizenship laws presume that the children of immigrants are fundamentally *foreigners*, despite having been born on Italian soil, having attended Italian schools, and speaking Italian as a first language.

But it is important to note that jus sanguinis in Italy was not inevitable. Rather, the shifting contours of Italian citizenship law were shaped by the contentious spatial project of Italian unification and nation building at the end of nineteenth century. The Risorgimento, or Italian national unification process, was completed in 1871 when Rome was incorporated as the country's capital. Nonetheless, the Italian nation-state has been characterized since its inception by deep and intractable political, economic, and cultural "fragmentation" between the economically prosperous and industrialized North and the agricultural, impoverished South.[22] Indeed, the debates that unfolded in the context of Italian national unification about the boundaries of citizenship closely paralleled those taking place in the post–Civil War United States, which faced similarly interlocking questions about the relationship between an agricultural South and industrial North, the place of Blackness within the nation, and the potential citizenship rights of long-subjugated, racialized, and economically exploited groups.[23]

The first attempt at a comprehensive Italian nationality law, the 1865 Codice Civile (Civil Code), allowed citizenship in some cases for those born in Italy; this was part of an effort to recognize the contributions of foreigners who fought in the wars of Italian unification.[24] Jus sanguinis only became enshrined in Italian law in 1912, with Law No. 55/1912. This new nationality law was enacted in response to the contradictory pressures of nation building, internal differentiation, and diaspora that plagued the new Italian nation-state. During this period, the fledgling Italian nation-state was engaged in the process of producing the contested category of "Italian citizen" in relation to multiple, racially fraught Southern Questions—northern Europe versus southern / Mediterranean Europe, northern Italy versus southern Italy, and Italy versus its new African colonies.[25] Shortly after national unification, millions of Italians began to leave Italy in search of work abroad, establishing emigrant *colonie* in countries across the Americas.[26] And even before the project of national unification was complete, Italy had also begun projects of "demographic colonialism" in the Horn of Africa, moving in step with the rest of Europe's scramble for African colonies.[27] From the time of Italy's humiliating defeat at the Battle of Adwa in 1896 up until the early twentieth century, the former model of "emigrant colonialism" was generally regarded as a "pressure release valve" for shunting off excess populations that was preferable to demographic colonialism in Africa—additionally, emigration would also extend Italian interests elsewhere in the world.[28] It was only after Italy's seizure of Libya during the 1911–12 Italo-Turkish War (and the overall improvement of the Italian economy at the beginning of the twentieth century) that the Italian government began actively attempting to recall Italian emigrants, who could then settle this new North African colony.

In this context, Cristiana Giordano argues, jus sanguinis (conferred via the paternal line) was seen by lawmakers as a way to construct "a notion of nationality as a tenacious bond that could endure emigration and be passed down to descendants in the diaspora."[29] Legal restrictions prohibiting the acquisition of citizenship by the children of white Italian men and Black African women from the Italian colonies in the Horn of Africa were not overturned until 1952.[30] In addition, until 1975, women could lose their citizenship if they married men with non-Italian citizenship.[31] Relatedly, it was not until 1983 that the ability to transmit Italian citizenship by birth was deemed to be the constitutional right of women in addition to men.[32] Prior to 1983, under Italian law a family's citizenship always followed that of the paterfamilias, or male head of household.

The legal boundaries of Italian citizenship have thus never been stable; instead, they have repeatedly expanded and contracted since the Risorgimento. The apparatus of citizenship via blood descent was not a "natural" outcome of Italian nation building, but was rather the product of a set of historically and geographically specific debates about the impacts of regional fragmentation, mass emigration, and colonialism on the bonds of the national community. While the 1912 nationality law was enacted in response to the challenges posed by an *outward-moving* Italian diaspora, debates about Italian citizenship since the 1980s have focused on the impact of non-Italian diasporas *entering* Italian space. In this context, the new boundary figures on which these newer citizenship debates hinge are *migranti* (immigrants), *stranieri* (foreigners), *extracomunitari* (non-EU citizens), and *rifugiati* (refugees, typically assumed to be African).

Today, however, Italian political commentators (including those who are generally supportive of a reform toward jus soli) frequently assert that citizenship was a relatively straightforward matter before Italy became a country of immigration in the 1980s and 1990s. As the epigraph at the beginning of this chapter from Jesuit journalist Francesco Occhetta suggests, this claim relies on the invention of a mythical Italian past characterized by a bounded and homogenous national body. This stable sense of *italianità*, the story goes, was rudely interrupted by the arrival of large numbers of postcolonial migrants at the end of the twentieth century. But the history of Italian nationality laws reveals that the question of citizenship in Italy is far more complex than these recent commentators would suggest. In fact, Italian citizenship has been more a question of *managing difference and spatial dispersal* than of maintaining internal homogeneity and national boundedness—from regional differences, to colonial encounters, to the spatially extended ties of large-scale emigration. It is for this reason that in her magisterial history of Italian nationality law from 1861 to 1950, Sabina Donati argues: "To be Italian, to become Italian and to exercise rights and duties in the peninsula as Italian citizens meant very different things at specific points. . . . Metaphorically, the changing laws and debates concerning citizenship can certainly be useful pencils for researchers when trying to give form to and grasp the historically evolving and changeable meanings of *italianità*."[33] As Donati goes on to explain, citizenship and national identity do not move in lockstep. At times, citizenship laws may reflect particular ideas and ideals of Italian nationhood, but generally speaking, "there is no causal link between national identity and nationality laws."[34]

Because jus sanguinis is not the natural outgrowth of a stable, unitary notion of *italianità*, it is open to challenges and transformation. In addition, this Italianness is not formally codified and transmitted through state institutions as in explicitly assimilationist countries such as France, so it is open to constant negotiation and contestation.[35] In this spirit, "second-generation" activists have argued that descent-based citizenship enshrines a racialized notion of Italianness that is sharply at odds with the country's increasing demographic diversity: a generation of new Italians who should have automatically earned the right to Italian citizenship by virtue of the fact that they were born on Italian soil are systematically disadvantaged by policies that enshrine a biologistic conception of Italianness. For many of these activists, the shared characteristics that define Italian citizenship today should not be blood, parentage, or descent, but rather the influence of birthplace and the bonds of culture and language.[36] In this way, citizenship reform activists have now become entangled in the processes by which the Italian state has historically defined who *is* (or should be) and who *is not* (or should not be) an Italian citizen.

"I Am Italy, Too!": The Jus Soli Citizenship Reform Movement

The implications of these new divisions became especially pronounced as effects of the 2015 Mediterranean refugee crisis began to intensify. Many of the most prominent citizenship reform activists in Italy are of African descent, and the majority of the refugees arriving in Italy via the Mediterranean are from sub-Saharan African countries such as Nigeria and Eritrea. As these "second-generation" activists were forced to resist their conflation with African refugees on the grounds that they are *Italians, not immigrants*, their strategies also raised challenging questions about the limits of nation-state citizenship as an approach to inclusion—and specifically, racial inclusion. These sorts of questions have intensified the debates around citizenship in Italy, not only between second-generation activists and politicians, but also among activists themselves.

Analyses of the Italian citizenship reform movement have tended toward one of two dominant narratives. On the one hand are celebratory accounts of second-generation activists who are attempting to radically transform and expand the definition of Italianness.[37] On the other hand are more skeptical accounts of activists who have naïvely linked their struggles for social justice to nation-state recognition.[38] The story I wish to tell, however, departs from both these frameworks. I am interested instead in the consolidation of the categories of "second generation" and "Italian without citizenship" as the basis for collective political action, and the way that these efforts in turn implicate activists in the contentious project of redrawing the boundaries of Italian inclusion and exclusion at a moment of perceived, interlocking "crises"—what Stuart Hall presciently described as the interplay between "positioning" and "being positioned."[39]

The number of children with non-Italian citizenship has grown by almost 300 percent since 2002, from a total of 288,950 to 1,087,016 *minori stranieri* in 2014.[40] Indeed, as the "problem" of immigration increasingly figured into political and academic debates about the borders of Italy, a quiet generational shift was gradually underway. Immigrants who settled in Italy in the 1970s, 1980s, and 1990s were now raising children on Italian soil—children who, despite having spent their entire lives in Italy, were not legally or socially recognized as citizens.

In 2005, a group of children of immigrants in Italy came together to form Rete G2. While this was not the first national Italian organization comprising the children of immigrants (Giovanni Musulmani d'Italia, or Young Muslims of Italy, was founded in 2001), it was the first to engage in political action around a shared "general identity as 'second generation.'"[41] Rete G2 was actually an outgrowth of informal social gatherings in Rome, during which a group of friends would meet regularly to discuss their shared experiences. They quickly found that while their parents had emigrated to Italy from many different countries, their own subjectivities converged on the shared condition of not being recognized as Italian. A common lament during these gatherings was that they found themselves being constantly asked the same question by strangers: "Ma, dove hai imparato a parlare così bene l'italiano?" ("Where did you learn to speak Italian so well?")—an Italian version of the spirit-crushing, Fanonian "Look! A Negro!" moment of interpellation.[42] It was in these sorts of exchanges that the hidden racial criteria floating beneath the supposedly neutral cultural markers of Italianness suddenly became evident—speaking fluent Italian was simply not enough to make one register as properly Italian.

During a conversation over spiced teas at an Eritrean bar in Milan during the summer of 2014, Zahra (herself Italian-Eritrean) fondly reminisced about the early days of Rete G2: "Rete G2 emerged from very personal needs, in Rome, in 2005—from things that touched our lives every day. The main objective [of citizenship reform] was selected because it's not useful to have ten items on your agenda and then not get to any of them. But at first, we started by doing mutual aid. It was like therapy. People would come together and chat, talking about the most basic things, like their hair, like having an Afro."[43] As a formal voluntary association, Rete G2 engages in two other broad sets of activities beyond advocacy for citizenship reform. First, they serve as a social network for the Italian-born and -raised children of immigrants who are scattered across the Italian peninsula. In fact, one of their first public initiatives was to establish an online forum for young people to connect, share their stories, and ask questions about the naturalization process.[44] For instance, a commenter once posted on the Rete G2 forum that he was having difficulty finding documents that would prove he had lived in Italy continually since birth. Another commenter responded with advice, noting that she had success using vaccination records as proof of residency in her own citizenship application.

In addition, the organization has also been involved in a series of national media campaigns that are intended to challenge public perceptions of who is Italian. Often, these projects (such as a collaboration with the children of midcentury Italian immigrants in Switzerland) show how Italy's own history of mass emigration has complicated questions of national identity. During an interview at a bookstore in Rome in 2014, Ibrahim, an Italian of Libyan descent and one of the founders of Rete G2, explained this prong of their strategy: "Citizenship is the main objective, but we have to also work on the image that Italy has of itself. Italy is only ever represented as white and Catholic. This has not changed in the last ten years. Changing the law also means putting this model into crisis. Italy is a country that still doesn't accept immigration."[45]

The organization's choice of name is significant as well. While the sociological concept of *second generation* has been subject to thorough academic critique, Rete G2 activists use this term rather differently from most mainstream scholars of migration.[46] For them, *seconda generazione* is not intended to serve as a stable sociological referent. Instead, it refers to the broader sense of demographic and social transformation represented by a new generation of young people who, in some way or another, have "non-Italian" backgrounds. In this way, Rete G2 has stretched the "second generation" label to include people who arrived in Italy as young children, as well as adoptees and children of mixed backgrounds. As Zahra elaborated:

> Back in 2005, people didn't talk about these things as much. In Italy, they have always talked about immigration, but about the children of immigrants? Never. And now there is criticism of the term "2G." I listen to the critiques, but the way I see it, it's a good thing that there is this debate. Because before, people didn't even have this identity, but now they can debate it. It's a privilege! We didn't invent the term; we just used it in the name Rete G2. Sociologists invented the term. We took it and expanded the definition, because people talk about all of the divisions in the second generation. We wanted to be more inclusive. We include people who were born here, who came here when they were very young, even people who were adopted. In Rete G2, we wanted to bring all of these people together. They are different ages, they come from different cities, they have different accents, but they are all Italian and something else.

For members of Rete G2, the term *seconda generazione* is in effect a political claim about the future of Italy. Rete G2 activists argue that Italy's dramatic transition from a country of emigration to a country of immigration in the 1980s and 1990s has produced an unstoppable demographic transformation that demands the country come to terms with its own history of colonialism and racism, and with the very tenuousness of Italian national identity itself.

In 2011, Rete G2 launched the L'Italia Sono Anch'io campaign along with a coalition of nonprofit partners and national labor unions. The goal of this campaign was to gather fifty thousand signatures (the threshold required to present a proposal by popular initiative to the Italian legislature) in support of a petition for a new citizenship law.[47] The campaign was an unprecedented success, ultimately collecting the signatures of two hundred thousand Italian citizens. The original proposal from the L'Italia Sono Anch'io campaign included automatic citizenship for any child born to an immigrant who had been legally resident in Italy for at least one year, as well as a simplified path to citizenship for those who arrived in Italy as children or who were born in Italy to parents without a residency permit.[48] The proposal also called for a reduction in the time required for naturalization for adult immigrants, from ten to five years. A second proposal developed for the L'Italia Sono Anch'io campaign would have also granted foreigners legally resident in Italy for at least five years the right to vote in local and regional elections.[49]

L'Italia Sono Anch'io's proposals were delivered to the Italian legislature in 2012. Finally, on October 13, 2015, the Camera dei Deputati (the Chamber of Deputies, the lower house of the Italian parliament) approved a citizenship reform bill that incorporated elements of the popular initiative proposal, along with parts of twenty other proposals related to citizenship.[50] Cécile Kyenge, Italy's then-minister of integration and the country's first Black government minister, contributed significant international attention and visibility to this campaign. In 2013, Kyenge (following the PD's list of legislative priorities for the first hundred days of the newly constituted Letta cabinet) established jus soli citizenship as a centerpiece of her agenda, publicly declaring several times in the media that "whoever is born in Italy is Italian."[51]

The law ultimately approved by the Camera dei Deputati departed in some significant ways from the original proposal developed by Rete G2 and the L'Italia Sono Anch'io campaign. Encouragingly, the Camera bill included an amendment that would have allowed people who were older than eighteen to retroactively obtain citizenship. On the other hand, however, the provision that would have reduced the residency requirement for naturalization was eliminated. In addition, whereas the original proposal only required parents to be legally resident in Italy for one year, the new proposal required at least one parent to be in possession of a long-term residency permit and to pass an Italian language test. Finally, the Camera's proposal emphasized a form of citizenship acquisition called *jus culturae* (right of culture). Jus culturae links citizenship for people who arrived in Italy as children to their time spent in the Italian school system. In other words, those who arrived in Italy before the age of twelve could become citizens after five years of school, while those who arrived between the ages of twelve and eighteen could acquire citizenship after living in Italy for five years, completing a full scholastic cycle, and obtaining an educational qualification (e.g., a high school or vocational school diploma). While the original L'Italia Sono Anch'io proposal did include one path to citizenship linked to school, jus culturae was hailed as an innovation of the Camera's bill, which emphasized this route while attenuating other possible paths to citizenship.[52]

The move toward jus culturae elicited a range of responses among citizenship reform activists. One founder of Rete G2 explained her ambivalence during a public forum in 2016: "We would have preferred a different form for the kids, something tied to the parents' *permesso di soggiorno* instead of school. Because school makes it seem like citizenship is a cultural thing." Yet this moment also signaled a significant shift already underway in the tone of citizenship reform activism. Activists had long sought to challenge the narrow conception of Italian national belonging enshrined in Italian citizenship law by pointing to both the historic and contemporary pluralities of Italianness.[53] But some groups had now begun to emphasize a "cultural citizenship" that could become the basis of a deracialized citizenship (see figure 1.1, for example). The proposal of jus culturae rests on the assumption that the Italian-born and -raised children of immigrants have been thoroughly infused with the "essential" cultural qualities of Italian national culture—that they are not foreigners, but practically (if not phenotypically) indistinguishable from white Italians in terms of language and habits. This was thus a timely and politically astute strategy that at once allowed activists to (1) subversively "talk back" to the structural racism of citizenship laws;[54] (2) refute the right's xenophobic claims that jus soli would lead to a "foreign invasion"; and (3) appeal to sympathetic centrist politicians with a liberal multicultural narrative of an ever-expanding Italian national family.

The 2012 documentary *18 Ius soli*, by Italian-Ghanaian filmmaker Fred Kuwornu, is emblematic of this kind of culturalist understanding of Italian citizenship. In one memorable promotional clip, an Italian-Nigerian rapper shares his Italian cultural bona fides against a bright blue background, the same shade used on the jerseys of Italian national sports teams: "I love pizza, I eat lasagna. . . . I mean, I sing Italian songs to my friends! So that makes me an Italian, just like my friends."[55] It is not surprising that these words were uttered by a Black Italian interview subject: Black Italians have long been overrepresented in the citizenship reform movement, precisely because Blackness and Black people are marked as the most extreme symbols of national nonbelonging in Italy.[56] For

FIGURE 1.1. "Cultural citizenship" in practice? A poster drawn by a multi-cultural group of children from an elementary school summer camp in Rome, displayed at a citizenship reform protest outside the Pantheon in 2017. Their text reads:

> *I AM ITALIAN BECAUSE:*
> *Monia: Italy is my reality.*
> *Hasanov: Italian is easier.*
> *Christian: There are more opportunities in Italy.*
> *Thomas: I like the landscapes.*
> *Arianna: I love pizza.*
> *Jeremy: I like soccer.*
> *Pierpaolo: Because in Italy there is safety and freedom!*

Source: Author photo.

this reason, global Black hip-hop style and other resources from across the Black diaspora have also figured prominently in citizenship reform activism.[57] In 2012, for instance, Rete G2 released a CD titled *Straniero a chi?* (Foreign According to Whom?), which featured a collection of original tracks by a group of *seconda generazione* musicians, the majority of whom were rappers, hip-hop producers, or reggae artists. The centrality of Black cultural products in the movement in fact speaks to the power of the "outernational, transcultural" politics of the Black diaspora, even beyond the Black Atlantic.[58]

At the same time, the circulation of images of Black Italians eating pizza and lasagne can also obscure the limitations of a culturalist approach to citizenship. At first glance, the turn to "common culture" does seem to offer the possibility of an Italianness delinked from race.[59] The Italian-Ghanaian soccer star Mario Balotelli, for instance, is frequently described by the Italian press as having a markedly *bresciano* accent (an accent typical of Brescia, the region in northern Italy where he grew up)—the assumption being that if one were not able to see the color of his skin, he could be mistaken for a white Italian.[60] The embrace of cultural citizenship similarly presumes "race" and "culture" to be diametrically opposed systems of categorization; in this understanding, culture is by extension a less rigid and essentializing means of defining the parameters of group membership than race.[61] As Stuart Hall argued, however, culture and race are really just "racism's two registers."[62] While biological understandings of "race" arguably reached their peak during the midcentury fascist regimes, race has historically been a polyvalent category that could never be reduced to just blood or phenotype. Rather, race can be more accurately understood as a power-laden, floating signifier that is made meaningful through religion, culture, geography, mobility, bodily practice, and social associations for the purpose of calcifying difference and arranging groups into hierarchies.[63]

Still, while activists admitted that the new reform bill did not contain all of their original demands, its approval by the Camera dei Deputati was nonetheless met with widespread celebration. And in fact, many children of immigrants actually supported the move toward citizenship via jus culturae because it gave them another way to legitimate their Italianness to a racist and xenophobic Italian public—specifically, through the "facts" of shared language and schooling. This optimism, however, sadly proved short-lived. By the time the group of activists had gathered in Rome for the meeting recounted at the beginning of this chapter, the reform bill had been languishing in the Italian Senate for over five months. The right-wing Lega Nord party had introduced thousands of nonsense amendments to the bill, simply to slow its progress through the Senate's committees.[64] Right-wing opposition to citizenship reform in the Italian parliament at this time conflated refugee arrivals via the Mediterranean, the threat of radical Islamic terrorism, and the supposed dangers of citizenship reform. Under the brash front-page headline "More Immigrants = More Attacks," the conservative Italian newspaper *Libero* argued that summer: "Italy has not yet been struck [by terrorists] because Islamists are less numerous. But above all because Italy does not give citizenship to people who are born here; that way we can drive them out if they do bad things. Too bad the Left wants to introduce jus soli."[65]

After the approval of the citizenship reform bill in the Camera, a group of older citizenship activists and younger recruits splintered off from Rete G2,

FIGURES 1.2A AND 1.2B.   Scenes from the October 13, 2016, flash mob in Rome.

Sources: Author photos.

demanding more direct action and public protests in support of citizenship reform. Expressing frustration with what they perceived as excessive backroom lobbying and legislative advocacy, this new group coordinated a series of flash mobs in major cities around Italy to mark the one-year anniversary of the citizenship reform bill's approval in the Camera. Organizing under the banner of Italiani senza Cittadinanza (Italians without Citizenship), large groups of activists descended on Padua, Bologna, Reggio Emilia, Rome, Naples, and Palermo on October 13, 2016, draped in ghostly white bedsheets to symbolize their status as forgotten, "invisible citizens" of Italy (see figures 1.2a and 1.2b).[66] The flash mobs were also accompanied by a national media campaign that included the distribution of "citizenship postcards" (see figure 1.3) featuring images of individual *italiani senza cittadinanza* as small children alongside their emotional, firsthand stories of growing up and attending school in Italy.

The flash mobs were incredibly successful in bringing wider public attention back to the subject of citizenship reform in Italy. But some children of immigrants saw these efforts as misguided, with the potential for unforeseen political consequences. As the mobilizations unfolded, one Black Italian researcher and filmmaker shared her reservations with me: "They are conflating

#ItalianiSenzaCittadinanza

Assita, Palermo

"Questa é una delle mie foto più belle di quando ero alle elementari. C'è tutta la mia classe. Ero tranquilla e felice con i miei compagnetti, ignara di essere una straniera nel Paese in cui sono nata e in cui sarei cresciuta. Oggi che sono finalmente cittadina italiana e continuo a studiare e investire sulla mia formazione, correndo da un corso all'altro, mi capita di riflettere ancora sulla mia condizione e su quella di altri giovani. Mi chiedo: vale la pena offrire il mio "sudore" intellettuale e le mie future competenze professionali ad un Paese che ha aspettato 18 anni prima di riconoscermi Cittadina?".

FIGURE 1.3. A citizenship postcard featuring the story of Assita, a Black Italian of Ivorian descent, surrounded by her elementary school classmates in Palermo. She writes:

"This is one of the best photos from when I was in elementary school. My whole class is here. I was relaxed and happy with my classmates, unaware that I was a foreigner in the country where I was born and raised. Now that I am finally an Italian citizen and I continue to study and invest in my education, running from one class to another, it has occurred to me to reflect again on my condition and that of other young people. I ask myself, Is it worth offering my intellectual 'sweat' and my future professional skills to a country that waited eighteen years before recognizing me as a citizen?"

Source: Italiani senza Cittadinanza Facebook page (https://www.facebook.com/italianisenzacittadinanza /photos/1839181636363233).

identity or belonging with a bureaucratic matter. Citizenship is bureaucratic; it doesn't mean that you feel that you belong. But part of the mobilization is proving that you are Italian in all of these different ways—with food, for instance." While I was at first taken aback by these comments, her words continued to echo in my mind—and she was also not the only Black Italian I know who had expressed these sorts of reservations (while still being supportive of the overall project of citizenship reform). Luca Bussotti argues that since 1912, Italian citizenship law has implicitly emphasized the "quality" of citizenship over the quantity of Italian citizens.[67] In a similar sense, my friend seemed to be arguing, *seconda generazione* activists were put in the position of having to articulate a set of claims about the "quality" of their Italianness in order to gain access to citizenship—that birth and schooling in Italy had produced a generation of unrecognized youth who were more "Italian" than their counterparts across the Italian diaspora.

I was also reminded of the words of conservative Italian politician Giorgia Meloni, leader of the Fratelli d'Italia (Brothers of Italy) party, who had expressed opposition to citizenship reform on the grounds that "becoming an Italian citizen should not be a bureaucratic matter, but an act of love."[68] Why were citizenship reform activists increasingly forced to prove their Italianness as a prerequisite for citizenship, when citizenship *is* a mere bureaucratic matter for white Italians? As the refugee crisis consumed the political debate, citizenship reform activists not only had to enumerate all of the ways that they had been thoroughly produced as culturally Italian, but also had to demonstrate that this quality in turn distinguished them from newly arrived African refugees. While citizenship reform activists since the early days of Rete G2 have justifiably emphasized that they are not foreigners, this message became increasingly urgent as politicians began to conflate refugees and the Italian-born children of immigrants.[69]

Along these same lines, Italiani senza Cittadinanza sought to challenge Italian ethnic absolutism by showing the public that they were "Italian-plus"—that their identities encapsulated multiple geographical itineraries within and beyond Italy.[70] Their mobilizations were also unfolding in relation to a burgeoning Black Italian postcolonial critique in literature and film, which approached contemporary Italian citizenship law as an enduring legacy of colonial governance and racial hierarchy.[71] Still, activists found that this rich and transgressive border consciousness had to be strategically grounded in some kind of recognizable "Italianness" for their citizenship claims to be taken seriously.[72] Indeed, as Lorgia García Peña observes, the fact that the children of immigrants must consistently perform their Italianness represents yet another way that the Italian nation-state normalizes racism not only through legal mechanisms, but through "symbolic actions" as well.[73] Italian journalists, as well as lawmakers from center-left parties such as the Partito Democratico (PD), had effectively wrangled the complex narratives of the *seconda generazione* (along with their withering critiques of the Italian nation-state) into a singular narrative that at once reified the Italian nation as a bounded object unified by a set of shared characteristics and elevated the standing of the Italian-born children of immigrants in relation to "unassimilable" refugees.

The following summer, Italiani senza Cittadinanza was facing another emergency: the citizenship reform bill would expire unless the Senate officially put the bill on its legislative calendar. Due to the 2016 constitutional referendum, which would have altered the size and composition of the Italian Senate, the PD had opted to indefinitely postpone any discussion or vote on the bill. On the final day the bill could be discussed before its expiration—June 15, 2017—opposition to citizenship reform came to a head in a series of racially charged confrontations unlike any seen previously. The neofascist CasaPound and the far-right Forza Nuova parties staged a demonstration in front of the Senate building, waving Italian flags and carrying large posters that explicitly linked jus soli and radical Islamic terrorism (see Figure 1.4 for the satirical response devised by some members of Italiani senza Cittadinanza). And the situation was no better on the Senate floor. As the Senate moved to open discussions of the citizenship reform bill, Lega Nord parliamentarians unfolded papers bearing the bolded words "NO JUS SOLI" and "STOP THE INVASION" as a small group of Black Italian activists looked on in horror from the public gallery above. A violent shoving match ensued, sending one senator to the emergency room. On the right, political commentators across Italy declared that if it were approved, citizenship reform would bring about "ethnic substitution"—a common refrain in the transnational circuits of white nationalist politics.[74]

The refraction of these racialized demographic concerns about the Italian population onto the question of citizenship was not entirely surprising. A year earlier, the Italian Ministry of Health's failed "Fertility Day" initiative had featured a campaign poster contrasting a stock photo of a white family with an image of a racially mixed group of young people apparently smoking cannabis, all above the unmistakably eugenic caption, "Correct lifestyles for the prevention of sterility and infertility" (see figure 1.5a).[75] For citizenship activists of color, the bitter irony was that the Italian government wanted to grow the Italian population, all while continuing to deny the children of immigrants access to Italian citizenship. Indeed, the Ministry of Health's pronatalist campaign seemed to foreshadow US congressional representative Steve King's 2017 declaration that America cannot "restore our civilization with someone else's babies."[76]

The day after the contentious Senate hearing, the Silvio Berlusconi–owned right-wing newspaper Il Giornale appeared on newsstands emblazoned with the headline "Easy Citizenship: ITALIAFRICA." It is important to note that while sub-Saharan Africans fleeing violence and political instability were overrepresented among the refugees arriving in Italy at that time, the majority of immigrants and their children in Italy are not Black.[77] Yet the supposed threat of a Black African invasion figured so prominently in debates about citizenship reform that the actual national backgrounds of the seconda generazione did not really matter. For opponents of the citizenship reform bill, Blackness and Islam together had come to stand in for everything that was "foreign" to Italy, and for all of the country's demographic, economic, social, and political woes.[78] Despite the fact that many Afrodescendants in Italy are also Muslim (particularly those with roots in countries such as Senegal, Nigeria, Eritrea, and Somalia), Blackness and Islam are understood in Italian public discourse to constitute two relatively distinct "racial" threats (see figure 1.5b).[79] The former threatens the demise of an unmarked Italian whiteness through racial contamination and biological degradation, while the latter stands in

FIGURE 1.4. A meme created by two members of Italiani senza Cittadinanza to poke fun at the figure of the Italian-American born in the United States, who can become an Italian citizen within a matter of months. The text reads, "Thank You Jus Sanguinis: Michael Rossi, 'Italian.'" This image was originally designed as a response to the signs carried by CasaPound protesters at an anti–jus soli demonstration in Rome in June of 2017. One widely photographed sign contained the text "Grazie Ius Soli: Jihadi John, 'inglese'" ("Thank You Jus Soli: Jihadi John, 'English'") next to an image of a man in a balaclava brandishing a serrated blade. The other CasaPound posters on display that day followed a similar visual formula.

FIGURES 1.5A AND 1.5B.   Race, sex, and the gendering of citizenship. On the left, a promotional poster from the Italian Ministry of Health's 2016 "Fertility Day" campaign. The large text reads, "Correct lifestyles for the prevention of sterility and infertility." On the upper photo, the caption says, "The good habits to promote"; below, "the bad 'company' to avoid."

On the right, an image used by the far-right Forza Nuova political party in 2017 that reads, "Defend her from the new invaders! She could be your mother, your wife, your sister, your daughter." This was originally a Fascist poster from 1944 intended to warn the Italian public about the sexual threat posed by Black American Allied soldiers in Italy; Forza Nuova only added the text "from the new invaders" and its logo.

Sources: Italian Ministry of Health and Monica Rubino, "Fertility day, bufera su opuscolo 'razzista': Lorenzin lo ritira e apre indagine," La Reppublica, September 21, 2016, http://www.repubblica.it/politica/2016/09/21 /news/fertility_day_mozione_di_sel-sinistra_italiana_cancellare_la_vecchia_campagna_-148217942/ (left); Forza Nuova, "Migranti, polemica sul manifesto di Forza Nuova: utilizza la progapanda fascista del Ventennio," Il Fatto Quotidiano, September 2, 2017, https://www.ilfattoquotidiano.it/2017/09/02/migranti polemica sul -manifesto-di-forza-nuova-utilizza-la-propaganda-fascista-del-ventennio/3831751/ (right).

for "the fear of violent death, the paranoia of Europe's cultural demise," and the annihilation of Italy as a Catholic nation (fears reignited most recently by the post–9/11 Global War on Terror).[80] Indeed, as David Theo Goldberg argues, "the figure of the Muslim, alongside that of the Jew, has historically bookended" Europe's long-standing preoccupations with its relationship to Blackness.[81]

While the citizenship reform bill survived the ominous June 2017 deadline, it ultimately died an untimely death in the Italian Senate that December—not from an insufficient number of votes in favor, but because the Senate continued to postpone a vote on the bill until December 23, when the parliament was scheduled to adjourn.[82] In the months leading up to that deadline, Italiani senza Cittadinanza had organized regular protests outside of Montecitorio in Rome; they also endured a brutal campaign of online harassment and misinformation targeting their activists and Facebook page. Ultimately, there were actually enough votes to pass the citizenship reform bill, but rather than risk adopting what could be interpreted as a politically divisive stance on the question of Italian citizenship, senators from across the political spectrum simply waited for the bill to expire. In fact, senators from the center-left Partito Democratico who had publicly expressed their support for the reform did not even present themselves in the Senate chambers that day. So, in a disturbing turn of events, a parliamentary *non-vote* had the effect of quashing the voting rights (among many other civil rights) of the Italian-born children of immigrants.

As one organizer told me a year and a half later, this day remains "seared in their memories." An open letter from Italiani senza Cittadinanza, addressed to Italian president Sergio Mattarella, expressed their outrage that the Senate had failed to uphold the Italian constitution. While this move could be read as an embrace of liberal constitutional values—with their intervention centered on the need for those values to be applied *equitably*—an alternative reading is that the open letter represents a subtle and subversive critique highlighting the hypocrisy embedded in the Italian state's deployment of the liberal category of "citizen":

> Today, December 27, marks seventy years since the promulgation of the constitution of our country. . . . We have all read, re-read, and rediscovered it during this year of mobilizations for citizenship reform; we recognized ourselves profoundly in its values, and particularly in Article 3 . . . : "It is the task of the Republic to remove the obstacles of economic and social order that limit the equality of citizens and prevent the full development of the human person and effective participation of all workers in the political, economic, and social organization of the country." . . . Dear President, you will agree with us that on December 23 the Republic failed in the removal of these "obstacles," maintaining a clear distinction between citizens and noncitizens, based on a purely elitist and economic conception of citizenship. Citizenship is more than a right. The great philosopher Hannah Arendt defined it as "the right to have rights" because only recognition as a citizen can transform an individual into a legal subject with rights.[83]

For citizenship reform activists, the demise of the bill in the Senate was perhaps the greatest setback in an exhausting political journey that had begun over a decade earlier. They had been abandoned by many of their allies, abused, and attacked. What could possibly come next?

Race, Nation-States, and the Politics of Citizenship

Two months earlier, the Italian philosopher Giorgio Agamben had penned a controversial editorial (in Italian) explaining why he did not sign a petition in favor of jus soli.[84] But unlike the concerns of other opponents of the citizenship reform movement, Agamben's skepticism had nothing to do with fears of "invasion" or cultural dilution. Rather, his opposition was grounded in the same prevailing concern throughout his work with the relation between sovereignty and biopolitics that is instantiated in modern understandings of citizenship.[85] For Agamben, sovereign power is based on the ability of the sovereign to enact a state of exception, within which the rule of law no longer applies and basic human rights are suspended. Citizenship represents one political-juridical technology by which such "bare life" is produced through sovereign exception; however, merely expanding citizenship rights does not automatically challenge the sovereign's power to reduce political, rights-based life to bare life. As Agamben elaborated in his open letter:

> We take for granted [the idea of citizenship], and we do not ever ask about its origins or its significance. It seems obvious to us that every human being from birth should be registered in a state order and in that way find themselves subjected to the laws and the political system of a state that they did not choose and from which they cannot disengage. . . . No matter the procedure used to determine this registration . . . the result is the same: a human being is subjected to a juridical-political order. . . . I fully recognize that the status of "statelessness" or "migrant" cannot be avoided, but I am not sure that citizenship is the best solution.[86]

Many activists perceived Agamben's open letter as yet another in a long series of betrayals from individuals and groups they expected to be allies—at the end of the statement, he noted that he would in theory support a petition urging all people to *give up* their national citizenship, though in reality he made no moves to renounce his Italian citizenship (symbolically or otherwise). Agamben's public opposition to jus soli represented a particularly stinging blow because he occupies the dual position of being both an elite and widely cited intellectual figure in the United States and Europe, *and* a prominent political figure. Agamben has made a number of recent forays into contemporary political debates and has emerged as a key point of reference in discussions about the so-called refugee crisis in Europe and migrant detention.

But despite the unpopularity of his stance, Agamben undoubtedly raised a series of challenging questions that are worth considering further—albeit from a different angle. Are there other political possibilities outside of this state-centric, juridical-political order? And following Alexander Weheliye's incisive critique of Agamben's *homo sacer*, what happens when we privilege *racism* in an analysis of citizenship and the state?[87] How might this change the way we understand political mobilizations that seek to question or challenge the normative arrangements of national citizenship, even when these actions may not "fundamentally alter the structured materiality of modern liberal juridical order and the political economy of . . . migration?"[88]

These are questions that, one way or another, will continue to shape citizenship mobilizations long after the crushing defeat of the reform bill in 2017. Many Black Italian activists and other people of color in Italy have come to understand citizenship reform as a means of contesting racialized national exclusion. And *opposition* to citizenship reform is almost always articulated in explicitly or implicitly racist terms (e.g., the threat of an African invasion). But *why* have the terms of racial inclusion and exclusion in Italy been articulated primarily through national citizenship, as opposed to other frameworks? Is it possible to contest a deeply restrictive Italian nationality law that disproportionality disadvantages people of color, while also articulating a political alternative that does not inadvertently reify the bounded nation? And what room is there for immigrants, refugees, and other "border crossers" in this citizenship story?

Citizenship remains so theoretically confounding because it is at once universalizing and differentiating. This profound political dilemma—of citizenship *both* as access to the promise of rights and recognition *and* as constantly generative of differentiation—has been increasingly taken up by scholar-activists in critical citizenship and migration studies. The 2015 Mediterranean refugee crisis and the subsequent fortification of the legal and territorial boundaries of Fortress Europe, in particular, has informed ongoing efforts by political theorists in Europe to re-evaluate citizenship not merely as a question of rights, but also—in a similar vein to Agamben—as a tool of exclusion and differential incorporation. These interventions are welded to a political economic critique in which borders and immigration and citizenship statuses are understood as tools of state power that condition, filter, and differentiate a global labor force.[89] In response to such trenchant critiques of nation-state citizenship, critical citizenship studies has attempted to delink citizenship from the state by instead highlighting a range of subaltern "acts of citizenship."[90] This is a response to the paradox Hannah Arendt described in *The Origins of Totalitarianism* as the "right to have rights" (which Italiani senza Cittadinanza also referenced in their open letter to Mattarella)—specifically, that access to what are commonly understood as universal human rights is always contingent on recognition by a spatially delimited, sovereign nation-state.[91]

In an attempt to untangle the Arendtian dilemma—and as a counterpoint to the state's exclusionary practices—critical citizenship studies has analyzed citizenship as a *process of claiming rights* rather than the rights themselves. As Ruth Lister explains, this work approaches citizenship as active participation, separate from rights—which could in turn become "the object of [political] struggle."[92] The goal of such a significantly expanded view of citizenship beyond the realm of the nation-state is to understand what alternative practices of community and obligation emerge when our analysis proceeds from the mutual constitution of "citizenship and its alterity."[93] But while the critical citizenship studies emphasis on both *exclusion* and *acts of citizenship* is profoundly generative, this approach has some important limitations.

For one, Sandro Mezzadra argues, attempts to broaden the concept of citizenship can inadvertently neglect its histories of violence and exclusion, with the result that "citizenship has been . . . cleansed of the burden of its historical past."[94] This is partly because the critical citizenship studies literature has downplayed the ongoing sovereignty of the state, as well as the significance of formal, nation-state citizenship in determining life chances and social opportunity for many racialized, precarious, and otherwise marginalized groups.[95] Indeed, much of the research that undergirds this body of literature has been conducted with migrants, refugees, and stateless people—groups for which national citizenship may in some cases be less materially significant than, for instance, an absence of direct violence and the freedom to move. But as Dorothy Louise Zinn points out, using the example of the Italian *seconda generazione*: "For many G2s, the problem of Italian citizenship simply looms too large for them to give much credence to theories of the irrelevance of the nation-state or the ascendancy of European supranationality."[96] Different marginalized groups related to national citizenship in divergent ways, Zinn suggests. For Black Italians born and raised in Italy, nation-state citizenship, even as a mechanism of differentiation, remains consequential—even in an age of globalization and transnationalism.

In addition, while these critical approaches to citizenship have analyzed citizenship in relation to exclusion and differentiation, exclusion is often approached as ontologically distinct from racism, or alternatively as a condition that can become "racialized" through external forces.[97] But even when national citizenship laws do not explicitly invoke racial categories, the apparatus of citizenship cannot be understood outside the intertwined histories of race, state, and nation.[98] Goldberg, for instance, argues that race has been central to the state since its conceptual and institutional emergence.[99] Specifically, the raison d'être of the modern racial state is to enforce internal homogeneity and expel heterogeneity from its boundaries.[100] When it comes to citizenship, this means that the state not only creates the conditions of possibility under which citizens can act as sovereign agents with free will; it is also a gatekeeper that, through the apparatus of law, determines who falls within the categories of "citizen" and "free agent" in the first place, through the deployment of various "racially ordered terms."[101]

Goldberg thus invites us to ask what happens to our account of citizenship when we flip the script: it is not that citizenship can become *inflected* by racism, but instead that our modern understandings of citizenship themselves derive from notions of racial difference—that racism is what molds the boundaries of citizenship. What emerges is not simply a story about fascist legacies in our current ethnonationalist resurgence, but a *longue durée* account of the dance of liberalism and racism.[102] Notions of racial difference are fundamentally embedded within the apparatus of liberal nation-state citizenship, which is why it is paradoxically both a location for the reproduction of racisms *and* a potent site of struggle for anti-racist activists in Italy.

Replanting the Seeds of Italian Racial Nationalism

To understand how citizenship became both the dominant means of advocating for racial inclusion *and* a means of producing new forms of racial differentiation and exclusion in Italy, we must return to an earlier set of debates. Italy did not have any formal immigration policies until the early 1990s. Before that time, migration to Italy was organized primarily through informal recruitment and resettlement by Catholic charities, or through the transnational social networks set into motion by Italian decolonization in the Horn of Africa.[103] In fact, what made Italy such an attractive destination for immigration in the 1980s was its relatively relaxed immigration laws in comparison with those of other European countries such as the United Kingdom.[104]

In 1989, the racist murder of South African asylum seeker Jerry Masslo in southern Italy prompted the enactment of Italy's first formal immigration law. Masslo, a thirty-nine-year-old anti-apartheid activist, had fled South Africa in hopes of eventually settling in Canada. At the time, however, Italy recognized political asylum applications only from Eastern Europe.[105] Because of his uncertain legal status, Masslo was forced to find informal work as a tomato picker in Villa Literno. While little is known about the precise circumstances of his murder, it is believed that he was killed while defending his meager salary from thieves. A flyer bearing the message "Permanent open season on Negroes" was found near the scene of the crime.[106]

Masslo's murder was incredibly shocking when it occurred. Many Italian commentators—as well as many African students in those early days of immigration to Italy—had hoped that Italy would be a relatively accommodating destination because of Italy's own history of mass emigration.[107] As Jeffrey Cole has observed, the late 1980s in Italy saw the publication of many books with predictions about Italian attitudes toward these new immigrants such as *Gli italiani sono razzisti?* (Are Italians Racist?) and *Oltre il razzismo: Verso la società multirazziale e multiculturale* (Beyond Racism: Toward a Multiracial and Multicultural Society).[108] Masslo's widely circulated reflections on Italian racism, drawn from an interview conducted the winter before his murder, were sobering:

> I thought in Italy I would find a space to live, a bit of civilization, a welcome that would allow me to live in peace and cultivate the dream of a tomorrow without barriers or prejudice. Instead, I am disappointed. Having black skin in this country is a limit to civilized coexistence. Racism is here, too: it is made up of bullying, abuses, daily violences against people who are asking for nothing more than solidarity and respect. Those of us in the Third World are contributing to the development of your country, but it seems that this has no weight. Sooner or later one of us will be killed and then they will realize we exist.[109]

Jerry Masslo's murder was met by massive, nationwide anti-racism demonstrations—demonstrations evincing the depth and breadth of the global, coalitional anti-apartheid politics that had initially emerged to support the full citizenship rights of Black folk in South Africa. In Rome alone, over two hundred thousand marchers descended into the streets—including Tommie C. Smith, the gold medal–winning sprinter who famously raised his fist in a Black Power salute at the 1968 Mexico City Olympics.[110] In addition, the public outcry surrounding Masslo's death set into motion the enactment of the Legge Martelli (Law 39/1990) in 1990. This was Italy's first formal immigration law, and its purpose was to regularize migrant workers in Italy by codifying a set of bureaucratic categories for migrants entering the country. Under the Legge Martelli, immigrants could apply for renewable two-year visas for the purpose of work, study, medical care, or family reunification; those who overstayed their visas were considered irregular migrants and could be summarily expelled from Italy within fifteen days.[111] At the time, lawmakers framed the Legge Martelli as an attempt to protect migrant workers from labor abuse by granting them official, legal status.[112] But this law worked in practice by reducing the number of immigrants who could legally enter the country. As the blog *Struggles in Italy* argues, by linking yearly immigration quotas to the job market, the Legge Martelli set into motion an "economic view of migration," one that has in turn served as the basis for all subsequent Italian immigration laws.[113]

On the coattails of the Legge Martelli, a restrictive reform of Italian citizenship law was enacted in 1992. When compared to the previous 1912 citizenship law, the new 1992 legislation made it easier for diasporic descendants of white Italians who had never lived in Italy to acquire Italian citizenship; at the same time, it became *more* difficult for immigrants and their children to naturalize under the 1992 citizenship law than the 1912 law.[114] Descendants of Italian emigrants living abroad (so-called latent Italians, or *oriundi*) could easily reacquire Italian citizenship, with no time or generational limits on this reactivation.[115] Italian emigrants and their descendants who had lost or renounced their Italian citizenship due to the nationality laws of their receiving countries could also regain citizenship with three years of residence in Italy.[116] For non-EU migrants, the time of residency required for naturalization was augmented from five years to ten years (EU citizens are required to have only four years of residency in Italy).[117] In this way, the new Italian nationality law explicitly doubled down on jus sanguinis citizenship at a time of increasing demographic heterogeneity in Italy, using geographical and cultural distinctions to draw a new set of racial boundaries around Italian membership.

The 1990s were thus a key turning point: they saw both the expansion of the bureaucratic categorization of migrants, linking their status to employment and economic contribution, and contracted access to citizenship. It is important to remember that at this moment Italians were coming to understand their country as one of *immigration*—a sharp departure from its much longer history as a country of mass emigration. These new debates about the need for "migration management" were thus shaped by a broader set of ongoing conversations about Italian racism, the possibility (or impossibility) of a multicultural Italian future, and the bases of a shared national identity. On the one hand, the Left invoked Italy's status as an historically poorer, racially ambiguous nation of emigrants and unsuccessful colonizers; on the other hand, the resurgent Right (symbolized by right-wing parties like the neofascist Movimento Sociale Italiano and Silvio Berlusconi's Forza Italia, as well as separatist parties such as the Lega Nord) embraced increasingly insular nationalist and regionalist politics.[118]

The Legge Martelli, but especially the 1992 citizenship law, can thus be read as expressions of modern racial nationalism. Through these laws, the connection between race and nation was framed by the legal apparatus of citizenship—a

link that was subsequently reinforced by legislation such as the 2002 Bossi-Fini Law (discussed in chapter 2). Once again, it is important to remember that "race" is not a stable ontological category that precedes racism; instead, racism itself produces the seemingly objective reality of race in the world, seizing on markers such as phenotypic difference, geography, culture, and economic activity.[119] This is especially important for understanding the various manifestations of state racism in postfascist Italy, where "race" became an "unspeakable" category of formal politics but *racism* did not disappear. Drawing on Goldberg's powerful theorization of "racial evaporations" in Europe, Caterina Romeo writes: "Race—historically a constitutive element in the process of Italian national identity—has 'evaporated' from the cultural debate in contemporary Italy as a result of the necessity to obliterate 'embarrassing' historical events. . . . The presence of race, like the presence of steam, saturates the air, rendering it heavy, unbreathable. Moreover, there is the constant threat that race could change its status back if challenged by new forces, thus becoming visible again."[120]

The contemporary articulations of race and citizenship in Italy must therefore be situated in the context of mid-twentieth-century liberal anti-racist arguments against the explicit invocation of "race" (understood in terms of essentialized, biological difference).[121] In Italy, for instance, the term *razza* (race) is associated almost entirely with Fascist-era racial theories. In this post–World War II retreat from "race," biological understandings of race have fallen out of official favor: center-left anti-racists advocate postracialism and color blindness, while right-wing separatists couch their xenophobia in the "acceptable" language of cultural difference.[122] But even when the legal architecture of explicit, biologically based racism has been dismantled, patterns of racialized disadvantage and exclusion persist, albeit under insidious new guises. Theorists have approached this "racial evaporation" using the analytics of "cultural racism," "cultural fundamentalism," "new racism," "racism without race," "differential racism," or "color-blind racism / racism without racists" to characterize the contours of these exclusionary discursive practices that order difference in cultural rather than purely biological terms.[123]

In this context, citizenship and nationality law became a way to re-border the Italian nation at a time of increasing heterogeneity, using facially neutral—but, as we have seen, profoundly racialized—categories. Italian citizenship law relies on notions of blood descent that implicitly link biological kinship and economic productivity to the construction of a shared, homogenous national cultural community.[124] For instance, in a widely circulated 2013 editorial written in opposition to jus soli citizenship, Italian political scientist Giovanni Sartori criticized minister of integration Kyenge's assertion that Italy is a "paese 'meticcio'" ("mixed" country).[125] With this assertion, Kyenge was drawing on a discursive repertoire favored by the Italian Left—one that vaunted Italy's historical-geographical position as a civilizational crossroads in the Mediterranean as a framework for approaching debates about the incorporation of racial "difference" into the contemporary Italian nation-state.[126] Sartori, however, disagreed; in his retort to Kyenge, he asserted that "Brazil is a very mixed country. But Italy is not. . . . Our alleged immigration expert [Kyenge] assumes that African and Arab youth born in Italy are 'integrated' citizens."[127] Indeed, as Tatiana Petrovich Njegosh astutely observes, "The terms ['jus sanguinis' and 'jus soli'] are significant . . . because they make visible that which the law invisibilizes through 'neutral' terms like 'descent' and 'ascent': the relationship between citizenship, racial categories, and the racialization of citizenship."[128]

It is worth noting that the re-embedding of racial nationalism within citizenship that occurred during the 1990s was distinct from the biological or phenotypic understandings of race and citizenship that characterized earlier periods in Italy. Nonetheless, this shift still elucidates why citizenship emerged as a primary means of advocating for rights and racial inclusion in Italy within the last decade. It also allows us to understand why citizenship creates a double bind for young activists, one in which solidarity between the *seconda generazione* and refugees is often perceived as politically infeasible and the newly arrived fall outside the racial boundaries of citizenship. It is a product of the way this very specific set of political, economic, and social conditions came together during Italy's transformation into a country of immigration.

Beyond Citizenship?

Racial nationalism did not disappear with the end of fascism in Italy. Rather, the racial underpinnings of citizenship have once again become visible, this time in the cauldron of contemporary struggles to reform Italian citizenship and recent mass migrations to Europe from sub-Saharan Africa. In this way, tracing struggles over citizenship can serve as a methodology for tracking continuities between liberalism, fascism, postracial color blindness, and the current far-right resurgence to reveal the various ways that race was "buried alive."[129] This is an important lesson to remember as the world grapples with the frightening resurgence of far-right ethnonationalism around the globe. It can be quite easy to approach these developments as a break from an earlier period of "color-blind liberalism," or the resurgence of cruder, more anachronistically overt racisms. But our current moment does not represent a historical rupture in a teleological march toward the disappearance of "race." Instead, this Italian story forces us to contend with the embeddedness of race within the nation itself.

The story of *seconda generazione* citizenship reform activists attempting to deracialize Italianness reveals the ways that citizenship constantly reproduces its own constitutive, racialized "outside." The shifting definitions and requirements for citizenship mean that it is also accompanied by a constant pattern of exclusion and differential incorporation, though the specific terms of that exclusion may shift over time—from descent, to length of residence, to cultural knowledge, and so on. In chapter 2, for instance, I will explore in greater detail how economic productivity has emerged as yet another racialized criterion through which "worthy" and "unworthy" citizens are differentiated. As citizenship reform activists fight to legally expand "who counts" as an Italian, they are thus faced with the possibility of a reformed Italian citizenship law that, in practice, actually consolidates Italianness in *new* ways.

This by no means suggests that citizenship is unimportant, or that activism for a reform of Italian citizenship law is misguided—far from it, in fact. Under the leadership of former deputy prime minister and interior minister Matteo Salvini of the Lega, access to citizenship was even *further* restricted. The 2018 Decreto Sicurezza (Security Decree) imposed new Italian language proficiency requirements, increased the fee for citizenship applications, doubled the waiting period between filing an application and receiving a decision from two to four years, and introduced a new series of conditions under which Italian citizenship can be revoked for naturalized citizens.[130] The need for a reform of Italian citizenship law is more urgent than ever.

The jus soli movement in Italy thus points to some of the limitations in contemporary critical theorizations of citizenship, as represented by Agamben's open letter and the radical dismissals of national citizenship so common among many other contemporary political theorists. As Charles T. Lee has argued, Giorgio Agamben's theory of sovereign power lacks an account of the ways the "abject" who are positioned on the constitutive outside of the politico-juridical order—including undocumented migrants, stateless people, refugees, and the children of immigrants—negotiate, extend, and reanimate "the life of citizenship from the very margins of abjection."[131] Lee's work suggests that even when there is no clear "outside" to liberal categories—even when all activism is fraught with varying degrees of contamination and complicity—the supposedly abject can still creatively reshape the terrain of possibility under liberalism, using whatever discursive tools might be at their disposal to craft more livable spaces.[132]

At the same time, the many difficult, sincere conversations activists in Italy are now having about the long-term implications of the jus soli movement also show the importance of remembering to ask, *Who is getting left behind?* and *What political possibilities and formations exist beyond the goal of nation-state recognition?* This is indeed the direction in which young "second-generation" activists in Italy are turning. Disillusioned by a series of betrayals by Italian politicians on the left and right, they have begun to reconsider their political strategies. Since the end of 2017, Italiani senza Cittadinanza have refused to ally themselves with any Italian political party. Rather than working within established political institutions, they have instead refocused their efforts on grassroots organizing, building alliances with teachers, and connecting with activists in other European countries. They have also emphasized cultural production as a way of bringing an analysis of institutional racism to the broader Italian public. In 2018, for instance, they released a short black-and-white film called *Io Sono Rosa Parks* (I Am Rosa Parks), which draws parallels between the civil rights movement in the United States and the jus soli movement in Italy. In addition, many activists I spoke to after 2017 have increasingly begun to deromanticize the goal of national citizenship, approaching it instead as a tool that provides access to a discrete set of rights and capabilities and delinking citizenship from the murkier philosophical and experiential matters of belonging (national or otherwise). In other words, they are not denying the power of the state, but are instead finding new ways to work in, with, and against the violent hegemony of the modern nation-state to articulate what Emilio Giacomo Berrocal has characterized as an "anti-nationalist" approach to citizenship reform.[133]

BLACK ENTREPRENEURS AND THE "(RE)MAKING" OF ITALY

> **We . . . have to define political and social action in different terms, and consider talented, deserving foreigners on the basis of an ethical foundation and a collective need. . . . Our system of production is incapable of taking up the challenges of globalization and transforming the human capital available to it into added value.**
>
> —Otto Bitjoka, *Talea: Il merito mette radici*

> **Attention to capitalism as a mediating force in social relations demonstrates how blackness is simultaneously differentiated and celebrated.**
>
> —Jordanna Matlon, "Racial Capitalism and the Crisis of Black Masculinity"

On July 4, 2016, a group of about thirty fashion designers, stylists, photographers, and journalists gathered in a modern, minimalist event space in southwest Milan.[1] It was a typically swelteringly hot and humid summer day, but the effortless chic of the crowd somehow remained unaffected. Inside the spotless space, dapper bartenders clad in shoulder straps served sparkling water, statuesque models practiced their walks, designers made last-minute adjustments to garments, and photographers lay in wait to snap photos (see figure 2.1). Dressed in a simple black sheath dress and disheveled from the heat and the crowded metro ride that had brought me to this far corner of the city, I was quite obviously unsuccessful in my attempt to blend in with this high-fashion crowd. After ordering a glass of ice water to calm my nerves, I located an inconspicuous seat toward the back of the room, pulled out my pen and notebook, and waited for the fashion show to begin.

This was a preview event organized by the AFRO Fashion Association, founded in 2015 by journalist and activist Michelle Francine Ngomno and obstetrician and fashion designer Ruth Akutu Maccarthy.[2] The following year, in 2017, Michelle, an Italian-Cameroonian raised in Ferrara, and Ruth, an Italian-Ghanaian raised in Seregno, would use the momentum of this capsule show to launch the first-ever Afro Fashion Week in Milan, the world's fashion capital. They have organized the AFRO Fashion Week every fall in Milan since, and continue to develop new initiatives showcasing the work of Black designers and entrepreneurs—from the 2019 FierAfric marketplace in Milan featuring Afrodescendant women designers, hair

FIGURE 2.1.   Models circle the runway during the AFRO Fashion preview event in Milan.

Source: Author photo.

product vendors, and chefs to local events across Italy and a training program for fashion students in Cameroon.[3]

Back at the AFRO Fashion preview event, the guests finished making their way indoors and Ruth took her place at the head of the impromptu catwalk. Despite her petite frame, she dominated the room in a uniform of towering heels, red sheath dress made from a star-speckled West African wax print fabric, turban, and dramatically oversized black glasses. As the low throb of techno music in the background died down, she greeted the crowd and proceeded to explain her philosophy of Afro fashion. The passion and urgency in her voice were palpable:

> Our goal is to promote a new culture, something we call "Afro." We are in a disastrous cultural and political situation right now, with immi-

gration and the plight of the *extracomunitari* [non–European Union immigrants]. This is the right time for this project, because fashion is not just a dress that you wear, a bag you carry, or a shoe you put on. Through fashion, we can show Italy the beauty of a new culture, "Afro": a marriage of colors, scents, and patterns that are African, with the style and elegance that are the special touch of Italian culture.

Ruth's emotional introduction to the fashion show represented one of many concurrent attempts to reframe Italian imaginaries of Africa in direct response to the ongoing southern European refugee crisis. That summer, the Italian news cycle was inundated with sensationalistic images of rickety boats of African asylum seekers capsizing in the Mediterranean, politicians making inflammatory declarations about "African invasions" and "ethnic replacement" in Italy, and acts of racist violence against African migrants. In fact, just two days after Michelle and Ruth's event, a Nigerian asylum seeker named Emmanuel Chidi Nnamdi was murdered in the Italian seaside town of Fermo by a fascist agitator (a story I will discuss in further detail in chapter 4). African refugees and asylum seekers were also being scapegoated at this time as the primary cause of Italian economic stagnation, by supposedly taking jobs and draining scarce welfare resources that should have been the sole entitlement of "native" (i.e., white) Italians.

For Michelle and Ruth, narratives of African cultural creativity constituted a potent strategy for countering this racist "single story" of Black life in Italy.[4] In her introductory remarks, Ruth explicitly rejected the idea of an undifferentiated Blackness, one that was characterized in the popular Italian geographical imagination solely by poverty, passivity, and unproductivity. Rather than desperation and abjection, the alternative vision of "Africanness" invoked by the AFRO Fashion Association that day was characterized by a colorful and happy cultural hybridity that, as a collateral benefit, could also awaken a moribund Italian economy from its prolonged slumber. Instead of showing images of drowning refugees, Ruth conjured a continent full of brightly patterned fabrics and rich creative traditions—a continent whose European-raised children could marshal their spatially extended "Afropolitan" networks and fluency in multiple languages as potent resources for revitalizing the storied tradition of "Made in Italy."[5]

Michelle and Ruth's AFRO Fashion initiative is but one example of a much broader trend of Black Italian women's cultural entrepreneurship in Italy. These varied projects, which have gained significant momentum and visibility during the last five years, encompass sectors such as apparel and accessory design, hair care, and cosmetics; they specifically target Black Italian women, and draw on materials, ingredients, and stylistic references from across the Black diaspora.

These initiatives have helped to advance alternative images of Blackness, and specifically Black womanhood, in Italy—images that depart from the more ubiquitous tragic or sensationalized media narratives that Ruth rejected in her speech. They have also enabled many women to achieve a relative degree of economic independence, particularly because (as described in chapter 1) a broad range of employment sectors are inaccessible to Black Italians without Italian citizenship. Entrepreneurship has thus afforded them the possibility of engaging in a broad range of political causes related to the rights of immigrants and their families in Italy.

In this chapter, I consider the ways that entrepreneurship has provided an unexpected opening for many Black Italian women to articulate claims to citizenship in Italy at a time marked by economic stagnation, virulent xenophobia, and anti-Black racism. As I suggested in chapter 1, discourses of economic productivity in Italy are profoundly interwoven with debates about immigration and citizenship. I expand on this argument here by revealing the ways that concerns about Italian economic stagnation have been mapped onto the figure of the "unproductive" Black migrant—a contemporary reworking of much older racialized and gendered distinctions between "proper citizens" and the "undeserving poor." Such distinctions are not only neoliberal in character, but constitutive of liberalism itself via the "boomerang effects" of European colonialism and imperialism.[6] In the second part of the chapter, I show how Black women's entrepreneurship has emerged as a strategy that is simultaneously *conditioned by* and *resistant to* these regimes of exclusion. I focus on the explosion of projects across northern Italy related to Black beauty and style, drawing on interviews with Black Italian businesswomen and participant observation at events related to Black cultural entrepreneurship in Italy.

Rather than dismiss outright the entrepreneurial activities of Black Italian women as mere "selling out"—by substituting the market for a more radical, anticapitalist agenda of Black politics—I argue that it is necessary to examine how the cultural politics of Blackness articulate with both structural conditions of precarity and creative practices of economic survival. After all, as Arlene Dávila (drawing on the work of Elizabeth Chin) argues, "the involvement of disenfranchised groups in consumer culture has long been pathologized as aberrant or apolitical, rendering any critique of consumption that is blinded of the structural forces that mediate such consumption largely misguided."[7] While Dávila's argument here is focused on consumerism and consumption, her point can also be extended to include the entrepreneurial production and market-based activities of marginalized communities more broadly. Indeed, beyond the more formal political mobilizations for citizenship that I described in detail in chapter 1, entrepreneurship has unquestionably emerged as one of the most active informal sites for the negotiation of Black citizenship in Italy. Following the reasoning of Dávila and Chin, this is precisely *because* long-standing racialized and gendered ideas about economic productivity and citizenship have shaped the current terrain of struggle for Black Italian women. This is an important reminder that citizenship, in all of its complexities, always exceeds purely state-centric analyses; the boundaries of citizenship are produced and contested not just through legislation and statecraft, but within the realms of political economy and cultural politics as well.

The women I profile in this chapter have used their entrepreneurial projects to connect to the global Black diaspora, insert Blackness into the story of "Made in Italy," and advocate for more cosmopolitan and open-ended understandings of Italianness. Many even explicitly ascribe a Black diasporic feminist politics to their work: they challenge constructions of the Black female body as a passive receptacle by demonstrating the agentive subjectivity of Black women through creative practices of bodily and sartorial transformation. And by remaking themselves in relation to the "Made in Italy" brand, they are in turn remaking what it means to be Italian today.

Yet entrepreneurship is also a deeply fraught and politically ambiguous strategy. This can be seen in the ways Black Italian women's entrepreneurship is reinterpreted in the public sphere by Italian media and politicians as local symbols of a transnational, hypercapitalist, and business-friendly Black "cool"—an economically desirable and thoroughly "modern" Blackness that only becomes legible in contrast to the abject figure of the African refugee. In addition, this kind of entrepreneurship is most accessible to those highly educated Black Italians who are able to access specific forms of material and cultural capital in a decidedly classed politics of respectability.[8] Given all of this, to what extent do efforts to decentralize the "refugee narrative" in favor of uplifting stories about Black entrepreneurs, as Ruth suggested in her AFRO Fashion speech, also inadvertently produce new sorts of racialized distinctions between "good/productive" Black citizens-in-waiting and "bad/unproductive" Black refugees? And by extension, what does it mean when the conditional inclusion of Black Italians (as creative cultural workers) becomes contingent on the marginalization of these refugees?

Citizenship, Blackness, and the Underserving Poor

Economic activity in general and entrepreneurship in the so-called creative industries in particular have emerged as key sites where ideas about Blackness, citizenship, and belonging are currently being articulated and contested by Black

Italians who were born or raised in Italy. It is important to note that conversations about who "counts" as an Italian do not always occur within the sphere of more traditional, collective forms of political activism. Italian social and political commentators often lament this development as evidence of a general depoliticization and individualization of youth, tied to rampant consumerism and systematic attacks on trade unions in Italy since the 1970s.[9] But the gradual turn away from political parties, social centers, and trade unions as privileged sites of activism for young people should also be understood as an expression of their profound frustration with the racism, paternalism, and many neoliberal compromises of the contemporary Italian Left since the decline of the Italian Communist Party.

There is in fact a long history in Italy of entrepreneurship being leveraged in struggles over the rights of immigrants and people of color, particularly by women. In the 1990s, as immigration became a major point of public concern (as noted in chapter 1, the country's first comprehensive immigration law was enacted in 1990), immigrant women were being stratified into racialized and gendered forms of labor such as care work, domestic work, and sex work.[10] In this context, interethnic feminist organizations in Italy often sought to create meaningful and dignifying spaces for immigrant women through entrepreneurship. As Heather Merrill has noted, while classic Marxist theory might portray the entrepreneur as an emblematic figure of the petite bourgeoisie, entrepreneurship in Italy is also tied to a genealogy of workerism and work cooperatives in which the radicalization of the working classes occurred through cooperatives.[11]

For many Italian-born and -raised children of African and Afro-Latinx immigrants, entrepreneurial activity today is closely tied to the articulation of claims for citizenship. This is a direct result of the way that the "integration" of immigrants and their children in Italy has been linked to the value created by their labor. As described in chapter 1, the differential inclusion or exclusion of immigrants based on their potential economic productivity was institutionalized in the 1990 Legge Martelli and has been reiterated in every subsequent Italian immigration law. The draconian 2002 Bossi-Fini Law, for instance, stipulates that Italian visas and residency permits for non-EU immigrants must be contingent on employment (or alternatively, enrollment in higher education). By the time of the 2009 Eurozone debt crisis, which set into motion an Italian "perma-recession" characterized by economic stagnation, austerity, and among the highest unemployment rates in Europe, legal and everyday scrutiny of the economic impact of immigration only intensified.[12] Many immigrants—who bore the disproportionate burden of the crisis—found themselves at risk of becoming undocumented because their employment contracts had been terminated, exposing them either to deportation or to exploitative forms of *lavoro nero*, or informal black-market labor. Although it is obvious, it is worth stating what is usually taken for granted: Italian citizens who were laid off as a result of the same structural economic conditions did not have their citizenship revoked or their status in Italy questioned.

But notions of economic productivity do not only suffuse immigration law; they also filter access to citizenship. Resistance in Italy to the legal and de facto recognition of the children of immigrants who were born and raised in Italy is frequently framed in terms of economic drain. For this reason, the naturalization requirements for both immigrants and their Italian-born children include exorbitant processing fees and evidence of a minimum income level. In a telling statement, Italian political scientist Giovanni Sartori lamented in 2013 that jus soli citizenship would be "a disaster in a country with high unemployment."[13] In other words, migrants and their children are seen as diverting state resources and taking jobs that should be the sole entitlement of "native" (i.e., *white*) Italians.

This phenomenon can be understood as a symptom of what David Theo Goldberg has characterized as "racial neoliberalism."[14] Under racial neoliberalism, Goldberg argues, the welfare state is attacked and gradually dismantled because it is perceived to be no longer serving its "intended" constituency of white citizens at a time when the demographic makeup of Western states is becoming increasingly diverse.[15] The Euro-American welfare state is seen as supporting only the undeserving—and the "undeserving" in this case are almost universally marked as Black and/or foreign.[16] As Goldberg writes, "Fear of a black state is linked to worries about a black planet, of alien invasion and alie*nation*, of a loss of the sort of local and global control and privilege long associated with whiteness."[17] But despite the many structural explanations for the comparatively weak Italian welfare state in relation to other European countries, "alien invasion" continues to serve as an all too convenient scapegoat.[18] This is, of course, contradicted by all available economic data: numerous studies have shown that immigrants and other noncitizens in Italy contribute more to the country's GDP than their actual share of the total Italian population; they open new businesses at a higher rate than Italian citizens; and their tax contributions help to rebalance an Italian pension system threatened by a graying population.[19]

In Italy, the "undeserving foreigner" is almost always embodied in the figure of the vampiric Black migrant who has come to Italy to take advantage of "free" welfare benefits without working. Blackness and foreignness are categories that are collapsed into each other and work to mutually reinforce one another—Blackness is fixed as geographically outside of Europe, and wholly external to European modernity. In one widely publicized case, a Lega Nord parliamentarian donned blackface on the floor of the Chamber of Deputies to protest government "handouts" that were supposedly being given to Black refugees while white Italian families suffered economic precarity.[20] Another notable example was the media-fueled national outrage over the alleged 35 euros per day allotted to refugees and asylum seekers in Italy (in reality, they are disbursed about 2.50 euros per day of "pocket money"—not enough to cover a round-trip public transportation ticket in most major Italian cities).[21] Despite the volumes of ink spilled on the supposed "problem" of refugee laziness in Italy, asylum seekers are legally prohibited from entering the Italian labor market for six months, and are instead conscripted into various forms of volunteer work designed to inculcate them with "Italian values" and prepare them for "integration" into Italian society. And many have actually sought out employment *in spite of* these structural barriers, for instance by using falsified documents to work as bicycle couriers for various food-delivery mobile apps.

Another jaw-droppingly absurd moment illuminated precisely how such images of an undifferentiated Blackness are linked to moral panics about scarce state resources and the undeserving. In August 2017, a photo circulated on social media of Black American actor Samuel L. Jackson and Black American basketball player Magic Johnson resting on a bench after a day of shopping at luxury stores in Tuscany, surrounded by shopping bags (see figure 2.2). As the photo made the rounds on Facebook and Twitter, outraged Italian commentators mistook Jackson and Johnson for refugees who had spent their 35 euros on an extravagant shopping spree.[22] To international observers, the bitter irony was that even the most powerful symbols of Black capitalism could be reduced to representations of undeserving poverty in the blink of an eye.

On the other hand, rosy stories of immigrants' economic resourcefulness are also used by liberal-left politicians to demonstrate the *benefits* of incorporating groups with foreign backgrounds into the national fold. Indeed, the figure of the industrious "immigrant entrepreneur" regularly factors into debates about immigration across Western Europe and the United States. Discussions about immigrant entrepreneurship hinge on the question of whether the diasporic, "hybrid" subjectivities of international migrants represent a threat to the integrity of a country's national culture, or whether they can instead function as a "smooth supplement to an ideology of free trade and markets."[23] For instance, when former president of the Italian Chamber of Deputies Laura Boldrini announced the 2016 MoneyGram Award for best immigrant entrepreneur in Italy, she also used the occasion to urge the Italian parliament to approve jus soli for the children of immigrants on the basis of their economic contributions: "The country should be grateful for the entrepreneurial contribution you make to our country. . . . The demographic crisis can be overcome with family policies and new arrivals, by providing the right to Italian citizenship."[24]

As these examples show, whether they are supposedly "gaming" the welfare state, stealing jobs from white Italians by voluntarily working for lower wages,

FIGURE 2.2. The meme of Samuel L. Jackson (left) and Magic Johnson (right). The text reads "Boldrini's resources at Forte Dei Marmi / Shopping at Prada with their 35 euros. Share if you are outraged!" Laura Boldrini, former president of the Italian Chamber of Deputies, has faced harsh criticism from the Right for her relatively progressive stance toward immigration policy in Italy. While the creator of this meme (which was seen and shared by thousands of Italians in a span of hours), admits that it was intended to be a joke that mocked the absurdity of racist panics surrounding African migration, he later remarked that "40 percent of people understood the provocation, [and] 30 percent were outraged."

Source: Maya Oppenheim, "Samuel L Jackson and Magic Johnson Mistaken for 'Lazy Migrants' by Italians after Shopping in Tuscany," Independent (UK), 21 August 2017, http://www.independent.co.uk/arts-entertainment /films/news/samuel-l-jackson-magic-johnson-lazy-migrants-italy-tuscany-forte-dei-marmi-louis-vuitton -a7905026.html.

or kick-starting the economy through entrepreneurship, immigrants and their children—and Black subjects in particular—are systematically evaluated as legitimate or illegitimate members of the Italian national community based on their economic productivity. But this is not only a symptom of entrepreneurial self-making under neoliberal governance and its associated "enterprise culture."[25] It is important to note that preoccupations with the "problems" of poverty and unproductivity are constitutive of liberalism itself. From the English

Poor Laws to the influence of Thomas Malthus on responses to the Irish Great Famine of 1845–52 to the 1965 Moynihan Report, a range of technologies of liberal and colonial governance have worked in concert to produce the category of the "undeserving poor" as beyond the boundaries of citizenship—a process that has also been caught up with ideas of racial and gendered difference.

Postcolonial feminist scholars such as Ann Stoler, Anne McClintock, and Zine Magubane have demonstrated that the citizenship of the white working classes in nineteenth-century Europe was not a foregone conclusion. Indeed, the category of "whiteness" has always contained within it internal differentiation and hierarchy.[26] Poor white women in particular were seen as threats to the racial integrity of European nations—unable to embody the upper- and middle-class values of domesticity central to the reproduction of whiteness, their economic status rendered them dangerously proximate to the racially "inferior" Black and Asian subjects in the colonies.[27] After Italian unification, for example, southern Italians were considered to be outside the racial and civilizational boundaries of the nation, their extreme poverty naturalized as racial difference rather than the product of internal colonization.[28] As a result, Italian politicians, colonial administrators, and scientists feared that any potential racial slippage between southern Italians and Africans in the new Italian territories in the Horn of Africa would undermine Italian colonial domination. This racialization of poverty was also deeply gendered, as seen in northern Italian criminologist Cesare Lombroso's preoccupation with the particular "cunning" of poor southern Italian women who engaged in prostitution and crime, and the racial traits they supposedly shared with Africans.[29] This history effectively explodes the unitary category of "white Italian." In addition, these examples suggest that class has never been an objective social phenomenon, but is instead constituted in and through the power-laden categories of race, gender, and nation.

By the late nineteenth and early to mid-twentieth centuries, poor whites were being systematically incorporated into Euro-American nation-states through access to the political franchise, welfare assistance, and—if not actual economic security—the "psychological wage" of full inclusion within the family of whiteness.[30] Colonized and enslaved subjects had long symbolized moral defects, laziness, and ungovernability that threatened to tarnish the racial status of poor whites.[31] But increasingly, these poor whites were being approached not as *potentially analogous* to people of color, but rather as their *foil*: they constituted the hardworking, deserving poor whose survival was imperiled by the undeserving Black poor. Even in Italy, as southern Italian immigrants in the United States were being targeted as racially proximate to Black, the Italian Fascist state increasingly sought to incorporate and uplift poor southerners in order to harden the distinction between Italians and African colonial subjects.

In the context of the resurgence of racist nationalisms in the twenty-first century, the category of the "white working class" has been consistently mobilized to dramatize the threats posed to the national body by immigrants, Blacks, and people of color generally. In Italy, these fears have condensed media and political attention into the figure of the single, young, Black male migrant; however, Black women are also targeted in unique ways by this politics of "exclusion and scapegoating."[32] This is because Black women represent the condensation of Italy's "triple crisis": economic stagnation, immigration, and declining birthrates / rising emigration of white Italians. They are portrayed as undeserving foreigners, and also as reproductive time bombs who will bring about an ethnic "great replacement." Italian politicians frequently warn that African women are arriving en masse to give birth on Italian soil—an iteration of the noxious "anchor babies" rhetoric used to stoke xenophobia in the United States.[33]

From liberal colonialism, through fascism, and up to our current neoliberal and ethnonationalist moment, race, gender, and class have worked as articulated categories that continually reproduce one another and give each other meaning. In turn, these categories have collectively shaped and redefined the boundaries of national citizenship. Contrary to common characterizations of neoliberalism as a sharp historical break that has effectively "economized" all aspects of private and political life, the linking of racialized and gendered notions of productivity to citizenship has actually been integral to the constitution of the liberal state itself. And this has in turn established a unique terrain of struggle for Black women in Italy today.

Black Businesses in Italy: From Foreign Contamination to Savvy (Afro) Cosmopolitanisms

Black Italian women's entrepreneurship seeks to disrupt the deeply entrenched teleology linking race, class, gender, and citizenship by refashioning Black womanhood as active, economically productive, creative, cosmopolitan—and quintessentially *Italian*. Since at least 2014, there has been a stunning proliferation of blogs, Facebook pages, YouTube channels, and traveling workshops encouraging Black women in Italy to embrace their natural features and hair textures, reject racist and Eurocentric standards of beauty, and assert themselves as legitimate members of Italian society. Natural hair care, beauty, and fashion are key sites of community building where Black Italian women can discuss the experiences of Black womanhood in contemporary Italy, and they also serve as powerful platforms for articulating citizenship claims.

When I first began this research in Italy in 2012, however, I did not expect entrepreneurship to be such an important hotbed of political activity—I imagined that I would spend most of my time marching in the streets at political demonstrations. Instead, over the course of months and years of fieldwork, I learned that there was a rapidly expanding microcosm of influential Black women entrepreneurs—women who were using their regional or national platforms to bring visibility to other Black Italians, serve as aspirational role models, advocate for citizenship, and mobilize against racism. I was surprised to find that many of the prominent Black activists I was meeting were also highly ambitious and driven businesswomen.

Yet, this unexpected development raised a number of questions that my Western Marxian political economic training (which, as Cedric Robinson argues, assumes a narrowly defined revolutionary working-class subject) proved insufficient to address.[34] Could entrepreneurship ever be considered a political act? Would the dynamics of market-based competition inevitably thwart the possibilities of Black solidarity? Did these projects simply reflect uncritical consent to the logics of neoliberal citizenship? Or, following Stuart Hall's analytical program from the inaugural issue of *New Left Review*, could Black women's entrepreneurship be understood as one example of the "imaginative resistances of people who have to live within capitalism"?[35]

Black Italian women's entrepreneurship is a geographically specific phenomenon, largely concentrated in the northern and central Italian regions of Lombardy, Lazio, Tuscany, Emilia-Romagna, Veneto, and Piedmont. This is due to the historically higher levels of economic prosperity and lower rates of unemployment in these regions, the existence of more extensive support networks for entrepreneurship (including "immigrant" entrepreneurship), and the presence of major urban centers and large immigrant populations.[36] In addition, while most immigrant families were devastated by the aftershocks of the 2009 economic crisis, the children of immigrants in northern Italy nonetheless continue to enjoy marginally greater economic stability when compared to their counterparts in the South.[37] This is because in many cases, their parents had settled in northern Italy in the 1970s, 1980s, and 1990s to pursue university education, work in large factories, or open ethnic shops, grocery stores, and other small businesses.

Black Italian businesswomen approach entrepreneurship as a complex terrain of struggle through which they can advance new representations of Black life in Italy and transform the meanings and practices of Italianness.[38] In doing so, they are challenging the aforementioned ideas of Black passivity and nonproductivity, and the ways these stereotypes cling to Black women in particular. Their projects draw on resources from across the Black diaspora, position Black women in relation to the "Made in Italy" brand, and advance cosmopolitan, Mediterranean understandings of Italian national identity. They are expanding the definition of *who* and *what* is made in Italy today by framing Blackness not as a problem of racial contamination and economic degradation, but as a solution to the problems of Italian productive (and reproductive) stagnation.

Natural Hair and Diasporic Connection

In January 2014, Italian-Ghanaian Evelyne Afaawua (who emigrated to Italy from France with her parents shortly after her first birthday) founded the first Facebook page in Italian about the care and valorization of natural, non–chemically straightened Black hair. Originally called "Afro Italian Nappy Girls" and based in Milan, the community now goes by the name "Nappytalia" and includes a robust, multiplatform social media presence (including a Facebook fan base of over sixteen thousand individuals as of August 2019), a blog, an e-commerce site, and offline meetups and workshops held in cities around Italy.[39] In 2018, after several years of planning and fundraising, Evelyne also launched a successful line of organic natural hair products called "Nappytalia Eco Bio Cosmetics." During our first meeting in Milan in the summer of 2014, shortly after the founding of Nappytalia, Evelyne described her decision to focus on hair:

> Once you've developed your ideas, you have to externalize the clarity that is inside. For me, for instance, I tried using skin-lightening creams. This was a period when I wanted to become lighter. There are all of these phases, which make you understand where your place is. And once you understand where your place is, you say, "*Va bene*, to be in that place I have to reflect it, right?" And for a girl, what does she think? Most likely, the first thing is hair. . . . You want the clarity inside to be visible outside. And so *hair*. . . . For me, it could be a question of money, but I have more to demonstrate than just money. Yes, we're Afro-Italians, and we are showing who we are, but we also want to show it on paper, to show off.

I had the chance to see just what this sort of "showing off" looked like when I attended a Nappytalia event in Milan two years later. The inaugural event of a fifteen-city tour across Italy, the Milanese edition of #NappyOnTour2016 was held in a room on the third floor of Gogol'Ostello, a mixed-use literary café owned by the Italian-Eritrean Asli Haddas. Although it was a bitterly cold January evening, the room's bright green carpet, white-and-pink striped wallpaper, and colorful hanging lamps lent the space a cozy ambiance. At the front of the room, a table with a pink tablecloth displayed an assortment of hair products wrapped in sheer pink gift bags, jewelry, and African print shirts. Another table practically groaned under the weight of a buffet of Italian and pan-African dishes. At the other side of the room, a group of photographers had set up an informal photo studio. The workshop attendees gradually filtered into the space, a group that also included three Black men, a white woman, and a biracial seven-year-old girl. As they shed their winter coats, it became clear that everyone had purposely dressed to the nines, many in outfits that featured African textiles. I came to a stunning realization: this was the first time I had ever experienced a space in Italy where I was surrounded almost entirely by other Black women.

And indeed, the space that Evelyne had curated that evening was intended to serve as a sort of refuge—and not just from the frigid winter air outside. As we took our seats in folding chairs, a member of the Nappytalia team distributed surveys with detailed questions about why we had decided to be "nappy," what hair products we used, what types of ingredients we preferred, and what hairstyles we enjoyed. As she read through the survey, one woman lamented that her hair was classified as "4C," the most tightly coiled curl according to the popular hair typing system developed by Oprah Winfrey's stylist, Andre Walker. But Evelyne was quick to intervene, immediately swooping over in her wax print skirt, Afro-Italian Nappy Girls t-shirt, and dangling pink earrings that matched her bubblegum-pink lipstick. "I'm a 4C, too!" she responded cheerily. "It even says in the Bible: 'The last will be first.'" Her words of encouragement recalled the justification for Evelyne's use of the word "nappy": she was inspired by the Black American cultural activists who had reappropriated the term from its association with unruliness, disorder, and incivility and given it a new meaning: "naturally happy."

After defusing what she interpreted as a momentary outburst of internalized anti-Black racism, Evelyne moved to the front of the room and began to tell her story, and the story of the Nappytalia community. She described herself as part of a new generation in Italy that had a doubled identity, one that spoke multiple languages and regional Italian dialects and was distinguished by having dark skin and Afro hair. The goal of Nappytalia, she explained, was to showcase the realities of a rapidly changing Italy, and to create a space that supported the self-expression of Black Italian women. "We exist," she said firmly. "If we are here," she continued, gesturing at the rows and rows of Black women seated before her, "then we exist." After Evelyne concluded her speech, she went on to provide tips about the care and maintenance of natural hair and demonstrated different hairstyling techniques on two volunteers from the audience.

When the scheduled program drew to a close, the workshop participants dispersed across the room to purchase hair products, treat themselves to snacks from the buffet, and pose for professional glamour shots. As I chatted with Evelyne, the Nappytalia team, and the workshop participants, I overheard conversations about topics ranging from the indignity of white Italians touching Black women's hair without permission to the challenges of obtaining Italian citizenship to the importance of showcasing all the ways Black women were contributing to Italian society. The topic of natural hair had created a rare space for Black Italian women to connect with each other and assert the beauty of bodily features that had been denigrated by Eurocentric standards of beauty and marked as foreign to Italian-ness. By engaging in communal acts of self-transformation (i.e., by making the decision to stop chemically altering their hair), these women had also begun to produce and express a collective Black Italian subjectivity.

The celebration of natural hair has also allowed Black women in Italy to ar-ticulate connections to a broader Black diaspora *beyond* Italy. Nappytalia builds on the momentum of an Internet-mediated Black natural hair movement that, since the mid-2000s, has linked together Black women across the globe.[40] As Ayana Byrd and Lori Tharps explain, social media has helped Black women learn new hairstyles and hair care practices that do not involve chemical straighten-ers and enabled them to connect with others who have also embarked on the journey of "going natural." Evelyne, for instance, spent almost a year researching Facebook pages and YouTube channels from Black hairstylists in the United States and France before settling on the importance of developing similar re-sources for Black women in Italy, *in Italian*. Indeed, in the early days of Nappyta-lia, she would frequently share images and videos from Black hairstylists and celebrities across the Black diaspora to the group's Facebook page. These dia-sporic resources were intended to serve as aspirational models for Black Italian women, who rarely saw themselves positively represented in the Italian media.[41] As one early member of the Nappytalia community explained to me in 2014, "Those of us who grew up in Italy, seeing only white people around us, thought that the only beautiful people were white. But with the Internet, we have seen that there are many places in the world where beauty doesn't just mean straight hair or white skin." Nappytalia's website also features articles about traditional Afri-can hair care practices, the cultural politics of Black hair, and the history of the transatlantic slave trade. These resources are intended to show Black Italian women that although they may experience social and political marginalization in Italy, they are not alone—they are members of a global Black community.

Nappytalia facilitates not only transatlantic diasporic connections, but trans-European and Mediterranean ones as well. In 2016, Evelyne attended the Black Europe Summer School, a two-week program in Amsterdam, the Netherlands, that brings together scholars and activists from across the diaspora to learn about the history and ongoing mobilizations of Black communities in Europe. Evelyne is also one of many young Black Italian entrepreneurs and activists who is an alumnus of the African Summer School, a program founded in 2013 by the Italian-Congolese journalist Fortuna Ekustu Mambulu and associated with REDANI (the Network of the Black African Diaspora in Italy), an influential network comprising mostly first-generation African immigrants in Italy. Held first in Verona and now based in Rome, the African Summer School is a one-week training program designed to prepare its participants to take advantage of the "African Renaissance" by developing microenterprises involving Africa or the transnational African diaspora.[42] But over the years, the program has also come to serve a second, more informal function. Specifically, it has allowed many of its Black Italian participants the opportunity to develop connections with their parental homelands on the African continent, countries they might not have been able to visit physically due to financial limitations or the strict residency requirements for Italian naturalization. In addition to seminars about business plan design, the African Summer School features lectures on African philosophy, history, economics, and ethics that draw on the intellectual legacy of Senegalese historian Cheikh Anta Diop to challenge European stereotypes of African backwardness. For Black Italians who participate in the program, it is very often the first time they have been taught by African professors and heard the African continent described as having history, wealth, and culture.

But what does it mean when these sorts of meaningful diasporic spaces are also mediated by consumption and capitalist market exchange? Writing about "African American beauty culturalists" during the civil rights movement in the United States, multiple scholars have pointed to the tensions that arose in the 1960s between Black pride and capitalism.[43] For instance, while many Black women salon owners did not see a contradiction between making money and promoting social causes, other activists contested what they saw as the gradual "commercialization" of natural hair.[44] Much like the African American beauty shop owners in the US South during Jim Crow studied by historian Tiffany M. Gill, Evelyne unambiguously characterizes herself as an "entrepreneur with social ethics." For Evelyne, natural hair is a diasporic resource that enables her to mobilize for the rights and dignity of Black women living in Italy. As one of the most visible Black Italians active in Italy today (she has been the subject of a documentary and countless magazine features and is regularly invited to speak at conferences about gender and the Black diaspora in Italy), she has used her platform to bring visibility to other Black Italians, call attention to anti-racism demonstrations in Italy, and mobilize support for citizenship reform.[45] She mentors aspiring Black Italian entrepreneurs and takes part in body positivity campaigns in Italy. The Nappytalia Facebook page, moderated by Evelyne and her collaborators, remains a rich site of conversation and debate about identity, racism, sexism, and the many obstacles faced by Black Italians without citizenship.

Since Nappytalia's founding, Evelyne has gone on to win Italian and European entrepreneurship awards, acquire local investors for her business, and connect to product manufacturers and distributors abroad.[46] In 2015, she was awarded the MoneyGram Award for foreign entrepreneurship in Italy under the *imprenditoria giovanile* (youth entrepreneurship) category—the first Afrodescendent entrepreneur to receive this honor. Later that year, she was awarded "Best Blogger" for the Nappytalia website at the annual Africa-Italy Excellence Awards. In fact, Evelyne recounted that attending the Africa-Italy Excellence Awards the previous year had been an important turning point for her—it was when she first began to take note of the way systemic racism had left untapped the economic potential of Black folk in Italy:

> Before the event, I had the idea that Africans were workers, street sweepers, *vu' cumprà*.[47] After that event, my idea of Africans was doctors, writers, bloggers, directors. Therefore, there was a possibility, an opportunity, to be African but to have the same occupations as many others without being limited by the color of your skin. But the problem is that for us young people, these examples are not as apparent. When I went to this event, I was like, wow . . . I started to dream: if there are people who at forty-five, sixty years old have been able to be doctors, gynecologists, bloggers, directors, then I say, well if the situation in Italy is like this, it's because these people are not employed at their full capacity.

She continued:

> I want to achieve my goals and dreams and become something. To create a position for myself in the society, regardless of whether I am white or Black. I want to be myself, with all of my characteristics, whether you accept them or not. . . . Whereas before I didn't acknowledge my Ghanaian side, now I try to show both. If you accept me, you have to accept me because I am Ghanaian, because I am Italian, *basta*. We have to . . . let people understand that we exist. I think that what could help would be to make them understand the utility that we have, the utility that we can give to the society. . . . If we talk about an Italian, an Italian can speak Italian well, can speak English, but what would be his approach toward an American, a Latin American, an African? It is probably much easier for an Afro-Italian to work with a foreigner than an Italian. Italians have a closed mentality.

As she spoke, Evelyne implicitly marked the racialization of Italianness as white, while also refusing to succumb to the equation of Blackness with foreignness. Rather, she suggested, "Afro-Italians" are Italians, too—but they have diasporic connections and an international outlook that make them *more* able to contribute to the economy than white Italians.[48] At the same time, her emphasis on "creating a position . . . in the society" through employment reflected the ongoing salience of economic activity in debates about Italian citizenship.

In this spirit, Evelyne has sought to build on the success of her Nappytalia brand by mentoring aspiring Black Italian businesswomen and linking together other fledgling entrepreneurs. And thanks in part to the path blazed by Evelyne, Italy now boasts a robust natural hair movement of its own—from stylists like "NaturAngi" (Angela Haisha Adamou)[49] and "Afro-On" (Belysa Shabani) to product vendors and manufacturers such as AfroRicci and Vanity Case Cosmetics to beauty bloggers and vloggers such as the women behind the multimedia site *Afroitalian Souls*. These women often import hair products from companies across the Black diaspora (typically the United States or the United Kingdom) to sell online to other Black Italians, filling a gap in the market in Italy for beauty products and cosmetics tailored to the specific needs of Black women.[50] But increasingly, they are looking not only to connect with Black diasporic networks abroad, but also to refashion "Made in Italy" at home.

New Geographies of "Made in Italy"

Since at least the 2008 economic crisis, discussions in Italy surrounding the future of "Made in Italy" have been met with uncertainty. "Made in Italy," a merchandise mark used since the 1980s to designate the uniqueness of Italian production in the "Four A's" of *abbigliamento* (clothing), *agroalimentare* (food), *arredamento* (furniture), and *automobili* (cars and other forms of mechanical engineering) and protected by Italian law since 1999, is a shorthand for the skilled craftsmanship associated with "traditional" Italian industries.[51] More recently, however, policymakers, journalists, and manufacturers' associations in Italy have expressed concern that this label (in its various iterations associated with luxury brands, quality manufacturing, and small-scale artisanship) is at risk. While the decline in prestige of "Made in Italy" has not been fully substantiated by the available economic data, various culprits have still been named: the economic crisis; fast fashion; the increasing availability of cheaper products from abroad (*cinese*, or "Chinese," is also a racially charged colloquialism in Italian that refers derisively to low-quality, mass-produced consumer goods); foreign counterfeiters; young Italians' lack of interest in traditional industries; the internationalization of product supply chains; and the stagnating effects of that peculiar Italian blend of bureaucracy and organized crime.[52]

This question of how to "produce" Italy is also intimately linked with fears about the *social reproduction* of the nation—from declining white Italian birth rates to the comparatively high birth rates of immigrants to the "brain drain" of highly educated and skilled young white Italians.[53] In other words, preoccupations about the state of traditional Italian industries and crafts are closely linked to nationalist fears about the impacts of porous borders, uncontrollable transnational flows, and growing racial or ethnic pluralism. In this sense, "Made in Italy" is more than just a national brand—instead, it signals a set of interrelated questions about *who* and *what* is made in Italy, and by extension, *who is making Italy* today and *who will make Italy* in the future. In the context of this uncertainty about the future of Italy—*Who will (re)produce the nation?*—economic activity has emerged as a key cultural and political touchstone. This is why immigrant-owned businesses are often singled out as the targets of protests and boycotts by Italian nativists, and also why the "Made in Italy" slogan is sometimes repurposed in campaign materials and sound bites for the Italian citizenship reform movement.[54]

Anthropologists such as Lisa Rofel, Sylvia Yanagisako, and Elizabeth Krause have studied the transformations of "Made in Italy"—and, by extension, Italianness—brought about by the insertion of Chinese entrepreneurs into the manufacturing of "Italian" textiles and clothing.[55] But any discussion of the "Made in Italy" brand must also be analyzed alongside the unfolding contestations about the place of Blackness within the symbolic and material boundaries of the modern Italian nation. Italian-Somali writer Igiaba Scego captured the layered racial meanings of "Made in Italy" in her award-winning 2003 short story "Salsicce" (Sausages). As the story's Muslim / Roman / Somali protagonist debates whether or not eating pork sausages will make her truly "Italian" in a way that her burgundy-colored Italian passport cannot, she wonders to herself: "Perhaps, by eating a sausage, I might go from neutral fingertips to real 'Made in Italy' fingerprints, but is this what I really want?"[56] Scego's story helps us understand why it is so meaningful for Black Italian entrepreneurs to affix the "Made in Italy" label to their Black natural hair products and African textile–inspired fashion designs.

Countless news features published within the last half decade have celebrated these Black Italian entrepreneurs for what is characterized as their creative and technologically forward-thinking contributions to the Italian economy.[57] Indeed, it is important to recognize that for many Black Italian businesswomen, their projects have *two* audiences in mind—an internal audience of other Black Italians who can come together around a particular theme (hair, fashion, beauty) to discuss their shared experiences and struggles, and an external audience of

Italians who can learn more about the lives and material contributions of the children of African and Afro-Latinx immigrants in Italy.[58] These counternarratives are intended to challenge the idea that Black bodies in Italian territory constitute an invasion, a threat, or a drain on resources—in other words, that they are perpetually "bodies out of place."[59] After all, the reasoning goes, by producing products that are "Made in Italy," you are in turn able to produce yourself as "Italian."

In 2011, the Italian-Nigerian-Russian entrepreneur and singer Alice Edun opened the first e-shop with products for Black hair in Italy. Several years later, along with her then-collaborator, Italian-Dominican stylist Reina Gomez, Alice's company AfroRicci (AfroCurls) launched the first "Made in Italy" line of products designed for curly or Afro-textured hair. AfroRicci products include a popular line of shampoos, conditioners, styling creams, and oils developed in painstaking collaboration with an Italian cosmetics laboratory. Today, the company boasts its own warehouse and office and exports to France, Canada, Spain, and the United Kingdom.

Like Evelyne's, Alice's and Reina's trajectories toward the world of natural hair care involved tangled, multisited journeys of self-discovery. I first met Reina in Milan in 2014, when she was a boisterous beauty blogger with a passion for Black history. The daughter of a white Venezuelan father and a mixed / Afro-Dominican mother, Reina was born in Venezuela, spent her early childhood years in Santo Domingo, and then came to Italy for elementary school. Reina explained that cutting off her straightened hair and letting her natural curls grow back in (the "big chop") was part of a broader attempt on her part to connect with the African roots of her Latin American identity—a process that had also involved careful study of the Haitian Revolution. She had been galvanized by her experiences of everyday gendered racism and nonrecognition in Italy to use *hair* as a platform for connecting other Black Italian women.[60]

Reina and Alice met in 2014, when Alice was searching for a hairdresser with whom to collaborate for various AfroRicci-related initiatives. Alice was born in Russia to a Black Nigerian father and a white Russian mother, grew up in Nigeria, and came to Italy as a young woman. Like Reina, Alice described her hair as an embodied way to assert pride in her African heritage. As Alice explained to me in 2016, shortly after Reina had introduced us:

> Hair is part of your identity, so when you talk about Afro hair, already the word "Afro" comes from "Africa." You are describing your hair, which comes from a place, a people. You are identifying with them, even if you were born here, or you were born there, or adopted, or are multiracial. When you describe Afro curls, you are saying that you are part

of that category of people. And so identity is part of that, in knowing where you come from, maybe a culture that you don't know well but that you want to get to know better.

Alice characterizes hair as the basis for a new form of Black Italian identity that refuses to subordinate "Afro" to "Italian" in the quest for broader social recognition. In addition to offering their hair products, Alice and Reina also organize workshops around Italy; often, they cater to young African adoptees and their white Italian parents. But a main source of pride for both women is the fact that they can claim the "Made in Italy" label as their own. Reina has since branched out to launch her own line of natural hair products in Italy, called "Authentic Afro Hair." But when we met over coffee at Alice's home in 2016, Alice and Reina shared their excitement at being able to promote the first "Made in Italy" product by, and for, Black women:

> ALICE: We are proud to say "Made in Italy." It is important to show the whole world that even in Italy, we are here. We're here, AfroRicci, and we have our own "Made in Italy" products.
>
> REINA: It's also a responsibility. "Made in Italy" is known all over the world as a sign of quality. It is a cultural thing, tied to a history of small artisans. . . .
>
> ALICE: From Italian shoes, stylists, fashion, to food, the finishing on our houses, furniture . . . "Made in Italy" is synonymous with quality. So the first cream for Afro hair in Italy has to be that way. It has to be a quality product.
>
> CAMILLA: It seems important to be able to say "Made in Italy" during this [economic] crisis, too.
>
> ALICE: The crisis, of course! I would like it if there were more support from the Italian state for "Made in Italy" . . . especially for innovative things. . . . Yes, it's a beauty product, but it's a niche product, for a particular group of people who are part of the Italian culture. Afro-Italians are part of the Italian culture. There needs to be support for "Made in Italy" products for Afro-Italians, too.

As Alice elaborated in a 2017 interview, AfroRicci "demonstrates that even I contribute at the social, economic, and cultural levels in *this* country. . . . It is important that Italy recognize the multiethnic woman."[61] Her comments imply that the meanings attached to entrepreneurship are deeply gendered, as Black Italian businesswomen seek to challenge both their *invisibility* (as unrecognized "citizens-in-waiting") and their *hypervisibility* (as sex objects or docile care workers) in Italian spaces and in the Italian racial imaginary.[62] Indeed, as geographers of migration have argued, the bodies of those perceived as "foreign"—but especially those of women—are systematically instrumentalized to mark the cultural boundaries of citizenship and belonging in European liberal democracies.[63] Through their work with AfroRicci, Alice and Reina were forced to contend with economic constructions of Italian citizenship and the pervasive model of the "useful" immigrant entrepreneur. Nonetheless, the act of producing "Made in Italy" conditioners and curl creams for Black women also allowed them to claim legitimacy as Italians while *simultaneously* asserting pride in their African heritage. But again, Alice and Reina are not simply advocating for their incorporation into "Made in Italy" (and, by extension, the Italian nation itself). They are challenging the perceived isomorphism of "Blackness" and "foreignness" by refashioning Italy as one nodal point of interconnection within a much broader, transnational Black diaspora. Their implication that "Italian" and "African" are not mutually exclusive categories represents a new understanding of Italianness—as well as a rekindling of much older notions of Italy as a cosmopolitan Mediterranean crossroads.

The Afro-Mediterranean Renaissance in Italy

In 2011, Italian president Giorgio Napolitano delivered a highly publicized and widely circulated address to a group of newly naturalized Italians who had grown up in Italy as the children of immigrants. In the most quoted sentence of the speech, he confidently asserted: "It is important to realize that young people of immigrant origins in our schools and in our society are not just an obstacle to be overcome; they are also a fruitful source of stimulation because they come from diverse cultures."[64]

At the gathering, timed to coincide with the 150th anniversary of Italian national unification, Napolitano proceeded to extol the ways that the "new Italian citizens" assembled that day would contribute to the collective well-being of Italy by sharing "languages, constitutional values, civic duties, and laws," citing as examples young Italian-Chinese entrepreneurs and the Italian-Somali writer Igiaba Scego (whose short story I mentioned earlier). For many activists, Napolitano's speech represented an important, yet limited, moment of institutional recognition in the growing movement for a reform of Italian citizenship law.[65]

At a time of economic crisis, declining Italian birth rates, and renewed mass *emigration*, Napolitano's speech implied, it was simply a matter of good business sense to bring the children of immigrants into the Italian fold: "Without their future contribution to our society and our economy," he declared, "the burden of national debt would be even more difficult to sustain." The marking of

Italy's 150th "birthday" was widely derided that year for being lackluster and somber, marred by shameful political scandals and intractable regional divisions.[66] Ironically, then, Napolitano seemed to be calling on the children of immigrants at a time of great national pessimism to stand in as the symbols for a new and economically revitalized Italy.

As the examples in this chapter have shown, however, the entrepreneurial projects of Black Italian businesswomen may make use of the "Made in Italy" label—but their products cannot be entirely subsumed within the staid realm of "traditional" Italian craft. Instead, these designers, stylists, and other cultural entrepreneurs frequently describe their products as "hybrids" of Italian and African influences—combining, for instance, West African wax prints with Italian sartorial techniques, or African raw ingredients like shea and cocoa butter with the quality standards of Italian cosmetics laboratories. These practices of cultural fluency, which position Black Italian women entrepreneurs as "cultural mediators," are often cited by outside observers as evidence that "Africa" and "Italy" are not mutually exclusive categories.[67]

In right-wing political discourse, Africa and Africans are ritualistically held up as representations of the unstoppable transnational forces of globalization that threaten Italian cultural particularity and the stability of the white Italian working class. As Douglas Holmes argues, these "integralist" politicians diagnose a social condition of *alienation* as the (white, European) popular response to the secular, cosmopolitan, and fast-capitalist orientation of the European Union.[68] This is a doubled form of alienation. "Alienation" indexes a condition of estrangement from a pre-existing wholeness or harmony, not only in the Marxian sense of socioeconomic stratification but also in terms of the loss of a mythical cultural and moral purity. But it can also be restyled as Goldberg's "alie*nation*"—the threat of a nation that no longer serves the needs of its citizens, understood to constitute an autochthonous and organic cultural unit.[69]

In 2017, for instance, protests broke out in Milan after a cluster of palm trees were installed near the Duomo di Milano, the largest cathedral in Italy. The palm trees had been funded by the Starbucks Corporation to set the stage for the nearby opening of the first Starbucks store in Italy (and the largest Starbucks in Europe). As they decried (and vandalized) the palm trees, protesters from the right-wing Lega party and the neofascist CasaPound deftly conflated the forces of transnational capitalism, the destruction of Italian cultural specificity, and "illegal" immigration from the African continent. Although palm trees are native to the Mediterranean region (specifically, *Chamaerops*, or the Mediterranean dwarf palm), and there were already palm trees in the Piazza del Duomo in the early nineteenth century, this flora came to stand in for the undesirable African contamination of pristine and bounded Italian national space: "NO to the

Africanization of the Piazza del Duomo!" the protesters' signs read.[70] The supposed insult was only amplified by the fact that the forty-two palm trees (and, eventually, fifty banana plants) were located steps away from a Catholic cathedral, an imposing "race-neutral" symbol of the unspoken whiteness of Italian national identity.[71]

In response to such sedentarist and enclosed understandings of Italian national space, Black Italian entrepreneurs and their supporters have sought to resurrect an alternative geography of Italianness, one that is unabashedly oriented toward the Mediterranean and emphasizes cultural porosity rather than boundedness.[72] In doing so, they suggest that rather than generating cultural dilution, the global diasporic networks of Black Italians can revitalize a stagnant Italian nation that has been insular and insufficiently cosmopolitan for much of its recent history.

This spatial strategy came to the fore in 2017, at a panel discussion composed of prominent citizenship reform activists during a cultural festival in Giavera (just outside the northeastern Italian city of Treviso). The discussion took place mere steps away from the festival's Afro Beauty and Fashion Expo, which featured booths for nine Black Italian fashion designers, hair product vendors, and stylists—including several of the women introduced in this chapter (see figure 2.3). As such, the connection between Black business, citizenship, and the shifting definitions of Italianness loomed in the minds of the panelists and the predominantly white Italian audience.

Bruno Baratto, the white Italian president of the festival, opened the discussion by noting that the "new generation of Italians" seated before him (and, it was implied, present at the expo) represented the resources of the world, something that Italy needed desperately at this moment. "This country is getting older, and is in need of a younger world that has capacities not just in terms of work but also in terms of creativity," he declared. Following his hopeful remarks, a lively conversation ensued among the panelists about just this sort of cosmopolitan outlook among the children of immigrants in Italy. An Italian-Moroccan activist noted that this "new generation" could act as a cultural bridge by engaging in international projects that linked Italy to the rest of the world. In a surprising historical parallel, his assertion also hearkened to the kinds of claims articulated by late nineteenth- and early twentieth-century Italian politicians about the potential economic and political benefits of Italian mass emigration (see chapter 1).[73] As she finished, an Italian-Moroccan educator took the microphone and, nodding enthusiastically in agreement, joked that white Italians are typically monolingual. As the audience tittered along self-deprecatingly with the panelists, an Italian-Ecuadorian organizer concurred, observing that the abil-

FIGURE 2.3. The Afro Beauty and Fashion Expo in Giavera, Italy.

Source: Author photo.

ity to speak more than one language (a skill that many, if not most, children of immigrants in Italy share) is good for business.

But while it might seem like a new political move, one that has only recently emerged to challenge the racism and parochialism of the "integralists," this strategy also aligns with a particular understanding of Italianness—one that sees the current insularity of Italians as a deviation from a much longer history of cross-Mediterranean mixing and exchange. Since Italian national unification at the end of the nineteenth century, politicians, scientists, and political theorists have debated the extent to which Italians were truly "white" due to centuries of Mediterranean mixing and their geographical proximity to Africa. But at various moments, this hybridity was not solely understood as a problem of racial impurity. It had also been heralded as the Italian nation's unique strength—one that differentiated it from northern, "Aryan" Europe. According to this Mediterraneanist vision of Italian national identity, the xenophobic, antiglobalist, and regionalist / nationalist turn in Italian politics dating back to the 1990s is the *real* historical aberration, not transnational trade flows and mass migrations.[74] This is because the Italian peninsula was geographically destined to serve as a cultural and civilizational crossroads.[75]

What Black Italian entrepreneurs are seeking to accomplish, then, is a centering of Black trans-Mediterranean and transatlantic diasporic connections as the key to a reinvigorated Italo-Mediterranean cosmopolitanism. In this reinterpretation, Blackness is figured both as Italy's past—as the multicultural Mediterranean utopia of classical antiquity, and the source of colonial resources during Liberal and Fascist Italy—*and* as the way toward a flexible, transnational future that will allow Italy to compete in a globalized economy. This could be seen, for instance, in a recent issue of *Vogue Italia*—a fashion magazine that is also notorious for its history of racist imagery and its erasure of Black models. Yet, in a move lauded by many as groundbreaking, the February 2020 cover featured the Italian-Senegalese model Maty Fall Diba holding a block-letter sign that reads "ITALIA," next to the lowercase, cursive subheading "italian beauty."[76] The "Bellezza Italiana" (Italian Beauty) editorial in that issue also featured other Italian models with diverse national backgrounds including countries such as Morocco and Germany. Despite their various hyphenations, these models were extolled as exemplars of a uniquely Italian *bellezza* that is both new and, one could argue, emblematic of a much older and quintessentially "Mediterranean" cosmopolitanism. But while seductive, Mediterraneanism is also not an entirely "innocent" reworking of Italianness. After all, Italy's position in the Mediterranean was vaunted by politicians and intellectuals as a legitimation for colonial expansion, and more recently has been used to promote advantageous Italian economic investments in Africa.[77] As in past iterations, this southward-looking reframing of Italian national identity is capable of absorbing certain racialized subjects, while discarding others as mere surplus.

"These Are Not the People I'm Talking About!"

If Black Italian entrepreneurs represent one possible vision for the future of Italy, what room is there in this future for the African refugees and asylum seekers arriving in Italy in the midst of the Mediterranean migration "crisis"? Sociologist Tamara Nopper has written about the ways that immigrants in the United States often articulate moral claims regarding their "character, productivity, and value" to the US economy, a strategy that echoes the assertions of many of my interlocutors in this chapter. Nopper argues that in the United States, these claims work to distinguish immigrants from Black Americans, who are cast as "lacking a work ethic, militant, xenophobic, and costly to society" and are seen as having squandered their right to American citizenship.[78] Nopper's argument about the racial and gendered character of claims for national inclusion via productivity is astute—but what would it mean to extend her analysis of the anti-Black racism in immigrants' rights organizing to Italy, where anti-Black racism and xenophobia cannot be so easily disentangled from one another? These differences shed light on the distinct dynamics of racial formation at work in the United States versus Italy. In the United States, Black subjects are coded as the undeserving poor who are nonetheless presumed to be citizens, and almost always in relation to immigrants who might be "brown," but are *not* Black.[79] In the Italian context, however, a significant proportion of the refugees arriving in Italy via the Mediterranean are from sub-Saharan Africa, and Black Italians are almost never assumed to be citizens.[80] Yet anti-Black racism is still present, perpetuated in this case through the production of racial essentialisms that distinguish between "assimilable" Black subjects (who are seen as able to marshal their diasporic networks for the benefit of the Italian economy) and "nonassimilable" Black refugees (who represent a drain on the economy).

This dynamic became visible during a highly publicized meeting of Milanese city officials in March 2016. This public event was organized by the Black Italian businessman Pascal, who is well known for promoting immigrant entrepreneurship in northern Italy based on the understanding that "immigrants are the true young labor force of this country."[81] Titled "Welfare Ambrosiano e Cittadini Globali" (Ambrosian Welfare and Global Citizens),[82] the gathering was intended to reframe the question of "immigration" to one of "global citizens" (and "welfare" to "employment"), with an emphasis on valorizing the unrecognized economic contributions of immigrants in Milan specifically and Italy generally. While the event was not explicitly concerned with the children of immigrants, it is worth noting that Milan is also a hub for AFRO Fashion, Nappytalia, AfroRicci, and many other "second-generation" Black Italian initiatives. A far grittier and less romantic city than more touristic Italian destinations like Rome and Florence, Milan has instead identified its particular niche as being "a city founded on work/labor."

The speakers at the Welfare Ambrosiano event represented an impressive swath of Milan's political set, including Giulio Gallera (assessor of welfare for the region of Lombardy); Stefano Dambruoso (a representative for Lombardy in the Chamber of Deputies); Alessandro Aleotti (entrepreneur, think tank director, and political commentator); and Piero Bassetti (former president of the region of Lombardy). A second panel even featured a debate among Milan's mayoral candidates about how the city should harness the talents of its substantial immigrant community—immigrants compose over 20 percent of Milan's population, and the Lombardy region has the largest immigrant population in Italy.[83] The caliber of the speakers pointed both to Pascal's extensive professional networks and to the municipality's investment in leveraging immigrants as resources to fuel Italy's financial capital and economic powerhouse.

Pascal was dressed for the event in an impeccable three-piece suit, with his trademark pocket watch chain and spectacles that lent him a professorial air. He introduced the speakers and prepared the audience to "use new words, words that don't create barriers . . . to develop a new perspective" on immigration. As the press release for the event announced, "Limiting ourselves to a discussion only about refugees and mosques would be misleading. The reflection should start from the new frontiers of international cooperation for development."[84] To Pascal's dismay, however, the presenters were not addressing the vision of "global citizens" that had been promised in the event's press release. Rather, the speakers proceeded to focus their remarks on the way that the city of Milan had responded to the unprecedented influx of African refugees in 2015 and 2016. Finally, visibly frustrated, he intervened and seized the microphone, his great booming voice echoing off the vaulted walls of the former cloisters where we were gathered: "You are talking about refugees escaping from war—these are not the people I am talking about. We have to stop reflecting on the people who are arriving on the boats! How do we create a situation where we *empower* the immigrants, transform them into paragons of success? We need a true meritocracy. But if we don't have a dialogical relationship, we will never get there. Because we have a shared destiny. We must live together in our differences. *That* is the challenge!"

Contrary to more common portrayals of a monolithic Blackness in Italy, Pascal's interjection called attention to the multiplicity of lived Black experiences in Italy—and the different meanings attached to these multiple Black*nesses*. As sociologist Jordanna Matlon argues, in the context of global political economy Blackness can function as a signifier that simultaneously represents the ravages of racial capitalism *and* capitalism's global reach (through the aspirational figures of exceptional Black athletes and performing artists).[85] Consider, for example, the case of white Anglo-Italian conceptual artist Vanessa Beecroft, a former collaborator of Black American recording artist and producer Kanye West. In an interview with *The Cut*, Beecroft explained that she felt such a profound affinity with Black people and Black artists that she took a genetic ancestry test hoping to confirm her hunch that she was not actually white. (The ravenous consumption of global Black popular culture by white Italians is often justified through similar references to Italian racial ambiguity via their geographical proximity to Africa.)[86] Yet despite her professed adoration of all things Black, Beecroft then went on to dismiss Africans in Italy as merely "in the street selling gadgets."[87] While itinerant street vending is a form of economic activity (and one that has a long history in Italy that predates the arrival of large numbers of African immigrants), in Beecroft's formulation this work did not carry the same dignity or creativity that she indexed as features of an authentic and desirable Blackness.

Similarly, at the Welfare Ambrosiano event, "the people arriving on the boats" were not those same immigrants who could be transformed into paragons of success and meritocracy. The differentiation between refugees on the one hand and Pascal's "global citizens" on the other constructed a racialized hierarchy of geographical itineraries and forms of mobility. "Refugees escaping war" were not agentic subjects, but rather fungible bodies moving reflexively in response to external political stimuli who could be cast aside as excess. "Talented, deserving foreigners" (as described in this chapter's epigraph), on the other hand, were sources of human capital whose transnational networks and global outlook held the key to Italy's uncertain future.

The Racial Politics of Productivity

This chapter has looked to Black Italian women's entrepreneurship to understand how the boundaries of Italian citizenship have been constructed and contested in terms of economic productivity. But rather than gloss this development as a symptom of what scholars have labeled "neoliberal citizenship"—the incursion of economistic logics into the realm of state politics—I situate these struggles against a longer historical backdrop. The connections among race, gender, and notions of economic productivity strike at the heart of liberalism itself, and its entanglement with colonial and imperial forms of governance. Just as Cedric Robinson argued that capitalism had inherited the racialism of the feudal system that preceded it, the liberal project was from its inception bound up with what Donna Haraway calls "productionist logics" that drew racialized distinctions between the rational and industrious subjects of natural rights and those incapable of transformative acts of self-making.[88]

By challenging the presentism of the neoliberal framework, I am suggesting that the liberal state cannot be so easily redeemed: nation-state recognition might produce tentative inclusion (or even differential incorporation) for some, but always at the expense of outright exclusion for others. Yet, as the examples in this chapter have shown, these are also not clear-cut forms of racial differentiation wherein people of African descent are unilaterally precluded from Italian membership. This is because "race" is not just a matter of epidermalization—it is coded sartorially and geographically, through forms of bodily habitus and webs of social association, via notions of labor and economic productivity. So, the question becomes not *whether* Blackness can be included within the boundaries of Italianness, but rather *what kinds* of Blackness can be rendered assimilable, and how the boundaries of what it means to be Italian might continue to be transformed through these struggles.

In the contemporary moment, the shifting boundaries of Italy are once again being remapped. Accordingly, the possibility of making space for Black subjects deemed capable of (re)producing Italy at a time of economic and demographic "crisis" is a contentious topic of debate among politicians and activists alike.

Black Italian women's entrepreneurship provides a unique window onto these contemporary contestations: their projects are directly implicated in wider struggles over the differentiation between "legitimate" European citizens suffering in the aftermath of austerity and economic contraction and "illegitimate" non-European bodies who constitute a threat to both national integrity and economic prosperity.

There is undoubtedly a risk that Black women are once again being conscripted (in a new form of colonial extraction) as the raw materials from which European nations can be rebuilt or reproduced at a time of stagnation, uncertainty, and political instability. Ananya Roy has argued that women are constructed in international poverty alleviation programs as ideal vehicles for economic development in the Global South—in contrast to their male counterparts, who are framed as anachronistic or abandoned by capital.[89] A version of this story is also unfolding in Italy, where the figure of the Black Italian woman entrepreneur is implicitly situated against the Black, immigrant, and male itinerant street vendor. Still, while Black Italian women's projects are frequently "domesticated" by politicians and journalists in the service of narrow nationalist political and economic interests, the capacious diasporic spatialities of their feminist politics continue to stretch far beyond the territorial boundaries of the Italian nation-state. Black Italian entrepreneurs are not "dupes," nor are they victims of false consciousness.[90] Rather, they are combining their strategies of economic survival with practices of Black diasporic interconnection, claims to Italian citizenship via the "Made in Italy" label, and creative reconfigurations of Italianness.

Valorizing immigrants (and their children) for "getting the job done" is undoubtedly a potent political strategy for countering far-right fantasies of a bounded and homogenous nation-state.[91] And in the Italian context, where the whiteness of Italians has always been an open-ended question, Black activists have encountered an especially unique opportunity to wrest open the boundaries of citizenship—one that approaches the contemporary Black Italian diaspora as a moment in a much longer history of Mediterranean cultural and economic mixing. But, as I will suggest in chapter 3, when nationalist integralism is simply substituted for a "digestive" model of citizenship—one in which elements of Mediterranean diversity can be absorbed for the purpose of bolstering the Italian nation-state but not necessarily challenging it—Black liberation is still no guarantee.

MEDITERRANEANISM, AFRICA, AND THE RACIAL BORDERS OF ITALIANNESS

> Finally, we discover that Italy, despite its political association with Europe, is essentially part of the African plate. Italy represents a promontory which indented Europe at the location of the Alps. Because the notions of Africa and Europe are relative, it is not possible to say whether Italy led the African assault on Europe, or if Europe impaled itself on Italy.
>
> —Larry Mayer, 2001

> Who better than the Italian citizen . . . to understand that a country that has perpetually expanded to include new complexions, inflections, and politics might (no, must) expand once more?
>
> —Taiye Selasi, *New York Times*, December 4, 2014

I took the high-speed train from Milan to Rome in early 2016 to attend the launch of Marilena Umuhoza Delli's autobiography, *Razzismo all'italiana* (Racism, Italian Style).[1] Marilena and I had met on Facebook after I stumbled across her blog *AfroItalian4Ever*, and we immediately bonded over the fact that we both had one Black parent (her mother is Rwandan) and one white parent from the northern Italian province of Bergamo. Her book talk was held in the Trastevere neighborhood in a small independent bookstore that specializes in Black history, immigration studies, African literature, and multicultural children's stories. The intimate space was far over capacity that evening, and the audience was squeezed precariously into rows of wooden chairs. A projector screen at the front of the room displayed a looping slideshow of Marilena's family photos. The racially diverse group listened intently as Marilena read excerpts from her autobiography. "My parents are from different cultures," she explained. "I grew up in Bergamo in the 1980s and saw very few other Black people. I was the only one in my school—in middle school, in high school. It was not easy, but I survived." Earlier in the presentation, she joked that the original title of her book was *Vaffanculo razzisti di merda!* (Go Fuck Yourselves, Racist Shitheads!), but her publisher ultimately made her change it. The audience burst out in laugher at the audacity of the rejected title, but also in recognition of its acerbic accuracy.

After Marilena finished her reading, an Italian postcolonial studies scholar serving as a discussant remarked that books like Marilena's are part of a new tradition of Italian postcolonial literature. Her book, and the proliferation of texts like it across Italy, provided timely reflections about what it meant to be Black in Italy today.[2] While most members of the audience nodded along in agreement with the professor's comments, one woman began whispering agitatedly to her neighbor. Her whispers grew louder, meeting disapproving stares from Marilena and the panelists, until she was finally asked to share her thoughts with the rest of the audience.

The woman, visible from where I sat at the back of the crowded room because of the way a dramatic shock of silver hair stood out against the rest of her black coif, asked how much of what Marilena experienced could be explained by the "southern" influence on Italian culture: "*Meridionali* have a culture of hospitality, of sensuality. I can say this because I am from southern Italy! So what you experienced might not have been hostility—it could have just been coming from this part of our culture. For instance, when people ask you questions about your hair, they might just be curious. At the end of the day, I think that Italians are just naturally open to people from other places—look at the mayor of New York, Bill de Blasio. He is married to an African American woman!" The professor sighed in frustration. "My book is a chronicle of everyday racism," Marilena explained calmly, yet firmly. "I am often asked if Italy is racist. I usually respond that Italy isn't inherently racist, but it *is* a country where racism is tolerated." This did not placate the southern Italian woman, who seemed ready to throw up her arms in protest: "We can't be racist!"[3]

In the bookstore that evening, the woman's claim about Italian "openness" represented an unwelcome interruption in a rare public discussion of the lived experience of anti-Black racism in Italy. Yet the implication behind her interjection—that Italian culture is characterized by a certain "southern influence" that is, at its core, antithetical to racism and insular nationalisms—was one that I encountered repeatedly during my research in Italy. A surprising number of my friends and interlocutors across the racial spectrum were deploying Italy's Mediterraneanness to make sense of racism, Italian national identity, and struggles over citizenship. Just over a week before Marilena's event, for instance, I had met an Italian-Ghanaian friend for breakfast at one of Milan's many train stations. As was typical of our conversations, we ended up ruminating on questions of diversity and Italian national identity. Very soon, we drifted to the subject of civilizational mixing in the Mediterranean basin—histories that converged on the Italian peninsula. "Italy is not *really* a country," my friend remarked slyly.

All of those things that we tended to think of as part of an "authentic" Italian culture, he went on to explain, really came from elsewhere: "If you look at history, you'll see that all of the popes and emperors had diverse origins—they were not 'Italian.'" Even my elderly white landlord in Sesto San Giovanni made use of Italy's peculiar racial geographies to talk about race and Blackness: when I told her the story of how my parents met, she responded that she could understand firsthand the prejudice my parents faced as an interracial couple because she was from northern Italy and her husband was a southerner.

These brief examples seemed to suggest that in response to the rising tide of racial nationalism and ethnic absolutism in Italy, a powerful counterargument was emerging from certain segments of the Left: Italianness is best represented not by purity of origin but rather by deep histories of civilizational cross-contamination across the Mediterranean.[4] These histories in turn throw into question the idea of a bounded and homogenous Italianness and point the way to a future in which citizenship is delinked from race. The idea of mixing, or *meticciato* in Italian—from the mixing of people of diverse backgrounds within a community to the mixing of people of different racial backgrounds in an intimate relationship to an individual "mixed-race" person—was being hailed as both the future of Italy and as one of its oldest traditions.[5]

As noted in chapter 1, former minister of integration Cécile Kyenge helped to repopularize this vision of Italy when she publicly declared that Italy was a *paese meticcio* (a mixed country) during her push for citizenship reform.[6] Even the traditionally conservative realm of Italianist scholarship has, in the last decade, witnessed a resurgence of interest in Mediterranean interconnections and in using concepts such as hybridity, inter- and transculturality, and *meticciato* to study Italian national identity.[7] Italianist scholar Vetri Nathan, for instance, described Italy as "a nation at the cultural crossroads of the Mediterranean . . . a geographical bridge, a long and narrow peninsula that not only spans North and South, but East and West."[8]

Beyond the realm of formal political discourse and the ivory tower of academia, assertions of Italo-Mediterranean hybridity suffuse cultural centers and business development plans, scientific research agendas, and political commentary across Italy. As the first two chapters of this book have shown, the children of immigrants often draw on histories of Mediterranean interconnection to challenge exclusionary citizenship laws, attempting to widen the racial boundaries of Italianness by pointing to the precariousness of Italian whiteness and national identity. But unlike the southern Italian woman at Marilena's book launch, this southern-facing gaze is used to *contest* Italian institutional racism—not to deny its existence. This has been a particularly potent strategy for Black Italians, who (as described in chapter 2) often marshal centuries of cross-cultural contact between the Italian peninsula and the African continent to suggest that a Black diaspora in Italy is anything but new. For them, Italy's history of racial liminality provides a unique political opening to mobilize for their inclusion within the historically unstable category of "Italian citizen." As Igiaba Scego wrote in an editorial for the *Guardian*, published after a horrific string of deadly attacks against Black migrants in Italy:

> I have often wondered how it is that in such a young country, only 150 years old, there is such pronounced and deeply rooted racism. I have my own theory. In its heart, as a Mediterranean state, Italy knows itself to be a country with strong links to Africa. It could be the perfect pivot between continents, between Europe and Africa, yet it persists in denying its mixed-race identity as a country made of diversity. Everyone has passed through here: Arabs, Austrians, Africans, the French, the Spanish. This is Italy, a mixture of different blood and skins. When it finally accepts this identity, it will once again be the Bel Paese we all love.[9]

The Rome-based association Neri Italiani—Black Italians brought these historical Mediterranean connections to life in the form of a playful reimagining of the Roman founding myth. According to the earliest written account of this story, which dates to the third century BCE, the vestal virgin Rhea Silvia (daughter of Numitor, the previous king of the Latin city Alba Longa) gave birth to twin boys named Romulus and Remus. The king of Alba Longa, Amulius, feared that the boys would have a legitimate claim to his throne and so he ordered them to be abandoned on the banks of the Tiber River. The twins were rescued by the river god Tiberinus, who delivered them to safety at the base of the Palatine Hill. There, the twins were discovered by a she-wolf, who suckled them. Thanks to *la lupa*'s act of interspecies mothering, the boys survived their death sentence and Romulus would go on to found the city of Rome around 750 BCE.

The bronze sculpture *La lupa capitolina* (The Capitoline Wolf), housed in Rome's Palazzo dei Conservatori, is today the most iconic rendering of this story (see figure 3.1a). Although it was traditionally attributed as an Etruscan work from the fifth century BCE, the statue of the she-wolf actually dates to the thirteenth century, and a fifteenth-century sculptor named Antonio Pollaiuolo later added figures of Romulus and Remus beneath her pendulous teats. But in the Neri Italiani version of the sculpture there is a *third* figure seated between Romulus and Remus, clasping their hands, a child with a beatific smile and a voluminous Afro (see figure 3.1b). If Rome is the beating cultural heart of Italy, then the insertion of a Black triplet into its mythological genealogy is a reminder that, from the *longue durée* perspective of the Mediterranean, Blackness in the Italian peninsula is nothing new. "We've *been* here," the third brother seems to say, with a sly wink.

FIGURES 3.1A AND 3.1B. Top: *La lupa capitolina*. Bottom: A reimagining of Rome's founding myth by the Black youth association Neri Italiani—Black Italians.

Sources: Wikimedia Commons, https://en.wikipedia.org/wiki/Capitoline_Wolf#/media/File:Capitoline_she-wolf
_Musei_Capitolini_MC1181.jpg (left); NIBI: Neri Italiani—Black Italians Facebook page, https://www.facebook
.com/neritaliani/photos/a.807752002613416/1337950559593555 (right).

As these varied examples suggest, the geography of the Mediterranean looms over popular figurations of Italianness and Italian citizenship. Today, the Mediterranean simultaneously represents the promise of a postracial future and a source of racial contamination; it is an alibi to deflect accusations of anti-Black racism and a way to create space for Black people within the Italian nation. Since Italian national unification at the end of the nineteenth century, the Mediterranean has been repeatedly mobilized in contestations over the symbolic and material boundaries of Italianness.[10] Italy's liminal geographical position—*not quite Europe, not quite Africa*—generated distinct dynamics of racial formation, as well as unique openings for contemporary Black activists seeking to challenge Italian ethnic absolutism.

This chapter takes a step back in time, examining the ways that the history of Italy's multiple "Southern Questions" has shaped contemporary understandings of Italianness. This genealogy of Italian racial thinking is a history of the present, one that helps to illuminate the current possibilities and closures for Black activism in a country where the boundaries between Italianness and Blackness have been anything but stable.[11] To be clear, I am not attempting to retrace African influences on Italian culture since antiquity—territory that has been well trod by studies such as Cheikh Anta Diop's *The African Origin of Civilization*, Martin Bernal's *Black Athena*, and Catherine Fletcher's *The Black Prince of Florence* (about the sixteenth-century nobleman Alessandro de' Medici). Instead, I consider the discursive mobilization of the Mediterranean in Italian racial formation across four key historical moments: Italian unification and colonial expansion; the rise of Fascism; postwar reconstruction; and Italy's transformation from a country of emigration to a country of immigration. In each of these moments, the Mediterranean was used to remap Italy's relationship to both Europe and Africa.

The story of Italy complicates theories of racial formation that northern Europe take as their (implicit) geographical reference point. In northern European countries such as France, Germany, and the United Kingdom, racial mixing was generally approached as dangerous and as a cause of degeneration—in other words, as a threat to the imperial order of things.[12] Only relatively recently, as Jin Haritaworn suggests, have multiraciality and multiculturalism come to be hailed as symbols of anti-racism and metropolitan progressiveness in these countries.[13] But the history of attitudes toward mixing are much more nuanced in southern Europe, where the geography of the Mediterranean effectively rendered claims to racial purity untenable. Indeed, the primary way that the Mediterranean has been figured by racial theorists and cultural commentators alike is as a symbol of confluence and exchange—of people, goods, and cultures.[14] Even Hegel considered the Mediterranean Sea to be "the center of World-History" because it facilitated frictionless communication and interaction across three entire continents.[15]

As Italy's relationship to the Mediterranean suggests, racism is reproduced not just through essentialized notions of culture (as the influential critiques of Europe's "new racism" have shown) but also through *geography* and practices of spatial differentiation.[16] An orientation toward the geographical politics of racism—in addition to the cultural politics of racism—thus provides an additional set of analytical tools for "identifying forms of differentiation that do not explicitly invoke blood . . . but nonetheless employ essentializing logics."[17] Race is not, and never has been, solely contained within the individual body or inscribed on the surface of the skin. For this reason, it is necessary to engage with the multiple geographically and historically specific racisms that (re)produce the category of race itself. As David Theo Goldberg writes, "If race is a virtually vacuous category, as many have insisted, it must act as a cipher rather than as a motor force with determining power of its own. Its modes of determination must derive from that for which it stands as shorthand. . . . The force of race assumes its power in and from the thick of contexts of the different if related geopolitical regions in which it is embedded, the specific conditions of which concretize the notion of race representing them."[18]

Italy's geographical proximity to the African continent prompted generations of Italian scientists, politicians, and colonial administrators to "measure, dissect, and classify" racially ambiguous Italians.[19] Their efforts to clarify the relationship between Italianness and Blackness resulted in a range of often contradictory practices of racial mapping and boundary drawing. Significantly, however, this Mediterranean *meticciato* was not always understood solely as a threat to the racial purity of the Italian nation-state. It was at times also approached as a source of racial and cultural invigoration—as a potential solution to the challenges of modernity.

This Mediterranean story represents an alternative genealogy of Italianness—the other side of an ethnic absolutist coin that privileges notions of a primordial, autochthonous Italian people with a culture (or regional cultures) that are deeply rooted and bounded in place. It suggests that Africa, Blackness, and Black diasporic routes are actually *constitutive* of Italianness, rather than external to it. But at the same time, political mobilizations of Mediterraneanness are not wholly innocent. Despite their apparent promises of multiracial and multicultural conviviality, discourses of Mediterraneanism and Italian hybridity can also work in practice to *exclude* Blackness by distancing Italy from sub-Saharan Africa, invoking historical relationships with North Africa while metaphorically severing the deep pan-African ties that traverse the entirety of the Mediterranean basin.

Italies and Southern Questions after the Risorgimento

In the summer of 2013, when I was beginning the research for this book, I met with a white Italian postdoctoral researcher to discuss my project. As we chatted in Italian, I explained that I was interested in the cultural politics of race and racism in Italy. But when she heard me utter the Italian word for race, *razza*, the color immediately drained from her face. Then, with careful condescension, she replied: "You must understand that in Italy, we don't use the word *razza*. It reminds us of Fascism. And really, 'ethnicity' is a much more accurate way to describe different human groups." Shocked, I rushed home that evening and drafted a panicked e-mail to one of my doctoral supervisors—I had clearly misunderstood the Italian context, I wrote, and was going to have to rethink my entire dissertation project. According to my "schooling" by the Italian postdoc, it seemed that my own Italian Blackness—which at first made me an ideal candidate to carry out this research—had been compromised by the influence of a perversely Anglo-American fixation on the concept of "race." But when I found myself repeatedly having versions of this same conversation in Italy, I realized that what I had initially mistook as a sign of my own incompetence as a researcher was actually a collection of valuable ethnographic moments. And this was what ultimately sent me hurtling into the archives of Cesare Lombroso in Turin.

The Italian-Jewish scientist Cesare Lombroso is hailed as the founder of modern criminology, best known for his articulation of the theory of the *delinquente nato*, or "born criminal." But while Lombroso is widely known today for his criminological studies, he was also a prolific racial theorist. Lombroso, who lived from 1835 to 1909, was active during and immediately following Italian national unification; before he published his most famous book, *L'uomo delinquente* (Criminal Man), in 1876, he penned a study of human races in 1871 titled *L'uomo bianco e l'uomo di colore* (The White Man and the Black Man). And, in fact, Lombroso's writings on crime and his scholarship on race cannot be separated, as his racial theories provided the intellectual scaffolding for his analysis of the atavistic "criminal type"—one who bears the physical residues of lesser-evolved and racially inferior human groups.

I begin my story of Italy's Mediterraneanisms with Lombroso and Liberal Italy—the period from Italian national unification until the rise of Fascism (1861–1922)—because far too often, racism (and by extension, xenophobia) in Italy are framed as historical aberrations. From this perspective, racism is either a foreign imposition by Nazi Germany during World War II or a knee-jerk response to the arrival of large numbers of sub-Saharan African migrants in the 1980s and 1990s. As Angelo Matteo Caglioti argues, while the scholarship on

racism and racial science in Italy has focused predominantly on the anti-Semitism of late Fascist racial science, this emphasis elides a domestic tradition of racial theorization that dates to Italy's Liberal period.[20] A closer look at the archives suggests that the entanglement of race and citizenship was in fact constitutive of Italian nation-state formation, in ways that remain deeply consequential to this day. As a matter of fact, debates about race in Liberal Italy were characterized less by anti-Semitism and more by an overwhelming preoccupation with Italy's trans-Mediterranean relationship to the African continent.[21] So, to understand the relationship between Italianness and Blackness (and how this relationship figures in contestations over the boundaries of Italian citizenship), it is necessary to begin with postunification Italy and efforts to consolidate the new nation's racial identity.

Rearticulating these lineages of pre-Fascist racial thought requires reading archives against the grain—in the University of Turin's Archivio Storico del Museo di Antropologia Criminale Cesare Lombroso (Historical Archive of the Cesare Lombroso Museum of Criminal Anthropology), for instance, there is no dedicated file for Lombroso's work on racial science. This points both to the evasion of race in the standard historiography of Liberal Italy and also to the way that racism suffused most aspects of Lombroso's scientific research such that it could never truly be separated out from the rest of his scientific oeuvre. The archivists and I instead had to follow an elusive trail of bread crumbs through Lombroso's notes, editorials, letters, and maps, as well as secondary commentary on his research. At one point, for instance, an archivist pulled out a large illustration of Sarah Baartman (the so-called Hottentot Venus) from a filing cabinet and turned to me hopefully: "Maybe this will be helpful for you?"[22] Although Baartman herself was never taken to Italy, her spectral presence in the archive suggests the centrality of Blackness in efforts to ascertain the racial parameters of Italianness at the turn of the twentieth century (see figure 3.2).[23] Indeed, as Stephen Small argues, "Blackness" in Europe includes not just the physical presence of people of African descent but also various forms of "race-thinking and racist thinking" that deploy negative stereotypes of African savagery and inferiority.[24]

The unification of Italy, also known as the Risorgimento, took place over five decades, culminating in the incorporation of Rome as the capital of the Kingdom of Italy in 1871. Yet this milestone was met with deep ambivalence in Italy, perhaps best captured by Massimo d'Azeglio's famous (and possibly apocryphal) quote, "We have made Italy. Now we must make Italians." At the time of the Risorgimento, Italy was a patchwork collection of city-states and languages that were not always mutually intelligible—it was little more than Metternich's mere "geographical expression." The most pressing challenge facing the new nation-state, however, was the so-called Southern Question. The Southern Question, discussed

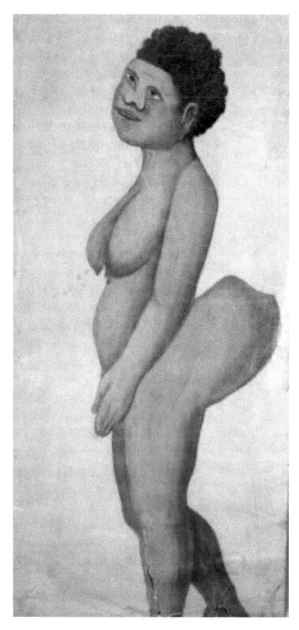

FIGURE 3.2. Painting of the *venere ottentota* (Sarah Baartman, the so-called Hottentot Venus).

Source: Archivio del Museo di Antropologia Criminale "Cesare Lombroso," University of Turin.

most famously by the Marxist intellectual Antonio Gramsci but predating him by several decades, refers to the significant differences between the northern and southern halves of Italy in terms of economic production, industrialization, infrastructure, income, literacy, public health, and criminal activity.[25]

Italian elites generally understood the divergence between northern and southern Italy through an Orientalist lens that emphasized the South's geographical and racial proximity to the African continent.[26] And this question of an "African" influence rendered precarious Italy's inclusion within a broader family of European nations. Most European nation-states traced their cultural and political origins to ancient Rome, locating the cradle of European civilization within the Italian peninsula.[27] Yet intellectuals of northern Europe—influenced by Aryanist or Nordicist racial theories that emphasized racial purity—looked down on *contemporary* Italians due to their proximity to the African continent. In his *Essay on the Inequality of Human Races* (1853), the French aristocrat Joseph Arthur de Gobineau famously contended that despite the Aryan racial origins of the Roman Empire, its collapse could be traced to the decadence and racial degeneration caused by the Aryan Romans' indiscriminate intermixing with Africans and Asians.[28] And recent archaeological discoveries along the Italian peninsula had also provided new, physical evidence of ancient Mediterranean migrations that converged on the Italian peninsula—making modern Italian claims to racial purity wholly untenable.[29]

This "problem" of racial equivocality was further exacerbated by Liberal Italy's colonial expansion.[30] Italy began acquiring territorial possessions in the Horn of Africa as the process of national unification was underway, which meant that Italy was actually faced with *two* racially charged Southern Questions.[31] If the racial character of the fledgling Italian nation was an open question, then what could possibly serve as the basis for Italian authority in the new African colonies? While Italian colonialism is today glossed as "weak" and "ineffectual," during the late nineteenth century the supposed failure of Italian colonialism had not yet been established. Italian elites thus found themselves contending with this question, summarized by historian Mary Gibson: "Could race mixing be invigorating rather than enervating and a signal of mongrelization and decline? If so, was race mixing useful only among 'whites'?"[32]

Italy's demographic heterogeneity, moral panics about the "backwardness" of southern Italians, geographical proximity to Africa, and colonial expansion generated a variety of approaches for apprehending Italy's racial character.[33] During the Liberal period, two competing arguments emerged: on the one hand, Italy was understood as comprising two distinct races—an Aryan Italic race in the North, and a Semitic Mediterranean race in the South; on the other hand,

Italy was said to comprise a unique Mediterranean race from which the rest of Europe emerged.

The former approach was championed by Lombroso and his student Alfredo Niceforo (1876–1960). In *Criminal Man*, Lombroso asserted that southern Italians shared specific physical and lifestyle traits (e.g., the abuse of women, resistance to authority, laziness) with Africans—as Daniel Pick writes, for Lombroso, Blackness "was not simply an external threat."[34] According to Gaia Giuliani, Lombroso characterized the southern temperament as one "defined by transnational raciologies . . . deterministically attached to the influence of those Arabic (Semitic) or 'African' (Hamitic) races that were also composing the racial background of the newly colonized populations."[35] For Lombroso, southern Italians' high rates of brigandage, organized crime, and murder was explained by the fact that they were racially mixed, the descendants of the many different populations who had conquered and settled in the South (see figure 3.3).[36]

But although Lombroso believed that northern and southern Italians represented two distinct races, this assertion did little to quell Italian uncertainties about their authority in the new African colonies. "It remains to be seen," he mused at the beginning of *L'uomo bianco*, "if we whites, who stand proudly at the peak of civilization, will have to one day bow our heads before the progna-

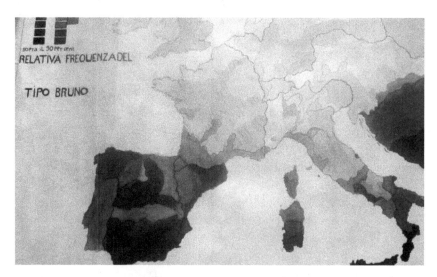

FIGURE 3.3. Map commissioned by Cesare Lombroso illustrating the geographical distribution of the *tipo bruno* (dark-haired type). For Lombroso, the Latin *tipo bruno* represented one of the two major racial groups in Europe, the other being the Germanic "blonds."

Source: Archivio del Museo di Antropologia Criminale "Cesare Lombroso," University of Turin: 3/1861 "Relativa frequenza del tipo bruno."

thous muzzle of the negro, or the yellow and ashen face of the mongoloid."[37] In the same book, he concluded that only the white race had achieved absolute physical and civilizational perfection.[38] But if southern Italians shared racial characteristics with Italy's colonial subjects in the Horn of Africa, what did this imply for Italian colonialism?[39]

Italy's humiliating defeat by the Ethiopian army at the Battle of Adwa in 1896 (the first African anti-imperialist victory) rendered these questions even more urgent. In this context, Lombroso's student, the Sicilian positivist Alfredo Niceforo, sought to systematize his mentor's methodology so that his arguments about race, crime, and degeneracy could be rendered more widely generalizable and politically actionable.[40] In *L'Italia barbara contemporanea* (Contemporary Barbarian Italy, 1898) and *Italiani del nord e italiani del sud* (Italians of the North and Italians of the South, 1901), Niceforo contended that apart from some racial fluidity in central Italy, it was in fact possible to differentiate between the northern and southern halves of the country.[41] The existence of these two Italies gave Niceforo a way to sidestep the question of Italian racial inferiority by externalizing Mediterranean contamination to southern Italy and the African continent. At the same time, this did not mean that national unity was impossible; rather, Niceforo held that the heterogeneous character of the Italian nation required regionally distinct forms of governance, with the South maintained as a sort of internal colony.[42]

Lombroso and Niceforo had responded to Gobineau's infamous charge of Mediterranean degeneration by distancing a more "civilized" northern Italy from southern Italy, Africa, and the racial contamination of Blackness. But other scholars during this period sought to upturn the racial geography of Europe by claiming instead that Aryan Europe actually derived from the Mediterranean itself.[43] The most influential proponent of this alternative theory in Italy was the Sicilian positivist physical anthropologist and polygenecist Giuseppe Sergi (1841–1936), founder of the Società Romana di Antropologia (Anthropological Society of Rome).

Sergi was a vehement critic of Aryanist racial theories. In *Origine e diffusione della stirpe mediterranea* (1895; published in English as *The Mediterranean Race: A Study of the Origins of European Peoples*), he argued that Italy was populated by a Mediterranean race with origins in the Ethiopian highlands of the Horn of Africa. This Mediterranean race had gradually spread into North Africa, across the Mediterranean, and into Europe and Asia (see figure 3.4).[44] Sergi thus traced the origins of European civilization to a Mediterranean stock that was formed through the commingling of many populations along the Mediterranean basin after an initial dispersal from the African continent.[45] In doing so, he cast doubt on the supposed Indo-European origins of Europeans, and on the idea of a pure Germanic / Aryan racial type. Contrary to popular depictions of the Mediterranean as a hotbed of

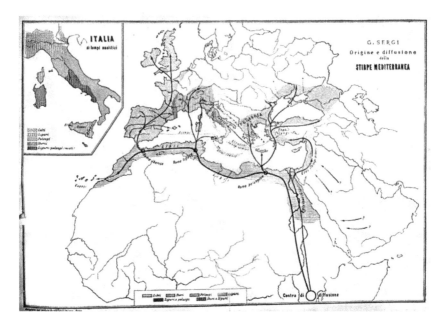

FIGURE 3.4.   Giuseppe Sergi's map illustrating the geographical diffusion of the "Mediterranean race/stock" from the Horn of Africa across the Mediterranean and into Europe and Asia.

Source: Giuseppe Sergi, Origine e diffusione della stirpe mediterranea *(Rome: Società Dante Alighieri, 1895).*

racial degeneration, for Sergi the unique geography of the Mediterranean actually created the "most favorable conditions for the development of a civilization more cosmopolitan than those born in the valleys of the great rivers."[46] He thus located "the mysterious goddess Isis who rises from the Black Hamitic land" at the heart of Western civilization, turning Gobineau's infamous race struggle on its head.[47]

Far from undermining Italian colonialism, the notion of a racial, civilizational, or cultural connection between Italy and Africa was used to bolster Italian colonial expansion. For instance, some commentators, including members of the Società Geografica Italiana (Italian Geographical Society), contended that the presence of a precolonial Christianity in the Horn of Africa made Ethiopia and Eritrea ideal "vehicles for Italy's civilizing mission."[48] In other words, the similarities between Italy and the Horn of Africa could strengthen Italy's territorial ambitions. But there remained enough of a racial difference to legitimate Italian colonial authority—while Sergi traced the deep historical origins of European civilizations to the Horn, he nonetheless concluded that *in the present day,* members of the African branch of the Mediterranean stock were simply less suited to civilization and social order than their European relatives.[49]

Despite these different geographic imaginings of Italy's relationship to the Mediterranean during the Liberal period, what they all shared was an attempt to use racial science to secure Italy's membership as part of Europe and resolve the questions raised by Italy's geographical position at the border of Europe and Africa.[50] Italian elites strove to access European modernity through the production of scientific knowledge, and specifically through the production of scientific knowledge that mapped Italy as unambiguously European—either by bracketing southern Italy as outside the racial and civilizational boundaries of Italianness, or by asserting the Afro-Mediterranean origins of all of European civilization. Italian scientists had been influenced by the groundbreaking research of Charles Darwin and were in conversation with theorists including Herbert Spencer and Francis Galton. In other words, they were active members of a vast global network of racial scientists and eugenicists engaged in the production of knowledge about Europe, Africa, and Blackness—what would eventually become, in the words of Stefan Kühl, an "international of racists" (*die internationale der Rassisten*).[51]

These debates about Italy's racial geography had implications that reached far beyond elite scientific squabbles, shaping Italy's relationship to multiple Southern Questions and the everyday lives of both southern Italians and colonial subjects. The theories of southern Italian degeneracy developed by Lombroso and his students were cited in the US Immigration Commission's 1911 Dillingham Report, which laid the foundation for the Johnson Act of 1921 and the Johnson-Reed Act of 1924, effectively barring most Italian immigration to the United States.[52] Italian immigrants who had taken up residence across the Atlantic in countries such as the United States were frequently regarded as racially ambiguous and morally suspect due to the transnational reach of studies by Lombroso and his contemporaries.[53] The positivists of Liberal Italy also played a key role in Italy's colonial endeavors, as the anthropological knowledge they produced shaped practices of colonial administration. The 1909 Civil Code for the Colony of Eritrea, for instance, held that the "mixed-race" children of Eritreans and Italians could be conferred Italian citizenship if their fathers were known to be "Aryan-Italian"; if the parents were unknown, then citizenship would be decided based on the anthropometric evaluation of the children's racial features.[54] As De Donno observes, this code bounded Italianness racially, as both Aryan *and* Mediterranean.[55] While the 1909 civil code was never formalized into law, it was still referenced by judges and provided guidance when they were adjudicating the citizenship status of "mixed-race" children from the African colonies who had not been legally recognized by their white Italian fathers.[56]

For Lombroso, Niceforo, Sergi, and their contemporaries in Liberal Italy, the Mediterranean represented the central "problematic" through which the racial character of the new Italian nation could be ascertained. Regardless of whether Italians were classified as Aryan or Mediterranean, white or Black, European or African, this racial character could then be used to support broad arguments about civilizational capacity, colonial governance, and the limits of Italian citizenship. For those scientists Gramsci derisively labeled "Southernists"—whom he recognized as partners of the northern bourgeoisie in the subordination of southern Italy—the Mediterranean had been transformed into a buffer zone that allowed the new Italian nation to digest and metabolize all forms of unruly racial, cultural, and civilizational mixing.[57]

Aryans, Mediterraneans, and the New Roman Empire

The rise of Fascism in Italy is frequently characterized as a sharp break from the Liberal period, marked by the rise of binaristic racial thinking and anti-Semitic legislation targeting Jews as the nation's internal enemies—a direct product of Italy's political alignment with Nazi Germany. The writings of historian Renzo De Felice, for instance, minimized the existence of racism and colonialism under Fascism, attributing Italian racial laws to Nazi influence and characterizing racism as a sharp deviation from the mentality and history of the Italian nation.[58] But what is so often overlooked is that the Italian Fascist state was just as preoccupied with the "problem" of the Mediterranean, and what this meant for the establishment of an Italian empire abroad and notions of citizenship at home. Indeed, figures like Niceforo actually *bridged* the eras of Liberal positivist science and Fascist eugenics.[59] If, as Rosetta Giuliani Caponetto argues, Africa has always played a role in Italian national identity, under Fascism it was increasingly viewed as the constitutive "outside" against which a consolidated Italian racial identity could be celebrated.[60]

The Fascist regime sought to overcome the international humiliations of both Italy's defeat at Adwa and the United States' restrictions on Italian immigration, both of which seemed to confirm Aryanist theories of Italian racial inferiority.[61] In response, Fascist doctrine, policies, and practices of positive eugenics sought to construct a "new fascist-imperial man" that was young, virile, fertile, and superior to the people of the African continent.[62] Southern Italian women, portrayed as backward and sexually licentious during the Liberal period, were now idealized by the state as symbols of fecundity, capable of propagating the Italian race.[63]

At the same time, lingering Italian racial uncertainties were increasingly directed outside the territorial boundaries of Italy onto the colonies, with the gradual consolidation of Italy as a singular people rather than a hierarchy of more or less pure or civilized races. Of course, as Lucia Re explains, the process of constructing Italians as a racially unified body was already underway by the latter part of the Liberal period, with the devastatingly destructive and genocidal Italian campaign in Libya that began in 1911 and lasted until 1932.[64] As Re argues, "The Libyan war sought to unify Italians by displacing racism from inside to outside the body of the nation and its people."[65] In a sense, then, the Italian colonial campaign in Libya also represents a bridge between the Liberal and Fascist geographies of Italian race-making.

This effort to racially unify the Italian nation did not result in an immediate embrace of racial *purity*, however. In the 1920s and 1930s, Benito Mussolini actually subscribed to the theory of Italians as a *razza ario-mediterranea* (Aryan-Mediterranean race), one based on the fusion and assimilation of many different populations across Europe and the Mediterranean.[66] According to Mussolini, this set Italy, and Italian Fascism, apart from the Nordicism that had shaped the Fascist regime in Germany.[67] And this Aryan Mediterraneanness was characterized not by homogeneity, but by mixing: in a 1932 interview, Mussolini entirely rejected the idea that pure races existed, asserting that "it is often . . . from happy mixtures that a nation derives strength and beauty."[68]

As Giuliani argues, these claims were directly related to the imperial ambitions of Fascist Italy.[69] Mussolini dreamed of reviving the ancient Roman Empire of the Mediterranean. With this goal in mind, the notion of an Aryan-Mediterranean race had the benefit of establishing a link between Italy and Africa, undergirding the imaginary of a benevolent colonialism in which Italy—as an advanced, modern nation—could help to rekindle the stagnant civilizations along the Mediterranean basin. The Italian Ministry of Foreign Affairs in fact contended that Italy should serve as a cultural and racial bridge, a more appealing and less overtly "racist" presence in Africa and the Middle East than Britain or Germany.[70] These arguments were based not solely on racial science, but on notions of religious and cultural unity: Mussolini and the intellectuals who bolstered the Fascist regime frequently pointed to the "universalist" political philosophies of both ancient Rome and Catholic Rome as Italian antidotes to the segregationist racial hygiene policies that characterized the imperial practices of Britain and Germany.[71]

The Italian Fascist marching anthem "Faccetta nera" (Little Black Face), written by Renato Micheli, exemplified the way notions of Mediterranean interconnection were used to legitimate imperialism. "Faccetta nera," sung by Italian soldiers during the reinvasion of Ethiopia, tells the story of an Abyssinian girl who is encountered by the Italians during the war, using masculine sexual conquest as a metaphor for (and invitation to) colonial conquest.[72] The lyrics implied that Italians would not deploy brutal domination, but would instead welcome Ethiopians into a family of shared laws and customs. "Faccetta nera" was one of the most popular songs of Fascist Italy and is still sung today despite its violent history. During the mid-1930s, it circulated widely, along with semi-pornographic postcards of Ethiopian and Eritrean women—representations of the sexual rewards awaiting Italian colonizers in the Horn of Africa.[73]

Faccetta nera, bell'abissina	Pretty little black face, beautiful Abyssinian
Aspetta e spera che già l'ora si avvicina!	Wait and see, for the hour is already on its way!
quando saremo insieme a te	When we are together with you
noi ti daremo un'altra legge e un altro Re	We shall give you another law and another king
La legge nostra è schiavitù d'amore	Our law is slavery of love

This idea of a Mediterranean racial, cultural, and civilizational unity accomplished several tasks. It allowed for the incorporation of internal Italian racial differences into a single national identity, while also fixing Italy's Mediterraneaness as one distinct from the Mediterraneanness of colonized Africans. And it appealed to revanchist territorial visions of a new Roman Empire.

These ideas held sway for the first decade of Fascist rule, thanks to the legacy of Sergi and the influence of more contemporary public intellectuals like Nicola Pende.[74] But the Mediterranean position, whether exemplified by the legacy of the "two Italies" thesis or Sergi's "Mediterranean stock," became increasingly untenable. A large number of male Italian settlers in Eritrea had taken advantage of a local custom known as *demoz*—temporary, "contractual conjugal arrangements" between men and women involving payment, relationships that coexisted alongside the more formal and religious institution of long-term marriage.[75] In the resulting colonial system of *madamato* or *madamismo*, an Eritrean woman would share a household with an Italian man (who was often already legally married to an Italian woman who had remained in Italy). The Eritrean *madama* would provide her Italian partner with "all the comforts of home," while also serving as a cultural intermediary of sorts.[76] The ubiquity of these conjugal interracial relationships in the colonies—and the children resulting from such unions—raised challenging questions for administrators, jurists, and scientists in Italy. How, if at all, should colonial administrators regulate intimate contact between Italian citizens and colonial subjects? And, given the ambiguities of Italian racial identity, to which category should the resulting *meticci* ("mixed-race" children) be assigned? While Mediterraneanists condoned interracial contact as another means to reinforce Italy's connection to their colonial subjects, Aryanists feared that miscegenation would only undermine colonial hierarchies.[77]

A major turning point came in 1936, when Italy successfully occupied Ethiopia and established Africa Orientale Italiana (Italian East Africa). For Mussolini, the reinvasion of Ethiopia avenged the 1896 Italian defeat at Adwa; as such, the newly established Italian empire could leave no room for intimations of Italian racial inferiority. Whereas during the Liberal period the Italian government had tolerated (and sometimes condoned) emigration as a "safety valve" for managing internal tensions after national unification, the Fascist state now began to support systemic "demographic colonialism" to stem the flow of Italians abroad and grant them their own "place in the sun" within the empire.[78] As southern Italians were being progressively incorporated into the Italian national body and imperial project, the Fascist regime began to embrace explicitly Aryanist understandings of Italian racial identity (which incorporated both northern and southern Italians) to bolster Italian authority in the colonies.

The resulting colonial codes and laws sought to eliminate any possibility of racial fluidity between the colonizers and the colonized, establishing varying degrees of racial apartheid across the empire. The 1933 Organic Law for Eritrea and Somalia had in many ways reflected a continuation of Liberal theories about the potentially porous boundaries between Italians and (certain) Africans. According to this law, "mixed-race" children who were recognized by their fathers could become Italian citizens, but unrecognized children could be granted citizenship only if their physical features showed substantial evidence of whiteness and they displayed evidence of Italian cultural assimilation.[79] But by 1937 (*before* racial laws were enacted in Italy), interracial relationships were officially prohibited in the Italian colonies. The goal of this new policy was twofold. On the one hand, the Fascist government sought to manage the racial threat posed by the practice of *madamato / madamismo* in the Horn of Africa and the "mixed-race" children resulting from these unions. On the other hand, the regime wanted to protect the "prestige" of the Italian Empire against any embarrassments caused by working-class Italian settlers.[80] And in 1940, the children of Italian settlers and colonized subjects from the Horn of Africa were completely precluded from access to Italian citizenship—a marked difference from the 1909 and 1933 policies.[81] Rather than emerging in the Italian metropole and then spreading outward, the earliest attempts by the Fascist state to legally calcify the racial categorization of Italians as white Aryans actually emerged *first* as a strategy to contain the Mediterranean contact zone, and only then served as the model for the 1938 racial laws targeting the Jews (as well as Romani and Sinti populations) as Italy's "internal enemy."[82]

It is no surprise that Mussolini ultimately attempted to ban "Faccetta nera"—no longer a rousing anthem that eroticized imperialism, it was now seen as a dangerous enticement to interracial mixing.[83] This was also the same moment when the term *meticciato* entered the popular lexicon in Italy.[84] Its centrality was a problem for the newly consolidated Italian overseas empire, reflected in a sharp uptick in Italian-language publications invoking the word (see figure 3.5). Visual and written Fascist propaganda and advertising at this time explicitly depicted

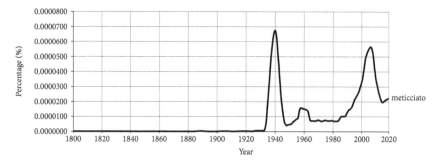

FIGURE 3.5.   Google N-Gram graph showing the frequency of occurrences of the word *meticciato* in Italian texts published between 1800 and 2019. Note the sharp increase around the late 1930s and early 1940s. Illustration by Mike Bechthold.

Source: https://books.google.com/ngrams (retrieved February 1, 2021).

Blackness as degenerate, dramatizing the supposed dangers of racial contamination and urging the importance of strict spatial segregation to limit contact between Italians (now officially depicted as white Aryans) and Blacks.[85]

During this latter period of the Fascist regime, the geographical center of gravity of Italian raciology also began to shift northward, from the Mediterranean toward northern Europe. Sergi was too old and sick to have much public influence by this time, and his work—along with the research of other positivists like Niceforo—was increasingly subject to virulent attacks by the younger scholars favored by the Fascist regime.[86] This was a trajectory encapsulated in the career of doctor and anthropologist Giovanni Marro (1875–1952). While Marro is lesser known than his contemporaries such as Lidio Cipriani, Julius Evola, and Guido Landra, like them he was a prolific public intellectual who published in both academic journals and in popular magazines such as the Fascist periodical *La Difesa della Razza.*[87] A student of Lombroso in Turin, Marro broke from his mentor and eventually went on to found the Museo di Antropologia ed Etnografia (Museum of Anthropology and Ethnography) in the University of Turin's biology department.[88] Marro, lumping together the Lombrosians *and* Sergians of Liberal Italy, condemned all research he saw as merely conceding to claims of Italian inferiority and argued that the theory of a Mediterranean race with African origins was nothing more than "Jewish internationalism."[89]

In 1938, the same year the racial laws were enacted in Italy, Marro was appointed to design the Sala della Razza (Hall of the Race) in Turin, a monumental exhibition illustrating the origins and history of the Piemontese people, who hail from the region directly south of Italy's western Alps.[90] While Marro (himself a native of Piemonte) admitted that the hall was designed with a particular

FIGURE 3.6.   Benito Mussolini at the inauguration of Marro's Sala della Razza in 1938.

Source: Giovanni Marro, La Sala della razza nella rassegna "Torino e l'autarchia" (Turin: Tipografia Silvestrelli e Cappelletto, 1939), 8. Archivio del Museo di Antropologia ed Etnografia, University of Turin: "Marro G. Questione Razziale."

regional focus, he argued that "the characteristics of [Piemonte's] population fit well within the Italian racial type, because their spiritual features shine from the same light that inflames each and every Italian."[91] In other words, the Piemontese were emblematic of the Italian people generally, and hence a careful study of their origins and achievements could serve as a template for the study of the Italian race as a whole. Marro's "temporal convening of space" was emblematic of efforts during this period to reorient Italy's national-racial identity away from Africa and the Mediterranean, while also challenging the fragmentation of the Italian nation into racially distinct populations.[92] It is telling that Mussolini, once a vocal proponent of a Mediterranean understanding of Italianness, attended the opening of Marro's Sala della Razza (see figure 3.6).

This gradual, tenuous, and nonlinear move toward Aryanism was also reflected in the "Manifesto degli scienziati razzisti" (Manifesto of Racial Scientists), published in the *Giornale d'Italia* on July 14, 1938.[93] The manifesto was written under the specific guidance of Mussolini in the Ministry of Popular Culture by ten scientists (including two anthropologists, Lidio Cipriani and Giudo Landra), and was signed by an additional 180 (including Giovanni Marro). This relatively concise statement was intended by Mussolini to prepare the Italian people for the enactment of the 1938 anti-Semitic racial laws, and was thus written with mass circulation in mind. The ten points of the manifesto asserted that Italians were part of an Aryan race:

1. Human races exist;
2. Large and small races exist;
3. The concept of race is purely biological [*national differences are, at their core, matters of biological race*];
4. The majority of the current Italian population is of Aryan origin and its civilization is Aryan [*there remain few traces of pre-Aryan civilizations in Italy*];
5. The idea of an influx of large masses of men in historical times is a legend [*unlike other European nations, the racial composition of Italy is the same today as it was thousands of years ago*];
6. There already exists a pure "Italian race" [*and race is a biological, not historico-linguistic or spiritual matter*];
7. It is time for Italians to declare themselves to be racist[94] [*Italy is Aryan-Nordic, but this does not mean importing German racial theories wholesale into Italy*];
8. It is important to draw a distinction between the Mediterraneans of Europe (the Westerners) on the one hand, and the Orientals and Africans on the other hand [*Sergian theories of a common Mediterranean race with origins in Africa are dangerous*];
9. Jews do not belong to the Italian race;
10. The purely European physical and psychological characteristics of the Italians must not be altered in any way [*mixing with non-European races is not permissible*].[95]

The manifesto effectively expunged any connection to Africa in the historical "making" of the modern Italian race and established the Jewish people as the new *internal* threat to Italian racial homogeneity. On the one hand, it seemed to seal the Fascist regime's growing embrace of Aryanism and its repudiation of the Mediterranean. But on the other hand, the manifesto still betrayed some significant moments of slippage when it came to Italy's relationship to Africa and the Mediterranean. The manifesto asserted that Italians are Aryans, but also that there is a pure Italian race; there exist Mediterranean Europeans (who are not to be confused with Oriental or African Mediterraneans), but Italians also have purely European characteristics.[96]

These continued debates among Italy's racial scientists into the late 1930s, the uncertainties about the wholesale importation of Nazi racial theories, and the extant inconsistencies in the manifesto were also reflected in the tiered system of Italian citizenship that took shape by the end of Fascism. Citizenship had been fragmented into discrete and ranked categories: mainland Italian citizenship; Libyan Italian citizenship; a special Libyan Italian citizenship for Muslim subjects; and colonial subjecthood for Eritreans and Somalis.[97] This distinction between North Africa and the Horn of Africa reflected the Fascist regime's ongoing support for pan-Islamism in the Mediterranean—the aforementioned idea of Roman civilizational linkages was used to challenge the British presence in North Africa, while simultaneously reiterating the existence of a deeper racial and cultural gulf between Italy and sub-Saharan Africa.[98] North Africa, in other words, occupied a higher position than the Horn of Africa on a civilizational hierarchy that culminated in the Fascist regime's vision of white, Romanic Italy. Just as in the Liberal period, the Mediterranean remained a crucial—yet politically confounding and ever-shifting—point of reference in identifying who truly "counted" as an Italian, and which groups remained beyond the boundaries of Italian citizenship.

Postwar Italy's Racial Evaporations

For all of Fascist Italy's preoccupation with the question of Africa and the Mediterranean, the postwar period was remarkably silent on these issues.[99] But this was a resounding silence, one that paradoxically worked to continue the "whitening" of Italians that had already been underway by the late 1930s. On the one hand, discussions of "race" as a marker of human difference, in the sciences and beyond, were more or less foreclosed.[100] On the other hand, an "unmarked" Italian whiteness was consolidated through popular media, advertising, and consumer culture.[101] As Italian society was forced to reckon with the social implications of the heterogeneity brought by colonialism and Fascism (namely, in the form of children of mixed origins, the presence of Black American soldiers from the Allied occupation of Italy, and early waves of postcolonial migration), references to Italy as a Mediterranean nation remained rare. The problems of Fascist state racism and Black racial contamination had merged in the Italian popular imagination; as Cristina Lombardi-Diop argues, both had to be externalized as geographically and temporally beyond the borders of Italy for the country to rebuild itself from the ashes of World War II.[102]

Kamala Visweswaran has argued that the evasion of "race" (in favor of supposedly neutral markers such as ethnicity or culture) in postwar Europe is linked to the global influence of mid-twentieth-century liberal American anthropology—represented by Franz Boas and his students, including Ruth Benedict and Ashley Montagu.[103] While there was considerable debate among the Boasians as to whether "race" could be salvaged as a valid—and value-neutral—biological category, they generally agreed that *in practice*, "race" implied negative valuation and should not be used to explain human social difference. This approach was ultimately enshrined in the 1950 and 1951 UNESCO Statements on the Race Question, which sought to counteract the horrors of state-sanctioned scientific racism and fascist eugenics, and which ultimately influenced the development of late twentieth- and early twenty-first-century anti-racism in Italy.[104]

In Italy, these attempts at post-Fascist reconstruction took as their objective the elimination of "race," rather than a reckoning with the historical construction of these racial categories. As Caterina Romeo argues, race was constitutive to the consolidation of Italian national identity, but it "evaporated" from public discourse in order to distance postwar Italy from the historical embarrassments of colonialism, Fascism, and even the racism enacted against Italian emigrants abroad.[105] This "de-fascistization of fascism," Miguel Mellino (drawing on Emilio Gentile) argues, "was promoted from within by postwar Italian political and cultural élites and from abroad by US geostrategic pressures"; it took many different forms, including the publication of revisionist histories of Italian Fascism.[106] Italy did not undergo any kind of post-Fascist attempts at reckoning and reconciliation like those seen in Germany. Instead, many of the institutions that had supported the work of racial scientists began to distance themselves from this research, characterizing those scientists as poor scholars, as not representative of Italian scientific culture, or as dedicated scientists whose research was misinterpreted and politicized. The leading figures of the Fascist regime were executed, and, as Lombardi-Diop notes, the legacy of the Italian anti-Fascist resistance provided a form of moral absolution for the crimes of Fascist imperialism.[107] Together, these developments helped bolster the powerful myth of *italiani, brava gente* (Italians, good people)—that Italy had no autochthonous tradition of racism.[108]

The foreclosure of "race" in the Italian public and academic spheres as a strategy of post-Fascist reconstruction functioned in tandem with the erasure of colonial traces within Italy. Colonialism, Fascism, and the "stain of racist persecution and apartheid" all needed to be sequestered safely outside the space-time of the nation so that Italy could move into the future unencumbered by its troubling past.[109] In postwar Italy, the unwelcome memories of this past were embodied in the presence of a generation of "mixed-race" children across Italy, including the children of Eritrean women and Italian men, and the children of Black American soldiers and Italian women (relationships that were demonized in Fascist-era propaganda posters like the one reproduced in figure 1.5b).[110] Thus, in practice Italian reconstruction entailed the metaphorical, and at times even literal, externalization of Blackness and Black subjects.

The 1949 Italian film *Il mulatto*, directed by Francesco De Robertis, fictionalizes one such removal. *Il mulatto* was one in a spate of postwar Italian films addressing, with varying degrees of directness, the racial remains of Italian colonialism and Fascism, as well as the Allied invasion of Italy.[111] In the film, Angelo is the product of a rape committed during World War II by a Black American soldier against a married Italian woman named Maria. Maria, whose husband Matteo had been serving a jail sentence during her violation and pregnancy, dies in childbirth. When Matteo is released, he first rejects Angelo, but then has a change of heart and attempts to raise the child. Eventually, however, Angelo's uncle (his father's brother) arrives from the United States to find him. Matteo is reluctant to part with Angelo, but Angelo hears his uncle sing a soulful melody—described in the film as the sad lament of the Black American people—and feels immediately drawn to him. Because of this innate, unspoken connection, Matteo and Angelo's American uncle concur that it is in the child's best interest for him to return to the United States and be raised there. The denouement neatly summarizes what was at stake in the racial geographies of postwar Italy: the possibility of Italian racism is sidestepped because Matteo accepts Angelo; however, the boy also cannot remain in Italy because his "true" racial home is in the United States.[112] Angelo's story—of sexual violation, of missing parents—implies that Blackness is incompatible with the normative heterosexual Italian family structure. With his brown skin and blond Afro, Angelo's mere existence is a complete impossibility in postwar Italy.

As Blackness was being pushed beyond the boundaries of Italy, Italian popular culture simultaneously promoted a vision of Italy as homogenous and white. Advertisements—accessible to increasingly large numbers of everyday Italians thanks to new radio and television programs—aggressively promoted the value of personal and domestic hygiene, linking soaps and other cleaning products with images of purity and whiteness.[113] As Lombardi-Diop explains, this new Italian consumer culture represented a form of "redemptive hygiene" that was oriented on the subliminal "whitening" of the Italian nation.[114] As Ilaria Giglioli's work has demonstrated, Italian state policies after World War II focused on the modernization of southern Italy, with assistance in the form of financial aid from the United States' Marshall Plan to rebuild Western Europe—a move that redirected the colonial civilizing mission inward, into Italy's internal periphery.[115] Southern Italians also began to migrate in large numbers to the urban areas of northern Italy during this same period, and doing so afforded them new opportunities to shed the lingering racial stigma of southern Italian poverty and civilizational backwardness through their spatial proximity to the more "modern" and "developed" industrial centers of northern Italy.

The silence surrounding "race" in postwar Italy was productive, in that it reinforced the notion of Italy as an implicitly white (or at best, racially unmarked), benevolent, and territorially bounded nation with no links—colonial or otherwise—to the Mediterranean and Africa. The "unspeakability" of race in postwar Italy also meant that Catholicism came to function as a convenient proxy for whiteness.[116] The process of distancing postwar Italian culture from the horrors of Fascist state racism meant bounding the metaphorical location of racism and race as outside of Italy, negating all the ways that Italy had been (and continued to be) produced through its trans-Mediterranean connections with the African continent since unification. Yet, Italy's racial ambiguities could not be fully contained. They stubbornly continued to burst forth, for instance when landlords in the industrial northern Italian city of Turin refused to rent apartments to southern Italian labor migrants, hanging large signs outside their buildings that announced, "*Non si affitta ai meridionali*" (We don't rent to southerners).[117] Nonetheless, these postwar efforts to cleanse Italy of racial difference—however unsuccessful—would have fateful consequences for the way that Italians made sense of their country's transformation into a site of immigration in the late twentieth century. This shift was heralded by the arrival of large numbers of sub-Saharan African migrants—including many from Italy's former (but forgotten) colonies.

The Return of Mediterranean *Meticciato*

On November 8, 2015, a group of leftist anti-racist and anti-fascist protesters from Bologna's social centers and student collectives descended on the city's iconic Piazza Maggiore to protest the arrival of Matteo Salvini. Salvini, leader of the political party that was at that time still called the Lega Nord, was in town to sponsor the candidacy of Lucia Borgonzoni (also from the Lega Nord) for mayor of Bologna. But Salvini also planned to use the occasion to call for greater unity among Italy's right-wing political parties, inviting Silvio Berlusconi of Forza Italia and Giorgia Meloni of Fratelli d'Italia in a bid to send a message to the country that "the majority of Italians are not on the Left."[118] The Lega Nord had risen to prominence in the 1990s on an antisouthern platform that cast southern Italy and the Roman central government as leeches on the prosperity of a hardworking, industrial North. Increasingly, however, the party had turned the weight of their ire toward a deeper South—one represented by African migrants who were arriving to Italy from the Mediterranean Sea.[119] By the fall of 2015, after a summer when record numbers of refugees and asylum seekers had landed on the country's southern shores, Salvini had gained international notoriety as one of the loudest voices in Italy decrying the supposed threats posed by the presence of *extracomunitari* from sub-Saharan Africa.

For Salvini and those of his ilk, the Mediterranean represents a dangerous source of invasion and racial contamination—it is a porous border that must be reinforced in order to protect the racial and cultural integrity of the Italian people. In other words, they have once against cast the Mediterranean as a "Black" threat to the racial integrity of the Italian nation, now symbolized by the arrival of thousands of African migrants, refugees, and asylum seekers. At the same time, a number of Italian politicians have explicitly attempted to once again consolidate Italianness as a distinct race—and a white one, at that.[120] And this political rhetoric has newly relegitimated "race-talk" among everyday Italians as well. For instance, at a family dinner in my mother's hometown in 2016, during a heated debate about immigration to Italy, my cousin's husband responded to my charges of xenophobia by declaring exasperatedly, "But shouldn't we have the right to *defend* our own race?" The links to Fascism in this racial bounding of the "we" of Italianness are undeniable—after all, *La Difesa della Razza* (The Defense of the Race) was the name of a popular Fascist magazine whose inaugural issue in 1938 sold eighty-five thousand copies.[121]

Bologna has long been known as a leftist stronghold in Italy, its nickname *La rossa* (The Red) alluding to its history of anti-fascist resistance, student activism, and Marxist organizing. In the days leading up to Salvini's arrival in 2015, posters and graffiti appeared on walls across the city urging residents to "defend Bologna from the Lega's invasion"—a clever reversal of the Right's xenophobic rhetoric of immigrant invasion. Expecting a violent clash between student protesters and supporters of Salvini—rumors circulated in the press of protesters preparing Molotov cocktails—the city enacted extensive security measures in the Piazza Maggiore, including the deployment of a large riot police presence. On the day of the protests, far-right supporters of Salvini gathered with Italian flags and crucifixes in hand, shouting racial slurs, raising their arms in the Fascist Roman salute, and chanting "Duce! Duce! Duce!" (Leader, Mussolini's title in the Italian Fascist state). On the other side of the police cordon, a racially diverse group of anti-racist protesters led by the Bolognese collectives Arte Migrante and Cantieri Meticci danced and sang, even as they were kicked and shoved by Salvini's supporters.

That Bologna's student radicals clashed with supporters of right-wing parties that fall day was not particularly surprising. But what *was* notable was the particular tactic that the leftist protesters chose to challenge the racism and xenophobia of the Right. As they leapt into the air and danced to drumbeats, they repeated the slogan "Bologna è meticcia! Bologna è meticcia!" (Bologna is mixed!).[122] As a video of the protest reveals, a number of the white protesters chanting this refrain had even daubed their faces with streaks of brown paint—it seemed that the protesters wanted to render themselves closer to brown by marking their bodies with symbols of racial ambiguity.[123] And this was not the only time that protesters in Italy had attempted to challenge a rising tide of racism and xenophobia by making broad declarations about *meticciato*. A brief survey reveals, among many other protests, conferences, cultural events, and festivals across Italy: a 2012 protest in Milan against the Lega Nord declaring Milan to be "meticcia";[124] a 2019 protest that defined Naples as "meticcia"; and a soccer tournament held in cities around northern and southern Italy called "Mediterraneo Antirazzista," which seeks to substitute discourses of Mediterranean invasion with a vision of Mediterranean interconnection.[125]

As these examples show, the Mediterranean has taken on two distinct, but connected, meanings in Italy today. For the Right, the Mediterranean represents an encroachment: as an aquatic conduit connecting the Italian peninsula to the African continent, it poses a threat to the precarious whiteness of Italians. This can be witnessed, for instance, in the Italian government's crackdown on the operations of NGO rescue ships in the Mediterranean because they allegedly facilitate illegal migration from the African continent.[126] But for the Left, the Mediterranean is used to challenge racism, xenophobia, and border fortification by opening up the category of Italianness—though often in ways that inadvertently cleanse Italy and the Mediterranean of their messier histories of racial categorization and colonial violence.[127] While the Right's view of the Mediterranean is undoubtedly hegemonic, it is clear that contestations about what it means to be Italian, and who is a legitimate member of the national community, are once again playing out via competing ideas about the implications of Italian proximity to the Mediterranean and Africa.

As Italy made the dramatic transformation from a country of emigration to a country of immigration in the 1980s and 1990s, a range of prominent activists, social theorists, and political figures began to reach back into the Mediterranean, retrieving older concepts such as Mediterraneanism and *meticciato* to construct counterhistories of the Mediterranean as a space of convivial mixing, civilizational exchange, and population movement.[128] In these figurations, the Mediterranean is reclaimed not as a symbol of racial contamination, but as an antidote to Italian ethnic absolutism. In the face of inflammatory political rhetoric about the need to protect a homogenous, white Italian race, the Mediterranean archive presents an alternative vision of Italianness, and of the future of Italy—one in which Italy is defined by rich heterogeneity and by the footprints of cross-Mediterranean migrations spanning millennia. This focus on the Mediterranean as the defining characteristic of Italianness (rather than a threat to it) works to denaturalize the Italian border, suggesting that Italy itself is less of a stable fact than an open-ended question.[129] As the Italian political scientist Pierfranco Malizia explained in a 2005 book: "The Mediterranean created a unique situation, that of a crossroads that developed everything we consider today to be the diverse possibilities of interaction, or assimilation, integration, the melting pot, the salad bowl."[130]

Indeed, for the Left it is not enough to simply claim that Italy has recently become "mixed" because of immigration; rather, these actors also recount a particular history of Italianness—one in which mixing itself, rather than the vision of cultural insularity promoted by political parties like the Lega, is a key element of Italian national identity. Unlike the *meticciato* that was of such concern in Fascist Italy, the *meticciato* of late twentieth- and early twenty-first-century white Italian anti-racists has come to stand in for cosmopolitanism, "colorful" urban environments, and mixed societies writ large. Its resurgence in the popular Italian lexicon is not about problematizing individual children of mixed backgrounds, but rather about celebrating these young people as exemplars of a cultural pluralism that is Italy's historical destiny.[131] In Bologna, anti-racist protesters contended that the real "invaders" were not immigrants but instead the xenophobic politicians, and that it was they who posed the *real* threat to Italy's innately heterogenous identity. And, as seen in some of those protesters' use of brown face paint, these types of claims often involve the assertion of a uniquely Italian proximity to Africa and Blackness. As Alessandro Portelli has suggested, the flip side of the Lega's pattern of conflating southern Italians and Africans is an *identification* on the part of Italians with Africans because of their ambiguous "southernness."[132] After a range of postwar efforts to separate metropolitan Italy from the heterogeneity of its colonial interconnections, it appeared that activists were now embracing Italy's Mediterranean history of racial liminality as a road map for the future.

Even scientists have been enrolled in the production of this renewed, rainbow vision of Italianness. One recent study, conducted by a team of geneticists partially funded by the Italian Ministry of Education, University, and Research and the Istituto Italiano di Antropologia—importantly, the same institute founded by Giuseppe Sergi in 1893—was released to the Italian press with great fanfare. Based on a sampling of fifty-seven linguistic minorities across Italy, the researchers concluded that Italy was home to some of the greatest human biodiversity in Europe.[133] Indeed, in response to a series of politicians declaring Italians to be a singular (white) race between 2017 and 2018, scientists such as Guido Barbujani were quick to clarify that there is no such thing as a "white race" because—genetically speaking—"we are all African."[134]

In 2008, on the seventieth anniversary of the publication of the 1938 "Manifesto of Racial Scientists," a group of scientists convened by Marxist geneticist and agronomist Marcello Buiatti in Pisa signed the "Manifesto degli scienziati antirazzisti" (Manifesto of Anti-racist Scientists).[135] Buiatti, the son of a Polish-Jewish mother and a white Italian partisan father who had fought in the anti-Fascist resistance during World War II, designed the 2008 document to serve as a point-by-point refutation of the Fascist-era manifesto. In something of a return to Giuseppe Sergi's original hypothesis, the new manifesto asserts that race does not exist, using as evidence Italy's geographical position as a peninsula in the Mediter-ranean: "The phenomena of social and cultural *meticciamento* that have charac-terized the entire history of the peninsula, and in which not just local populations have participated but also the Greeks, Phoenicians, Jews, Africans, Spaniards, in addition to the so-called barbarians, have produced the hybrid that we call Italian culture."[136] The 2008 manifesto rejects the late Fascist imaginary of the Mediter-ranean as a space demarking a solid boundary between Italy and the "threat" of Africa; however, it bears no mention of Italian colonialism, nor of Africans them-selves, as integral to the construction of Italianness in the *present*. Following the structure of the original manifesto, the 2008 document notes that "Italian Jews are both Jewish and Italian," but it does not make a similar claim about Black Italians. Indeed, by attempting to directly refute each point of the "Manifesto of Racial Scientists," the authors of the "Manifesto of Anti-racist Scientists" find them-selves trapped by its same logics. While the 2008 manifesto suggests that Africa played a role in the making of Italy in the deep past, this African presence is van-ished from an understanding of contemporary Italianness.

As these examples suggest, the return of the Mediterranean as a framework for understanding Italianness has been fraught and politically ambiguous. Laura Harris observes that the theories of Italy's internal racial differentiation that had developed in the late nineteenth century in tandem with Italian colonialism were "recycled" in the late twentieth century, mapped onto the African migrants arriv-ing in Italy from the other side of the Mediterranean.[137] But because of the racial evaporations set into motion after World War II, the historical continuities in these processes of racial formation were effectively delinked—the "problem" of racial difference was displaced onto the body of the immigrant (specifically, Afri-can) Other, rather than understood as central to Italian nation-building itself. Instead, the Mediterranean is preserved either as a source of racial contamina-tion or as a site of innocent mixing, rather than a contentious object of knowledge production tied to the construction of Italian citizenship.

While far-right anxieties surrounding Mediterranean invasion are clearly alarming, the Left's reappropriation of the Mediterranean is not without conse-quence, either. Without the analytical tools to engage with the historically sedi-mented racisms that continue to animate contemporary conversations about the African presence in Italy and the boundaries of Italian citizenship, what remains is a depoliticized Mediterranean cosmopolitanism in which Italians as a "mixed" people have no racial identity and hence no capacity for perpetrating racism.[138] Such invocations of the Mediterranean frequently locate "race" as ontologically prior to "racism," assuming that the solution to racism is to merely remove the word "race" from circulation—indeed, those same scientists continuing Sergi's legacy in Rome by studying Italian genetic diversity have also been actively engaged in a campaign to remove the word "race" from the Italian constitution.[139] Sante Matteo, in the introduction to the 2001 volume *ItaliAfrica*, echoed this hopeful sentiment by recounting the long history of contact between Africans and Italians due to their geographical proximity: "Racism based on skin color has not been an entrenched, institutionalized aspect of Italian culture," he wrote; therefore, "diversity and equality may be easier to achieve under conditions that are not tainted by a previous history of master/servant relationships."[140] The bitter irony is that for all of the violent, explicit racisms that marred Liberal and Fascist Italy, these periods were nonetheless characterized by an explicit recognition of the centrality of Africa and Blackness in defining the parameters of Italian citizenship. In resurrecting the Mediterranean as a reference point for an inclusive and anti-racist Italianness, however, contemporary white Italian anti-racist activists risk once again marking Blackness as external and invasive, just like their right-wing counterparts did—except in their figuration, people of African descent can only be incorporated into the nation through what have been reterritorialized as distinctively *Italian* histories of mixing and Mediterranean conviviality.

Toward the Black Mediterranean

Popular understandings of Italianness today are characterized by an implicit, "unspoken whiteness."[141] Yet as Angelica Pesarini notes, translating an argument by Tatiana Petrovich Njegosh, "Italians travel, inhabit, transform, and shift the color line divide between Black and White by reshaping and re-signifying both Blackness and Whiteness, and the boundaries between these two categories."[142] As this chapter has shown, the process of "whitening" Italians was in fact anything but straightforward, characterized instead by a long, fraught, and violent history of struggle over Italy's relationship to Africa and the Mediterranean.[143]

Italy has always defined itself in relationship to Blackness via the Mediterranean, even before Italy became a major destination for migrants from sub-Saharan Africa.[144] This is evinced in the way that the ancient Roman notion of the Mediterranean as *mare nostrum* (our sea) became the Fascist vision of *mare nostrum*, which sought to establish a new Roman Empire through the imperial conquest of Africa, and in the twenty-first century became the name given to the Italian government's now-defunct aquatic search-and-rescue program for managing migration from the African continent. Indeed, rather than Hegel's vision of the Mediterranean as the center of World-History (a vision which, it should be noted, negated the historicity of Africa), we would be advised to heed Aimé Césaire's warning about the oft-romanticized civilizational encounter: "It is an excellent thing to blend different worlds; that whatever its own particular genius may be, a civilization that withdraws into itself atrophies; that for civilizations, exchange is oxygen; that the great good fortune of Europe is to have been a crossroads. But then I ask the following question: has colonization really *placed civilizations in contact*? Or, if you prefer, of all the ways of *establishing contact*, was it the best? I answer no."[145]

But just because Mediterraneanism is tied to a history of Italian racial boundary drawing, this does not mean that these ideas must be relegated to the dustbin of history. The Mediterranean is a site of profoundly contradictory imaginaries—at once home to a long history of transcultural contact and transformation, and also the site of Fortress Europe's most extreme violences. Drawing on precisely this ambiguity, Black activists have also used the Mediterranean as the basis for claims to citizenship. Italy's history of racial equivocality has in fact generated a unique terrain of struggle for activists seeking to expand the racial boundaries of Italianness and Italian citizenship. After all, if modern Italy is little more than an amalgam of Mediterranean peoples and civilizations, if Italians themselves were once regarded as proximate to Black and southern Italians were not considered as fully legitimate members of the nation, and if Italy itself had colonized the African continent, then what real grounds are there for denying the citizenship of Black Italians today?

Citizenship reform activists regularly make note of the fact that there is no such thing as a singular "Italian" people, with the implication that this is the result of Italy's position in the Mediterranean. In a Facebook post about a newspaper article that described Italians as little more than "an aggregation of a geographic type," Italiani senza Cittadinanza commented with the concise formula "#*ItaliaDiOggi* = #*ItaliaDiIeri*" (#ItalyOfToday = #ItalyOfYesterday).[146] Italiani senza Cittadinanza's hashtags challenge the idea that demographic heterogeneity is new to Italy (the children of immigrants are frequently described in the press as "new Italians" or as representatives of a "new Italy"). Instead, their comment suggests that the children of immigrants simply represent a new chapter in a much longer story, one in which Italy's boundaries and modes of self-definition have repeatedly expanded and contracted throughout history.

In yet another example, the Milan-based multiracial youth activist collective Il Comitato per non Dimenticare Abba e Fermare il Razzismo (The Committee to Remember Abba and Stop Racism), formed after the racist murder of nineteen-year-old Italian-Burkinabe Abdul Guibre in 2008, has reappropriated the idea of *meticciato*. But rather than as a color-blind vision of peaceful hybridity, they approach *meticciato* as a political strategy for jettisoning discriminatory categories such as *integrazione* (integration), *immigrato* (immigrant), and *extracomunitario* (non–European Union migrant). These latter categories, they argue, presume Italy to be a bounded and homogenous unit and take for granted the existence of national borders. In place of them, the activists seek to build up a new, radical language for dismantling the interconnected power structures of racism, militarism, border fortification, and capitalism that threaten Black lives in Italy today.

These efforts suggest that Black Italians are using the Mediterranean in novel ways: to demonstrate the historical continuities of a Black presence in Italy, *and* the historical continuities in the violence of Italian racial formation (which has always used Africa and Blackness as points of reference). An Italian-Afro-Brazilian citizenship activist from Rome astutely linked historical struggles over Italian national unity to the racism faced by Black people in Italy today:

> There is no such thing as a typical Italian. And this makes things more difficult. Already from Milan to Naples, they see each other as a threat. They hate each other, they discriminate against each other, they insult each other. So if you add a Black person . . . it disrupts the whole order of things. There is a perception of invasion. . . . But Italians don't have their own "space." It doesn't exist. And because they don't have this, when someone even *more* different appears, their reaction is "Oh god, what are we going to do?"

These activists are advancing a vision of a *Black* Mediterranean. This Black Mediterranean politics is not afraid to contend with the racial histories that were part of Italian unification, colonialism, and Fascism. It locates Blackness at the heart of Italianness, but also draws on an alternative archive of Black diasporic struggle to imagine a very different sort of future for Italy.

The first part of this book has focused on struggles over Italian citizenship, with attention to the historical and contemporary ways that citizenship has been constructed and contested as a fundamentally *racial* category—through invocations of blood, birthplace, and culture; through notions of economic productivity and the "undeserving poor"; and in relation to Italy's ambiguous Mediterranean geographies. But Black Italians are not only seeking to expand the boundaries of Italian citizenship—they are also imagining other possibilities for political solidarity and community that stretch beyond the limits of the nation-state itself. These Black Mediterranean visions and practices constitute the focus of the second part of this book.

Part 2

DIASPORIC POLITICS

TRANSLATION AND THE LIVED GEOGRAPHIES OF THE BLACK MEDITERRANEAN

> All had to acknowledge that try as they may, the children had become something many of them would never be, for better or worse, new Italians. An emergent Black Italia.
>
> —Donald Martin Carter, "Blackness over Europe: Meditations on Cultural Belonging"

> What am I? Who am I? I am Black and Italian. But I am also Somali and Black. So am I Afro-Italian? Italo-African? At the end of the day, I am just my story.
>
> —Igiaba Scego, *La mia casa è dove sono*

Misrecognition, in Three Stories
Trescore, Italy: Late 1980s / Early 1990s

When I was little, my mother would take me to Italy each summer to visit her family (my father was only able to join us for one week of these annual trips due to his unrelenting work schedule). One summer afternoon when I was a toddler, my mother and I went to the local *mercato* to shop for produce. We approached a market stall run by an elderly white Italian woman. She took one look at my *cappuccino* skin and enormous head of Afro curls, and then turned to my mother with a smile that radiated grandmotherly benevolence: "*Ma che brava!* You adopted a little girl from Africa!" My mother, always a bit hot-tempered, raised her chin defiantly and announced proudly, to anyone within earshot: "I didn't adopt her. She is *my* child, and my husband is Black!"

Sesto San Giovanni, Italy: March 8, 2016

I was living in Sesto San Giovanni, a working-class suburb just outside of Milan that was once affectionately known as "Italy's Stalingrad" (due to its history of anti-Fascist resistance and labor organizing). My apartment was located just downstairs from the flat that belonged to my cousin Mara, her husband, and their two sons. Mara and I would often walk over to Sesto's community pool together in the evenings for open lap swimming hours; we treasured this time together, when we could catch up and blow off some steam after a long day of work. One evening, as I was standing at the shallow end of my lane and adjusting my fluorescent latex swim cap, one of the swimming coaches walked over to me. "Are you from New Zealand?" he asked earnestly. With what I am sure was a look of utter bafflement on my face, I responded that I was actually from California, and that I was half Italian and half African American. "My mother is *bergamasca*, and she is actually my cousin," I explained further, pointing to Mara floating in the lane next to me. Sensing my confusion, the coach unpacked his "New Zealand" theory: my swim cap said, "Oakland Triathlon Festival," but he read *Auckland* instead of *Oakland*. I realized, too, that the "clue" of my dense Afro curls was hidden away underneath the swim cap. Plus, he said, I looked *mulatta*, so it made sense to him that I would come from a place like New Zealand.

Bergamo Città Alta, Italy: October 23, 2016

My mother and I took a spontaneous day trip to Città Alta, the walled medieval portion of Bergamo that sits in the hills overlooking the newer, lower city. My mother went to high school in Bergamo; the upper city, with its panoramic views and meticulously preserved historic architecture, has always held a special place in her heart. We decided that day to peruse a sprawling, open-air craft market. My mother stopped to look at some handmade earrings, and I wandered over to a stall displaying knit scarves and hats. The person manning that booth, an elderly white Italian gentleman, noticed me eyeing his wares. "What strange hair you have," he mused. I responded flatly: "It's just my natural hair; it grows like this." "And so you don't have to do anything? It just comes out like that?" he asked, squinting. I nodded. "Where are you from?" he continued. I was so used to answering this question that I did not need to consciously formulate my response. I simply repeated the same tired refrain: "I was born in California, but my mom is *bergamasca*." By this time, my mother had walked over to us, and threw an arm around my shoulders; she overheard the tail end of this interaction as it echoed between the cobbled street beneath our feet and the vaulted portico above our heads. Sensing that this man doubted my Italianness, she elaborated on my curt reply with evidence of my local Italian credentials: "Yes, she is half *bergamasca*. She even likes to eat polenta!" Still, the man was not satisfied. "*Boh!*" he retorted, an exclamation whose meaning lies somewhere at the intersection of confusion, not-knowing, and indifference. "I've never seen hair like *that* in Bergamo."

The Politics of Belonging in the Black Mediterranean

Who gets to belong in Italy?[1] What does it take for a person who is racialized as "Black" to be met with a reaction other than surprise, bemusement, or hostility? As the previous chapter suggested, the answers to these questions are anything but straightforward. Italy's historical and geographical position as a Mediterranean crossroads, as well as its own internal heterogeneity, complicate any attempt to bound Italianness as pure and racially homogenous. This deep history of connections traversing sub-Saharan Africa, the Mediterranean, and southern Europe has presented Black Italians with a powerful political opening for claiming Italian citizenship. Yet at the same time, invocations of Italy's Mediterraneanness can also work to buffer the country's ambiguous geographical-racial-national identity from the perceived threat of Black contamination. This occurs most obviously in the far Right's hyperbolization of encroaching "African invasions" arriving on Italian shores from the Mediterranean. But even liberal anti-racist Mediterraneanisms are not wholly immune. Romantic portrayals of Italo-Mediterranean mixedness produce a strategic distancing of Italianness from the category of whiteness, a move that enables pernicious claims to Italian racial innocence and, by extension, the "disavowal and denial of racism."[2] This *Italian-innocence-as-product-of-Mediterranean-racial-liminality* does not acknowledge the many ways that racism (and specifically, articulations of racism that were centered on Italy's relationship to Africa and Blackness) has historically defined the boundaries of Italian citizenship. In both instances, Blackness remains an "absented presence"[3]—constitutive of Italianness itself, yet vanished from its symbolic and material boundaries. This is why my own claims to Italianness—whether they are articulated through kinship, cultural practice, local knowledge, geography, or language—are so often met with confusion. The fact that I actually carry a burgundy Italian passport—and that this physical symbol of my Italian citizenship is accessible to me through blood kinship with a white Italian (my mother)—suggests that citizenship itself does not necessarily produce racial inclusion.

Still, as I alluded at the end of part I, there are alternative ways that Black activists in Italy today are drawing on the unique histories of racial formation in the Mediterranean. They are not holding up the Mediterranean as a racially innocent category, nor are they merely positioning themselves as the newest form of "diversity" to join Italy's vast Mediterranean melting pot. Indeed, a key question facing Black Italians today is how precisely to contextualize the specificities of their lived experiences of racism within the overlapping histories of Mediterranean interconnection, colonialism, and migration. Their varied responses to this question suggest that it is indeed possible to take seriously the unique fluidity of racial borders in Italy and the wider Mediterranean, while also acknowledging that this very liminality can itself be generative of particularly virulent forms of anti-Black racism and nationalism. In addition, these Black Italian activists are challenging Italian exceptionalism by linking the Mediterranean to a wider set of geographical referents—in terms of both the circulation of global racisms and the international networks of Black diasporic resources and modes of resistance.

This chapter draws on the voices, experiences, and activism of a group of Black Italian political activists, artists, and entrepreneurs in the wake of the murder of Nigerian asylum seeker Emmanuel Chidi Nnamdi in July 2016—an event that shattered the lingering myth of Italian racial conviviality. This horrific event congealed a set of emergent conversations about Blackness in Italy and what it means to organize around the category of "Black" or "Afro-Italian" (as opposed to "second generation," "immigrant," or any number of national appellations such as "Italian-Nigerian" or "Italian-Ghanaian"). The range of responses to Nnamdi's murder brought to light the profound tensions and challenges in the articulation of a collective, coherent Black Italian political project in Italy today. More specifically, it provided a clear vantage point onto the ways that Black activists are currently struggling to craft a language that can attend to the specific contours of racism and exclusion in Italy, while also attempting to situate the lived realities of Black Italy within a much wider, global Black diasporic context.

These emergent conversations about Black Italianness signal an important shift, which I take up as the central concern of the second part of this book. Afrodescendants who were born or raised in Italy are focusing not only on access to national citizenship but also on the political collectivities that can be forged through a shared sense of *Blackness*—and the way that this orientation on the Black diaspora necessarily throws into question the limits of national citizenship as a means of ameliorating the most severe insults of the Italian racial state. But at the same time, Blackness is not a unitary, self-evident category. Who constitutes "Black Italy," and whose interests are represented by the new politics mobilized around "Black Italianness"? What work does this category do, and who is left out? And, as Black Italian activists look beyond the Italian context for solidarity and political inspiration, how are they mapping Italy's place within a global Black diaspora that has been overrepresented by the United States? My analysis of Black Italians' responses to Nnamdi's murder is thus centered on a productive tension: the tension Black Italians encounter as they articulate the specificities of Black subjectivity (and anti-Black racism) in Italy in relation to (1) the myth of a supposedly "color-blind" Mediterranean Italy on the one hand; and (2) the overwhelming dominance of Black Atlantic geographies and North American understandings of race in conversations about Blackness on the other hand.

While lively (and often contentious) conversations about Black Italy are happening within activist and informal electronic spaces thanks to the increasingly visible activities of Black Italians, they are also beginning to take place on a very limited scale within academia—particularly around the concept of the Black Mediterranean. For this reason, I approach both everyday activist and academic spaces as interconnected and equally valid spheres of inquiry and attempt to toggle between the two in order to foreground the multiple sites in which knowledge production about "Black Italy" currently takes place. The Black Mediterranean in particular is an emergent analytical framework that foregrounds the complicated histories of racism and race in Italy, and in the broader Mediterranean. It makes room for the possibility of Blackness in Italy, but also stresses the urgency of anti-racism by emphasizing the constitutive racist violence and subordination undergirding Italian national formation in relation to the Mediterranean.[4] The Black Mediterranean stitches Italy's history of racial formation to its present resurgence of racial nationalism, with the purpose of articulating the possibilities for Black life in Italy's future—in other words, it is both an analytic *and* a powerful ethical-political demand.

Fermo and the Lived Experience of Blackness in Italy

On July 5, 2016, a thirty-six-year-old Nigerian asylum seeker named Emmanuel Chidi Nnamdi was beaten to death by Amedeo Mancini, a thirty-nine-year-old white Italian soccer *ultra* (hooligan) associated with a local chapter of the neo-fascist CasaPound Italia political movement.[5] Nnamdi and his wife, Chinyere, had fled the violence of the Boko Haram insurgency in Nigeria after losing their parents and a two-year-old daughter when their village church was set on fire. They undertook the dangerous journey through Libya and across the Mediterranean on a smuggler's boat, during which Chinyere suffered a miscarriage, and finally arrived in Palermo.

The harrowing story of Emmanuel and Chinyere is far from an isolated case. UNHCR estimates that in 2016, over thirty seven thousand Nigerians arrived in Italy via the Mediterranean.[6] That year, Nigerians made up approximately 21 percent of sea arrivals, followed by Eritreans at 11 percent. The journey across the Sahara and Mediterranean to southern Italy is characterized by extreme racist violence, sexual assault, extortion, exploitation, and unfree labor; in fact, most sub-Saharan Africans who begin the trans-Mediterranean journey never make it beyond North Africa.[7] Deaths and near fatalities along the extended borders of Europe, argues activist and political theorist Maurice Stierl, "point to the diffuse but connected registers of death-inducing violence that underpin the contemporary EUropean border regime."[8]

Emmanuel and Chinyere had been living at the bishop's seminary in the small central Italian seaside town of Fermo since the previous September and were married in January.[9] Six months later, on the afternoon of July 5, the couple was going for a stroll when two men began shouting insults at them. At one point, one of the men grabbed Chinyere and called her *una scimmia africana* (an African monkey).[10] When Nnamdi intervened to defend his wife from this assault, Amedeo Mancini attacked him with a street sign ripped out of the ground nearby. Nnamdi fell into an irreversible coma from the beating and died the following day. While Chinyere immediately volunteered to donate her husband's organs, her incredibly selfless act of generosity was soon overshadowed by unsubstantiated claims that she had fabricated elements of her testimony to police, and that Nnamdi had attacked Mancini in an unprovoked act of aggression.[11] Chinyere (who herself suffered bruises during the assault in Fermo) was subjected to severe harassment and death threats after her husband's murder, and was eventually moved to an undisclosed Italian town for her own protection.[12]

To some white Italian observers, the murder of Emmanuel Chidi Nnamdi only confirmed their suspicions of the Black body in Italy as out of place and always-already dangerous.[13] In a widely circulated Facebook post published shortly after Nnamdi's death, Matteo Salvini of the Lega opined that this violence was clear evidence that "clandestine immigration is out of control; actually, this organized invasion will not bring anything positive."[14] While not going so far as to explicitly *condone* the attacks on Emmanuel and Chinyere, Salvini's statement implied that Black immigrants and refugees in Italy will inevitably incite violent backlashes from white Italians because their mere presence implies a cultural or racial invasion. In a bizarre echo of the reasoning behind the enactment of the Legge Martelli, Italy's first comprehensive immigration law, in 1990 (i.e., Jerry Masslo's death could have been prevented had there been robust immigration regulations in place—see chapter 1), Salvini used the occasion of Nnamdi's murder to call for stronger "controls, limits, respect, and rules" governing immigration into Italy.

The murder of Emmanuel Chidi Nnamdi rapidly, albeit fleetingly, brought together two groups in Italy who were normally not in direct dialogue, at least not at the level of formal political activism—that is, newly arrived immigrants and refugees from sub-Saharan Africa on the one hand, and the Italian-born or -raised children of African and Afro-Latinx immigrants on the other.[15] It also temporarily dissolved some lingering differentiations among Black Italians along national lines, bringing Eritreans and Nigerians and Ghanaians and many others together into the *piazze* to express their indignation. As an Italian-Congolese stylist told me on the way to an anti-racist demonstration in Milan, with a grim sigh, "We're all in the same boat now." This is because the brutal attack made shockingly apparent the precariousness of what Frantz Fanon in *Black Skin, White Masks* famously called "the lived experience of the Black man" (often mistranslated into English as "fact of Blackness") in Italy.[16] For Fanon—who, it is worth remembering, was drawing from his own experiences of anti-Black racism in Europe—violence is constitutive to the formation and lived experience of the racialized subject. And the lived experience of Blackness in Italy in many ways transcends immigration and citizenship status—arguably, the primary ways that questions of difference are framed institutionally because (as noted in chapter 3) outright references to "race" have been largely silenced in postwar Italy. Despite the "self-reflexive color-blindness of Italians," however, people of African descent are systematically denied recognition as de facto Italians and are thus situated in a Fanonian zone of nonbeing.[17]

The outpouring of horror, grief, and anger that was expressed in the wake of Emmanuel Chidi Nnamdi's murder over private text message exchanges and phone calls, and across public-facing social media postings and calls to action, always condensed into a single, nightmarish point: *This could have been any one of us.* Merely for committing the violation of being Black in public, Nnamdi's name had been added to the ever-growing roll call of Black victims of racist violence in Italy—one stretching from Jerry Masslo in 1989 to Abdul "Abba" Guibre in 2008 to Samb Modou and Diop Mor (the two Senegalese immigrants murdered in Florence by another member of the CasaPound) in 2011, uniting them in a gruesome family tree of anti-Black violence.[18] This, in the land of *italiani, brava gente*: the perpetrators of a supposedly more "gentle" and "mild" form of colonialism in Africa, the underdogs of Europe who, thanks to their own national experience of large-scale emigration and history of being racialized as Mediterranean, had less of an innate capacity for racism than their counterparts in northern Europe or across the Atlantic.

#BlackLivesMatter and Anti-racist Praxis in Italy

As in most summers in Italy, everyday life began to grind to a halt by July 2016. By this time of year, Italian families typically begin to prepare for the summer school holidays and plan trips to the beach or mountains where they can escape the heat and heavy humidity. Against this backdrop, the death of Emmanuel Chidi Nnamdi disrupted the gradual, peaceful wind-down of midsummer and immediately sent shockwaves across the country. Many scholars have critiqued the general tendency whereby only instances of extraordinary racist violence become legible to national publics. This process, they suggest, both elides the more mundane realities of institutional racism and implies that racism can be understood as an exception to the "normal" state of affairs in modern liberal states.[19] Nonetheless, Nnamdi's murder and the subsequent smear campaign against his grieving wife Chinyere were able to capture the Italian public's imagination and (at least temporarily) direct a laser-like focus on the persistence of Italian racism in a way that crude anti-refugee propaganda and the steady stream of Black deaths in the Mediterranean could not. The horrific attack catalyzed important conversations precisely because it demonstrated the interconnections between the intersecting forms of quotidian violence that, while invisible to most white Italians, constantly besiege the bodies and souls of Black folk in Italy.

As anti-racism protests rippled across Italian cities that hot and sticky summer, from Fermo to Milan to Rome, demonstrations under the banner of #BlackLivesMatter were also mushrooming across the United States and in European cities such as London, Paris, Berlin, and Amsterdam in response to the extrajudicial murders of Black men and women at the hands of police officers. Indeed, multiple news outlets subsequently referred to 2016 as the year that #BlackLivesMatter "went global." Some of these marches were organized in solidarity with Black Americans who took to the street in response to the deaths of Alton Sterling and Philando Castile.[20] But other marches also attempted to shed light on anti-Black state violence *within* Europe. In France, the death of twenty-four-year-old Adama Traoré in police custody incited marches in Paris that drew links between anti-Black police violence in the United States and Europe and also sought to challenge the enduring myth of French color blindness.[21] In the United Kingdom, nationwide #BlackLivesMatter marches were timed to coincide with the fifth-year anniversary of the murder of twenty-nine-year-old Mark Duggan, who was shot by police in London while unarmed.[22]

Many Black Italians earnestly followed these global struggles against anti-Black violence from the international window afforded them by Facebook, noting to me the ways that their struggles against everyday and institutional forms of racism in Italy seemed to be so clearly intertwined with the mobilizations of their Black sisters and brothers in other countries. The issues that interested activists in Italy may not have precisely mirrored the main violations that were mobilizing protesters in other corners of the Black diaspora. Instead of—or perhaps in addition to—police brutality, they faced realities such as restrictive, structurally racist citizenship laws and the systematic "letting die" of Black migrants in the Mediterranean.[23] Still, my friends and interlocutors in Italy all expressed a shared sense of their very Blackness being under siege in the context of both micro-level interactions and large-scale bureaucratic encounters.

In Milan, an anti-racism and anti-fascism protest was organized less than a week after Nnamdi's death, with the help of the youth organization Il Comitato per non Dimenticare Abba e Fermare il Razzismo. The Comitato, housed in an occupied collective space in Milan's northwest known as Centro Sociale Cantiere (Construction Site Social Center), was formed by a multiracial collective of young people in 2008 in response to the racially motivated murder of Abdul "Abba" Guibre. To this day, the group works to maintain Abba's legacy by organizing language workshops, protests, soccer tournaments, and public events in Milan about the relationship between racism, xenophobia, militarism, borders, and capitalism. The Milan-based DJ Marvely Goma Perseverance expressed the continuities (and disjunctures) stretching from Abdul Guibre to Emmanuel Chidi Nnamdi in a wrenching open letter addressed to the deceased Abba, published on July 9, 2016, in the online Black Italian arts and culture magazine *GRIOT*:

> A lifetime spent with a finger pointed at us, condemned to excel so that we don't fall into the category of the "usual immigrants" or the "usual blacks," as if we had chosen to be born "black," as though we had chosen that label—which, among other things, I never understood. . . . Goodbye Abba, I miss you so much and here nothing has changed. The other day they beat and killed Emmanuel. I didn't know him but unlike you, who was born Italian, he had a different story that was similar to that of our parents, a refugee in search of Christian charity and calm where he could nurture his own hopes.[24]

On the day of the protest organized by the Comitato in Milan, I was walking with my Italian-Ghanaian friend Isabelle, who was that day clad in her trademark red dashiki and a fresh twist-out, as we headed to make handmade posters in her office near the iconic Piazza del Duomo.[25] As Isabelle and I commiserated about the social and logistic challenges of organizing political demonstrations in Italy, she proceeded to whip out her smartphone, open up the Facebook application, and proudly swipe through photos of a #BlackLivesMatter march that had taken place not long ago in London. We paused to take refuge from the beating sun in the shade of a portico near an empty café, huddled over her phone near a teetering stack of chairs. As we rested, she explained to me that the black-clad activists posing solemnly with raised fists in the photos before us were actually Black Italians living, working, and studying in London. Several had met each other for the first time through their involvement in that demonstration—and others had confessed to me earlier that their first encounters with Black radicalism and concepts such as institutional racism or intersectionality did not occur until they had left Italy for the United Kingdom.

Isabelle, like so many other Black Italians born or raised in Italy, had found some inspiration in the model of autonomous Black political action represented by #BlackLivesMatter. Her breathless description of the protest in London echoed the damning statement released by the European Network against Racism, which declared that Emmanuel Chidi Nnamdi's murder was a "wake-up call" for the formation of a pan-European #BlackLivesMatter movement: "It's time to say out loud that Black and migrant lives matter—not only at sea, but also in the streets of our cities and in the hearts and minds of all of us. The murder of Emmanuel is yet another wake-up call to Europe to take racism and violence seriously. When will it start listening?"[26] Isabelle personally saw #BlackLivesMatter as an incitement to build similar types of anti-racist movements in Italy, even if the specific contours of anti-Black racism in Italy differed from the primary issues centered by activists in the United States and in the emerging UK-based offshoot of the #BlackLivesMatter movement. Even the posters we carried reflected the transnational mixture of political influences we were drawing on: from the obvious "Black Lives Matter" to "Nessuna Pace Senza Giustizia" ("No Justice, No Peace," adopted from a 1967 speech by Dr. Martin Luther King Jr.), to "Siate Umani" ("Stay Human," a riff on "Restiamo Umani," the sign-off of Palestine-based Italian journalist Vittorio Arrigoni that was subsequently adopted by immigrants' rights activists in reference to the current Mediterranean refugee crisis).[27]

But for other Black Italians, the connection between these struggles was far less self-evident. And the uncertainty that some activists and bloggers felt about the prospect of subsuming their own struggles within an increasingly global but still largely US-centric movement against anti-Black state violence pointed to the doubly marginal position of Black Italians both in Italy and within the wider African diaspora. Along these lines, a prominent Italian-Ugandan-Sudanese blogger based in Milan, who over the last year has gained a substantial online following for her smart social commentary, slickly produced anti-racism videos, and curation of beauty tutorials for Black women, posted an incitement on Facebook in the midst of the Emmanuel Chidi Nnamdi protests. Her colorful commentary brought to a head the unspoken tensions within a new generation of politically conscious youth that has only very recently (and very tentatively) begun to collectively refer to itself as "Afro-" or "Black Italian":

> Guys, we are not in America and we are not Americans #chill you're more concerned, shouting, and crying for the injustices suffered by African Americans than for things that are happening in the country where you live, your country of origin, and many other places where injustice and discrimination run rampant . . . #blacklivesmatter here

blacklivesmatter there, you're acting as though in the United States your complaints would be taken seriously by someone. Americans NEVER look beyond their own backyard. . . . And they call their president the "Leader of the Free World."[28]

A heated debate quickly ensued under the blogger's indignant message, one I heard directly referenced in passionate conversation over countless aperitifs and coffees over the subsequent weeks. But on that sleepless summer night, I was affixed to my laptop screen as I tried desperately to piece together news reports of racist violence and Black resistance from Minnesota, Louisiana, London, Amsterdam, Paris, Rio de Janeiro, and Fermo.

And with each new and increasingly irate addition to the discussion about Black Italians and their connection to #BlackLivesMatter, my browser emitted an incongruously cheery two-tone notification alert. *BA-BING!* "I am half American, so I feel the injustices and hypocrisies of both countries," replied a writer from Reggio Emilia, the daughter of a Black American father and a white Italian mother. *BA-BING!* "Afro-Italians simply need to stop emulating African Americans. . . . Afro-Italians can create something better, which hopefully won't be based on skin color and the stupid 'one-drop' rule," retorted another commenter. His comment was quickly met with statements of approval that remarked on the heterogeneity of Afrodescendants in Europe. This heterogeneity, it was implied, distinguished Black politics in Italy from their stateside counterparts— unlike Black Italians, Black Americans supposedly cannot trace their African ancestry to a specific country or ethnic group due to the genealogical rupture of the transatlantic slave trade. *BA-BING!* "This is why I don't agree with the use of the term 'Afro-Italian,'" responded an Italian-Afro-Brazilian student activist from Rome. "It refers to African Americans, but here in Italy and in Europe . . . there is no 'Afro' in common," she continued, arguing that it is more typical for Afrodescendants in Italy to identify with their or their parents' country of origin. *BA-BING!* Another young woman took issue with the blogger's original post: "#Blacklivesmatter not just for America but for the rest of the world. Maybe in Italy they don't physically kill us like in America, but they kill us morally every day through discrimination."

An Italian-Ghanaian medical student from Verona with a keen interest in Black diasporic cultural politics attempted to mediate between the various positions that had been expressed in this ever-expanding Facebook thread: "It is true, yes, that we and Black Americans swim in different waters. Just as it's true that we are able to take our first steps thanks to them. *They are different waters, but at the end of the day they all flow into the same sea.*"[29]

Diaspora, Power, and the Interconnected Seas of Struggle

These debates left me feeling profoundly uncertain about my own positionality as a self-identified Black Italian by a set of roots and routes different from those of most of my interlocutors in Italy—specifically, as a Black American with ancestry linking her to the transatlantic slave trade who also happens to be an "ethnic" Italian with birthright citizenship. My friends' emphasis on the importance of tracing family lineage to specific African countries seemed to both invoke a strand of anti-Black racism based on the "taint" of slavery and re-inscribe the importance of blood kinship—ironically, the very same principle that limited their access to citizenship in Italy.[30] Early on in my fieldwork, I became accustomed to answering the question "But where *exactly* in Africa is your father's family from?" with a shrug. If pressed, I might continue, "We don't know for sure. Somewhere in West Africa, probably what is today Ghana or Nigeria."

While existentially troubling, these questions and debates about the characteristics and possibilities of a shared Black identity in Italy were not surprising. Indeed, I had begun to take note of two broad themes in nascent Black Italian cultural politics. On the one hand, Black Italian activists often look to the United States for inspiration, ideas, practices, institutions, strategies, and cultural forms in what sociologist Stephen Small calls *diasporic resources* and anthropologist Jacqueline Nassy Brown alternatively terms *diaspora's resources*—this includes literature like *The Autobiography of Malcolm X*, hip-hop and rap, cultural icons, self-care practices, and political strategies.[31] Over the past decade, this transnational circulation has been facilitated by the Internet and social networking sites such as Facebook, Instagram, YouTube, and Twitter.[32] These platforms have allowed for the rapid sharing and remixing of music, videos, memes, images, hashtags, slogans, and political movements.[33]

On the other hand, activists also assert to me that there is something unique about the Black experience in Italy—from limited access to citizenship to their own personal and familial entanglements with immigration politics; from the immediacy of colonialism to their lived experiences to a direct sense of attachment to specific African countries. Indeed, I sometimes found my questions about American influences brushed off with the assertion, "We are *not* copying Black Americans, but simply trying to work for the benefit of Afro-Italians!" While such a statement could be easily dismissed as a case of misplaced nationalism, I believe that it is more indicative of the oft-overlooked power relations *within* global diasporic communities. Black Italians are resisting being reduced to "junior partners" within the Black diaspora due to their distance from the formative geographies of the Middle Passage and the Black Atlantic.

A friend in Milan, the son of a Black Gambian father and a white Italian mother, who grew up nearby in the posh town of Monza, explained it to me this way one afternoon:

> I didn't have any cultural reference around me. There was no one else who was having the same feelings. . . . And so, you know, that was when I started to look at Black America, because it was the thing you could relate to more, you could find more, you know? And you could also relate more because it was closer to you, because it was the time of hip-hop; it was the time of b-boys. . . . So yeah, I turned to America, and you know, I started like, reading Malcolm X, and all of those things. . . . And my mom was getting worried. But my father was laughing—he said, "This has nothing to do you with you, it's not your history!" . . . And so, in a way, my identity struggle and journey started there. And there were different episodes, of growing up in the only country that you know, but that country did not recognize you as part of this country.

This conversation was part of a longer discussion this friend, Daniel, and I shared over several long lunches in 2016.[34] And it seemed to me that he was uniquely situated to comment on the uncertain crosscurrents of diasporic identification: his father was part of the informal network of Senegalese and Gambian immigrants who settled in northern Italy and became politically active in the 1980s (a cohort that also included the writer Pap Khouma and the educator and artist Mohamed Ba); and he was educated in Switzerland and travels frequently to New York, Paris, and Johannesburg for his work in an Italian foundation promoting African arts. Daniel spoke a subtly accented English peppered with Black American slang and cultural references; even though our conversations usually began in Italian, we always found ourselves gravitating back to English because, as he put it, "Italian just doesn't have the vocabulary to talk about these things yet."[35]

Yet, despite the affinities he expressed with Black America, in Daniel's view the cultural products that had been so formative in his youth were now part of a broader capitalist, imperialist power structure. And, he noted, racism simply operates differently in Italy than in the United States. He gave two examples to illustrate his point. He first noted that an Albanian might appear to be whiter than the average white Italian, but would still face discrimination. He then recalled that when he was much younger, he had a North African friend who was called a "n****r" by a southern Italian classmate who (Daniel chuckled) actually had darker skin than him; however, when this friend turned to Black American culture and began hanging out with his Black classmates, his mother demanded to know why he was spending so much time with "*those* n****rs." In other words,

Daniel was implying, the social mechanics by which "race" functions in Italy are shaped by complicated histories in which multiple "Souths"—from southern Italy to sub-Saharan Africa—overlap and collide to produce unexpected lines of alliance and fracture.

This insistence on difference, which in Daniel's anecdote was first articulated by his father but later became something he himself would firmly assert to me, is an important reminder that diasporic unity is not a given, and that Blackness cannot be reduced to a single, universal condition. This is the second chapter of the "coming to consciousness" narrative that I heard so frequently when speaking with Black Italians about their histories of self-identification.[36] This story frequently began with seeing oneself as solely Italian and having that mutual recognition denied, then looking to the other side of the Atlantic for guidance, and eventually realizing that what used to serve as a mirror no longer offered back a perfect reflection. My friend's story is reminiscent of Black studies scholar Michelle Wright's call in *Physics of Blackness* for a form of Black studies that can attend to the complex catalog of histories by which Black Americans and Black Europeans and other diasporans intersect.[37] This is an important matter for the emerging study of "race" in Italy, which in many cases is still caught between the poles of asserting an Italian exceptionalism with regard to racial tolerance and overrelying on models and concepts transposed directly from the United States or Britain (for instance, an emphasis on transatlantic slavery as the linchpin of Black identity and lived experience).

My attention to the United States here is not a forced comparison, nor is it an attempt to suggest that there exists a normative teleology by which Black diasporic subjects achieve proper "consciousness."[38] But these debates among Black Italians about their relationship to Black American cultural politics suggest that Black America remains a powerful reference point, an inescapable center of gravity in discussions about the contours of global or transnational Blackness. Indeed, within the field of Black European studies the notion of "African American hegemony" is a major source of contention, pointing to the uneven access to academic resources and recognition across the diaspora, as well as Black Americans' deeply equivocal entanglement with (or rather, conscription into) "the most powerful nation on earth."[39] It is for this reason that Wright has called into question the anchoring of global Blackness in what she refers to as the "Middle Passage epistemology," a framework that "points to the Atlantic slave trade as the crucial moment that separated blacks in the West from their ancestral origins, and then locates all preceding and subsequent events, from the classical world to the modern day, in relation to the Middle Passage."[40] This epistemology, she argues, begins to lose some of its relevance in the context of Black Europe. Within Black Europe, many people of African descent did not arrive via Middle Passage geographies and therefore use different timelines and historical markers (such as World War II and the role of colonial soldiers in the Allied armies) to recount their community "origin stories."

These questions point to the limitations of conceptualizing the Black diaspora solely in terms of "roots" and "routes." Instead, the story of Black Italians suggests that diaspora can be more accurately addressed as a relation or process rather than a static state of exile or displacement—what Stuart Hall describes as the play of "difference" within diasporic cultural identity.[41] Scholars of the global Black diaspora are increasingly attending to the question of what precisely constitutes unity or connection across diaspora; how the particularities of place shape distinct diasporic relations; and how contradiction and tension manifest in diaspora just as often as (if not more than) harmony and accord. As Jacqueline Nassy Brown (whose book *Dropping Anchor, Setting Sail* explores the geographies of racial formation in Liverpool) warns, "The association of diaspora with worldwide Black kinship, as it were, can actually render certain kinds of Black subjects, experiences, histories, and identities invisible."[42] Indeed, in a thoughtful and generative critique of Paul Gilroy's theorization of diaspora, she argues that Gilroy sometimes takes for granted the universality and translatability of Black American culture without attending to the power relations that stymie the realization of harmonious diasporic connections.[43] These differences, and the way they shape Black social practices across different geographical contexts, are constitutive of what Brown calls "counter/*part*" relations.[44]

But this emphasis on difference is also complicated by the fact that claims to "Italian exceptionalism" are frequently invoked by everyday white Italians and politicians to *deny* the existence of racism.[45] In other words, racism and racist violence are regarded simply as things that happen "out there" in the United States, with its burdensome legacy of slavery. While the murder of Jerry Masslo in 1989 disrupted some of the dangerously naive assumptions about racism in Italy that proliferated during the immigration debates of the 1980s, these ideas continue to carry political weight today.[46] The conservative Milanese daily *Il Giornale* (part of the Berlusconi media empire), for instance, ran a headline on July 11, 2016, boldly declaring, "The Government Invents 'Racist Italy'" (see figure 4.1a).[47] This announcement was juxtaposed with a subheading about anti-police violence protests in the United States that implicitly externalized racism as a specifically *American* problem: "Black revolt in the USA: 200 arrested in a few hours." This was not the first time the Italian Right had framed Italian "race relations" through a national comparison with the United States: a widely infamous Lega Nord propaganda poster uses Native American imagery to draw a parallel between the dispossession and displacement of indigenous communities by US settler colonialism and the supposed impact of immigration on white

FIGURES 4.1A AND 4.1B. The racial geopolitics of comparison. Left: *Il Giornale* front page from July 11, 2016, reading "The Government Invents Racist Italy." Right: Lega Nord poster depicting a Native American man in a war bonnet, with the text, "They had to endure immigration / Now they live in reservations!"

Sources: Polizia di Stato, http://www.poliziadistato.it/rassegna/rassegna11_07.pdf (left); Melina Melchionda, "'Bounce the Illegal Immigrant.' The Lega Nord's Discriminatory Propaganda Becomes a Game on Facebook," i-Italy, August 24, 2009, http://www.iitaly.org/magazine/focus/facts-stories/article/bounce-illegal-immigrant-lega -nords-discriminatory-propaganda (right).

Italians (see figure 4.1b).[48] In both cases, the United States stands in as a cautionary tale for white Italians—it is a place where "difference" and "diversity" have run amok.

But such pernicious claims to innocence conveniently neglect Europe's own complicity in enslavement—including the Mediterranean slave trade and the Genoese bourgeoisie whose trade networks helped to pave the way for the triangular transatlantic slave trade.[49] Still, in the wake of Emmanuel Chidi Nnamdi's murder, I was confidently told by numerous white Italians over casual dinner conversation that Italy is not a racist country—and really, how could I *dare* to make such a brash accusation when the police were gunning down my own people with impunity back home in the United States? Indeed, as Crystal

Fleming has observed, the lack of state statistical data on racial discrimination and racist violence in most European countries (and the public delegitimation of data collected by grassroots and nongovernmental organizations) has made it comparatively difficult for Black European communities to have their mobilizations against racism taken seriously by state authorities and their white co-nationals.[50]

Alongside this denial of racism in Italy (which functions by way of bounded geographical comparisons and a methodological nationalism that presumes nations to be hermetically sealed units) are almost-as-common assertions about Italy's status as a *meticcia*, or hybrid / mixed nation—particularly among white leftists and self-proclaimed anti-racists.[51] These assertions are by no means geographically delimited to southern Italy, as heard in the "Bologna è meticcia" chants at a demonstration against Lega Nord in 2015 (described in chapter 3), or as seen in a 2016 program sponsored by the Italian Ministry of Cultural Heritage celebrating the artistic production of "hybrid Italians" in Milan.[52] As I discussed in the previous chapter, one response to the political prominence of absolutist northern Italian identities over the last two decades has been to reappropriate discourses of Italian mixedness and hybridity, vaunting Italy's regional patchwork of dialects, cuisines, and local cultures to suggest that there can be ample room for immigrants and their families within this already heterogeneous nation.[53] But in practice, the aforementioned Italian "hype of hybridity" has become a subtle form of Italian nationalism and even colonial nostalgia.[54] It is a Mediterraneanism that constructs Italy as a crossroads of civilizations, a Hegelian center of World-History that benefits from a more fluid and flexible approach to identity than the United States and its infamously restrictive rules of racial hypodescent.[55]

For decades, in fact, apologist historians claimed (erroneously) that the frequent violations of Fascist racial segregation laws in the colonies of Italian East Africa by white Italian settlers could be interpreted as evidence of a lack of widespread racial prejudice among everyday white Italians.[56] And since World War II, largely due to the centrality of Italian communists in anti-Fascist resistance and Third Worldist solidarity movements, many white Italians have come to view themselves as inherently opposed to racism, which is in turn understood as "hostility, violence, or intolerance directed against culturally and physically different populations."[57] Indeed, the concept of institutional or structural racism is still relatively obscure in Italy; if explained, it would likely conjure up images of Jim Crow segregation or South African apartheid. Instead, racism is commonly understood as operating either at the level of banal, individual prejudice or at the extreme level of Nazi genocide. (Significantly, the concept of institutional racism has begun to gain some traction in Italy, in part due to jurisprudence scholar Clelia Bartoli's publication of the book *Razzisti per legge* [Racists by Law] in 2012.)[58]

It is important to remember, however, that the imaginary of the United States as the foil to a more tolerant or racially fluid Italy is itself a relatively recent phenomenon. During the Italian Fascist regime, for instance, the United States was frequently represented as a place where dangerous forms of racial intermingling took place. A 1941 issue of the Fascist magazine *La Difesa della Razza*, for instance, printed an unflattering picture of New York mayor Fiorello La Guardia eating a hot dog while standing next to a Black woman (see figure 4.2). While La Guardia was the son of a white Italian father and an Italian-Jewish mother, in the photo's caption he is referred to only as "the Jew La Guardia"—in keeping with the late Italian Fascist regime's policy that "Jewish" and "Italian" were two mutually exclusive racial categories. This front-page tableau was intended to convey to the Italian public a grotesque "spectacle" of degeneration and interracial fraternizing.

But even today, Italy's regional diversity, the history of internal North / South differentiation, and new state-sponsored research on the country's genetic-ethnic-linguistic diversity (as discussed in chapter 3) are marshaled as evidence that racial categories are simply less calcified in Italy than they are in the United States. The problem of bounding "race" as a concept that is territorialized in specific places (even when this is the unintended result of leftist European solidarity with Black liberation movements in the United States, as Sabine Broeck discusses in the context of West Germany in the 1970s), however, is that it has helped to stymie the development of critical conversations about racism's existence *within* Europe.[59] It is perhaps for this reason that so many of my interlocutors in Italy, including but not limited to both Black and white Italians, would unfailingly ask me to weigh in on the same question: "Which country is more racist, the United States or Italy?"—subtly nudging me to concede that American racism is more crude or violent in comparison with the Italian tendency toward simple *chiusura*, or close-mindedness.

In Italy, appeals to a sort of universal, color-blind hybridity have as their main consequence the invisibilization of the specificities (and historical sedimentations) of racism and anti-Black violence. Even after the murder of Emmanuel Chidi Nnamdi—a clear, explicit case of Italian anti-Black racist violence if ever there was one—I saw numerous signs employing universalizing rhetoric such as "We are all evolved apes" (remember that his wife was called an African monkey) and witnessed protesters declaring, "We are all Africans!" One widely circulated commentary even claimed that the most disturbing aspect of the murder was not "the death of a human being . . . but the death of the human inside us all."[60]

FIGURE 4.2. Front page of the Fascist Italian magazine *La Difesa della Razza* (1941), showing New York mayor Fiorello La Guardia eating next to a Black American woman. The caption next to the photo reads: "The Face of the United States. Here is a faithful portrait of the Jewified and anti-racist United States: the Jew La Guardia provides a spectacle of vulgarity, next to whites and n****rs mixing fraternally." In chapter 3, a woman from southern Italy used the interracial intimacies of a *different* Italian mayor of New York—Bill de Blasio— to argue that "Mediterranean" Italians were not inherently racist.

Source: *Archivio del Museo di Antropologia ed Etnografia, University of Turin: "Marro G. Questione Razziale."*

From the Black Atlantic
to the Black Mediterranean

Given all this, how are Afrodescendants to articulate their distinct Black Italian political subjectivities without denying the existence of racism in Italy, neglecting the global scale of anti-Black racism and racial formation, or falling victim to an overly romanticized vision of Mediterraneanism or multicultural mixing?[61] After all, in Italy we have to take seriously the histories of racial boundary-drawing that were caught up with the process of national unification, as well as Italy's own colonial history (all of which, significantly, *preceded* the rise of Fascism)—and the reverberations of these histories in the present. Indeed, drawing on Stuart Hall's own engagement with Antonio Gramsci, it is important to acknowledge the existence of multiple, geographically and historically situated—yet deeply interconnected—racism*s*.[62] And actually, I would argue that the link across time and space between Gramsci and Hall is one powerful example of how a rich body of scholarship on racism from Britain (and the United States) can be deployed transgressively to challenge the color-blind logics that dominate continental Europe, while also recognizing the particular racial formations that have "settled" in Italy.[63] Even though Hall claimed that "Gramsci did not write about race, ethnicity or racism in their contemporary meanings or manifestations," Pasquale Verdicchio notes that Gramsci was actually quite attuned to these questions precisely because Italy's "Southern Question" had already been cast in terms of an immutable, ahistorical racial and ethnic difference.[64]

As I noted earlier, the question of how to engage an Anglophone analytic vocabulary of racism in Europe is a central concern both for Black European studies and for the practice of organizing against anti-Black violence in Europe. Fatima El-Tayeb notes that one tendency among European scholars has been to take as a matter of fact the silence surrounding "race" in Europe and suggest that any invocation of race as a category of social analysis is mere "U.S. cultural imperialism."[65] Instead of such a wholesale rejection, she argues, what is necessary is a "contextualized understanding" of processes of racialization.[66] For this, she turns to David Theo Goldberg's concept of *racial regionalizations* and specifically, *racial europeanization*.[67] Goldberg argues that racist configurations in Europe show the limitations of an "incessant focus on the logics of unqualifiedly racially repressive cases such as the US."[68] This is not because "race" as such does not exist in Europe, but rather because the "European experience is a case study in the frustrations, delimitations, and injustices of political racelessness."[69]

Goldberg argues that these distinct yet interrelated racist configurations derive from "their embeddedness, from the particularities that count for socio-specific determinations"—a claim that echoes Hall's insistence on the way general features of racism are "modified and transformed by the historical spec-ificity of the contexts and environments in which they become active."[70] Here, I want to suggest the importance of thinking not just in terms of racial *europe-anization*, but also of the Mediterranean and southern Europe specifically—what Ian Law (also drawing on Goldberg) refers to as *racial mediterraneanization*.[71] This is not to endlessly subdivide the world into self-contained analytical cate-gories (a problem with some "polyracism" arguments), but rather to recognize the contours of racism and its denial in a region that has been either vaunted or denigrated as ethnically mixed or culturally plural.[72]

This is where, I believe, emerging work on the Black Mediterranean can be in-structive. Today, scholars such as Alessandra Di Maio argue that the Black Mediter-ranean is no longer just a precondition for modern racial capitalism; it is being reproduced every day at the nexus of anti-Black violence (seen in immigration pol-icy, citizenship law, and everyday racisms) and Black liberation struggles across the Mediterranean basin.[73] Admittedly, the Mediterranean might seem like an odd geographic referent to employ in light of the fact that most people of African de-scent still live in the northern half of Italy, and especially when southern Italy is the region most traditionally associated with "Mediterranean culture."[74] I argue, how-ever, that the Mediterranean (and the Black Mediterranean specifically) is still con-ceptually relevant for several reasons: because of the way imaginaries and discourses of Mediterranean difference shaped Italian racial theorization in ways that distin-guish it from northern Europe; because of the enduring trans-Mediterranean lega-cies of Italian colonialism; because the large-scale internal labor migration of southern Italians into northern Italian cities after World War II has helped to blur sharp divisions between the two regions; because the journeys of Africans into It-aly are in most cases trans-Mediterranean and postcolonial rather than transat-lantic and tied to enslavement; and because tracing these historic and contemporary trans-Mediterranean connections can challenge the ethnocentrism inherent in dominant narrations of the origins of Italy and Europe.

New research in fields such as comparative literature, history, Italian stud-ies, Black studies, sociology, anthropology, and geography is engaging with the production of Blackness and the distinct contours of Black subjectivity in Med-iterranean Europe; the erasure of Black histories and the dense networks of cul-tural creolization linking Africa and Europe; and the practices by which African diasporas in Italy engage with and expand the circuits of global Black-ness. P. Khalil Saucier and Tryon Woods, for instance, mark the histories of anti-Black racist violence in the Mediterranean basin as conditions of possibility for "contemporary forms of policing Europe's borders."[75] Drawing on their work, Christina Sharpe has located the Black Mediterranean within a broader "wake" of anti-Black terror, dispossession, criminalization, and forced migration.[76] In an adjacent move, Ida Danewid argues that Black Mediterranean histories of racial capitalism are obscured by the deployment of abstract humanisms in white European refugee solidarity movements.[77] Timothy Raeymaekers has in turn approached the Black Mediterranean in his work as a layered, fluid landscape of "overlapping and often contradictory histories of mobility and exchange" that produce differentiated regimes of racialized labor.[78]

But academia is by no means a privileged site of knowledge production on the Black Mediterranean. Black Italian writers such as Igiaba Scego, Gabriella Ghermandi, and Cristina Ali Farah, as well as documentarians including Medhin Paolos (whose work will be discussed in chapter 5), Fred Kuwornu (whose work was highlighted in chapter 1), and Ariam Tekle have all articulated sophisticated analyses of Blackness through Mediterranean crosscurrents via the arts. Following the powerful exhortations of Black Italian activists, these contemporary engagements with the Black Mediterranean provide an emergent framework for foregrounding the interconnections between Italy and Africa without relying on romantic images of unfettered mobility and conviviality. They are powerful examples for how to link Italy to a wider Black diaspora without privileging the Atlantic as uniquely generative of Black diasporic cultures.

As an analytic, the Black Mediterranean is focused on linking sub-Saharan Africa to the wider Mediterranean basin, past and present—from the historical connections between Nubia and Egypt to the "often violent and discriminatory migration control regimes" that characterize today's migration control collaborations between North African states and Fortress Europe.[79] This is significant because most (though certainly not all) Afrodescendants in Italy today have arrived via trans-Mediterranean geographies. These journeys might entail the aftermath of Italian colonialism in the Horn of Africa, plane flights from Dakar on student visas, or voyages across the Sahara to Libya followed by maritime passage across the Mediterranean to Lampedusa. In addition, the capacious geographic referents of Black people in Italy cannot be fully subsumed within Atlantic geographies of Blackness, as they also maintain direct familial, cultural, economic, and often political connections to their parents' countries of origin on the African continent. The Black Mediterranean therefore allows for both historically and geographically situated engagements with the complex material and symbolic networks of Italian Blackness.

Centering the irrepressible connections between sub-Saharan Africa and the Mediterranean can also facilitate a critical rethinking of European modernity itself by challenging the separation between sub-Saharan African Blackness and the imaginary of the Mediterranean as the cauldron within which a presumably white, European civilization was produced. As Robin D. G. Kelley writes in his 2000 foreword to Cedric Robinson's *Black Marxism*, "The exorcising of the Black

Mediterranean is about the fabrication of Europe as a discrete, racially pure entity solely responsible for modernity, on the one hand, and the fabrication of the Negro, on the other."[80] Iain Chambers, drawing on Fernand Braudel, notes for instance that the entire Mediterranean region relied on gold from sub-Saharan African before the "discovery" of New World bullion: "While European textile goods went south, across the Sahara, gold and slaves traveled north to the Mediterranean shoreline and European cities."[81] As Black European scholars Olivette Otele and Nathaniel Adam Tobias Coleman suggested at a symposium on the Black Mediterranean held at Birmingham City University in the United Kingdom during the fall of 2016, recentering the complexities of Black life in the story of Euro-Mediterranean modernity can also work to undermine the dangerous pretentions of European ethnic absolutism.[82]

Historian Gabriele Proglio takes on Kelley's provocation about Europe and the Black Mediterranean in his evocative essay "Is the Mediterranean a White Italian-European Sea?" The Mediterranean, he writes, is not intrinsically anti-Eurocentric; rather, it has been

> the repository of de-territorialization and re-territorialization processes (Deleuze and Guattari ([1975] 1983) of the colonial and postcolonial elsewhere and of the reinvention of Italianness (Proglio 2016). Indeed, the Mediterranean may be viewed as an archive of Italian / European cultural memories (Assmann 1992) or as the domain of Italianness, first symbolic and then physical, first as mental concept / idea / representation of Mediterranean-ness, the mythical realm of Italian progeny and then as an assortment of intersubjective practices linked with feelings of belongingness to the Italian imagined community. . . . Actually, this narrative process that is always conceived in contrast to what is deemed black, non-Italian, non-European has a circular pattern, as argued by Edward Said with regard to the category of Orientalism (Said 1979:127) and Dabashi with reference to the new global conflicts (2008).[83]

Indeed, from Hegel to Mackinder to Braudel himself, the Mediterranean has been conceived chiefly as Europe's political, cultural, and economic incubator.[84] Yet, as Proglio argues in his introduction to the 2016 edited collection *Decolonizing the Mediterranean*, "Sub-Saharan African migration to Europe has unveiled the existence of a Black Mediterranean" with a long history that is systematically neglected in the historiography of both Europe *and* the global Black diaspora.[85] Focusing on these connections does not mean privileging narratives of hybridity as an antidote to the myth of European purity, however—the violence of the ever-shifting Euro-Mediterranean border and the persistence of structural anti-Black racism in Italy suggest otherwise.

Traduttore, Traditore: Translating Black Italy

The Black Mediterranean elucidates two urgent questions for the study of an emergent Black Italy: What is unique about the crosscurrents that produce trans-Mediterranean racial formations?[86] And how are they at once distinct from, but also in intimate conversation with, transatlantic diasporic formations? These questions certainly pose interesting intellectual puzzles, but what does it mean to engage them *practically*? The activists, artists, and entrepreneurs I spoke with in Italy repeatedly asserted that the problem ultimately came down to one of language.

As Isabelle told me the first time we met, "It seems stupid, but vocabulary is really important. In the Italian dictionary, these terms don't exist. I think that we have to invent, we have to Italianize, we have to find terms—even in dialect." The lack of an Italian vocabulary that can address the specificities of racism was a lament that I heard frequently, as was a concern that the only terms of collective self-identification available ("Afro-Italian," "Black Italian," etc.) were "just copied" from other contexts with different Black histories. Sonia, an Italian-Liberian musician based in Rome, explained the lexicological challenges facing Black Italians this way:

> I think that at the historical level, the United States has endured an entire journey, so there have been lots of movements, whereas in Italy there is nothing. So we still need time, at least fifty years. But I am trying to study in order to try and understand which terms have been used in the African American movements, so that I can bring them here to Italy. I think that one term I would start to use is "diaspora." I think that, yes, we have to build our own language, but we can also take it from other cultures that have already arrived at some solutions, some changes. . . . We need terms here that are stronger, proud, constructive, positive.[87]

I observed a similar conversation between two Italian-Ghanaian friends from Verona about the limited available terms of self-identification in Italy. Esther and Marcus were notably less optimistic, however, about the usefulness or relevance of the Black American experience:

> ESTHER: Well, I am afraid that these associations of "new Italians" always focus on the word "Italian" and less on the concept of double identity. That is what is happening: there is an assimilationist model. And so those who were born without citizenship, they say we are

Italian, *punto*, to affirm themselves in the society. [Young people] don't think about "Black Americans," "Black Italians." A person born here will say "Italian," but they will not say "African," so that they can be accepted. A person born here can't accept having a double identity. . . . But I say that I am Afro-Italian. It is a passage that still has to happen for the new generations in these movements and associations about citizenship and about identity.[88]

MARCUS: I don't think that you can use the term "Black Italians." It is not correct. There is the Italian context; it is not the American context. In America, you can say "Black American." It makes sense, because the society was born in a particular way. But here, it was born in a different way. . . . We need to use the correct terms; we have to look at reality with different filters. If you look at the Italian reality with American filters, then it is difficult to understand. I have seen that in America, if you'll allow me, you even have difficulty defining what Blackness is among yourselves! So if you, who are the experts with this term, have problems, then let's leave it there and *ciao*.

In *The Practice of Diaspora*, cultural historian Brent Hayes Edwards suggests that translating even "a basic grammar of blackness" posed key obstacles for the development of Black internationalist movements during the interwar period.[89] Thus, while the turn to an expansive sense of shared Black struggle had the potential to challenge restrictive nation-state borders, practical efforts to articulate this sort of tenuous unity often foundered on those very same boundaries. Edwards's magisterial work suggests that language is not an abstraction, but is instead drawn from concrete experience and in turn shapes a group's available political horizons. For that reason, the politics of translation provide a privileged vantage point from which to observe the cultures and disjunctures of Black diasporic politics. Even the process of documenting the "fact of Blackness"—and by extension, centering "race" as an important node of insurgent knowledge production—Edwards writes, can be deeply contentious.[90]

What, then, can collective Black anti-racist organizing in Italy look like when Italian does not have a readily available translation for the word "Blackness" (the closest substitute is *negritudine*, which refers more to the Francophone literary movement initiated by Aimé Césaire, Léopold Senghor, and Léon Damas, and translators are still debating whether to introduce *nerezza* or *nerità* as alternatives); or when use of the word "race" is still generally publicly unacceptable and the term *di colore* (of color) is employed to avoid race rather than to express solidarity among racially marginalized groups; or even when self-identification as "Black" or "Afro-Italian" can be a controversial matter?[91] One need only to remember the shock and surprise that reverberated through the Italian press when Cécile Kyenge declared, "Sono nera, non di colore, e lo dico con fierezza" (I am Black, not "of color," and I say it with pride).[92]

These were the questions that Isabelle and Imani posed to me during the 2016 Black Europe Summer School in Amsterdam.[93] After meeting Black activists from countries such as Britain and the Netherlands, and reading Black diasporic texts from even further afield, they approached me both heartened and deeply distressed. "We need to translate these texts into Italian," Isabelle said with great urgency. "This language doesn't exist in Italian; people who want to talk about these topics use English words, and so we need to construct this groundwork together." What Isabelle was calling for was a version of VèVè Clark's "diaspora literary"—the ability to access and engage with literatures from across the global Black diaspora while also situating them within their particular "historical, social, cultural, and political" contexts.[94]

With these concerns in mind, we collectively hatched a plan: we would translate a selection of chapters from books we found particularly inspiring, post our "guerilla translations" on the Internet, and bring together Black Italians to share their experiences and reflect on the readings. Our group quickly expanded from three to six to ten to twenty collaborators, most of whom identified in some way as Afrodescendant Italians—from founders of national advocacy organizations to internationally recognized bloggers; from fashion designers to medical students. Our collective included people with ties to Ghana, Nigeria, Senegal, Gambia, Eritrea, Ivory Coast, Sudan, and Uganda, as well as individuals of mixed backgrounds like myself. After much deliberation, we settled on three texts: the introduction to *Black Europe and the African Diaspora*, James Baldwin's "Stranger in the Village," and some selections from Grada Kilomba's wrenching *Plantation Memories: Episodes of Everyday Racism*.[95]

Beforehand, Marcus sent the group a set of provocative guiding questions: Is the idea of "Afro-Italians" an Afro-Americanization of the circumstances in Italy? How can we focus attention on the experiences of Afrodescendant women in Italy? How can we think about the connection between a "global Blackness" and the specificities of the situation in Italy? He signed off his message with a quote from the Afro-German poet May Ayim: "It is important that we as Black people create spaces in which we can be among 'ourselves,' in order to comprehend our commonalities and differences, to exploit them in our everyday lives and political work. But also . . . to create some moments of relaxation and release for ourselves."[96] Marcus's use of the Ayim quote gestured toward the second, unstated purpose of our gathering: to create a new kind of Black space for an "emergent Black Italia" that does not have a singular geographical referent, but rather emerges from within the interstices of everyday life.[97] And in many ways, our modest project did in fact draw indirect inspiration from the work of Audre Lorde and Afro-German writers such as May Ayim in the 1980s and 1990s, when they began to "organize as a community and . . . define their multiple biracial identities"—a process that culminated in the publication of the groundbreaking collection of Afro-German women's writing titled *Showing Our Colors: Afro-German Women Speak Out.*[98]

Finally, one chilly evening in December we gathered at Daniel's apartment near the Basilica di Sant'Ambrogio in Milan. To our surprise, people had arrived for the meeting from across Italy—from northern cities such as Verona and Padua, from Rome, and even from as far south as Palermo, Sicily. Daniel cued up a smooth playlist of jazz and R&B as we picked at chocolates, poured ourselves ample glasses of wine, and sprawled across the tiled floor of his painstakingly appointed loft apartment. We were mindful of the time because the rapper Tommy Kuti, our beloved Italian-Nigerian "hometown hero" from nearby Brescia, would be stopping by later in the evening to film scenes of the group for his new music video (aptly titled "#AFROITALIANO"). After Daniel formally welcomed us all to his home, and Marcus recapped our project and the discussion questions, our conversation quickly turned from a more academic reflection on the translated readings to a lively exchange about a different kind of translation—specifically, the possibility of articulating a collective "Black" identity in Italy. As we reflected on the "Afro-Italian" and "Black Italians" labels, it was clear that we all shared this collective "we" in different ways—that there was no essential, unitary Black (Italian) subject.

> ALMAZ: It makes sense that in a particular moment, a person or a group of people might choose to organize around a particular term—in that case, it has a use, and that use can change over time—like the term "second generation." If you want to historicize things, then yes, there have been many migrations of Africans into Italy, but in our times this term serves a purpose. But there can be a forced correlation with some terms, for instance, with the movements of African Americans. If you look on paper, yes, we are Italian, and we are also African. But it's a generalization. We also belong to specific communities.
>
> MARCUS: I don't often use "Afro-Italian" to define myself.
>
> ALMAZ: I do, for simplicity's sake.
>
> MARCUS: There's also the matter of general belonging, and also of pride.
>
> ALMAZ: That's true. I grew up in Milan. I remember when you would say "hi" to someone from across the street because they were Afro "something." But with these new groups like "Black Italians," I feel the need to push harder, to do some more specific research.[99] These general

terms aren't sufficient anymore. Looking at African Americans is okay, but what about histories of colonialism, in order to understand an Afro-Italian identity? I'm not worried about fragmentation—we've already seen this happen with the Senegalese community.

DANIEL: But I'm Italian-Senegalese-Gambian. So I've never had a specific "community" that I am a part of. It's important to find points of commonality. . . . Our generation has a language that is not based on our own experiences, but on borrowings from other places.

IMANI: I've never liked the term "Afro-Italian." . . . I have a lot of Afrodescendant friends—Senegalese, Nigerians—but they are all very different. I've never seen this sentiment of "Africa United." The only thing they have in common is that they are Italian—but then that valorizes the Italian part and not the Senegalese or Nigerian part. Putting the African American myth on a pedestal takes you away from Italian history. There is an Italian colonial history! We have to study it, to focus on that.

CAMILLA: Yes, it's important to think about these colonial legacies. And also about histories of racism in Italy, to combat the idea that there is no racism in Italy. But it seems like there is a tension here between our different individual self-identifications, and a shared experience of being "racialized" as Black by a white supremacist society.

MARCUS: Some people use "Afro-Italian" to copy Americans, sure. But I don't really see it as trying to emulate them. It's just about finding a common identity. An Ivorian girl and an Angolan girl *do* have something in common; they have similar experiences.

DANIEL: There are two inflections to this conversation: self-identification, and the external gaze. I'm comfortable with all of these terms. It's like a hat—I can choose which one I want to put on every day. I feel profoundly Afro-Italian; I feel profoundly Black Italian; I feel Italian; I feel white European; and so on. All these things can coexist. The possibility we have is to not accept a basic framework of dichotomy (either / or). We have to find a form of self-identification we can all share, and from there build a sense of community amongst ourselves.

Eventually, tensions cooled as more bottles of full-bodied wine were circulated among the group. Several hours later, the night ended in dancing, singing, and teary-eyed goodbyes. The words of a Black American Fulbright scholar from Bologna who came to participate in the discussion echoed in my mind as I rode home on the train (a space that, for both Fanon and Du Bois, was marked by racial insult): "When I hear people share their stories, despite the differences, there is *still* something we all have in common." She was referring specifically to Isabelle, and how the emotional stories Isabelle had shared about her journey of self-acceptance through natural hair resonated with her own struggles against racialized beauty standards in the United States. So, not only was Black Italy being seen as a distinct cultural formation with specific histories, languages, and politics, the young scholar seemed to suggest, it was also beginning to emerge as a rich source of diasporic resources that it could in turn share with Black America, one of the primary cultural beacons of global Blackness.

The task of articulating a shared sense of Blackness in Italy is already underway, despite the profound tensions inherent in this project—tensions that became particularly visible that long evening at Daniel's apartment. One need look no further than to the proliferation of blogs and books and songs and activist collectives addressing "Afro-" or "Black Italian" identity, or to the way that incidents like the murder of Emmanuel Chidi Nnamdi force individuals with disparate lived experiences into an uneasy solidarity with one another and with worldwide Black communities as a matter of survival. It is a project of mapping the lived geographies of the ever-shifting Black Mediterranean—of remapping the boundaries of inclusion and exclusion in Italy.

Transforming Citizenship in the Black Mediterranean

A new generation of Black activists is currently seeking to assert itself, gain national visibility, combat Italian racism, and acquire legitimacy as Italians by birth *who are also Black*. Their efforts in turn raise challenging questions about the promises, limitations, and contradictions of national citizenship. How can Black Italians mobilize for citizenship when the Italian nation-state is a thoroughly racial formation? Where does global Black diasporic solidarity intersect with the politics of local or national belonging in Italy? Can Black Italians enact forms of Blackness that resist an all-too-easy incorporation into race-blind Italian Mediterraeanisms? As Gaia Giuliani writes, drawing on the work of Fatimah Tobing Rony: "In Italy the white gaze has an anthropophagic posture which turns it into a 'scopic regime' that, while producing some subjects as racialized, includes them within the 'colour line' that marks the boundaries of the imagined space of whiteness. To be included within the imagined (racialized) community of the Nation, these subjects need to be transformed in appropriable objects."[100]

The ways that Black Italians are beginning to come together to discuss their shared experiences, develop a language for grasping the particularities of Italian racism, and connect with Black struggles in other countries speaks to the emergence of a set of Black Mediterranean diasporic practices whose ethical horizon stretches far beyond Italy. In the next chapter, I consider the ways these emergent Black Mediterranean diasporic politics have the potential to bring together not only Black people who were born and raised in Italy, but also newly arrived sub-Saharan African immigrants and refugees who are not necessarily connected through shared birthplace. These are alternative visions of community that are far more capacious than those captured by the framework of national citizenship, and yet at the same time, they have the potential to radically transform the meanings and practices of Italianness today.

REFUGEES AND CITIZENS-IN-WAITING

**The historical origins and political lineage of immigration control . . .
lie in its colonial bureaucratic assembling of populations as racially
different.**

—Barnor Hesse, "Raceocracy"

**These actions . . . are hard to assess, or even recognize, since they
do not involve grand gestures of state overthrow, the rise to power
of charismatic leaders, or the development of the large-scale social
projects characteristic of modernist statecraft. Yet they still
manage to have profound impact, even in their moments of purported
failure.**

—Yarimar Bonilla, "Freedom, Sovereignty, and Other Entanglements"

It was the summer of 2016, and I was in Amsterdam for the ninth annual Black
Europe Summer School. In a spacious and sunny conference room, three Black
Italian women activists and entrepreneurs were sharing their stories with the
assembled participants from the program. The group hailed from a wide swath
of European countries with very different histories of Black presences, including Portugal, Switzerland, Belgium, Britain, and the Netherlands, as well as various cities across North America. The testimonies from the Italian delegation
centered on their shared experience of being born and raised in Italy, yet being
perpetually perceived as foreigners simply because of the color of their skin. This
pervasive sense of Blackness as always "out of place" in Italian space, they argued, suffused debates about citizenship reform in Italy.

For instance, they explained, many politicians had argued that citizenship for
the children of immigrants should be based on an Italian language proficiency
test. But the Black Italian activists argued that this proposal was based on a conflation of all "second-generation" Italians with the refugees and asylum seekers who
were currently arriving in Italy by boat from the African continent. As they explained, this suggestion was clearly absurd (not to mention deeply offensive): Italian was their first and primary language—the Italian they spoke was so obviously
inflected with the accents typical of the places where they were raised in Italy, and
they even spoke specific regional Italian dialects. In a country where *national*

belonging is frequently articulated in terms of *local* cultural practices, regional accents and dialects are a potent way of asserting that one is not a newcomer. According to the Black Italian activists and entrepreneurs, the largest obstacle to citizenship reform (and more generally, to the recognition of Black people as legitimate members of the national Italian community) was that the Italian public continued to conflate them with first-generation immigrants and newly arrived refugees from Africa.

A Black activist from Portugal, who organizes Freire-inspired Theater of the Oppressed workshops for African migrants in Lisbon to explore issues such as everyday racism and the surveillance of immigrant neighborhoods, raised her hand after this explanation. "But what about Pan-Africanism?" she asked, with great urgency and a hint of annoyance. "Doesn't this split between citizenship and migration just create more divisions in the Black community?" A passionate debated erupted among the activists and scholars gathered in the room:

> Isabelle (Italian-Ghanaian): We are stuck with the immigrants, the boats—that is the image that is cast on me. I don't want that for my children.[1]
>
> Imani (Italian-Brazilian): The problem is that we don't exist in Italy. That makes the politics of the government and the institutions and the parliament go in the wrong way. They say, "They have to integrate." I'll give you one example. If you say we are like immigrants, that we are all the same, we are all foreigners—some people may have been in Italy for more or less time, but at the end of the day we are all foreigners—then the government will respond by saying, "Then they need to learn the language." We don't need that. Immigrants need language courses, but we don't need that. That is one example of the politics that have been made in Italy for the last thirty years about immigration, but not about citizens.
>
> Anna (German-Turkish): I understand this distancing from migrants, but at the same time, many people are traveling back and forth, which troubles the distinction.
>
> Imani: When I said that we want to separate from migrants, I mean in terms of the politics regarding us, not because I'm saying "ugh." Because there are a lot of Italian citizens who have foreign backgrounds. This gap must be filled, not with migration politics, but with the specific politics of *us*. Because there are more than a million of us in Italy . . . there are more than five million immigrants in Italy. But there are no politics for us, for this kind of "migration

consequence," or whatever you want to call us. Of course we are all immigrants, but in a different way, and these differences must be acknowledged, and must have specific politics.

INES (AFRO-PORTUGUESE): But this is still perpetuating a difference, instead of seeing a connection. The Portuguese constitution, for instance, shows that we are always immigrants—it maintains a distinction between migrants, natives, and stateless people. Look at your own constitutions and see how fundamental these distinctions are. I encourage you to think *beyond* these categories!

The debate that day remained largely unresolved. Yet, the divergent viewpoints expressed during that gathering were reflective of a larger set of tensions running through the emergent politics of Blackness in Italy: tensions between citizenship reform and refugee rights, between national inclusion and transnational Blackness, and between the liberal politics of inclusion and systemic critiques of the racial state. These are not merely abstract intellectual exercises. Rather, they are urgent questions that suffuse Black European life and political organizing. And these dilemmas will only continue to grow in urgency as established Black communities are increasingly confronted with the arrival of more recent migrants, refugees, and asylum seekers.

These dilemmas have seemingly led, frustratingly, to an impasse, with no clear political alternatives in sight. On the one hand, Black activists have proven that liberal notions of citizenship are not fixed—they are in fact flexible and can be negotiated within the context of claims for the recognition and formal inclusion of historically marginalized racial subjects. On the other hand, efforts to stretch the legal boundaries of citizenship to include criteria such as birthplace, schooling, cultural and linguistic knowledge, or economic productivity also inadvertently create new sets of constitutive exclusions. Citizenship seemed at first to open up a new set of possibilities, challenging narrowly defined understandings of the modern nation-state by emphasizing heterogeneity and the porosity of borders. But in the context of an ethnonationalist resurgence in Italy that has linked the arrival of migrants from sub-Saharan Africa to a general sense of Italian national malaise, Black activists are increasingly confronting the limitations of citizenship as a strategy for combatting institutionalized, state racism in Italy.

Here I should note that I am not advocating for an uncritical, essentialist notion of universal Black solidarity. It is not my objective to claim that all Black people in Italy share the same interests, political leanings, or lived experiences. Nor do I assert that they *should* constitute a "natural" political collective on the road to a proper diasporic consciousness. I am also not grasping for an ideal-type

Black radical politics in Italy to uphold as a model. Rather, I am interested in the ways that the dominance of liberal notions of citizenship and nationalism can in practice preclude certain critiques of the racial state—critiques that see restrictive notions of citizenship, everyday racism against Black Italians, and the marginalization of sub-Saharan African immigrants and refugees all as different facets of the same larger phenomenon. What sorts of new possibilities and alliances might be opened up when we begin to look beyond national-scale mobilizations that intentionally or inadvertently draw tenuous distinctions between Black citizens (including citizens-in-waiting) and Black migrants in Italy?

Activists, artists, and entrepreneurs across Italy have been working tirelessly in attempts to untangle these dilemmas. One important strategy has been to distinguish between institutional legitimation and national belonging. In other words, Black Italian activists might approach the struggle for citizenship as an effort to gain access to the specific rights and protections granted by the Italian state, all while minimizing the *affective* significance of citizenship as an expression of identity, national belonging, loyalty, or pride. This move, while subtle, has helped to create an opening for the expression of new kinds of capacious, global Black diasporic ties. But although this approach produces powerful new possibilities for reimagining Black Italy in terms of what Heather Merrill (drawing on the work of geographer Doreen Massey) calls "relational place," it still cannot fully undermine the power of state categories to produce distinctions among the families and communities that make up contemporary Black Italy— differentiations such as "immigrant" and "second generation," or alternatively, "born here" and "newly arrived."[2]

Yet these various struggles also suggest that the dominant liberal frames of nation-state and citizenship are beginning to fray at the seams. If chapter 1 of this book asked how Black Italians' experience of *being a problem* could generate transgressive insights about Italian racial nationalism, this process has now led them to question the boundaries of the broader political "problem-space" in which they are currently organizing.[3] Young activists who were deeply invested in making claims through the national community as a means of becoming legally recognized by the Italian state have increasingly become disillusioned with this political project. After all, if the history of the liberal nation-state suggests that it is a thoroughly racial formation, then any articulation of citizenship in relation to the nation-state will be by definition fraught and limited.[4] This does not mean that Black activists have abandoned the struggle for the reform of Italian citizenship law—far from it. But at the same time, they are actively developing alternative ways of understanding themselves in relation to space, nations, borders, and diasporas.

Another quandary remains, however. Nation-state citizenship is by definition exclusionary. But while scholars and activists have attempted to craft alternative forms of non-national citizenship that are more open and flexible (global citizenship, diasporic citizenship, urban citizenship, insurgent citizenship, etc.), the nation-state still holds hegemony over the legal apparatus of citizenship. So, if the state is the primary arbiter of citizenship and rights—and the state itself cannot be understood outside deeper histories of racial differentiation—what alternatives remain, beyond deploying a strategic form of nationalist essentialism or embracing a non-nationalist sense of transnational belonging with no real legal "teeth"? Are there other meaningful ways of practicing community, membership, or citizenship? Postcolonial theorists such as the anthropologist David Scott have responded to these sorts of dilemmas by characterizing our current moment as one of "tragedy," "disenchantment," and "stuckness."[5] Disillusionment and dashed hopes suffuse the politics unfolding at liberalism's limits around the world—from the southern shores of Europe, where refugees are confronted with an onslaught of legal categories that condition their movement, to the cities of Italy's industrial triangle, where Black Italians are facing racial exclusions within the category of "citizen."

In this chapter, I draw on Caribbean anthropologist Yarimar Bonilla's generative notion of *strategic entanglement* to explore alternative forms of Black political organizing, ones that do not regard citizenship or nation-state recognition as a primary or singular objective. Bonilla defines strategic entanglement as "a way of crafting and enacting autonomy within a system from which one is unable to fully disentangle."[6] The notion of strategic entanglement is not meant to invoke a new kind of liberal, instrumentalist, and thoroughly Machiavellian political actor, but instead describes the process of crafting diasporic politics and projects in the long shadow of state sovereignty.[7] These practices do not always contain coherent, explicitly articulated political visions, nor do they necessarily rise to the level of directly challenging the sovereignty of the modern nation-state. But entanglement, I will argue, provides a useful analytic for comprehending the ways that Black activists make use of shifting alliances and tactical engagements with the state for purposes that may include, but also extend beyond, the objective of nation-state recognition.[8] The future of these movements remains uncertain, but they are nonetheless wrenching open powerful new visions of solidarity—what I call "Black Mediterranean diasporic politics." This emergent Black Mediterranean diasporic politics aligns with W. E. B. Du Bois's prophetic vision in *Dusk of Dawn* of political community based not on the fascist dyad of blood and soil, but on shared social histories of subordination and resistance.

I focus in particular on the work of a group of Italian-born Eritreans who began to self-organize as large numbers of Eritrean refugees and asylum seekers started to arrive in Milan in 2015. Rather than drawing boundaries between themselves and newly arrived refugees on the basis of birthplace or Italian belonging, they crafted new forms of solidarity based on the shared links of diaspora and anticolonial struggle. I conclude by considering what new kinds of Black Mediterranean alliances may continue to emerge in Italy, which was recently rocked by the 2018 electoral victory of far-right and neofascist political candidates, as well as a new spate of racist attacks against Black migrants. Taken together, these examples suggest that we are not trapped in an iron cage of exhausted possibilities—and indeed, that the current liberal impasse has also generated a moment characterized by great political effervescence and radical experimentation.

Overlapping Borders: The Eritrean Diaspora in Italy

The story of the Eritrean community in Italy provides a helpful lens through which to view the tensions between citizenship and national membership on the one hand, and diaspora and transnational Blackness on the other. While the narrative that follows is by no means an exhaustive account of the varied diasporas from the Horn of Africa in Italy, it links together colonial histories, contemporary migrations, immigration and citizenship law, and the current southern Mediterranean refugee crisis.[9] The multigenerational Eritrean community in contemporary Italy represents a powerful example of the complex and nonlinear ways that notions of identity, community, and borders have been increasingly compelled to respond to both legacies of colonialism and contemporary border management practices.

In 1869, an Italian commercial company (with the backing of the Italian government) purchased the town of Assab, located strategically on the Red Sea in what is now Eritrea. In 1882, control of Assab was formally handed over to the Italian state, marking the establishment of the first official Italian colony—hence Eritrea's nickname, *la colonia primogenita* (the first-born colony). Italy then took over the port of Massawa in 1885 with the support of the British, who so feared French expansion in the Horn of Africa after Egypt's defeat in the Ethiopian-Egyptian War that they were willing to violate their own treaty with the emperor of Ethiopia. Italy continued to seize land in the Horn of Africa, gradually piecing together the colony of Italian Somaliland. These territorial ambitions reached a temporary threshold in 1895, when Italy invaded Ethiopia but was soundly defeated by the armies of Ethiopian emperor Menelik II in 1896 at the Battle of Adwa.

By the 1880s, the Italian government had begun to launch large-scale infrastructural and development projects in the Horn of Africa. Nonetheless, living conditions for Eritreans under Italian rule remained among the poorest on the African continent.[10] Around this same time, Italians began to settle these newly colonized territories. From a few dozen settlements around the turn of the twentieth century, the white Italian population in Eritrea ballooned to approximately four thousand by the start of World War I, and to over seventy thousand settlers in 1939.[11]

A range of different forms of interracial interaction were common in the Italian colonies of the Horn of Africa, most notably the practice of *madamato*, or common-law relationships between Eritrean women and Italian men.[12] Yet, these interactions coexisted with everyday, legal, and spatial systems of separation, hierarchization, and violence deployed to maintain colonial control, as well as the widespread circulation of stereotypical (and in the case of women, hypersexualized) images of Blackness across Italy.[13] Italy also conscripted many of its colonial soldiers from Eritrea (the so-called *Ascari*, derived from the Arabic term *ascar*, or soldier).[14] These repressive conditions intensified under Fascism, when Italy reinvaded Ethiopia and declared the establishment of the Italian Empire (including Italian East Africa) in 1936.[15] During the Second Italo-Ethiopian War, for instance, Italian soldiers deployed chemical weapons and violently crushed anticolonial resistance.[16] The Fascist period was also marked by spatial apartheid and the enforcement of strict racial laws—including antimiscegenation policies.[17]

Following Italian defeat in World War II and the subsequent dissolution of the Italian Empire, historian Angelo Del Boca argues that "the Italian government not only eluded their obligations to clarity [about the realities of Italian colonialism] but actively impeded the emergence of truth."[18] Del Boca notes that for decades, the only systematic historical account of Italian colonialism was contained in an apologist fifty-volume series called *L'Italia in Africa*, published by the Italian Ministry of Foreign Affairs. These "definitive" texts (fifteen of the twenty members of the editorial committee were former colonial officials), he explains, simply reinforced the whitewashed narrative of *italiani, brava gente*, and argued that Italian colonialism was more benevolent than the colonial endeavors of other European countries.[19] While scholars inside and outside Italy have increasingly devoted critical attention to Italian colonialism, this subject continues to be neglected in formal school curricula and popular discussion in Italy. But the material and symbolic legacies of Italian colonialism endure, from widespread "racial clichés and prejudices" to the streets and monuments across Italy bearing names and symbols of former colonies to ongoing border conflicts between Eritrea and Ethiopia.[20]

Yet perhaps the most powerful and enduring legacy of Italian colonialism in the Horn of Africa has been the establishment of a large and vibrant Eritrean diaspora in Italy. It was not entirely uncommon for Ethiopians, Eritreans, and Somalis to travel to Italy during the colonial period. These voyages were facilitated in part by the presence of the Aeroporto Civile di Asmara, first established by the Italian colonial authorities in 1922 as a military airport. The Aeroporto Civile was one of the first airports built in the Horn of Africa and served as part of an international connection linking Mogadishu, Asmara, Khartoum, and Tripoli to Rome. But Italian decolonization after World War II also set into motion a new wave of migration across the Mediterranean from former colony to metropole. Yet, unlike countries such as France, Britain, or the Netherlands, which actively recruited a postcolonial labor force in the wake of World War II's economic collapse, Italy never implemented policies favoring or facilitating immigration from its former colonies, nor did it extend full citizenship to colonized (or formerly colonized) subjects.[21]

The first Eritreans to settle in Italy were largely women, who came to Italy in the 1960s and 1970s to work as in-home domestic workers—sometimes for the same white Italians they had served in the former colonies, after those families left the Horn of Africa.[22] The coup d'état of Mengistu Haile Mariam in 1974, and the subsequent intensification of conflict between Ethiopia and Eritrea, also catalyzed another wave of Eritrean emigration to Italy. This network of Eritreans in Italy assisted subsequent waves of Eritrean settlement in Italy during the war for independence and in the aftermath of the brutal Isaias Afwerki regime. While Eritreans currently make up only a small percentage of Italy's total African population, in the 1970s they constituted a significant portion of the country's burgeoning Black community.[23] In addition, many of the Eritreans who settled in Italy during this period were of mixed racial backgrounds, with a Black Eritrean mother and a white Italian father—the latter having returned to Italy without his Eritrean family and without formally recognizing his paternity.

The Eritreans who arrived in Italy during the second half of the twentieth century settled primarily in Milan and Rome and remain largely concentrated in these bustling metropolitan areas today. Indeed, while it is currently popular in Italy to speak about the fate of the so-called second generation, or children of immigrants, the Eritrean community is in many cases now in its *third* generation of residence in Italy. Because of this long physical presence, as well as their colonial connections, Eritreans often narrate their relationship to Italy in terms of shared language, culture, and sometimes lineage.[24] They constitute something akin to Homi Bhabha's mimic man: "almost the same, but not quite / white," a partial presence that both reproduces (post)colonial hierarchies and also threatens to rend them asunder. This is significant considering the legacy of one strand of Italian colonial racial theory, which posited that populations from the Horn of Africa were not Black Africans but descended from white Semites.[25]

These sorts of ambiguous proximities to Italian colonialism have also produced varying degrees of identification with Blackness among the Eritrean diaspora in Italy, and as a result have sometimes complicated their relationships with other African communities. A young Eritrean man who was born in Asmara but grew up in Milan explained it to me in this way: "The first generation [of Eritreans in Italy] would call people from Senegal *negro*. . . . We don't look like people from Senegal; we are Black, but with European features like yours [*he gestures at my face*], the narrow nose . . . we're not big and tall. The second generation gets along with all of the African communities—Senegalese, whatever, without problems. There is a symbiosis. Sports like basketball bring people together. That's the second generation." An event held in Milan during the spring of 2016 further illuminated these tensions. At a public forum on Black Italian cultural entrepreneurship, a heated debate erupted between a group of younger Black Italians and an older Eritrean woman. Following a presentation by a group of young Black women entrepreneurs with families from Haiti, Ghana, Nigeria, and Uganda, the Eritrean audience member stood to tell her story. In her mid-forties or early fifties, dressed in a red dress and a black cardigan, with a red-tinged bob and matching red lipstick, she cut an exceedingly elegant and regal figure. She explained that she had lived in Italy since 1976, but did not experience the sort of discrimination recounted by the young Black women who had spoken earlier. She told the audience that, while unfortunate to hear, their stories simply did not resonate with her own experiences as "an African woman in Italy." In fact, she noted, she had been hired for many high-profile positions, including an appointment at the Vatican in Rome.

As she spoke, the young Black Italian women who had presented earlier began to audibly sigh, grumble, and shake their heads in frustration. The forum had already run thirty minutes over schedule, and the room was quickly becoming stuffy as the afternoon sun filtered in through the windows. We were all sweating through our clothes, yet the audience was crackling with energy—this was quickly becoming the liveliest conversation of the day. The moderator struggled to keep up with the ensuing volley of comments, dashing back and forth across the spacious room with a cordless microphone in hand. An Italian-Haitian woman raised her hand and responded that different shades of skin color produce different levels of social acceptance in Italy—an implicit reference to the Eritrean woman's lighter complexion. The Italian-Congolese woman sitting next to her agreed, adding that in her opinion, Eritrean women enjoyed greater acceptance than women from other African countries. Yet, these differences aside, Eritreans in Italy also draw heavily on the cultural and political influences of the global Black diaspora—often in direct response to their experiences of state-sanctioned and everyday racisms.[26]

The density of the co-constitutive connections between the Horn of Africa and Italy also extends beyond the level of everyday experience to encompass postcolonial geopolitics. For instance, the annual Eritrean festivals held in Bologna were key sites in the international struggle for Eritrean independence, bringing together thousands of Eritreans from across Italy, Europe, the United States, and other countries around the world.[27] Indeed, anthropologist Victoria Bernal notes that at the time of Eritrean independence in 1991, one in three Eritreans (approximately one million people) lived outside of the country—many having taken up residence in Italy.[28]

These transnational connections certainly challenge the racialized notion of bounded national spaces, and of Europe and Africa as discrete and hermetically sealed geobodies. But the bureaucratization of the Italian immigration apparatus in the 1990s began to fragment this multiplicity of overlapping colonial, migratory, labor, and familial relations linking Eritrea to Italy. The institution of Italy's first comprehensive immigration laws, as well as the tightening of Italian citizenship law, helped to calcify distinctions between citizens and noncitizens, and between different legal categories of migrants. Among other new regulations, the Legge Martelli formalized visa requirements for noncitizens seeking to enter Italy for extended periods of stay.[29] Of course, this is not to idealize a period of (post)colonial cosmopolitanism and mobility between Italy and the Horn of Africa that never actually existed. Rather, I am suggesting that the underlying conditions of Eritreanness and Blackness in Italy shifted in important ways after the 1990s. In particular, the Italian state's interpellation of postcolonial subjects as "migrants" worked to further invisibilize the colonial past, obscuring the ways that Italian colonialism in North Africa and the Horn had laid the groundwork for a range of northward, cross-Mediterranean migrations in the late twentieth and early twenty-first centuries—what Derek Gregory calls the "colonial present."[30]

This sort of spatiotemporal disjuncture was brought to life in *S.I.C: Stranieri in casa* (Strangers at Home), a short independent film directed by Marco Luzzi and the Eritrean activist and social center / concert venue director Alem Abbai.[31] *S.I.C.* was filmed in Milan in 1998 and features a cast of amateur actors drawn from the city's tightly knit Eritrean community. In the film, a group of young Eritrean men and women leave a Milanese nightclub after an evening of revelry, only to be stopped by the police as potential suspects in a car robbery. The police officers order them to line up against a wall and demand that they produce identification documents. When several members of the group brandish their Italian identity cards, one officer responds suspiciously in an interpellative moment that is classically Althusserian: "You've been here for *how* long? And how is it that you have Italian citizenship?"[32]

The direct colonial relationship between Italy and the Horn of Africa, as well as the relatively long history of the Eritrean presence in Italy, distinguishes the Eritrean diaspora from other African communities in Italy. These characteristics are precisely what make the Eritrean diaspora such an important site for engaging with alternative responses to the refugee "crisis" in Italy. How does a Black community that has been firmly established in Italy for multiple generations respond to the arrival of large numbers of refugees who also share their same national background? How are the possibilities for political solidary conditioned by the imposition of legal, state-sanctioned categories? To what extent does citizenship status produce new divisions, and when can it instead facilitate transgressive acts of solidarity?

Tales from Porta Venezia and Beyond

The summer and fall of 2015 witnessed the worst refugee crisis in recent memory: nearly eight thousand people daily arrived to Europe, fleeing violence and upheaval in sub-Saharan Africa and the Middle East.[33] Italy—and specifically the tiny island of Lampedusa, located seventy miles away from Tunisia—was a key point of arrival for thousands of refugees and asylum seekers from Eritrea.[34] That same year, the Mediterranean Sea was designated "the most deadly sea crossing in the world" and "the most deadly border in the world."[35] By April, the official tally of deaths in the Mediterranean had surpassed seventeen hundred (for comparison, the total number of recorded fatalities by the end of April 2014 was ninety-six).[36] Italy had abandoned its Mare Nostrum maritime search-and-rescue program in 2014 to comply with the EU Triton border securitization operation, with the result that horrifying reports of refugee deaths at sea became a grim fixture in the summer news cycle.[37]

By the fall, large numbers of Eritreans who had survived the grueling Mediterranean crossing began to appear in Milan, most notably in the Eritrean neighborhood of Porta Venezia. The specific circumstances of those who had made it as far north as Milan varied widely. Most had arrived in Italy by sea, traveling across the desert to Libya and then traversing the Mediterranean by boat to land in Lampedusa or Sicily. By passing through Libya, a former Italian colony and one of the key transit nodes along the central Mediterranean migration route, Eritrean asylum seekers were actually retracing a much older Italian colonial route (see figure 5.1).

A fraction of those Eritreans who arrived in Sicily subsequently registered asylum applications with the Italian immigration authorities.[38] Those who did not go through these formal channels of international recognition effectively "disappeared" once they landed in Italy, using informal networks to gradually travel

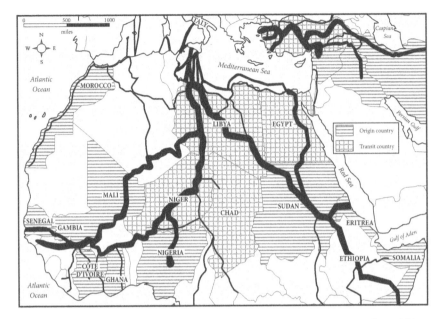

FIGURE 5.1. Map showing central Mediterranean migration routes from Africa to Italy. Thick lines represent more heavily traveled routes. Note that one route from Eritrea to Italy passes through Libya, another former Italian colony. Map by Mike Bechthold.

Source: European Political Strategy Centre (European Commission), "Irregular Migration via the Central Mediterranean," Strategic Notes 22 (February 2, 2017).

north in search of jobs and in some cases, family reunification. But even those who had filed applications (and whose applications were approved) found that compliance did not guarantee easier mobility within Europe. The European Union's Dublin Regulation states that asylum seekers must apply for refugee status in the first EU country they enter. This meant that Eritreans who landed in Italy were not allowed to apply for asylum anywhere outside Italy. Given the weak state of the Italian economy and the requirement that asylum seekers must wait for six months before they can access the Italian labor market, this meant that Eritrean migrants were effectively trapped in legal limbo. Unable to work and unable to leave Italy, the majority went underground, dropping out of the Italian asylum system in an attempt to travel clandestinely to more economically robust countries in northern Europe.[39] But whether they sought to stay in Italy or traveled onward to Germany or Sweden, Milan was a logical stopping point because of Porta Venezia's Eritrean community.[40]

Porta Venezia, located three metro stops northeast of the central Piazza Duomo, draws its name from the enormous stone gates built in the nineteenth century along the former medieval and Roman walls of the city. Lined with stately neoclassical and art nouveau palazzi, Porta Venezia's streets are now home to numerous Eritrean restaurants and cafés as well as nightclubs and underground clubs serving Milan's youthful, stylish set. The neighborhood has also become a major hub for Milan's queer community; it contains some of the city's most popular gay venues and also hosts Milan's annual pride parade. These same qualities have also spurred the rapid gentrification of Porta Venezia over the course of the last decade.[41]

Long-term Eritrean residents of Porta Venezia quickly took notice as refugees began sleeping on the streets and in nearby Montanelli Public Gardens and washing their bodies and clothes in public drinking fountains. These gardens were named after the famous Italian journalist and historian Indro Montanelli, and they are home to a towering bronze statue erected in his honor. Montanelli had volunteered in the Second Italo-Ethiopian War of 1935–36, and subsequently wrote a column about the conflict for the national Italian newspaper *Corriere della Sera*. Notably, for years Montanelli also denied the Italians' deployment of poisonous gas during the "pacification" of Libya and the Italian reinvasion of Ethiopia.[42] While in Ethiopia, he infamously purchased a twelve-year-old Eritrean girl as a "child bride," and until his death denied any allegations that this "relationship" constituted rape because, as he argued, "European" norms pertaining to childhood and sexuality simply did not apply in Africa.[43] The Montanelli Gardens thus formed a sort of unintentional imperial palimpsest, linking histories of Italian colonial violence with the postcolonial border violence of Italy and Fortress Europe.

Many of the refugees who began to gather in Porta Venezia had not eaten in days, and others bore visible injuries left over from their perilous journeys across the Sahara to Libya, and across the Mediterranean to Sicily. At first, reactions among the local Eritrean community to these newcomers were mixed. Some residents feared that these tattered and weathered new arrivals would damage the reputation of the neighborhood and jeopardize their already precarious standing in Milan. Yet others, who continued to support the Afwerki regime despite its track record of human rights abuses, saw these refugees as defectors who had betrayed the embattled cause of Eritrean nationalism and had instead taken up residence in the land of their former European colonizer. But most Porta Venezia residents responded to the influx of refugees from Eritrea by beginning to launch informal networks of support, collecting food and clothing, providing rudimentary first aid, and arranging places for refugees to sleep.

The everydayness of these efforts was both striking and inspiring. One evening in early 2016, I happened to be meeting an Eritrean friend from Porta Venezia for an *aperitivo* in the historic center of Milan. As we snacked on finger foods and sipped Aperol spritzes in a trendy bar atop a large department store, his cell phone started to ring. Our conversation paused as he answered the call, speaking quickly and seriously in Tigrinya. When he put down his phone, he explained that a woman had arrived in Milan from Eritrea six months ago and was stuck in a precarious housing situation with her brother. Reluctantly, he agreed to take her in because he had a spare couch in his apartment where she could sleep. Noting the look of surprise on my face—he had agreed to house a complete stranger over the course of a rapid-fire, two-minute phone call—he explained that these sorts of phone calls had become extremely common over the last several months. Members of the Eritrean community in Porta Venezia regularly reached out to friends and family to arrange temporary housing for those who had just arrived in Milan.

What is unique about these sorts of interventions in Porta Venezia is twofold. First, longtime Eritrean residents are subtly resisting the legally produced division between second-generation Black Italians and newly arrived refugees. Second, they are not working with an abstract subject of "human rights" in mind—the dominant framing of the southern European refugee emergency adopted by sympathetic, left-leaning organizations—but rather are engaging with Eritrean refugees through historically and geographically situated understandings of diaspora, urban inequality, postcolonialism, and Black Mediterranean interconnection.

In the section that follows, I trace the story of a group of Eritreans born and / or raised in Italy who, in 2013, began bringing meals to Eritrean migrants and refugees on the streets of Porta Venezia.[44] The group quickly grew into a "citizens' committee" that semiautonomously coordinated service provision for refugees in the neighborhood; as they began to formalize their structure, they took on the organizational name "Cambio Passo." I focus on the ways that two of the original Porta Venezia volunteers narrate their "strategic entanglements" with municipal and national politics, as well as the spatially extended obligations of diaspora. This is not intended to serve as an exhaustive account of the refugee crisis in Milan and of the city's various resettlement efforts.[45] Rather, I wish to engage with the ways certain Black refugee rights activists have thought through their own involvement in this "crisis" in relation to broader questions of citizenship, belonging, political subjectivity, and diaspora.

"To Porta Venezia They Only Sent the Police": Swerving Visibility and Representation

In July 2016, shortly after the gathering in Amsterdam I described at the beginning of this chapter, I met Medhin Paolos in Porta Venezia's sprawling Montanelli Public Gardens. Medhin had also been present for that heated exchange between Black European activists about citizenship and refugees, and I was eager to hear her own evaluation of the debate. As an Italian-Eritrean native of Porta Venezia, one of the founders of the Rete G2 (described in chapter 1), a student of Black radicalism, and an advocate for newly arrived Eritrean refugees in Milan, she seemed uniquely situated to think across these different strands of Black Italian mobilization.

After exchanging pleasantries near the gardens' graffiti-covered planetarium, we headed over to a patch of grass near a large wrought iron gazebo. Medhin produced a tie-dyed blanket out of her canvas bag, along with two cups and a plastic bottle of lukewarm but flavorful tea given to her by an Eritrean acquaintance. Medhin, whose long braids were tied back in a light blue scarf, gestured toward the gazebo in front of us while simultaneously swatting away aggressive tiger mosquitoes. The gazebo's dark balustrades were draped with a rainbow of clothes and linens—a zebra-striped towel, a blue shirt, white singlets. Next to the gazebo, an African man in a red t-shirt sat on a bench, nodding along to the music from his white earbuds. Nearby was a group of African men and women washing their feet and drinking water from a public fountain. This was a refugee encampment, Medhin explained. Some of the men looked to her to be Eritrean, but not all of them—Medhin was even fairly certain that she recognized some of them from her years of community organizing in the neighborhood.

Medhin explained that she became involved in refugee activism three years ago, as part of the original grassroots group of volunteers who had come together to provide care and advocate for refugees in Porta Venezia (some of whom later went on to found the group Cambio Passo). But when I asked Medhin if there were many *seconda generazione* like her who were involved in refugee activism, she shook her head. There was one exception, however: many Syrians who had grown up in Italy became involved in advocacy for Syrian refugees escaping civil war through the extensive network of Islamic organizations in Milan, including the Coordinamento Associazioni Islamiche di Milano (Coordination of Islamic Associations of Milan, or CAIM). CAIM's close connections to the municipality also ensured that the city of Milan was attuned to the needs of Syrian refugees.

But Medhin and several of her Eritrean friends soon noticed that the refugees from Eritrea—who lacked the same level of institutional recognition by city officials—had been largely sidelined in terms of service provision.[46] Indeed, some of the city's only official engagements with Porta Venezia during the refugee influx were conducted under the auspices of neighborhood security: the police regularly surveilled shops and restaurants in the neighborhood, issuing citations for cleanliness concerns and asking workers for their immigration documents without due cause. The assumption of the police, Medhin and others I spoke to concurred, was that Eritrean residents of Porta Venezia were harboring and possibly even exploiting refugees and irregular migrants.[47] Sordid stories of Eritrean smuggling rings in Milan belied a more mundane reality, one in which long time Porta Venezia residents were providing food and shelter (and sometimes arranging travel) for undocumented Eritreans. "The city of Milan *loves* to talk about how great it is with refugee resettlement," Medhin said sardonically, with an exaggerated sigh. "But the reality is that this is thanks to the mobilizations of its citizens."

Medhin's comment could at first glance be dismissed as a symptom of what anthropologist Andrea Muehlebach has characterized as "neoliberal morality," in which post-Fordism and the retreat of the Italian state have generated a voluntary labor regime in northern Italy that dovetails ambiguously with both Catholic and autonomist worker traditions.[48] The *modello lombardo del welfare* (Lombardian welfare model), Muehlebach argues, produces a normative citizen-subject who is responsible for producing social cohesion and public good. As Medhin explained, the initial goal of the volunteers was to first open a space that would provide services to Eritrean refugees, and then eventually hand the "keys" over to the city of Milan—until the volunteers realized how resource- and expertise-strapped the municipality actually was.

But while Muehlebach's study was conducted a mere ten metro stops away (in my neighborhood of Sesto San Giovanni), her story of neoliberal morality does not square neatly with the picture Medhin conjured of Porta Venezia. For one, neither those giving nor those receiving voluntary services fell within the normative scope of citizenship. Even for those who, like Medhin, were able to naturalize through Law No. 91/1992, at the level of daily interactions Black Italians were still not recognized as legitimate members of Italian society. In addition, the informal efforts of Porta Venezia's Eritrean residents were not always valued by municipal officials as signs of proper neoliberal morality, and in fact were often criminalized under the rubrics of "smuggling" or "human trafficking."[49] Indeed, these mutual aid projects were not so much about the social reproduction of abstract urban, regional, or national Italian space, but about the obligations of other kinds of affective ties and connections. Medhin explained:

> As the children of immigrants (or immigrants who have been in Italy for a long time), they can help more easily, even if they are not formal cultural mediators. It's not just a question of being able to speak the necessary languages, although that matters. I am not comfortable conversing in Tigrinya, but there is still some common ground. . . . I want to see more *seconda generazione* get involved because these people are their relatives. There are people who are arriving who are my age. If they

weren't Eritreans, I might not have gotten as involved doing this work. When you are in the story, it's hard *not* to care.

This did not mean that Medhin and the other volunteers were only preoccupied with the struggles of Eritrean refugees—rather, they welcomed anyone who came to them for assistance. Still, her experience as an Eritrean in diaspora, and the realization that she herself could have also been a refugee, galvanized her to "put her privilege to good use" by engaging in mutual aid and solidarity work.

Medhin was quick to note, however, that activism around citizenship reform was still important. At the practical level, she explained, it made sense for activists to focus on a specific, liberal policy intervention so as not to exhaust their limited energy, resources, and political goodwill. But at the "cultural level," as she put it, it was still possible for second-generation Black Italians to widen the scope of their concerns through the discursive production of shared interests between themselves and African refugees. In effect, Medhin was questioning the tightly bounded notion of "us" that drove the Black Italian activists in Amsterdam at the beginning of this chapter to distinguish themselves from newly arrived refugees. But this was a challenging tightrope walk to navigate, Medhin explained with great empathy, eyes narrowing behind her glasses:

> As far as the question of Blackness goes, our generation is still figuring it out. We've been going on this journey of identity, of trying to get documents, and so on. But there is a new risk—that whoever achieves a certain level of status will become part of the mainstream (even though we will always be Black). They acquire privilege, like expats compared to immigrants. It's a similar story with immigrants from southern Italy—they eventually achieved a certain status and now they have no more problems. It's the same narrative for the children of immigrants, except for the legal documents. But at the quotidian level, it's more or less the same. So the risk is that we will enter into the same mechanics as the other groups. . . . The citizenship discourse is glamorous; there are so many theses and events about the second generation. The risk is leaving out the newly arrived. Can you enlarge your circle of privilege, or will you do what those before you did? . . . A refugee who arrives when he is fifteen, because many are arriving when they are that young . . . I see him as a 2G, though with a different journey. This can't just end with me and my experiences.

Medhin described her commitment to both the citizenship and refugee struggles as one of articulating multiple (and sometimes, seemingly contradictory) entanglements. On the one hand, she explained, "I am trying to say that I am

Italian and this [citizenship] law should include me, to widen a community." But on the other hand, *not* being perceived as Italian could also help her when working with refugees. "So, you're a shape-shifter!" I exclaimed, both of us collapsing onto the tie-dyed blanket in raucous laughter. Medhin agreed: "You stretch your muscles based on what you have to do. It seems opportunistic, but we all do it. For instance, I have to be able to show the administration that I can speak to [the Eritrean refugees] in a way that they can't."

In adopting my characterization of herself as a shape-shifter, Medhin was not invoking a romanticized hybridity in which she could don and shed identities completely unencumbered by relations of power. Nor was she drawing on the liberal language of "free choice." Rather, she was attempting to explain the different political openings and closures that were generated by her strategic entanglements with the liberal and state-centric politics of national citizenship, the transnational politics of Blackness, and the postcolonial politics of the Eritrean diaspora in Italy. These are the same themes that Medhin explored in her successful independent documentary film with Alan Maglio, *Asmarina* (2015), which tells the story of the Eritrean community in Porta Venezia.[50] In fact, the final section of the documentary focuses specifically on the work of Medhin's generation to assist newly arrived Eritrean refugees. As she explained to me, while the film does address the various divisions that cut across Milan's Eritrean and Ethiopian communities, she added this section to the end of the film precisely to challenge the tendency (among both white and Black Italians) to separate the concerns of the second generation from those of refugees.

A couple of months later, I met with Rahel Sereke in the same public gardens in Porta Venezia. It was a temperate fall day; the summer humidity had finally broken and although it was sunny out, the air was no longer unbearably hot. We took a seat on a chipped green bench overlooking the gardens' pavilion and again watched as groups of Eritrean men strolled through the gardens, stopping to wash in a public fountain and hang their clothes to dry on the balustrades of the wrought iron gazebo. Rahel, also Eritrean, was born in Rome and raised by a white Italian family; she moved to Milan fifteen years ago to study urban planning at the Politecnico (Polytechnic University of Milan). She had worked for a time in Asmara as an urban planner, but ultimately returned to Italy when the political instability in Eritrea made her profession increasingly untenable.

Rahel was one of the founding members of Cambio Passo, along with Medhin. Several years ago, Rahel began working as a community organizer in Porta Venezia, where she brought together merchants from the neighborhood to challenge the criminalization of their informal *accoglienza* activities by local authorities.[51] Like Medhin, Rahel was also frustrated that these activities were regarded as little more than refugee exploitation. "I told city councilman [Pierfrancesco] Majorino that without the Eritrean community, there wouldn't be any refugee *accoglienza* in Milan," she said, scrunching her chin as if to emphasize her point. While there were reception centers in Milan where refugees could find shelter indoors, Eritreans were still disproportionately sleeping outside, for a variety of reasons: the centers did not have cultural mediators who spoke Tigrinya; the centers controlled their inhabitants' movements and daily activities in ways that were often highly restrictive and infantilizing; and those who had dropped out of the formal asylum system could not—or were afraid to—engage with certain Italian institutions. These concerns eventually laid the groundwork for Cambio Passo: "People like Medhin, mostly Eritreans and Ethiopians who were hanging out here, saw this problem. We saw groups, first ten of them, then twenty, then fifty, then one hundred in precarious conditions, skinny, poorly dressed, sick. So we began to activate our networks. The group started to converge daily on Porta Venezia to collect clothes, goods, and organize medical assistance. When the refugees were at Milano Centrale, the city provided *accoglienza*, but to Porta Venezia they sent the police."[52]

As Rahel explained, these community-based efforts often swerved the politics of representation. Unlike the Muslim community, which was comparatively well represented through formal associations by the centrist Partito Democratico, the Eritrean community did not have such strong connections to local government.[53] Syrians in particular were also perceived as white (or at the very least, white-adjacent), arriving in Italy with families and small children—factors that in practice seemed to outweigh any potential institutional Islamophobia. Islam has long occupied an ambivalent position in Euro-American racial discourse, higher in the civilizational hierarchy than Black Africans (who, in those same discourses, are *biologically* fixed as racially inferior), but nonetheless culturally suspect.[54] It was this same system traffic in racial / cultural meaning-making, for instance, that afforded Libyan Muslims—but not Black colonial subjects from the Horn of Africa—a qualified form of Italian citizenship in the Italian Empire (see chapter 3). Thus, at the height of the Mediterranean refugee crisis, Syrians were often popularly constructed as more sympathetic refugees than the "single young Black men" arriving from the Horn of Africa. From these conditions, a two-tiered system of refugee reception soon emerged in Milan: one for Arabs, and another for everyone else. When Rahel and her fellow members of Cambio Passo confronted municipal officials about this situation, they only demurred. "They were all just excuses," Rahel explained. "They said these people weren't planning to stay in Italy . . . one high-ranking official said that maybe Eritreans just prefer sleeping outside!"

Milan had already seen three housing occupations between 2004 and 2009, during which Somali, Eritrean, Ethiopian, and Sudanese migrants claimed housing by squatting in abandoned buildings. Yet, Black migrants and refugees were perpetually regarded as temporary and transient figures, not potential long-term residents and certainly not connected in any way to the longer history of the Italian nation. And even if these migrants did intend to leave economically stagnant Italy in search of greener pastures in northern Europe (as many certainly did), they were precluded from consideration because of dominant, sedentarist understandings of belonging. Ironically, they were trapped by the same spatial politics that were shaping the citizenship reform debates unfolding simultaneously in Italy: Black Italians were *also* regarded as perpetual migrants and outsiders, and they sought formal state recognition by asserting their claim based on the duration of their residency in Italy.

In this way, the Cambio Passo activists from Porta Venezia sought to call out the limits of the state's immigration apparatus, and specifically the way that the EU and Italian asylum systems intersected with municipal service provision to produce a situation of benign neglect at best, and slow violence at worst. Significantly, they were *not* seeking incorporation into the formal bureaucratic apparatus of *accoglienza*. While Cambio Passo's efforts filled in for the state's racialized neglect of Eritrean refugees, the group did so in a way that also subverted the state's very categories and systems of differentiation. Rahel believed (and I am strongly inclined to agree with her) that neither the institutional Left nor Right was invested in a broader sense of justice, and would never deign to challenge the state's restrictive migration and citizenship policies. "And as long as you define the problem like that," Rahel said, running her hands pensively along her braids, "I won't get involved." Several volunteers insisted against the institutionalization of Cambio Passo precisely because the group sought to engage tactically with the municipal apparatus in order to "legitimize spaces of pre-existing action" (and thus curtail policing). Indeed, the question of whether to establish Cambio Passo as an official *associazione* (voluntary association) was the subject of lengthy debate among the group's thirteen members. While Cambio Passo ultimately decided to formalize its structure, some of the group's members still contend that this choice has left them with somewhat less flexibility.

Today, Cambio Passo's efforts have shifted from a focus on new arrivals to a focus on refugees who are already in Milan. This is because the Italian government's crackdown on migrant rescue at sea, along with a new partnership with the Libyan coast guard to prevent migrants from leaving the North African shore, has curtailed new arrivals to Italy by 80 to 90 percent.[55] The group's volunteers are now working to help move Eritrean refugees out of underfunded, carceral reception centers; they also physically accompany refugees as they navigate labyrinthine webs of service provision in Milan. Cambio Passo's efforts have also taken on an increasingly transnational dimension, through collabo-

rations with groups outside of Italy to monitor humanitarian corridors and migrant travel routes and contest forcible repatriations.

Like Medhin, Rahel worried that the citizenship reform movement would fragment these tenuous connections between the Eritreans who had grown up in Italy and recently arrived refugees. I explained that I was interested in speaking to her precisely because so many Black Italians I had talked to were careful to emphasize their *difference* from refugees when presenting themselves to the Italian public. Rahel furrowed her brow, responding pointedly: "But this is a distinction produced by the society. This is the fear I have with the citizenship law—that it will cut the ties between immigrants and their children. This is a racist country, to the roots. There are so many distinctions, and now there are different levels, starting from those who are absolutely 'not integratable.'" Indeed, Rahel longed for a different understanding of citizenship that could hold together multiple, overlapping, and intersecting attachments. "Our ties are stronger than those of *volontarismo*," she said, echoing Medhin's comments from earlier. "Community ties are not so liquid. We can't just help for six months and then move on to something else." It is important to note here that Rahel was not simply replacing one narrow form of nationalism (Italian) for another (Eritrean). Quite the contrary: Rahel, Medhin, and many other organizers had in fact embraced the category *habesha* as a way of uniting Eritreans and Ethiopians in diaspora, and they did not actively distinguish between the two groups when conducting everyday outreach activities in Porta Venezia. This move represented a subtle way of undercutting the histories of betrayal and conflict stemming from the border disputes that were catalyzed by Italian colonialism in the Horn of Africa, producing a new kind of "us" based instead on shared diasporic roots and routes.

These engagements can be read as yet another way of understanding the contemporary conditions of Black Italianness. Both Medhin and Rahel emphasized the fact that Black Italians who were born and raised in Italy—those who were still not considered by society to be full Italian citizens—were the ones providing services for "uprooted" refugees who had been cast aside by the state, thus exposing the limits of liberal universalism. The connections they articulated to newly arrived refugees were framed in terms of postcolonial interconnection (what Olivia C. Harrison refers to as "transcolonial identification"), diaspora, and spatially extended kinship—not normative liberal European humanitarianism or neoliberal Italian voluntarism.[56] It is for this reason that Rahel dreams of eventually expanding the scope of Cambio Passo, using refugee *accoglienza* as a jumping-off point to engage other Black Italians in critical discussions about identity—for instance, by reading and reflecting on the autobiographies of immigrants. These sorts of gatherings, Rahel explained, could help

Black Italians come to terms with the multiple relations in which they are entangled, relations that render them "familiar strangers"—neither fully Italian nor immigrant.[57] Unlike the dominant framing of citizenship reform, this conceptualization of Blackness in Italy is not oriented on birthplace *or* culture, but on the intersections of what Rahel evocatively called "spaces of uncertainty."

Spaces of Uncertainty, From Emmanuel to Idy

While the previous section focused primarily on the narrations of two individuals, the reflections from Medhin and Rahel about Cambio Passo suggest that the interactions between second-generation Black Italians and newly arrived refugees can begin to produce spaces of rupture that trouble the assumptions and divisions embedded within state-sanctioned categories such as "migrant" and "citizen." Cambio Passo provides a provocative, albeit limited example of entanglement: Eritreans born and raised in Italy are exposing the limits of a liberal politics of recognition, but they are not disavowing engagements with the state altogether.

This does not mean, however, that the Italian-Eritrean activists are merely cynical and steely-eyed practitioners of "strategic cunning" or "pragmatic vision."[58] Their involvement in both citizenship reform and refugee *accoglienza* suggests that at the level of everyday practice, Black Italians are questioning the liberal promises of visibility, recognition, and citizenship—even as they are still compelled to respond to these same frameworks.[59] Their activities may not always read as clearly articulated political philosophies. Nonetheless, they reflect a preoccupation with the enactment of capaciously envisioned diasporic solidarities, along with a careful attention to the way that different Black subjects are situated in relation to the very categories they are putting into question. This ambivalence is captured in the self-reflexive question posed to me by an Italian-Eritrean journalist and citizenship reform activist: "Does it make sense to focus on the 'second generation' while [refugees] are dying?"

This kind of self-questioning among Black Italians may seem politically inconsequential because it does not call for a total revolution, comprising the complete eradication of nation-state borders and state categories. Indeed, there has recently been a vogue of sorts among scholars upholding the abstracted figure of the refugee as a symbol of political refusal who embodies an immanent radicalism deriving from his (and in these accounts, it is usually *his*) position within the exceptions of liberalism—as seen, for instance, in Agamben's controversial stance on Italian citizenship reform as described in chapter 1 of this book.[60] But beyond the fact that this approach commits narrative violence against the complex and varied stories of *actual* refugees, it also paradoxically upholds the same modernist vision of self-sovereignty and independence that these intellectuals are seeking to subvert through the refugee.

While the activists in this chapter have not extracted themselves from legal categories, we must remember to heed Stuart Hall's warning against mistaking "outcome" for "impact."[61] Black Italians are grappling with their entanglements in the liberal politics of recognition as well as other more transversal relations, and in navigating these "spaces of uncertainty" they have opened up new spaces of solidarity and care in the interstices of a moment characterized by widespread political immobility. Their ongoing actions provide one inspiring answer to the question raised by Gilmore about the constraints of recognition politics: "How do people actively come to identify in and act through a group such that its trajectory surpasses reinforcing characteristics . . . or protecting a fixed set of interests . . . and instead extends toward an evolving, purposeful social movement?"[62]

But what is happening beyond the old stone gates of Porta Venezia? The Eritrean community of Milan is a unique example because of its long colonial and postcolonial ties to the Italian nation. But are there other spaces in Italy where new understandings of Black Italianness are emerging that look beyond the liberal categories of citizenship? Earlier in this book, I discussed the wave of organizing and debates spurred by the death of Nigerian asylum seeker Emmanuel Chidi Nnamdi. I observed that this horrific event seemed to bring young Black Italians who were born in Italy and seeking recognition as *Italian* into direct conversation with Black migrants and refugees. But this opening proved to be short lived. At a protest in Rome the week following Nnamdi's murder, the old fault lines seemed to be cracking open once again.

About one hundred people had gathered under the beating sun in the Nicola Calipari Gardens of Piazza Vittorio Emanuele II on July 12, 2016. The crowd was arranged around a raised platform, and demonstrators could add their names to a list to deliver brief, impromptu speeches. While the majority of those present were white Italians, I recognized many familiar faces from among Rome's African associations, as well as the citizenship reform movement and the burgeoning Black Italian movement. One person in particular caught my eye: a Black Italian musician I had previously interviewed, dressed that day in a bright yellow top, with voluminous twists wrapped in an elaborate, colorful turban. She turned to me, a look of exasperation on her face: "I'm ready to leave." After listening to almost an hour of improvised speeches, she was certain that there was deep confusion about the purpose of this protest, and about the workings of racism in Italian society: "They're talking about refugees, but we live it differently as members of the second generation. [African migrants] experience racism when they arrive, but we live it every day, for twenty, thirty years here." Earlier that day, on the way to the protest, I had asked an Italian-Haitian journalist and a Cameroonian activist why it seemed that so few people were turning out for these demonstrations—and why so many Black Italians felt disconnected from these efforts. The Cameroonian activist noted, wistfully, that there had been an enormous march in Rome after the murder of Jerry Masslo in 1989. His journalist companion responded, with a sigh of resignation, "But that was a different time. There wasn't yet this media discourse of 'invasion.'"

Two years later, in 2018, Italy was embroiled yet again in racially charged national election campaigning. Political parties across the right-wing spectrum continued to direct everyday Italians' economic woes toward animosity against the scapegoat figure of the Black / African migrant, using the same rhetoric of invasion my journalist friend had lamented in 2016. Against this backdrop, on February 3 a twenty-eight-year-old white Italian man named Luca Traini (who had previously run for local office on a Lega Nord ticket) carried out a shooting spree against Black migrants in the central Italian town of Macerata.[63] Traini claimed that he was acting in retaliation for the death of an eighteen-year-old white Italian woman at the (alleged) hands of a Nigerian gang member; after the rampage, he wrapped himself in the Italian flag, raised his arm in the fascist Roman salute, and shouted "Viva l'Italia!" (Long Live Italy!).[64] While, miraculously, none of Traini's targets were killed, he injured five men and one woman—Black migrants from Nigeria, Ghana, Gambia, and Mali.

One month later, as Italians were waking up to the national election results, a sixty-five-year-old white Italian man in Florence shot and killed a Senegalese itinerant street vendor named Idy Diene. Roberto Pirrone was unemployed and had originally planned to commit suicide to relieve his family of the financial burden of his care; he ultimately decided to go out into the streets of Florence and kill the first person he encountered.[65] Yet, as additional reports of the murder surfaced, it became clear that Pirrone had actually crossed paths with a white Italian woman and her child *first*, and then decided to shoot Diene instead. In a cruel twist of fate, Diene's widow had also been the partner of Samb Modou, a Senegalese man who was killed in a racist attack in Florence in 2011 now known as the *Strage di Firenze*, or "Florence Massacre."

This series of explicitly anti-Black acts of violence prompted enormous demonstrations across Italy. But one moment in particular from a protest in Florence on March 11, 2018, stood out. A young Italian-Senegalese woman in a blue puffer coat inaugurated the event, standing against a somber gray sky. She began with her recollections of being a small child in 2011 and hearing the news of two Senegalese migrants being shot in the street "like animals." She remembered hoping to herself that this would be a one-time event, something that would never happen again. Her voice cracking, she described her subsequent horror on hearing the news from Macerata and then Florence: "I am afraid of walking through the streets because my skin is black. Those of us born and raised here, we all need to fight together." Applause erupted from the audience as she attempted to exit the stage. But the next speaker, an older Senegalese woman, summoned her back up. "I want to speak directly to you," said the older woman into the microphone, a supplicating tone of motherly compassion radiating from her voice. "You said you were born here. You said that you were afraid. But you were born here, and you have rights. If all of us are here," she said, gesturing to the hundreds of African men and woman gathered around them, "it means that we, too, are a part of this country. And we should not be afraid."[66]

The aftermath of Macerata and Florence suggests that once again, the intertwined crises of economic stagnation, refugee arrivals, and anti-Black violence may yet produce an opening for a new politics of Black solidarity that unites Black Italians, migrants, and refugees. Drawing on the insights of anthropologist David Scott, I am not arguing that Black activism around citizenship or national recognition is a fundamentally misguided project, but rather that these efforts represent tentative interventions into the particular, liberal-modern "problem space" into which Black Italians have been involuntarily conscripted.[67] But at the same time, events from Porta Venezia to Macerata to Florence suggest that this liberal frame is coming apart, and something yet to be determined is emerging in its place. The activities of Eritreans in Cambio Passo and the dialogue between two generations of Senegalese women in Florence are evidence of a multiplicity of efforts to craft new kinds of relations between mobility and membership, between citizenship and diaspora, and between rights and borders.

These moves, I suggest, are immanent expressions of a Black Mediterranean diasporic politics: of anti-racist struggle oriented not on the nexus of citizenship-integration-migration-xenophobia, but rather on the structural embeddedness of racism within postcolonial Italy. They provide alternative answers to the questions "What do we owe to one another?" and "From what bases do these obligations to one another extend?" As the examples from this chapter have shown, these ties of ethical obligation emerge not from the universalist presupposition of a shared human condition of vulnerability, nor from the racial-patriarchal "nation as family." They instead build on a radical tradition of coalitional politics that can itself be understood as a Black (as well as Black *feminist*) diasporic resource.[68]

In chapter 5 of *Dusk of Dawn* ("The Concept of Race"), W. E. B. Du Bois famously disavowed his earlier, German-Hegelian understanding of race as shared blood and spirit. "What is it between us that constitutes a tie which I can feel better than I can explain?" he asks.[69] What connected him to Africa, he realized, was not the color of his skin or the texture of his hair—it was a common history of struggle. "These ancestors of mine have suffered a common disaster and have one long memory," he wrote.[70] Moving away from arborescent family trees and blood kinship, Du Bois argued that while the actual ties of heritage might vary, this was actually less important than a (nonlinear, nonarborescent) form of kinship based on the shared social heritage of slavery and discrimination. And this notion of "social heritage" in turn allowed for more capacious practices of political community that had the potential to unite (in his words) "yellow Asia," the South Seas, and Africa. Du Bois's own life put this particular understanding of diasporic politics into practice. As Gilroy notes, Du Bois was above all a diasporic intellectual whose scholarly formation and political commitments were also forged through extensive travels in Europe, and particular via his philosophical studies in Germany, as he traversed the United States, the United Kingdom, continental Europe, and West Africa as a scholar-activist.

This sort of radical internationalist orientation has long been a hallmark of Black diasporic politics. The negritude movement championed by Aimé Césaire and Léopold Senghor in the 1930s similarly articulated diasporic solidarities that yoked together the Caribbean, France, and West Africa in circuits of anticolonial revolutionary praxis. And the Pan-Africanist conferences that took place over the first half of the twentieth century—of which Du Bois was also a key organizer—saw the forging of wide-reaching diasporic connections as Black activists came together in European metropoles (i.e., Paris, London, Manchester) to collectively diagnose shared conditions of racist injustice across a range of formerly and ongoing imperial sites.

The emergent diasporic politics of Black Italians are similarly oriented on shared trans-Mediterranean histories of racial dispossession rather than on naturalized notions of citizenship, birthplace, descent, culture, or territory. Italy after all, along with the rest of Europe, was complicit in the formation of a colonial, sociospatial racial order that served as the condition of possibility for restrictive demarcations of "Italianness" and for the racist violences of Fortress Europe.[71] These dense and power-laden webs of connection across the Mediterranean have been traced back and forth through the centuries by Italian colonial invaders and Eritrean domestic workers, by Nigerians crowded aboard barely seaworthy boats and forcibly removed through EU-sanctioned deportations. They echo (though they are not immediately reducible to) the Middle Passage, another violent sea passage etched into the geographical history of the Black diaspora.[72] But like the Black Atlantic, the Black Mediterranean is not only an archive of death, grief, and trauma. These interconnected spaces and histories—

the same ones that allowed a Senegalese woman in Florence to declare that, regardless of immigration status, *we are here and unafraid*—can also be read against the grain to summon wellsprings of hope and care. They are resources that will allow Italy's multigenerational Black community to imagine futures and craft spaces otherwise.

CONCLUSION

Looking South

In Naples they call me Zulù;
I arrived on a boat from Area Nord to the middle of Gesù.
The tattoo on my stomach says *terrone di merda*,
And I wear that blue-blooded name with pride.

. . .

But in Naples they already know this story.
Those elegant gentlemen who passed through here:
They called everyone who wasn't with them a *brigante*,
And cleansed with fire anyone who rebelled.

—Terroni Uniti, "Gente do sud"

It is well known what kind of ideology has been disseminated in myriad ways among the masses in the North, by the propagandists of the bourgeoisie: the South is the ball and chain which prevents the social development of Italy from progressing more rapidly; the Southerners are biologically inferior beings, semi-barbarians or total barbarians, by natural destiny; if the South is backward, the fault does not lie with the capitalist system or with any other historical cause, but with Nature, which has made the Southerners lazy, incapable, criminal and barbaric.

—Antonio Gramsci, "Some Aspects of the Southern Question"

In early March 2018, Italian voters were still rubbing their eyes in disbelief at the results of the country's recent parliamentary elections.[1] In a frightening parallel with the US presidential elections a year and a half earlier, center-right and far-right parties, along with the populist Movimento Cinque Stelle (M5S), swept both the Senate and the Chamber of Deputies.[2] Luigi Di Maio of M5S and Matteo Salvini of the Lega, two controversial figures previously considered to be political outsiders, had suddenly entered the mainstream.[3] M5S won 32 percent of the vote in the parliamentary elections, while the Lega claimed another 17.69 (almost 14 percentage points higher than their results in the previous elections).

For comparison, the centrist Partito Democratico (PD) saw a decline of 6.5 percentage points in its share of the vote, to a mere 18.9 percent. And this was no small shift—more than nine hundred parliamentary seats had been at stake that year.

The lead-up to the vote had been particularly grueling. Beyond the typical international ridicule that accompanies any mention of Italian politics, the electoral campaigning had taken on an undeniably racist and xenophobic tenor by the early spring of 2018. Politicians explicitly sought to channel the economic anxieties and frustrations of everyday white Italians into unbridled hostility toward African immigrants and refugees, resulting in the episodes of deadly racist violence described at the end of chapter 5. Political commentators around the world feigned surprise at the resurgence of far-right parties in Italy, chalking up this political tectonic shift to a groundswell of "anti-establishment" protest votes.[4] But in reality, the seeds of this neofascist resurgence had been planted over a century ago, in the very foundations of the liberal Italian racial state. They were then watered with the bloodletting of Italian colonialism. They were fertilized with the "racial evaporations" of post–World War II Italy, and again with the re-entrenchment of racist exclusion in post-1990s immigration and citizenship laws.

For many Black Italians, the election results were a source of deep pessimism, fear, and insecurity. Many of my friends spoke openly of being afraid to walk in public spaces for fear of their mere presence provoking racist aggression and violence. While many Black Italians and other children of immigrants had already begun emigrating out of Italy in search of better employment opportunities since at least the late 2000s, I heard more people than ever speak of leaving in search of safe havens abroad. There was nothing left for them in Italy, they seemed to be saying. One citizenship reform activist in Rome explained to me, with great sadness, that many of her comrades had become deeply depressed—between the double-punch of the citizenship reform bill's defeat and the recent election results, they were losing hope. She lamented that some of her longtime activist friends were making concrete plans to leave Italy for their parents' home countries.

But beyond this desire to emigrate, there is another significant geographical shift underway in the emergent Black Italia. I carried out the majority of the research for this book in major northern Italian cities, from Milan to Rome. The children of immigrants to Italy who have come of age in the last two decades reside primarily in these cities, which were major sites of industrial employment opportunities for migrants who arrived in the 1980s and 1990s. Even today, the majority of Italy's immigrant population (and their Italian-born children) resides in the North.[5] But as new arrivals—especially refugees and asylum seekers—are increasingly incorporated into the informal economies of southern Italy, there is now a growing (albeit younger) "second generation" of Black Italians in the South as well. In 2011, Istat found that since the Italian national census ten years prior, southern Italy had experienced the largest increase in foreign-born population of all Italian regions, though the vast majority of immigrants still live in northern and central Italy.[6]

While the explosion of a laboring migrant underclass in southern Italy has received significant attention in recent years—most notably in books such as Sagnet and Palmisano's *Ghetto Italia*—Black youth born in Italy have been largely neglected in these accounts.[7] Indeed, the 2016 citizenship reform flash mobs described in chapter 1 represented one of the first times that these types of mobilizations had taken place outside northern and central Italy. This can be explained in part by the fact that the children of immigrants in southern Italy are significantly younger on average than their counterparts in the North. But beyond that, life is also notably harder for Black youth living in this doubly marginal corner of Europe. As a Black Italian student activist from Palermo explained, "Palermo is a world apart. There is such a distance. There is some solitude—you feel foreign to the rest of Italy, and to the rest of the [second-generation activists'] network. You have to exert triple the effort." As one of the organizers of the flash mob in Palermo, she described an observer's surprise that citizenship activism extended to one of Italy's southernmost outposts: "Who would have thought that an idea that good could have come from someone in Palermo?" she was asked with incredulity. Young Black Italians like my friend in Palermo also intersect more directly with newly arrived migrants and refugees, generating a regionally distinct cauldron of racial and labor politics.

But what are the implications of this geographic shift for the various challenges facing Black Italy today? Without naturalizing southern Italy as a hybrid space of unrestricted mixing and racial boundary-crossing, I want to advance some tentative ideas about how the changing circumstances in the South may open up different sorts of Black political imaginaries and practices. I start by considering some of the distinct challenges Black youth in southern Italy face in this geographically, economically, and politically subordinated region of Italy, and the diverse political tactics and survival strategies they have adopted as a result. Like their counterparts in the North, Black Italians in southern Italy must also contend with the ambiguities of a liberal, rights-based framework of national citizenship. But Black Italians in the South are also multiply "southernized," and as such, they confront multiple, overlapping Gramscian Southern Questions: from the historical "internal colonization" and racialization of southern Italy by the North to Italy's own political-economic peripheralization in relation to northern Europe to the relative marginalization of Black Italians within the global currents of the Black diaspora.

The seemingly unique conditions of the South can actually offer powerful lessons for Italy, Europe, and beyond. In the tradition of radical Black Caribbeanist thought, I believe that a reorientation toward southern Italy—and the Black Mediterranean generally—has the potential to unsettle both hierarchical geographies and teleological narratives of liberalism and modernity. And this is a profoundly urgent task: As an Italian-Nigerian activist from Castel Volturno—a town outside Naples known as "the little Africa in Italy," famous as the place where Miriam Makeba held her final concert in honor of six West African immigrants massacred by the Camorra during the *Strage di San Gennaro*—told me gravely in 2016, "Questi sono anni difficili ma importanti."[8] These are difficult times, but they are important ones as well. They are important times precisely because the intensification of the deadly trifecta of nationalism, racism, and xenophobia has given Black politics in Italy a new urgency, galvanizing activists to defamiliarize taken-for-granted categories and develop new forms of diasporic community.

View(s) from the South(s)

In September 2016, I took the train south from Milan to Naples. Earlier that year, I had encountered a powerful video of an anti-racist performance organized in Naples in June 2015. In the widely circulated video that was posted to Facebook (see figure 6.1), twenty Black Italian activists from the group Culture Connection Castel Volturno marched into the historic center of Naples and, after a moment of deafening silence, declared in both English and Italian:

> In a non–colored man's country, we fight for equal rights.
> Silence.
> My silence is power; my silence rules.
> We are people.
> We are humans.
> We deserve equal rights.
> Tell me who you are and I will tell you who I am.
> My mind is powerful, strong, kind, generous, peaceful, soulful.
> We are genius.
> We are educated!

The aesthetics of the march seemed to have been influenced by the protest styles of #BlackLivesMatter, but I was curious to understand what had motivated this public action. I connected with one of the group's founders, James, an Italian-Nigerian jurisprudence student, actor, and model.[9] After a lengthy discussion

FIGURE 6.1.   Culture Connection C. V. activists in Naples.

Source: Culture Connection C. V. Facebook page (https://www.facebook.com/cultureconnectioncv/videos /1622609424618433/).

over coffee one afternoon in Naples, he agreed to show me around his home-town and introduce me to some of his friends and fellow activists.

The following day, a Saturday morning, I met James outside of his university, and together we hopped onto the M1 bus connecting Naples to Castel Volturno. The passengers on the bus that morning were primarily African men; as the bus lumbered north along the fifty-kilometer road, more and more people boarded until it was standing room only. Behind James, a man in a Rasta cap was dozing quietly, his head repeatedly nodding almost onto the shoulder of the person sit-ting next to him. As we drove past endless overgrown cornfields and the occa-sional hotel, more men in the back of the bus tried to catch quick catnaps. Every now and then, the bus would pause at an isolated stop for one of the riders to exit. This bus was an important conduit, James explained to me—it provided a link to work in Naples for people who lived in the adjacent province of Caserta. After about an hour, we finally arrived in Castel Volturno—specifically, at a stop marked by a red-and-black bench that had been installed as part of a mu-nicipal public arts project. Above the bench hung two colorful, mosaic-like metal panels, one of the African continent and another of a Black woman in hoop earrings and a towering head wrap (see figure 6.2).

James and I met up with his friend Susie, and the three of us made our way through town. We strolled down a street lined with African grocery stores and turned left onto a dusty, unpaved road that led through walled housing compounds. They pointed out one at the end of the road—the Centro Miriam Makeba. The Centro Makeba was founded in 2011 by a Ghanaian woman named Mary, three years after the death of Miriam Makeba in Castel Volturno. Makeba had become an important cultural and political icon for the city's large African

FIGURE 6.2. A bench at a bus stop in Castel Volturno.

Source: Author photo.

community because she performed her final concert here in solidarity with the West African workers who had been killed during the *Strage di San Gennaro*— there is even a monument dedicated to Makeba in town. Castel Volturno represents one of Makeba's several political connections to southern Europe—after all, her song "A Luta Continua" was inspired by the Mozambican struggle for independence from Portuguese colonialism.

The Centro Makeba itself comprises a colorful, two-story building and an oasis-like courtyard flanked by palm trees. Drapes made from African textiles hang from the open windows and flutter gracefully in the breeze. In the back of the building, Mary grows peppers, tomatoes, eggplants, fruit trees, sugar cane, and even a fledgling baobab tree. That day, the courtyard was filled with folding tables piled high with clothes that had been collected for African migrants. Mary explained that the following day was the anniversary of the *Strage di San Gennaro*, and so she was planning a ceremony for the city's African community. Through her work at the center, Mary also organizes workshops, community discussions, and concerts. On a typical day, however, the Centro Makeba serves as a tranquil meeting place for people of African descent to socialize—from recent West African migrants to Black youth who were born in Castel Volturno.

Inside the building, the walls were covered with posters of African leaders, descriptions of various plants and seeds, anticapitalist and anticolonial messages, motivational memes, and images of Bob Marley and Miriam Makeba. We were soon joined by James's sister Iris, and the four of us gathered in the kitchen to fry plantains and prepare an aromatic, spicy meat and tomato stew for lunch. As we cooked and snacked, James, Susie, and Iris (all of whom are university students in their late teens and early twenties) began to open up about everyday life in southern Italy. As we talked about the challenges of Black youth political organizing in Castel Volturno, my interlocutors oscillated between fond descriptions of the "sweetness" of southern Italians and Mediterranean culture and accounts of their own everyday experiences of brutal racism and misogynoir.[10]

"You know why the [Black Italian] movement is stronger in the North?" James had asked me earlier, during our bus ride from Naples. "It's because they are older. Only more recently are immigrants coming to the South, so the second generation here is young. The median age is ten to fifteen years old. I know someone who is twenty-eight, but that's about it." Indeed, there had been a trickle of African migrants coming to work in Castel Volturno as early as the 1970s and 1980s, many of whom had found jobs in construction. But in recent years, this trickle had expanded as increasing numbers of West African migrants fled economic and political instability in their home countries. Today, the employment opportunities in Castel Volturno are not as promising as they once were. As a result, Black immigrants are being inserted into exploitative, informal agricultural labor, as well as the organized crime–controlled sectors of the illicit economy. Indeed, while recent reports have shown that labor exploitation of migrants is a more significant problem in northern Italy than previously thought, there is still something of a broad (though by no means neat or exhaustive) geographical distinction between the cultures of Black entrepreneurship in northern Italy that I described in chapter 2 and the patterns of structural economic hyperexploitation that characterize Black labor in southern Italy.[11]

After we ate, Gabriela burst out of the building, white braids piled atop her head and wide eyes lined in electric blue. Gabriela is also a student and a close friend of James's—they first met when she organized an event at the Centro Makeba on the *seconda generazione* and citizenship. While her friends teasingly characterize her as *vivace* (lively), Gabriela's carefree attitude belies an incredibly sharp wit and acute political clarity. She began to tell me about her university studies in African postcolonial studies and a project she recently worked on related to trash collection in Castel Volturno. As Gabriela described it, the Black community in Castel Volturno was faced with multiple, overlapping forms of invisibility and nonrecognition. Beyond the children of African immigrants who are unable to obtain citizenship, Gabriela explained, thousands of people in Castel

Volturno are unaccounted for by the municipality, living in unregistered villas: "And how can you collect trash from a community that doesn't exist?"

These various scales of economic and social marginalization in southern Italy, and their deep historical antecedents in both Italian national unification and European colonialism, did not dissuade my interlocutors from political engagement. Gabriela and her friends are but a few of the Black activists in Italy who are beginning to rethink the possibilities of political resistance emanating from the South. To do this, they are drawing on the overlapping stories of southern Italian dispossession, migrant labor exploitation, and Black youth struggles for inclusion that have converged on places like Naples and Castel Volturno. But rather than deploy the historic marginalization of southern Italians to downplay anti-Black racism in the present, they are instead drawing on these parallels to activate new sorts of alliances: for instance, between Neapolitan university students and their Black Italian counterparts who are struggling to pay tuition in the wake of austerity and are taking on odd jobs to make ends meet; or between Black Italian youth and newly arrived African migrants who, in different ways, remain unseen by the state; or between migrant laborers and southern Italians fighting back against the stranglehold of organized crime. This articulation of radical solidarity between multiple Souths is grounded in the specific histories of nationalism, racism, and capitalism that have shaped Italy and the wider Mediterranean region—as well as the ways these categories have been multiply reconfigured from the Risorgimento through to the ongoing Mediterranean refugee "crises."

One example of this work has emerged from the musical collective Terroni Uniti, a supergroup of sorts comprising thirty well-known Neapolitan artists (see figure 6.3a).[12] The members of the group include white Italians, African immigrants, and "second-generation" Black youth, and through music they are attempting to craft a new form of political solidarity based on their shared "southernness."[13] Their single "Gente do sud" (People of the South in Neapolitan), quoted in the epigraph at the beginning of this chapter, identifies the singers in the collective as "people of the sea" who have shared—though not fully equivalent— histories of oppression, seafaring, border crossing, and resistance. The proceeds of their compilation were intended to benefit Watch the Med's Alarm Phone, a hotline for migrants and refugees traversing the Mediterranean.[14]

A similar artistic effort to rethink Italy and Italianness from the South can also be seen in the breathtaking work of Vhelade, a Sardinian-Congolese vocalist. She has described her debut album, *AfroSarda* (Afro-Sardinian, 2017), as an exploration of her two "motherlands"—Sardinia and Africa.[15] In the music video for the album's titular single, Vhelade dons traditional Sardinian folk costumes as she sings in front of famous archaeological sites such as the Tumba de Zigantes

(Giants' Tomb) and the Domus de Janas (House of Witches), surrounded by African animist dancers (see figure 6.3b). As she buries her hands in the white sand of a windswept beach, Vhelade metaphorically reconnects Sardinia and Africa, two spaces whose histories are profoundly entangled in the racial geographies of the Italian nation-state. After all, Sardinia was derided by nineteenth-century racial scientists after Italian national unification for being civilizationally backward, racially proximate to Africa, and in need of colonial forms of governance on the part of northern Italy. Stuart Hall even argued that Antonio Gramsci's upbringing in Sardinia profoundly shaped his approach to the relationships among region, class, culture, and nationalism in political struggle. This was because Sardinia, as Hall explained, "stood in a 'colonial' relationship to the Italian mainland."[16] As geographer Allan Pred writes,

> The social construction of space becomes one with the social construction of race. The now-segregated becomes the further racialized. Spatial meanings derived from racialization become racially reinscribed, the confirmation of racial difference. The physically Elsewhereized and Isolated become further discursively Othered. . . . Those exiled to enclaves beyond the metropolitan core become further scapegoated. Where you are becomes who you are, becomes how you are [under]classed. Yet another feat of ontological magic. Yet another dirty trick.[17]

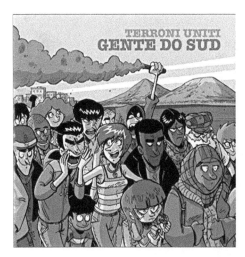

FIGURES 6.3A AND 6.3B. Left: Cover art for the Terroni Uniti single "Gente do sud." Right: Vhelade dons a traditional Sardinian folk costume for the *AfroSarda* music video.

Sources: "Terroni Uniti," Open DDB, https://www.openddb.it/artisti/terroni-uniti/ (left); "Vhelade–Afrosarda–Nalingi Yo (Official Video)," YouTube video, https://www.youtube.com/watch?v=4BYr85k7g2U (right).

But in *AfroSarda*, Vhelade wields the proximity of Sardinia and Africa transgressively, to help us demystify this "dirty trick": her easy, embodied slippage between her own Sardinian and Congolese heritages forces the viewer to confront the slipperiness of "Italianness" itself.

Reorienting the Geographies of Black Resistance

In contemporary Europe, it has become all too common to associate Blackness with death. Activists on the left repeatedly conjure ghastly images of boats of Black refugees capsizing in the Mediterranean, while at the same time, far-right xenophobes claim that an encroaching Blackness heralds the death of a racially pure Europe that never actually existed.[18] But to accept the facile equation that Blackness signifies only death is to concede to the very same chant that was hurled at Mario Balotelli, perhaps the most internationally famous Black Italian: "Non ci sono neri italiani!" (There are no Black Italians!). After all, as Katherine McKittrick powerfully reminds us, "Racial violences . . . shape, *but do not wholly define*, black worlds."[19]

Against such invocations of death and ontological nonbeing, this book has sought to show instead how an emergent Black Italy has formed and survived—even thrived—at a moment when the logics of Fortress Europe would have us believe that it should not exist at all. The mobilizations of Italian-born and -raised Black youth for national recognition, citizenship, and capacious non-national forms of racial justice have entailed complex negotiations of the boundaries of Italianness, Mediterraneanness, Europeanness, and Blackness. In some instances, these activists have been able to expand the boundaries of who "counts" as an Italian, beyond narrowly biological conceptions of race. At other times, they have become entangled in the process of rebounding Italianness on the basis of birthplace, economic productivity, or cosmopolitan connectivity. These ambiguous reconfigurations have sometimes inadvertently worked to generate racialized distinctions *within* Italy's Black community, pitting those born in Italy against the newly arrived. And as new forms of exclusion are continually reproduced within the seemingly color-blind category of "citizen," the meanings of race and Blackness in Italy continue to shift as well. But as Black youth seeking to deracialize the Italian nation are increasingly confronted with the limits of liberal citizenship at a time of rising ethnonationalism, they have also turned toward other sorts of political imaginaries and practices. Indeed, Black Italians are increasingly looking *beyond* the nation-state, tentatively exploring the new political formations that emerge from their own strategic entanglements not only with the politics of liberalism, but also with more capacious African and Black Mediterranean diasporas.

While this book has focused primarily on Black Italian activism in northern Italy, I turn my gaze toward the South here because it offers rich opportunities for further reflection. This account is not meant to be exhaustive or conclusive—instead, I want to offer a set of questions. After all, southern Europe is now becoming a hothouse for the many, seemingly apocalyptic forces shaping our present: from economic precarity and austerity to ethnonationalism and fascism to global mass migrations met by deadly border regimes and walls. And southern Italy *in particular* provides an oft-overlooked window into the overlapping systems of racial nationalism, border fortification, and labor exploitation that have shaped our modern world.

Many of the questions about race and the intertwined politics of Blackness and southernness facing Black youth in the Mezzogiorno parallel ones that have been taken up by intellectuals working in the long tradition of radical Black Caribbeanist thought. Indeed, the Mediterranean shares many geographical, political, economic, and social characteristics with the Caribbean. Most strikingly, both seas are upheld as spaces of interconnection that have been profoundly shaped by processes of mixing, hybridity, *métissage*, or creolization—histories that are inextricable from extreme forms of racial-capitalist and gendered violence. And just as the writings of intellectuals such as C. L. R. James, Frantz Fanon, and Sylvia Wynter emerged from a moment of political emancipation across the global African diaspora, the current unfolding of Black Mediterranean politics has been shaped by emancipatory visions intended to challenge various forms of racist violence along Europe's southern shores.[20] So what sorts of transgressive knowledges from the Caribbean can be "made to the measure" of the contemporary Mediterranean?[21] In *European Others*, Fatima El-Tayeb argues that Caribbean theories of creolization offer powerful analytical tools for mediating between the uncritical imposition of US understandings of racism on the one hand, and the assumption of European "raceless" universalism on the other.[22] This is because Caribbean discourses on race, nation, gender, and sexuality emphasize the *relationality* of "specific circumstances and universal conditions, local applications and global connections."[23]

The Caribbean and its relationship to the Black Radical Tradition have also provided a way to "provincialize" linear, diffusionist stories of European capitalist modernity.[24] Thinkers from Sidney Mintz to Edwidge Danticat have attempted to reorient world history on the islands of the Caribbean, "places where phenomena we think of as belonging to our own age—mass migration and mass industry and transcontinental trade—have been facts of life for centuries."[25] According to C.L.R. James's 1963 appendix to *The Black Jacobins*, for

instance, the brutal, racial political economy based on the transnational sugar trade thrust enslaved Black folk into "a life that was in its essence a modern life."[26] Just as Paul Gilroy later crafted a counternarrative of modernity based in the foundational violence of the transatlantic slave trade in *The Black Atlantic*, James's location of modernity in the particular socioeconomic relations of the seventeenth-century West Indies became central to anti- and postcolonial claims about modernity and the position of Black life specifically within the West, liberalism, and capitalism.[27]

But what happens when we reorient the story once again—this time to the Mediterranean? This does not mean succumbing to the historiographical retconning that served to construct the Mediterranean of antiquity as the cradle of a white, Western, and Christian European civilization. Rather, it means acknowledging that the Mediterranean Sea (like the Caribbean Sea and the Atlantic Ocean) can serve as one of many rhizomatic starting points for telling different kinds of stories about modernity, racial capitalism, and even Blackness itself.

In *Poetics of Relation*, Édouard Glissant described the Caribbean archipelago as emblematic of the idea of "Relation." He even explicitly contrasted the Caribbean to the Mediterranean: "Compared to the Mediterranean, which is an inner sea surrounded by lands, a sea that concentrates (in Greek, Hebrew, and Latin antiquity and later in the emergence of Islam, imposing the thought of the One), the Caribbean is, in contrast, a sea that explodes the scattered lands into an arc. A sea that diffracts."[28] But what if, in an expansive and reparative rereading of Glissant, we were to think the Mediterranean differently—not as an empty expanse hemmed in by land, but as full of contradictory and interrelated meanings, place-making practices, subjectivities, and struggles?[29] For Glissant, the Mediterranean's almost claustrophobic geography is generative of monotheistic religions, ontologies of boundedness, and the overwhelming will to annihilate difference ("the One").[30] But we can *also* read the Mediterranean as a site of relation—as another explosive archipelago of porosity that throws into question the pretension of unitary and totalitarian identities and histories.

And just as writers from the Caribbean have attended to the poetics and world-making practices that emerge from conditions of horrific violence and domination, we are also witnessing radical new political formations emerging from the Mediterranean. Caribbean intellectuals from C.L.R. James to Édouard Glissant to Françoise Vergès to Sylvia Wynter have grappled with the "composite reality" of Caribbean societies—with the ways that diverse groups, languages, religions, and cultural practices have come together under conditions of extreme exploitation and dispossession to collectively generate new, durable forms of life.[31] Even Stuart Hall used his experiences of hybridity and creolization in Jamaica as analytics to understand debates about multiculturalism and racism in Europe. Similar sorts of claims about the relationship between racist violence and creolization can be made for the Mediterranean today—which is why I understand the Black Mediterranean as simultaneously a descriptive project, an analytic, and (perhaps most importantly) an ethical demand.

Echoing my engagements with Cedric Robinson's *Black Marxism* in chapter 4, we can no longer approach the Black Mediterranean as a (now-defunct) precondition for a racial capitalist order centered on the North Atlantic. Nor is it sufficient to approach the dynamics of the contemporary Mediterranean as merely derivative of Black Atlantic afterlives of slavery. Instead, it is urgent to study the *ongoing* reproductions of the Black Mediterranean in the present, along with all of its ongoing, nonlinear articulations with the Black Atlantic (as well as the Black Pacific and the Black Indian Ocean). Doing so requires engaging with a broad and unconventional archive that includes the experiences and testimonies of activists, popular and material culture, digital media, and literature—as well as traditional historical archives that are read against the grain. But in this way, we can begin to shift our stories of Black resistance to one of the spaces where liberal assumptions of equality, citizenship, freedom, and postracialism are perhaps most obviously and dramatically beginning to fray. After the 2018 elections, Matteo Salvini, then deputy prime minister and minister of the interior, enacted additional restrictions on the acquisition of Italian citizenship, further criminalized the activities of NGO rescue boats assisting migrants in the Mediterranean, closed refugee camps and assistance centers, and cut off access to a range of public services and programs for migrants.[32] Although the Salvini government collapsed in August 2019, there is no sign that this trend will abate.[33]

But where the fabric is fraying, something new is emerging. Since I began this research in 2012–13, Black Italians have continued to mobilize and raise their voices in movements that include and stretch beyond national citizenship. And we have much to learn from them. In the Black Mediterranean, we can clearly see that immigrants' rights and postcolonial struggles are not separate from the project of Black liberation; that "identity" and political economy do not exist on separate planes; that multicultural mixing and state recognition do not automatically beget justice. For these reasons, I believe that the political practices and solidarities emerging from Black youth spaces in southern Italy will inform struggles and strategies elsewhere in the world during this profoundly critical moment—an interregnum, a time of monsters. The entangled, nested, and overlapping geographies of southern Europe—from the Mediterranean to Italy to the Mezzogiorno to Sicily and Sardinia to Lampedusa—offer lessons in the spatial reproductions of racisms and nationalisms, as well as the possibilities of transgressive solidarity.

CODA

On February 3, 2020, I flew from California to New York for a presentation of the book *Future: Il domani narrato dale voce di oggi* (Futures: Tomorrow Narrated by the Voices of Today) at the Calandra Institute of Italian American Studies at Queens College.[1] *Future*, edited by Igiaba Scego, was the first-ever Italian-language collection of writing by Black Italian women; I had the honor of writing the book's preface. I was met in New York by Angelica Pesarini and Marie Moïse, both of whom had flown to New York City from Italy to discuss the short stories they had contributed to the volume, and Candice Whitney, who had written an English-language review of the volume and was currently in the process of translating it into English.

The trip was a thrilling whirlwind, the four of us buoyed by the excitement of this cross-country and transnational reunion of beloved comrades. In addition to attending a successful (and over-capacity) public presentation of the book at the Calandra Institute—the volume's official "launch" in the United States—we spent three days exploring the many confluences of Black and Italian cultures in New York City. We chatted up Italian waiters in the Financial District, debated the legacy of Cesare Lombroso over dinner with a group of Italian studies professors, devoured Cajun food in Tribeca, and paid our respects at the African Burial Ground National Monument.

At the end of the trip, I returned to Santa Cruz, and Angelica and Marie flew back to Italy. Just over two weeks later, Italy recorded its first COVID-19–related deaths. On March 9, 2020, Italian prime minister Giuseppe Conte announced a mandatory lockdown for the entire country. Supermarkets and pharmacies were among the only businesses that could remain open; all residents were strictly required to remain at home, except to carry out essential activities such as grocery shopping. I watched from afar as the novel coronavirus tore through Italy, and it seemed as though those beautiful days in New York had taken place in an alternate reality, or a beautiful dream. I received regular dispatches over WhatsApp from Angelica, who—just weeks after her trip to the United States— was now trapped in her apartment in Florence, watching her neighbors fall ill to the virus. This disjuncture was even more striking because while the death toll in Italy continued to mount and the Italian government was adopting increasingly rigid quarantine measures, the United States had not yet fully come to terms with the deadliness of COVID-19. The devastation in Italy seemed to provide an ominous porthole view into the future—a terrifying glimpse of what was to come as the pandemic began to spread across the United States.

The sites in Italy where I conducted my research have been among the hardest hit by the COVID-19 pandemic. In the region of Lombardy, where most of my Italian family lives, over thirty-four thousand people have died from the virus at the time of my writing in October 2021 (the pandemic has claimed over one hundred and thirty thousand lives in Italy so far).[2] The sound of ambulance sirens became a constant backdrop to daily life; army trucks were deployed to remove coffins from over-capacity morgues and crematoriums for storage in remote, refrigerated shipping containers; mayors turned into micro-celebrities on social media for berating constituents caught taking superfluous walks outside; and neighbors in lockdown performed music for each other from their socially distant balconies.

It is not surprising that Italy's immigrant communities have been impacted by the pandemic on multiple levels. While a 2020 Fondazione ISMU report shows that some immigrant communities experienced higher COVID-19 infection rates than the general population (for instance, Peruvians and Ecuadorians in the Lombardy region), this data includes only cases that were reported to the Italian National Institute of Health, and for which nationality data was available.[3] This suggests that we have not even begun to scratch the surface of the impact of COVID-19 on some of the most vulnerable communities in Italy—namely, undocumented immigrants, refugees, and asylum seekers. Indeed, migrants and those working in solidarity with them have raised alarms about the spread of COVID-19 in immigrant detention centers, as well as the quarantining of asylum seekers on offshore boats.[4] These discussions parallel similar ones unfolding in the United States about the urgency of decarceration as a response to the deadly spread of COVID-19 in jails and prisons.[5]

While northern Italy has borne the brunt of the COVID-19 pandemic, southern Italy has by no means been immune. In southern Italy, concerns about restrictions on mobility and the closure of borders in response to the pandemic prompted agricultural lobbies to demand the implementation of "green corridors" to facilitate the movement of migrant labor across the country—a disturbing appropriation of the language of "humanitarian corridors" popularized during the migrant crises to assist the movement of refugees across borders. These efforts ultimately culminated in the announcement of a six-month, partial amnesty for two hundred thousand undocumented immigrants working in the agricultural and fishing industries. This move was praised by many observers as a positive step, one that would curb some of the most egregious abuses committed against undocumented workers. Italy's minister of agriculture, the former trade unionist Teresa Bellanova, declared that this move would make "the invisible . . . become less invisible."[6] Migrants' rights activists, however, raised concerns that this temporary amnesty would only subject precarious immigrant laborers to new forms of state surveillance and regulations on their mobility (this time, under the guise of containing COVID-19)—yet another example of the double-edged sword of state recognition and visibility.[7] In addition, these activists have drawn attention to how the dynamics of racial capitalism have once again led to the determination of who "counts" as a worthy, rights-bearing subject based on racialized notions of economic productivity.

The COVID-19 pandemic in Italy also reignited racist fears of transnational contamination—the same xenophobic sentiments that have spurred such virulent backlashes against immigrants, refugees, and their children in Italy. What former US president Donald Trump derisively referred to as the "China virus" contributed to a spike in anti-Asian racism across Italy—even though one of the earliest recorded cases of COVID-19 in Italy was from a *white* Italian man who had traveled to Wuhan, China, and brought the virus back to Italy with him.[8] In fact, while the Chinese community in Italy is disproportionately concentrated in Lombardy (Milan's Chinatown, established in the 1920s, is the oldest and largest Chinese neighborhood in Italy), their rates of COVID-19 infection (0.3 cases per 1,000) were among the lowest of any national group in Italy—including Italian citizens.[9]

Before the pandemic reached Italy, a new wave of anti-racist activism had swept the country in response to the explicit xenophobia of Matteo Salvini's right-wing government. Calling themselves the *sardine* (Sardines) because of their strategy of packing as many protesters as possible into public spaces, thousands of Italians descended on the main square of Bologna, and later in additional towns across Italy, from the fall of 2020 through early 2021 to condemn racism and populism. While the *movimento delle sardine* (Sardines movement) received international attention, and even inspired similar protests in other countries, this movement was also rightfully criticized for its nonpartisan approach, undemocratic leadership structure (particularly for a group initially described as "grassroots"), and general unwillingness to take clear, explicit stances on policies and laws criminal-izing immigration to Italy.[10]

In response to the liberal anti-racism of the Sardines movement, another group soon emerged in Naples called the *sardine nere* (Black Sardines), composed of African migrants who had originally been denied the opportunity to speak at a Sardines demonstration in Naples. Through a productively agonistic rela-tionship with the mainstream Sardines movement, the Black Sardines advanced an alternative analysis of racism as *structural* (rather than mere populist *rhe-toric*), illuminating the reproduction of racisms through border fortification in their demands for the regularization of their immigration status and a repeal of the 2019 "security decree" that further criminalized undocumented migrants and asylum seekers.[11] But because both of these movements were focused on physical proximity and the dense occupation of public spaces, the COVID-19 pandemic quickly caused them to lose momentum. Indeed, as Italians went into lockdown and everyday life was increasingly consumed with the "new normal" of the pandemic, the massive upwelling of protest surrounding Salvini seemed to fall into a lull.

On May 25, 2020, a Black American man, George Floyd, was murdered in broad daylight by a police officer in Minneapolis, Minnesota. His death, along with the murders of Ahmaud Arbery, Breonna Taylor, Nina Pop, James Scur-lock, Tony McDade, David McAtee, and many others, relit a spark in the United States—the flames of which quickly fanned out to Italy. And this upwelling of protests cannot be understood separately from the pandemic. It was a powerful response to the sense of atomization and social isolation of shelter-in-place orders, and it also reflected a general sense of Blackness being under siege from all angles, including from those institutions that are commonly understood as sources of safety and care—from the police to the medical establishment. The disproportionately high COVID-19 death rate among Black Americans, along with highly visible cases of murder by police (or, in the case of Arbery, by a for-mer police officer), brought into sharp relief the necropolitical regimes that con-stitute liberal modernity.

As I discussed in chapter 2 of this book, the Black Lives Matter protests of the summer of 2020 were not the first time that the Black Lives Matter move-ment had "gone global." Nonetheless, there was still something distinct about the way the banner of Black Lives Matter was taken up by Black activists in Italy in 2020. My comrades who participated in the demonstrations in Milan, where thousands of protesters descended into the streets, said that they had never be-fore participated in or even witnessed an anti-racist action in Italy of that mag-nitude.[12] While the demonstrations across Italy were frequently characterized in the Italian press as rallies for George Floyd in solidarity with Black Americans, they were also about drawing attention to Italy's many own "George Floyds." Indeed, some protesters even carried signs that declared, "l'Italia non è innocente"—Italy is not innocent. The Black Lives Matter demonstrations that spread across Italy during the summer of 2020 also renewed conversations about the legacies of Italian colonialism in Africa. Just as Black Lives Matter in the United States re-energized efforts to remove Confederate monuments and statues of Columbus in the United States, the protests in Italy also helped to draw attention to the monumentalization of Indro Montanelli in Milan (discussed in chapter 5).[13]

At the same time, we should be careful not to assume that Black Lives Matter simply emanated outward from the United States in a sort of linear, transnational diffusion of diasporic resources—a perspective that implicitly, and mistakenly, assumes that Black Italians did not (or could not) reach proper Black political consciousness until they were given direction by Black Americans. While the diasporic circulation of culture, ideas, and political strategies has undoubtedly shaped the politicization of Black Italians, it is also the case that there have been many generations of Black struggle across Italy and the Black Mediterranean, including resistance to Italian colonialism in Africa. Black Italy is not an offshoot, nor is it derivative.

Yet, the ways that Black Italians have taken up the banner of Black Lives Matter raise the question of what this call means specifically in the Italian context. While immigrants (including African immigrants) are overrepresented in Italian prisons, police violence and incarceration have not been the primary focus of the movement in Italy.[14] Instead, activists have drawn connections between Black Lives Matter and the citizenship reform movement, positing that racialized citizenship in Italy is a chief way that Black lives are structurally and systematically "unmattered."[15] At the same time, Angelica Pesarini warns that

> it is essential not to separate [the citizenship] struggle from the question of immigration—the militarization and racialization of the Mediterranean border, a neoliberal process that filters access based on the color of one's passport. And sometimes, not even a passport with the "right" color can protect our bodies from racist violence. . . . It is necessary to be aware of our own positionality and privilege. When we say "Black Lives Matter" in Italy, we cannot only be thinking about those people who were born in this country, or who arrived as "documented" immigrants.[16]

While abolition, as both a political demand and framework for radical world-making, has become part of the mainstream lexicon in the United States since the summer of 2020, this concept has not yet been taken up to the same extent in Italy. Yet, it is easy to image abolitionist demands from Black Italy that center on the abolition of the violent border regimes of Fortress Europe, the abolition of immigrant detention, and even the abolition of citizenship itself as a means of conferring rights, recognition, mobility, and personhood.[17] This, I believe, is the greatest lesson Black Italy—and the wider Black Mediterranean—has to offer in this moment of global Black uprisings. Because most Black Italians are also postcolonial subjects who have intergenerational experiences with border violence and exploitative labor regimes, their mobilizations necessarily link together struggles against racism, borders, coloniality, and capitalism. The remarkable florescence of Black Lives Matter in Italy thus reminds us that any movement for substantive racial justice—one that seeks to build a world based on the radical understanding that, as Ruth Wilson Gilmore says, "Where life is precious, life is precious"—must also contend with, and seek to dismantle, the deadly entanglements of racial capitalism, border fortification, and coloniality.[18]

METHODOLOGICAL APPENDIX

I briefly sketched my methodological approaches in the introduction to this book; however, I have included this methodological appendix to more thoroughly flesh out my fieldwork practice. I recall that during the first half of my time in graduate school, I would typically read ethnographic texts in graduate seminars with the goal of zeroing in on their central theoretical interventions. It was only later, when I was planning my own fieldwork and, subsequently, attempting to write a dissertation, that I returned to these beloved texts with an eye toward the way their authors stitched together elegant and apparently seamless narratives out of empirical data—and only *then* leveraged those insights into contributions to theory. In the spirit of that sort of demystification, I share how this process worked for me in the crafting of this monograph.

Research Timeline

I began this project in 2012, when I started the PhD program in geography at UC Berkeley. At the time, I was keenly interested in the ways that West African immigrants in Italy made use of digital technologies to reinforce transnational diasporic networks and also navigate structural racism in Italy. I spent the summer of 2013 in Italy with the goal of conducting preliminary fieldwork on these questions; it was then that I first learned about the citizenship reform movement in Italy, and this completely changed the course of my research. I returned to Italy for the summer of 2014 and began conducting more interviews with citizenship reform activists, cultural workers, and entrepreneurs across a number of Italian cities such as Milan and Rome.

In January 2016, I moved to Sesto San Giovanni (next door to Milan), which became my home base for a year. This was when I conducted the bulk of the ethnographic and archival research for my dissertation and, eventually, the book you are currently reading. That year, I also formally affiliated with the department of philosophy, sociology, education, and applied psychology at the University of Padua (under the mentorship of Dr. Annalisa Frisina), an opportunity that also provided me with a valuable source of academic community and comradeship. I subsequently returned to Italy during the summers of 2017, 2018, and 2019 to conduct additional follow-up research.

Methods

In the writing of this book, I drew from four key sources of empirical data: archival research; media and policy analysis; semistructured and unstructured interviews; and participant observation. I discuss each of these elements in greater detail below.

ARCHIVAL RESEARCH

While I am not trained as an historian, during my fieldwork I repeatedly encountered moments of "pushback" from some of my white Italian interlocutors, who fervently asserted to me that Italy did not have a history of racism on the scale of the United States, and that to talk about racism as such was to impose a distinctly "American" problem onto the Italian context. As such, I became invested in developing my own deeper understanding of the specific histories of race-making within Italy, and especially how notions of Mediterraneanism were mobilized in the past and still continue to resurface today in contemporary Italy as a way of explaining "difference."

My first stop was the Archivio Lombroso at the University of Turin's Archivio del Museo di Antropologia Criminale "Cesare Lombroso." Archivist Cristina Cilli provided incredible guidance and direction as we collectively read "between the lines" of the files and folders in the archive to identify reports, articles, letters, and notes pertaining specifically to Lombroso's racial theorization and their national (and even global) influence. Giacomo Giacobini, scientific director of the neighboring Archivio del Museo di Anatomia Umana "Luigi Rolando" also provided invaluable historical context for Lombroso's ideas by situating him in relationship to many of his contemporary scientists (like Carlo Giacomini). Drs.

Cilli and Giacobini subsequently connected me to Dr. Gianluigi Mangiapane at the Archivio del Museo di Antropologia ed Etnografia at the University of Turin, who had been collecting and organizing the papers of the museum's founder, Fascist-era anthropologist Giovanni Marro. The researchers in Turin also put me in touch with Giorgio Manzi of the Italian Institute of Anthropology (founded by Giuseppe Sergi, as I mentioned in chapter 3), where I received a private tour of Sergi's scientific collections, borrowed an original copy of *The Mediterranean Race*, and interviewed Dr. Giovanni Destro Bisol about the institute's ongoing research into human genetic diversity.

In addition to this archival research, I also spent time at a number of specialized Italian libraries with resources specifically dedicated to the topic of immigration and cultural diversity in Italy, including the Centro Studi Emigrazione—Roma (CSER), the Fondazione Iniziative e Studi sulla Multietnicità (ISMU), and the Biblioteca della Camera dei Deputati.

MEDIA AND POLICY ANALYSIS

From 2012 to 2019, I collected mainstream newspaper and magazine articles, blog posts, public social media posts, YouTube videos, and other cultural artifacts to track the growing prominence of "Black Italian" or "Afro-Italian" identity. I used discourse analysis to analyze the multiple ways that Black Italianness was being narrated in relation to a range of contentious subjects—Italian national identity, Mediterraneanism, immigration, racism, colonialism, and the United States (and other sites of the global Black diaspora). I also maintained a collection of novels, memoirs, and documentary films by Black Italian artists. Similarly, I conducted document analysis of Italian immigration and citizenship laws from the 1990 Legge Martelli to the present, with a focus on how the conditions for immigration and naturalization have shifted over time in relation to notions of race, gender, birthplace, descent, cultural competency, and economic productivity.[1]

INTERVIEWS

I conducted semistructured interviews with a range of different interlocutors. These were audio recorded (with consent); however, I also took copious notes in my notebook or on my iPhone. These notes served as backup in case my recording device failed, but I also used them to capture forms of nonverbal communication (a furrow of the brow, a dramatic drag on a cigarette, an explosive laugh) as well as the broader situational contexts of the interviews. Six of the interviews took place over Skype—these were typically instances when, for whatever reason, I was unable to meet an interlocutor in person.

I arranged interviews with three key groups of interlocutors. The first was Black Italians who were born or raised in Italy. This group included people who have two Black parents (immigrants from sub-Saharan Africa or Latin America) and people from mixed backgrounds with one white Italian parent or one Black American parent. Because I was interested in the mobilization of the category "Black" or "Afro-Italian," I focused on interviewing people who were active in the spheres of political activism, entrepreneurship, cultural production, and mutual aid. This inevitably meant that my interlocutors tended to be of a relatively higher class or educational background—in other words, their experiences cannot be generalized or used to stand in for *all* Black Italians. I met my first interlocutors in 2013 and 2014 through mutual friends and colleagues (including my adviser Annalisa Frisina at the University of Padua); others I contacted directly after seeing their posts on social media sites like Facebook. From there, my group of interlocutors rapidly snowballed as people began to introduce me to their friends, colleagues, and comrades. In interviews, I followed an open-ended protocol, asking questions about my interlocutors' life histories, their modes of identification, their sources of inspiration, how they became involved in political or cultural work, and what they saw as the biggest challenges facing Black people in Italy.

Beyond this core group of interlocutors, I also conducted interviews with first-generation African or Afro-Latinx immigrants to Italy. These interviews provided me with valuable historical context about an earlier generation of Black activism in Italy. Our conversations also helped me to parse out the various ways that the terrain and terms of Black struggle in Italy had shifted over the previous two decades. Finally, I interviewed social workers, NGO workers, and others (usually white Italians, though not exclusively) who work with immigrants in Italy. These interlocutors shared helpful institutional context for understanding the immigration and citizenship bureaucracy in Italy, and they also provided me with a window onto mainstream liberal approaches to managing "difference" in contemporary Italy.

In addition to these more formal, semistructured interviews, I also carried out a large number of informal, unstructured interviews. These typically took the form of shorter conversations after leaving an event, on the sidelines at demonstrations, or while riding public transportation on the way to a meeting. The notes I kept from these interactions provided context and ethnographic texture for the events and debates I had observed that day. Altogether, I conducted over one hundred semistructured and unstructured interviews for this project.

PARTICIPANT OBSERVATION

The most significant part of the research for this book took the form of participant observation. Participant observation gave me insight into the everyday ways that Black Italianness is constructed, enacted, and contested in Italy today. Sites of participant observation included activist meetings; protests and demonstrations; public forums about immigration law, citizenship reform, and refugee rights; Black hair care workshops; and cultural festivals. Because the networks of Black Italian organizing are so dense and interconnected, I quickly became a reliable fixture at these types of meetings and public events, to the extent that my friends would joke that if there was an event about race and Blackness somewhere in Italy, I could be counted on to be there. In addition, I have extensive family networks across Italy. As such, my experiences listening to a typical middle-class white Italian family talk openly about the political issues of the day yielded insights that also informed the background of this project. When conducting participant observation, I took copious and detailed notes. At the same time, in writing, I was very judicious about what sorts of details to include and which to exclude, as I was often privy to sensitive conversations and interpersonal disagreements about ongoing political struggles.[2]

Reflections on Diaspora, Power, and Research Praxis

The multiple ways that I was entangled with my research subject raise not only methodological questions, but also theoretical, ethical, and political ones. A short anecdote—a snapshot in time, if you will—illustrates precisely this inseparability of research and the personal.

On March 25, 2016, I was preparing to fly back to California from Milan for a short break from my dissertation fieldwork. I was on my way to attend a conference in San Francisco and then spend Easter with my parents and my now-husband. Just three days earlier, a series of coordinated suicide bombings had been carried out at Brussels Airport in Zaventem and the Maalbeek metro station in Brussels city center. As I walked to the American Airlines check-in counter with my overstuffed suitcase in tow, bleary-eyed and squinting in the harsh fluorescent airport lights, I noticed a larger-than-usual police presence in the terminal. When it was finally my turn to check in for the flight, I slid my Italian / EU passport across the counter to a perfectly starched and coiffed Italian gate agent. She opened the passport, glanced at the photo page, and then looked up at me. She looked back down at the passport and again at me, searching the features of my face, her quizzical expression hardening into a look of stern suspicion:

- Are you a resident of Italy?
- I'm a resident of California, but I am living in Italy for the year.

- Then why do you have an Italian passport?
- Because I am an Italian citizen.
- Well, were you born *here* or *there*?
- I was born in California.
- Well excuse me, then *why* do you have Italian citizenship?
- My mother is Italian, so I am an Italian citizen.
- Ah! So there *is* a reason why you have Italian citizenship.
- Well, yes, it's quite simple. My mother is Italian, so I have Italian citizenship.
- Ma'am, that may be true but I can ask you whatever questions I deem necessary for reasons of security.

Still unsatisfied with my responses, the agent proceeded to ask me what I was doing in Italy, and whether I planned to return. After several more minutes of tense question-and-answer in rapid-fire Italian, she finally relented and handed me my boarding pass with a dramatic huff.

The motive behind this intrusive line of questioning was quite simple, I realized. To the woman behind the counter, I did not look sufficiently "Italian"—there was a disconnect between my brown skin and my burgundy passport. And at a moment when panicked reports were circulating about terrorists obtaining fraudulent EU passports, and about "second-generation" immigrants automatically obtaining European citizenship and then pledging allegiance to ISIL, this supposed incongruity made me a potential security risk. Of course, my story of disrupted conference travel did not compare to the forms of outright border violence endured by migrants seeking to cross the threshold of Fortress Europe. After all, I always had the option of unsheathing my US passport as a way of solidifying my security "credentials." Nonetheless, the way that I had been momentarily ensnared in a broader web of racial profiling at the border showed that for all hopes of a postracial Europe, Italian citizenship was still normatively being conflated with whiteness.[3] And in fact, once I posted about this incident on Facebook, it spread like wildfire across the social media pages of citizenship reform groups and Black Italian activists, who, knowing me personally, pointed to my story as evidence that even an Italian citizen "by blood" can be denied recognition on the basis of skin color.

The (a)symmetries of my own Black Italianness afforded me a unique opportunity to engage intimately with the spatial politics of Blackness and diaspora.[4] In practice, my research resembled what Tina Campt, in her work on Black Germans, describes as "intercultural address":

> This term describes a series of eruptions / interruptions that I encountered repeatedly in the process of interviewing: as an African-American, I often became the object of "address." . . . These unexpected exchanges

were moments where I became aware of gaps of translation and moments of interpellation between us, as well as how we actively produced Black identity in our dialogues. My informants repeatedly made strategic use of Black America to articulate their assumptions of our similarities and commonalities as Black people while always emphatically insisting on the specificity of our culturally distinct experiences of race in our respective societies.[5]

Indeed, the myriad ways that my Black-American-Italianness resonated, clashed, and harmonized with the experiences of my Black Italian interlocutors yielded profound, situated insights about the geographical and historical specificities of Black cultural politics in Italy on the one hand, and the global scale of anti-Black racism and resistance on the other. But while it presented an incredible opening for inquiry, this proximity could often be painful. In one instance, a Black Italian comrade once introduced me to a friend at an event as "Camilla, an American who came to Italy for a year to study Black Italians"—unintentionally invisibilizing my own Black Italianness in just a few words. On a different occasion, another Black Italian friend asked me pointedly over drinks if Black Americans were *really* part of the African diaspora, since (in his words) we had no real cultural connection to the African continent. On these occasions—when I, as Ashanté Reese writes, "did not meet the expectations that are sometimes affixed to racial solidarity"—I would have to swallow the lump in my throat, take a deep breath, and remind myself to just "save it for the dissertation [or book]."[6] While they were challenging, I ultimately came to understand these moments of mis- / de-identification as significant, because they actually revealed the ways that people understood the relationships among race, place, nation, citizenship, and diaspora. They also pointed to the relative privilege of transnational mobility and access that accrued to me by virtue of my *Americanness*—a reminder to take seriously power differentiations within and across the Black diaspora. These uncomfortable moments surfaced the continued, yet oft-overlooked relevance of citizenship status to Black anti-racist politics; they also shed light on the ways that the nation-state might condition, but can never fully contain, the capacious spatial reach of Black diasporic imaginaries and practices.

But for these same reasons, the boundaries between my personal life (as someone with family and close friends in Italy), my political life (as an anti-racist activist), and my professional life (as an academic researcher) frequently blurred in ways that were simultaneously generative and challenging. As noted above, I actively participated in activist meetings and demonstrations about citizenship reform, helped to organize events and workshops about Black Italianness, and even cofounded a Black Italian meet-up group based in Milan. In any of these moments, was I participating as an ethnographer? As an activist? As a friend? As a politically engaged citizen? Or some combination of all of the above? In a sense, this degree of entanglement is actually central to my research praxis: I believe that it is my responsibility to make use of my own academic capital by supporting the mobilizations of Black Italians and amplifying their voices wherever possible—also because in many ways their struggles are *mine* as well! But at the same time, this unique level of access comes with a great deal of ethical and political responsibility. For this reason, I sought to ensure throughout that I maintained transparency as a researcher, always explaining to new interlocutors why I was in Italy, the research I was conducting, my study methods, and the forms in which my research would ultimately appear when complete. Like Steven Gregory's description in *The Devil behind the Mirror* of performing a particular kind of "seriousness" in the field, I sometimes made a point to conspicuously wield my pen and notebook (or the iPhone Notes app) during conversations, meetings, and other gatherings.[7]

During my research, I also regularly gave public lectures and spoke on panels in Italy and wrote for public-facing audiences (through blogs, books, and more) in Italian—ensuring that my work would not remain siloed in the inaccessible "ivory tower" of American academia, and that I maintained a certain level of accountability to the interlocutors and communities in Italy who had supported my research for so many years. This is a practice that I continue to this day. Indeed, as this manuscript was taking shape, I actually traveled back to Milan to meet with a group of friends, interlocutors, and other stakeholders in the Black Italian community for a chapter-by-chapter discussion of my book project, during which I could preview the ways that my years of research in Italy would finally take shape in the form of an academic monograph.

It is my sincere intent that this project proves to be as useful for my friends, comrades, and interlocutors in Italy as it has been for me and my lifelong effort to reconcile my own Blackness with my Italianness. I hope that my interlocutors will see their voices and stories reflected faithfully in the narrative of this book, and that my offerings prove to be politically useful for ongoing efforts to challenge the hegemony of the Italian racial state, undo border violence, and support the conditions of possibility for Black livingness and liberation.

Notes

FRONTMATTER

1. "Chimamanda Ngozi Adichie—Afroitalini e cittadinanza," *Il Razzismo è una Brutta Storia*, November 18, 2019, http://www.razzismobruttastoria.net/2019/11/18/chimamanda-ngozi-adichie-a-bookcity-milano-2019-afroitaliani-e-cittadinanza/.

2. "Chimamanda Ngozi Adichie—Afroitalini e cittadinanza."

3. Cristiana Giordano, "Practices of Translation and the Making of Migrant Subjectivities in Contemporary Italy," *American Ethnologist* 35, no. 4 (2008): 588–606, https://doi.org/10.1111/j.1548-1425.2008.00100.x.

4. Tina Marie Campt, *Other Germans: Black Germans and the Politics of Race, Gender, and Memory in the Third Reich* (Ann Arbor: University of Michigan Press, 2005), 9.

5. Igiaba Scego, ed., *Italiani per vocazione* (Fiesole, Italy: Cadmo, 2005).

6. As Stephen Small and Rebecca C. King-O'Riain note in the introduction to *Global Mixed Race*, "'mixed race' should be read with assumed scare quotes around it, to signify recognition of its socially bound nature." See Stephen Small and Rebecca C. King-O'Riain, "Global Mixed Race: An Introduction," in *Global Mixed Race*, ed. Rebecca Chiyoko King-O'Riain, Stephen Small, and Minelle Mahtani (New York: New York University Press, 2014), vii–xxii. For a history of the social production of the "mixed-race body" in Italy, see Angelica Pesarini, "'Blood Is Thicker Than Water': The Materialization of the Racial Body in Fascist East Africa," *Zapruder World: An International Journal for the History of Social Conflict* 4 (2017), http://zapruderworld.org/journal/past-volumes/volume-4/blood-is-thicker-than-water-the-materialization-of-the-racial-body-in-fascist-east-africa/.

7. "Key Migration Terms," International Organization for Migration, January 14, 2015, https://www.iom.int/key-migration-terms.

8. Cristiana Giordano, *Migrants in Translation: Caring and the Logics of Difference in Contemporary Italy* (Berkeley: University of California Press, 2014); Miriam Iris Ticktin, *Casualties of Care: Immigration and the Politics of Humanitarianism in France* (Berkeley: University of California Press, 2011). On the politics of distinguishing between "migrants" and "refugees," see Teju Cole, "Migrants Are Welcome," *Verso* (blog), September 7, 2015, https://www.versobooks.com/blogs/2226-teju-cole-migrants-are-welcome; Jørgen Carling, "Refugees Are Also Migrants. All Migrants Matter," *Border Criminologies* (blog), September 16, 2015, https://www.law.ox.ac.uk/research-subject-groups/centre-criminology/centreborder-criminologies/blog/2015/09/refugees-are-also.

9. Alessandro Portelli, "The Problem of the Color Blind: Notes on the Discourse of Race in Italy," in *Crossroutes—The Meanings of "Race" for the 21st Century*, ed. Paola Boi and Sabine Broeck (Hamburg: LIT, 2003), 29–39.

10. Pesarini, "Blood Is Thicker Than Water."

INTRODUCTION

1. Timothy Raeymaekers, "Introduction: Europe's Bleeding Border and the Mediterranean as a Relational Space," *ACME: An International Journal for Critical Geographies* 13, no. 2 (2014): 163–72.

2. Margaret Evans, "Europe Tut-Tuts While African Migrants Die on Its Doorstep," CBC, November 18, 2013, https://www.cbc.ca/news/world/europe-tut-tuts-while-african-migrants-die-on-its-doorstep-1.2425050.

3. Valentina Pop, "Italy Grants Citizenship to Lampedusa Dead," *EUobserver*, October 7, 2013, https://euobserver.com/justice/121681.

4. Martina Tazzioli, "Spy, Track and Archive: The Temporality of Visibility in Eurosur and Jora," *Security Dialogue* 49, no. 4 (August 1, 2018): 272–88, https://doi.org/10.1177/0967010618769812.

5. The original quote from Gramsci's *Prison Notebooks* reads, "La crisi consiste appunto nel fatto che il vecchio muore e il nuovo non può nacere: in questo interregno si verificano i fenomeni morbosi più sviariati" (The crisis consists precisely in the fact that the old is dying and the new cannot be born; in this interregnum a wide variety of morbid phenomena appear). It is often stylized in English as "The old world is dying and the new world struggles to be born. Now is the time of monsters." See Antonio Gramsci, *Quaderni dal carcere* (Turin: Einaudi, 2001), 311; Antonio Gramsci, *Selections from the Prison Notebooks*, ed. Quintin Hoare and Geoffrey Nowell Smith (New York: International Publishers, 1971), 276.

6. Nick Cumming-Bruce, "Number of People Fleeing Conflict Is Highest since World War II, U.N. Says," *New York Times*, June 19, 2019, https://www.nytimes.com/2019/06/19/world/refugees-record-un.html.

7. Adam Taylor, "Why Italian Governments So Often End in Collapse," *Washington Post*, August 20, 2019, https://www.washingtonpost.com/world/2019/08/20/why-italian-governments-so-often-end-collapse/.

8. Over one and a half million refugees and asylum seekers, many originating from countries in sub-Saharan Africa, have crossed the Mediterranean Sea since 2015. See UNCHR, "Mediterranean Situation," Operations Portal: Refugee Situations, 2020, https://data2.unhcr.org/en/situations/mediterranean.

9. *Breitbart News* founder and one-time Trump adviser Steve Bannon had sought for many years to build a right-wing training academy in Italy. See "Italy Revokes Lease for Site of Bannon's Right-Wing Academy," Reuters, June 1, 2019, https://www.reuters.com/article/us-italy-monastery-bannon-idUSKCN1T235I.

10. Marc Morje Howard, *The Politics of Citizenship in Europe* (Cambridge: Cambridge University Press, 2009); Guido Tintori, "Naturalisation Procedures for Immigrants in Italy," European University Institute (Florence: EUDO Citizenship Observatory, February 2013); Chiara Marchetti, "'Trees without Roots': The Reform of Citizenship Challenged by the Children of Immigrants in Italy," *Bulletin of Italian Politics* 2, no. 1 (2010): 45–67.

11. Angelica Pesarini and Guido Tintori, "Mixed Identities in Italy: A Country in Denial," in *The Palgrave International Handbook of Mixed Racial and Ethnic Classification*, ed. Zarine L. Rocha and Peter J. Aspinall (Cham: Springer International, 2020), 359, https://doi.org/10.1007/978-3-030-22874-3_19.

12. Uday S. Mehta, "Liberal Strategies of Exclusion," *Politics & Society* 18, no. 4 (1990): 427–54, https://doi.org/10.1177/003232929001800402; Domenico Losurdo, *Liberalism: A Counter-History* (London: Verso Books, 2014); David Theo Goldberg, *The Racial State* (Malden, MA: Blackwell, 2002); Charles W. Mills, *The Racial Contract* (1997; repr., Ithaca, NY: Cornell University Press, 2014).

13. See, for instance, Patricia Hill Collins, "It's All in the Family: Intersections of Gender, Race, and Nation," *Hypatia* 13, no. 3 (1998): 62–82; Audre Lorde, *Sister Outsider: Essays and Speeches* (1984; repr., New York: Penguin, 2020); M. Jacqui Alexander, *Pedagogies of Crossing: Meditations on Feminism, Sexual Politics, Memory, and the Sacred* (Durham, NC: Duke University Press, 2005); Nira Yuval-Davis, *Gender and Nation* (1997; repr., London: SAGE, 1997); Paola Bacchetta, Tina Campt, Inderpal Grewal, Caren Ka-

plan, Minoo Moallem, and Jennifer Terry, "Transnational Feminist Practices against War," *Meridians* 2, no. 2 (2002): 302–8.

14. Gaia Giuliani, "L'Italiano Negro: The Politics of Colour in Early Twentieth-Century Italy," *Interventions* 16, no. 4 (2014): 572–87, https://doi.org/10.1080/1369801X.2013.851828.

15. I generally refer to racial "subjectivity" and "subjects" rather than racial "identities" throughout this book—following Jacqueline Nassy Brown, "subjectivity" captures the way that "race" is made intelligible through intertwined processes of spatial differentiation, community struggle, and cultural practice. According to the critiques of scholars such as Kim TallBear, "identity" often privileges *individual* self-making instead of the web of (profoundly spatial) practices of domination and resistance that produce racial subjectivity. "Subjects" and "subjectivities," on the other hand, complicate the notion of a stable, innate sense of self that exists prior to power. The conditions of possibility for Italian Blackness are shaped by the particular historical, geographical, legal, and political conditions in Italy and the Mediterranean—conditions that link up with the global circulation of anti-Black racisms and Black diasporic resistance but are also not wholly reducible to them. In this way, I am again moving away from an undifferentiated Blackness or Black politics toward a geographically and historically situated analysis of the emergent Black politics in Italy. See Jacqueline Nassy Brown, *Dropping Anchor, Setting Sail: Geographies of Race in Black Liverpool* (Princeton, NJ: Princeton University Press, 2005), 91; Sam Spady, "Reflections on Late Identity: In Conversation with Melanie J. Newton, Nirmala Erevelles, Kim TallBear, Rinaldo Walcott, and Dean Itsuji Saranillio," *Critical Ethnic Studies* 3, no. 1 (2017): 90–115, https://doi.org/10.5749/jcritethnstud.3.1.0090; Kim TallBear, *Native American DNA: Tribal Belonging and the False Promise of Genetic Science* (Minneapolis: University of Minnesota Press, 2013); Michel Foucault, "The Subject and Power," *Critical Inquiry* 8, no. 4 (1982): 777–95.

16. Engin F. Isin, "Engaging, Being, Political," *Political Geography* 24 (2005): 183.

17. A number of scholars have traced a similar set of dilemmas around the possibilities and limitations of politics oriented on "human rights" and "humanitarianism." See, for instance, Ticktin, *Casualties of Care*; Talal Asad, "What Do Human Rights Do? An Anthropological Enquiry," *Theory & Event* 4, no. 4 (January 1, 2000), https://muse.jhu.edu/article/32601; Inderpal Grewal, *Saving the Security State: Exceptional Citizens in Twenty-First-Century America* (Durham, NC: Duke University Press, 2017); Caren Kaplan, *Aerial Aftermaths: Wartime from Above* (Durham, NC: Duke University Press, 2017).

18. Robbie Shilliam, *Race and the Undeserving Poor: From Abolition to Brexit* (Newcastle upon Tyne, UK: Agenda, 2018); Satnam Virdee and Brendan McGeever, "Racism, Crisis, Brexit," *Ethnic and Racial Studies* 41, no. 10 (August 9, 2018): 1802–19, https://doi.org/10.1080/01419870.2017.1361544.

19. Patrick Lyons, "Trump Wants to Abolish Birthright Citizenship. Can He Do That?," *New York Times*, August 22, 2019, https://www.nytimes.com/2019/08/22/us/birthright-citizenship-14th-amendment-trump.html.

20. Annie Karni and Sheryl Gay Stolberg, "Trump Offers Temporary Protections for 'Dreamers' in Exchange for Wall Funding," *New York Times*, January 19, 2019, https://www.nytimes.com/2019/01/19/us/politics/trump-proposal-daca-wall.html.

21. Zeke Miller, Jill Colvin, and Jonathan Lemire, "Trump Digs in on Racist Tweets: 'Many People Agree with Me,'" Associated Press, July 16, 2019, https://apnews.com/9924c846abf84cfeabb76e6045190b42.

22. Ruth Wilson Gilmore, "Fatal Couplings of Power and Difference: Notes on Racism and Geography," *Professional Geographer* 54, no. 1 (2002): 15–24, https://doi.org/10.1111/0033-0124.00310.

23. See, for instance, Irene Bloemraad, *Becoming a Citizen: Incorporating Immigrants and Refugees in the United States and Canada* (Berkeley: University of California Press, 2006); Rogers Brubaker, *Citizenship and Nationhood in France and Germany* (Cambridge, MA: Harvard University Press, 2009); Stephen Castles and Alastair Davidson, *Citizenship and Migration: Globalization and the Politics of Belonging* (London: Routledge, 2020); Ruud Koopmans, Paul Statham, Marco Giugni, and Florence Passy, *Contested Citizenship: Immigration and Cultural Diversity in Europe* (Minneapolis: University of Minnesota Press, 2005); T. H. Marshall, *Citizenship and Social Class* (1950; repr., London: Pluto Press, 1987); Christian Joppke, *Immigration and the Nation-State: The United States, Germany, and Great Britain* (Oxford: Oxford University Press, 1999).

24. Irene Bloemraad, Anna Korteweg, and Gökçe Yurdakul, "Citizenship and Immigration: Multiculturalism, Assimilation, and Challenges to the Nation-State," *Annual Review of Sociology* 34, no. 1 (2008): 153–79, https://doi.org/10.1146/annurev.soc.34.040507.134608.

25. Roberto G. Gonzales and Nando Sigona, "Mapping the Soft Borders of Citizenship: An Introduction," in *Within and Beyond Citizenship: Borders, Membership and Belonging*, ed. Nando Sigona and Roberto G. Gonzales (London: Routledge, 2017), 1–14; Dimitris Papadopoulos and Vassilis S. Tsianos, "After Citizenship: Autonomy of Migration, Organisational Ontology and Mobile Commons," *Citizenship Studies* 17, no. 2 (April 1, 2013): 178–96, https://doi.org/10.1080/13621025.2013.780736; Sandro Mezzadra and Brett Neilson, *Border as Method, or, the Multiplication of Labor* (Durham, NC: Duke University Press, 2013).

26. See, for instance, Raymond A. Rocco, *Transforming Citizenship: Democracy, Membership, and Belonging in Latino Communities* (East Lansing: Michigan State University Press, 2014); Evelyn Nakano Glenn, *Unequal Freedom* (Cambridge, MA: Harvard University Press, 2002); Arely M. Zimmerman, "Contesting Citizenship from Below: Central Americans and the Struggle for Inclusion," *Latino Studies* 13, no. 1 (March 1, 2015): 28–43, https://doi.org/10.1057/lst.2014.71; James Holston, "Insurgent Citizenship in an Era of Global Urban Peripheries," *City & Society* 21, no. 2 (2009): 245–67, https://doi.org/10.1111/j.1548-744X.2009.01024.x.

27. Engin F. Isin and Greg M. Nielsen, *Acts of Citizenship* (London: Zed Books, 2013).

28. Orlando Patterson, *Slavery and Social Death: A Comparative Study* (Cambridge, MA: Harvard University Press, 2018); "Unwelcomed Immigrants, Birther Lies, Windrush Atrocity and Trumpism: Orlando Patterson on Blacks in America and Britain," *Jamaica Global Online* (blog), July 18, 2019, https://www.jamaicaglobalonline.com/unwelcomed-immigrants-birther-lies-windrush-atrocity-and-trumpism-orlando-patterson-on-blacks-in-america-and-britain/; Martha S. Jones, *Birthright Citizens: A History of Race and Rights in Antebellum America* (Cambridge: Cambridge University Press, 2018).

29. Claudia Rankine, *Citizen: An American Lyric* (Minneapolis: Graywolf Press, 2014); Aimee Meredith Cox, *Shapeshifters: Black Girls and the Choreography of Citizenship* (Durham, NC: Duke University Press, 2015).

30. Kwame Nimako and Stephen Small, "Theorizing Black Europe and African Diaspora: Implications for Citizenship, Nativism, and Xenophobia," in *Black Europe and the African Diaspora*, ed. Darlene Clark Hine, Trica Danielle Keaton, and Stephen Small (Urbana: University of Illinois Press, 2009), 212–37.

31. This historically myopic perspective on the part of European societies denies the deep entanglements of Europe and Africa, ties of colonialism and enslavement that generated the famous chant, "We are *here* because you were *there!*" See Stephen Small, *20 Questions and Answers on Black Europe* (Amsterdam: Amrit Publishers, 2018).

32. Barnor Hesse, "Afterword: Europe's Undecidability," in Hine, Keaton, and Small, *Black Europe and the African Diaspora*, 291 (emphasis in the original).

33. James Baldwin, *Notes of a Native Son* (1955; repr., Boston: Beacon Press, 1984).

34. Theophilus Marboah (@Theoimani), "Perché la storia del nero americano è unica anche in questo . . ." Instagram story, November 27, 2019 (emphasis in the original).

35. Baldwin, *Notes of a Native Son* (emphasis in the original).

36. Along similar lines, the Black Swiss scholar Jovita dos Santos Pinto notes, "As a Black European, who has worked on rendering visible a historical Black presence in Switzerland, I would argue Baldwin's U.S.A./Europe comparison presents a risk. It might feed into the figure of the 'stranger,' of the person of color being 'an eternal newcomer' to Europe." See Jovita dos Santos Pinto, Noémi Michel, Patricia Purtschert, Paola Bacchetta, and Vanessa Naef, "Baldwin's Transatlantic Reverberations: Between 'Stranger in the Village' and *I Am Not Your Negro*," *James Baldwin Review* 6 (2020): 184–85.

37. Frantz Fanon, *The Wretched of the Earth* (1963; repr. New York: Grove Press, 2007), 5. Re "swerving it," I thank my adviser and mentor Donald Moore for his colorful phrasing.

38. Charles T. Lee, *Ingenious Citizenship: Recrafting Democracy for Social Change* (Durham, NC: Duke University Press, 2016), 29; see also Annette K. Joseph-Gabriel, *Reimagining Liberation: How Black Women Transformed Citizenship in the French Empire* (Champaign: University of Illinois Press, 2019).

39. Heather Merrill, "In Other Wor(l)ds: Situated Intersectionality in Italy," in *Spaces of Danger: Culture and Power in the Everyday*, ed. Heather Merrill and Lisa M. Hoffman (Athens: University of Georgia Press, 2015), 78.

40. Paul Gilroy, *The Black Atlantic: Modernity and Double Consciousness* (Cambridge, MA: Harvard University Press, 1993); Philippe Fargues, "Four Decades of Cross-Mediterranean Undocumented Migration to Europe: A Review of the Evidence" (Geneva: International Organization for Migration, 2017).

41. David Theo Goldberg, "Racial Europeanization," *Ethnic and Racial Studies* 29, no. 2 (2006): 331–64, https://doi.org/10.1080/01419870500465611; Brandi Thompson Summers, *Black in Place: The Spatial Aesthetics of Race in a Post-Chocolate City* (Chapel Hill: University of North Carolina Press, 2019), 14.

42. Aliza Wong, *Race and the Nation in Liberal Italy, 1861–1911: Meridionalism, Empire, and Diaspora* (London: Palgrave Macmillan, 2006).

43. Thongchai Winichakul, *Siam Mapped: A History of the Geo-Body of a Nation* (Honolulu: University of Hawaiʻi Press, 1997).

44. Luigi Carmine Cazzato, "Fractured Mediterranean and Imperial Difference: Mediterraneanism, Meridionism, and John Ruskin," *Journal of Mediterranean Studies* 26, no. 1 (2017): 69–78; Jane Schneider, "The Dynamics of Neo-Orientalism in Italy (1848–1995)," in *Italy's "Southern Question": Orientalism in One Country*, ed. Jane Schneider (New York: Bloomsbury Academic, 1998), 1–23; Michael Herzfeld, "Practical Mediterraneanism: Excuses for Everything, from Epistemology to Eating," in *Rethinking the Mediterranean*, ed. William V. Harris (Oxford: Oxford University Press, 2005), 45–63.

45. Giuseppe Mazzini, "Intorno alla questione dei negri in America," *Scritti editi ed inediti di Giuseppe Mazzini* (Imola, Italy: Cooperativa Tipografico-Editrice P. Galeati, 1940), 27:163–65; Enrico Dal Lago, *William Lloyd Garrison and Giuseppe Mazzini: Abolition, Democracy, and Radical Reform* (Baton Rouge: Louisiana State University Press, 2013). The Italian historian Pasquale Villari also compared the plight of southern Italian peasants under Bourbon rule and after Italian unification to that of enslaved Black Americans. See Nelson J. Moe, *The View from Vesuvius: Italian Culture and the Southern Question* (Berkeley: University of California Press, 2002), 233.

46. Gaia Giuliani and Cristina Lombardi-Diop, *Bianco e nero: Storia dell'identità razziale degli italiani* (Milan: Mondadori Education, 2013).

47. Etienne Balibar and Immanuel Maurice Wallerstein, *Race, Nation, Class: Ambiguous Identities* (London: Verso, 1991), 61.

48. Katherine McKittrick, "On Plantations, Prisons, and a Black Sense of Place," *Social & Cultural Geography* 12, no. 8 (2011): 947–63, https://doi.org/10.1080/14649365.2011 .624280; Ruth Wilson Gilmore, *Golden Gulag: Prisons, Surplus, Crisis, and Opposition in Globalizing California* (Berkeley: University of California Press, 2007). See also bell hooks, *Feminist Theory: From Margin to Center* (London: Pluto Press, 2000).

49. Robin D. G. Kelley, foreword to *Black Marxism: The Making of the Black Radical Tradition*, by Cedric J. Robinson (1983; repr., Chapel Hill: University of North Carolina Press, 2005), xi–xxvi; Cedric J. Robinson, *Black Marxism: The Making of the Black Radical Tradition* (1983; repr., Chapel Hill: University of North Carolina Press, 2005).

50. Ida Danewid, "White Innocence in the Black Mediterranean: Hospitality and the Erasure of History," *Third World Quarterly* 38, no. 7 (2017): 1674–89, https://doi.org/10 .1080/01436597.2017.1331123.

51. Katherine McKittrick, *Demonic Grounds: Black Women and the Cartographies of Struggle* (Minneapolis: University of Minnesota Press, 2006), xv.

52. Emma Graham-Harrison, "Migrants from West Africa Being 'Sold in Libyan Slave Markets,'" *Guardian*, April 10, 2017, https://www.theguardian.com/world/2017/apr/10 /libya-public-slave-auctions-un-migration; Ampson Hagan, "Algeria's Black Fear," *Africa Is a Country* (blog), August 2017, https://africasacountry.com/2017/08/algerias-black-fear/.

53. Muriam Haleh Davis and Thomas Serres, *North Africa and the Making of Europe: Governance, Institutions and Culture* (London: Bloomsbury, 2018); Peo Hansen and Stefan Jonsson, *Eurafrica: An Untold Story* (London: Bloomsbury Academic, 2014).

54. Angelo Del Boca, "The Myths, Suppressions, Denials, and Defaults of Italian Colonialism," in *A Place in the Sun: Africa in Italian Colonial Culture from Post-Unification to the Present*, ed. Patrizia Palumbo (Berkeley: University of California Press, 2003), 17–36.

55. Robinson, *Black Marxism*, 102.

56. Robert Davis, *Christian Slaves, Muslim Masters: White Slavery in the Mediterranean, The Barbary Coast, and Italy, 1500–1800* (London: Palgrave Macmillan UK, 2003).

57. Robinson, *Black Marxism*, 16; Salvatore Bono, *Schiavi: Una storia mediterranea (XVI–XIX secolo)* (Bologna: Il Mulino, 2016).

58. Robinson, *Black Marxism*, 104.

59. Robinson, *Black Marxism*, 104.

60. Small, *20 Questions and Answers*. Italian colonialism in the Horn of Africa will be discussed in greater detail in chapter 5.

61. Cristina Lombardi-Diop and Caterina Romeo, "Introduction: Paradigms of Postcoloniality in Contemporary Italy," in *Postcolonial Italy: Challenging National Homogeneity*, ed. Cristina Lombardi-Diop and Caterina Romeo (New York: Palgrave Macmillan, 2012), 1; Stephanie Malia Hom, *Empire's Mobius Strip: Historical Echoes in Italy's Crisis of Migration and Detention* (Ithaca, NY: Cornell University Press, 2019); Gaoheng Zhang, *Migration and the Media: Debating Chinese Migration to Italy, 1992–2012* (Toronto: University of Toronto Press, 2019); Alessandro Di Meo, *Tientsin, la concessione italiana: Storia delle relazioni tra Italia e Cina (1866–1947)* (Rome: Ginevra Bentivoglio editoriA, 2015).

62. Lombardi-Diop and Romeo, "Introduction: Paradigms of Postcoloniality," 1.

63. Corrado Bonifazi, Frank Heins, Salvatore Strozza, and Mattia Vitiello, "Italy: The Italian Transition from an Emigration to Immigration Country," IDEA working paper no. 5 (Brussels: European Commission, March 2009), 8, https://www.researchgate.net /publication/267773953_Italy_The_Italian_transition_from_an_emigration_to_immi gration_country; Heather Merrill, *An Alliance of Women: Immigration and the Politics of Race* (Minneapolis: University of Minnesota Press, 2006).

64. Heather Merrill and Donald Martin Carter, "Inside and Outside Italian Political Culture: Immigrants and Diasporic Politics in Turin," *GeoJournal* 58, no. 2/3 (2002): 167–75.

65. Wendy A. Pojmann, *Immigrant Women and Feminism in Italy* (Aldershot, UK: Ashgate, 2006). See also Jacqueline Andall, *Gender, Migration and Domestic Service: The Politics of Black Women in Italy* (Aldershot, UK: Ashgate, 2000); Merrill and Carter, "Inside and Outside Italian Political Culture," 167–75; Sabrina Marchetti, *Black Girls: Migrant Domestic Workers and Colonial Legacies* (Leiden: Brill, 2014).

66. Merrill, *Alliance of Women.*

67. Asale Angel-Ajani, "Italy's Racial Cauldron: Immigration, Criminalization and the Cultural Politics of Race," *Cultural Dynamics* 12, no. 3 (2000): 331–52, https://doi.org/10.1177/092137400001200304.

68. Elena Ambrosetti and Eralba Cela, "Demography of Race and Ethnicity in Italy," in *The International Handbook of the Demography of Race and Ethnicity*, ed. Rogelio Saenz, Nestor Rodriguez, and David Embrick (London: Springer, 2015), 457–82; Pesarini and Tintori, "Mixed Identities in Italy," 351, 358–59.

69. Istat, "Cittadini non comunitari: Presenza, nuovi ingressi e acquisizioni di cittadinanza," press release, October 30, 2016, https://www.istat.it/it/archivio/223598.

70. Giorgia Papavero, "Minori e seconde generazioni," Fondazione ISMU, 2015.

71. While Italy never adopted formal policies of assimilation or multiculturalism like France or the United Kingdom, the Italian model of immigrant reception has been frequently characterized as one of "diffusion." See Umberto Melotti, "Immigration and Security in Europe: A Look at the Italian Case," in *The Frontiers of Europe: A Transatlantic Problem?*, ed. Federiga M. Bindi and Irina Angelescu (Washington, DC: Brookings Institution Press, 2011), 107–26; Francesco Grignetti, "'Immigrazione diffusa,' la risposta italiana alle banlieue," *La Stampa*, May 2, 2016, http://www.lastampa.it/2016/05/02/esteri/immigrazione-diffusa-la-risposta-italiana-alle-banlieue-8p5OH0i0xLdTcN0uFaWuPM/pagina.html.

72. This section, as well as the previous two paragraphs, are adapted from my article "In Search of Black Italia: Notes on Race, Belonging, and Activism in the Black Mediterranean," *Transition* 123, no. 1 (June 17, 2017): 158–62.

73. Merrill and Carter, "Inside and Outside Italian Political Culture."

74. W. E. B. Du Bois, *The Souls of Black Folk* (1903; repr., Oxford: Oxford University Press, 2007); Frantz Fanon, *Black Skin, White Masks* (1952; repr., New York: Grove Press, 2008), 90. For a discussion of the relationship between these concepts, see Paget Henry, *Caliban's Reason: Introducing Afro-Caribbean Philosophy* (London: Routledge, 2002).

75. Du Bois, *Souls of Black Folk*, 3 Satnam Virdee, "The Second Sight of Racialised Outsiders in the Imperialist Core," *Third World Quarterly* 38, no. 11 (November 2, 2017): 2403, https://doi.org/10.1080/01436597.2017.1328274.

76. Jacqueline Andall, "Second-Generation Attitude? African-Italians in Milan," *Journal of Ethnic and Migration Studies* 28, no. 3 (2002): 389–407, https://doi.org/10.1080/13691830220146518.

77. Andall, "Second-Generation Attitude?," 403.

78. All interview excerpts were originally in Italian and were translated by the author, unless indicated otherwise.

79. Susi Meret, Elisabetta Della Corte, and Maria Sangiuliano, "The Racist Attacks against Cécile Kyenge and the Enduring Myth of the 'Nice' Italian," *OpenDemocracy* (blog), August 28, 2013, http://www.opendemocracy.net/can-europe-make-it/susi-meret-elisabetta-della-corte-maria-sangiuliano/racist-attacks-against-c%C3%A9cile.

80. Liisa Malkki, "National Geographic: The Rooting of Peoples and the Territorialization of National Identity among Scholars and Refugees," *Cultural Anthropology* 7, no. 1 (1992): 24–44.

81. See the Methodological Appendix at the end of this book for a more detailed description of my research process.

82. Gilroy, *Black Atlantic*.

83. Heather Merrill, *Black Spaces: African Diaspora in Italy* (New York: Routledge, 2018).

84. Katherine McKittrick, "Commentary: Worn Out," *Southeastern Geographer* 57, no. 1 (2017): 99, https://doi.org/10.1353/sgo.2017.0008.

85. Katherine McKittrick and Clyde Woods, eds., "No One Knows the Mysteries at the Bottom of the Ocean," in *Black Geographies and the Politics of Place* (Boston: South End Press, 2007), 1–13.

86. "Cittadini stranieri in Italia—2019," Tuttitalia.it, 2020, https://www.tuttitalia.it /statistiche/cittadini-stranieri-2019/.

87. See, for instance, Steven Salaita, *Inter/Nationalism: Decolonizing Native America and Palestine* (Minneapolis: University of Minnesota Press, 2016); Jasbir K. Puar, *Terrorist Assemblages: Homonationalism in Queer Times* (Durham, NC: Duke University Press, 2007); Lisa Marie Cacho, *Social Death: Racialized Rightlessness and the Criminalization of the Unprotected* (New York: New York University Press, 2012); Lee, *Ingenious Citizenship*.

88. I am grateful to Jacqueline Nassy Brown for this insight into the practice of ethnography.

89. Fanon, *Black Skin, White Masks*; see also Merrill, *Black Spaces*. David Scott, *Conscripts of Modernity: The Tragedy of Colonial Enlightenment* (Durham, NC: Duke University Press, 2004).

90. Trica Danielle Keaton, *Muslim Girls and the Other France: Race, Identity Politics, and Social Exclusion* (Bloomington: Indiana University Press, 2006).

91. Yarimar Bonilla, *Non-sovereign Futures: French Caribbean Politics in the Wake of Disenchantment* (Chicago: University of Chicago Press, 2015).

1. ITALIAN ETHNONATIONALISM AND THE LIMITS OF CITIZENSHIP

1. In the past, Italy has responded to the perceived threat of "radicalized Islamic terrorism" swiftly, with harsh security and surveillance measures. After the 2004 train bombings in Madrid and the 2005 attacks on London's public transportation system, for instance, the Italian government immediately enacted some of the strictest Internet regulations in Europe. These regulations, which among other provisions targeted Internet cafés for heightened surveillance, led to the disproportionate policing of immigrant and Muslim communities. For more information, see Camilla Hawthorne, "Dangerous Networks: Internet Regulations as Racial Border Control in Italy," in *DigitalSTS: A Handbook and Fieldguide*, ed. Janet Vertesi and David Ribes (Princeton, NJ: Princeton University Press, 2019), 178–97.

2. Du Bois, *Souls of Black Folk*.

3. Du Bois, *Souls of Black Folk*; Virdee, "Second Sight of Racialised Outsiders."

4. Pseudonyms.

5. In one notable example from 2017, a fifteen-year-old Italian-Senegalese student and aspiring fashion designer named Mbayeb "Mami" Bousso designed an Italian flag–draped gown, which she wore to greet Italian president Sergio Mattarella in Mirandola (a town that had been devastated by an earthquake in 2012). Images of the meeting were circulated widely, to the celebration of the Italian Left—who elevated the young woman as a symbol of a new, multicultural Italy—and to the horror of the Right—who reported her to the police for "insulting" the Italian flag. See Paolo di Paolo, "Mirandola, quella ragazza nera vestita con il tricolore," *La Repubblica*, June 9, 2017, https://bologna.repubblica.it/cronaca /2017/06/09/news/mirandola_ragazza_tricolore-167693538/; Claudio Cartaldo, "Immigrata veste col Tricolore: Denunciata per vilipendio," *Il Giornale*, June 11, 2017, http://www

.ilgiornale.it/news/cronache/immigrata-veste-col-tricolore-denunciata-vilipendio-1408137.html.

6. All conversations and interviews originally took place in Italian and were translated by me into English, unless otherwise specified.

7. Giorgio Agamben, "Perché non ho firmato l'appello sullo ius soli," *Quodlibet*, October 18, 2017, https://www.quodlibet.it/giorgio-agamben-perch-on-ho-firmato-l-appello-sullo-ius-soli.

8. Michel Foucault, *The History of Sexuality*, vol. 1, *An Introduction*, trans. Robert Hurley (1984; repr., New York: Vintage, 1990).

9. Katharyne Mitchell, "Different Diasporas and the Hype of Hybridity," *Environment and Planning D: Society and Space* 15, no. 5 (1997): 533–53, https://doi.org/10.1068/d150533.

10. Patrick Weil, "Access to Citizenship: A Comparison of Twenty-Five Nationality Laws," in *Citizenship Today: Global Perspectives and Practices*, ed. T. Alexander Aleinikoff and Douglas Klusmeyer (Washington, DC: Carnegie Endowment for International Peace, 2001), 17–35.

11. Mohamed Abdalla Tailmoun, Mauro Valeri, and Isaac Tesfaye, *Campioni d'Italia? Le seconde generazioni e lo sport* (Rome: Sinnos, 2014); Papavero, "Minori e seconde generazioni."

12. European Convention on Nationality, European Treaty Series No. 166 Council of Europe § (1997), https://rm.coe.int/168007f2c8. The other seven countries that did not ratify the convention are Croatia, France, Greece, Latvia, Malta, Poland, and Russia.

13. Acquisto della cittadinanza, Pub. L. No. Legge n. 91 del 1992 (1992), https://www.senato.it/japp/bgt/showdoc/17/DOSSIER/941909/index.html?part=dossier_dossier1-sezione_sezione11-h1_h14.

14. It is important to note that many children of immigrants are not aware of this one-year window. Until an initiative spearheaded by Rete G2, municipalities made no effort to inform youth of the naturalization process.

15. A similar fate befell the elderly members of the Windrush generation in the United Kingdom, under former home secretary Theresa May's "hostile environment" policy. Sonya Sceats, "Opinion: Theresa May's Legacy Is the Hostile Environment—How Can She Evoke Nicholas Winton in Her Resignation Speech?," *Independent* (UK), May 25, 2019, https://www.independent.co.uk/voices/theresa-may-resigns-hostile-environment-nicholas-winton-immigration-windrush-scandal-a8929966.html; Jacqueline Andall, "Second-Generation Attitude?," 394.

16. Andall, "Second-Generation Attitude?," 394.

17. "Cittadinanza italiana, boom di richieste e tempi di attesa interminabili," *ModenaToday*, February 18, 2016, http://www.modenatoday.it/cronaca/numeri-richieste-attese-cittadinanza-italiana-modena.2015.html.

18. For more information on the distinction between citizenship as a *right* and citizenship as a *concession* in Italian nationality law, see "La concessione e l'accertamento della cittadinanza italiana," Progetto Melting Pot Europa, September 13, 2009, http://www.meltingpot.org/La-concessione-e-l-accertamento-della-cittadinanza-italiana.html.

19. Pesarini and Guido Tintori, "Mixed Identities in Italy," 359.

20. There are over eight hundred thousand children with non-Italian citizenship in Italian schools, 61 percent of whom were born in Italy. They make up 9.4 percent of schoolchildren in Italy. See Cristina Nadotti, "Crescono gli studenti non cittadini italiani: Il 61% è nato in Italia," *La Repubblica*, March 29, 2018, http://www.repubblica.it/scuola/2018/03/29/news/crescono_gli_studenti_non_cittadini_italiani_il_61_e_nato_in_italia-192524586/.

21. Isabella Clough Marinaro and James Walston, "Italy's 'Second Generations': The Sons and Daughters of Migrants," *Bulletin of Italian Politics* 2, no. 1 (2010): 8.

22. Giordano, "Practices of Translation," 590; John Agnew, "The Myth of Backward Italy in Modern Europe," in *Revisioning Italy: National Identity and Global Culture*, ed. Beverly Allen and Mary J. Russo (Minneapolis: University of Minnesota Press, 1997), 23–42; Schneider, "Dynamics of Neo-Orientalism," 1–23.

23. Moe, *View from Vesuvius*; Wong, *Race and the Nation*.

24. Tailmoun, Valeri, and Tesfaye, *Campioni d'Italia?*

25. Mark I. Choate, *Emigrant Nation: The Making of Italy Abroad* (Cambridge, MA: Harvard University Press, 2008); Wong, *Race and the Nation*; Rhiannon Noel Welch, *Vital Subjects: Race and Biopolitics in Italy, 1860–1920* (Oxford: Oxford University Press, 2016).

26. Between 1876 and 1976 alone it is estimated that over twenty million people left Italy. In fact, the Italian diaspora is regarded as one of the largest mass exoduses in modern history. See Francesco Cordasco, "Bollettino Dell'Emigrazione (1902–1927): A Guide to the Chronicles of Italian Mass Emigration," in *The Columbus People: Perspectives in Italian Immigration to the Americas and Australia*, ed. Lydio F. Tomasi, Piero Gastaldo, and Thomas Row (Staten Island, NY: Center for Migration Studies, 1994), 499–509; Donna R. Gabaccia, *Italy's Many Diasporas* (London: Routledge, 2013).

27. Bonifazi et al., "Italian Transition"; Giordano, "Practices of Translation," 591; Pojmann, *Immigrant Women*.

28. Choate, *Emigrant Nation*; Teresa Fiore, "The Emigrant Post-'Colonia' in Contemporary Immigrant Italy," in Lombardi-Diop and Romeo, *Postcolonial Italy*, 71–82.

29. Giordano, "Practices of Translation," 591.

30. Pesarini, "'Blood Is Thicker Than Water." I will discuss Italian colonial citizenship policies in greater detail in chapter 3.

31. Scholars such as Ann Stoler have explored the articulations of race, gender, kinship, and coloniality through the apparatus of citizenship law. See Ann Laura Stoler, *Carnal Knowledge and Imperial Power: Race and the Intimate in Colonial Rule* (Berkeley: University of California Press, 2002). In Italy, the reforms that granted Italian women the right to pass on citizenship to their children via jus sanguinis were the product of protracted Italian feminist struggles that were also linked to social issues such as divorce, abortion, and labor force participation.

32. I was born in 1987. Had I been born just a few years earlier, I would not have been automatically eligible for Italian citizenship through my mother.

33. Sabina Donati, *A Political History of National Citizenship and Identity in Italy, 1861–1950* (Palo Alto, CA: Stanford University Press, 2013), 8.

34. Donati, *Political History of National Citizenship*, 14.

35. Keaton, *Muslim Girls*.

36. Candice Whitney, "Race, Culture and Colonial Legacy in Today's Italian Citizenship Struggles," *Kheiro Magazine*, June 20, 2017, https://kheiromag.com/race-culture-and-colonial-legacy-in-todays-italian-citizenship-struggles-27b6d9f9649f.

37. See, for instance, Leonardo de Franceschi's important account of the citizenship reform movement in relation to struggles over media representation. Leonardo De Franceschi, *La cittadinanza come luogo di lotta: Le seconde generazioni in Italia fra cinema e serialità* (Rome: Arcane Editrice, 2018).

38. S. A. Smythe, "The Black Mediterranean and the Politics of the Imagination," *Middle East Report* 286 (Spring 2018), https://merip.org/2018/10/the-black-mediterranean-and-the-politics-of-the-imagination/.

39. Stuart Hall, "Cultural Identity and Diaspora," in *Colonial Discourse and Post-Colonial Theory: A Reader* (London: Harvester Wheatsheaf, 1994), 227–37.

40. Papavero, "Minori e seconde generazioni," 3.

41. Enzo Colombo, Luisa Leonini, and Paola Rebughini, "Different But Not Stranger: Everyday Collective Identifications among Adolescent Children of Immigrants in Italy," *Journal of Ethnic and Migration Studies* 35, no. 1 (2009): 37–59, https://doi.org/10.1080/13691830802489101; Annalisa Frisina, *Giovani musulmani d'Italia* (Rome: Carocci, 2007). See Giovani Musulmani d'Italia GMI, Facebook page, accessed March 19, 2020, https://www.facebook.com/GiovaniMusulmanidItaliaGMI/; Dorothy Louise Zinn, "'Loud and Clear': The G2 Second Generations Network in Italy," *Journal of Modern Italian Studies* 16, no. 3 (2011): 374, https://doi.org/10.1080/1354571X.2011.565640.

42. Fanon, *Black Skin, White Masks*.

43. Pseudonym.

44. This forum was originally housed on Rete G2's website, *secondegenerazioni.it*; it has since migrated to Facebook. See also Dorothy Louise Zinn, "Italy's Second Generations and the Expression of Identity through Electronic Media," *Bulletin of Italian Politics* 2, no. 1 (2010): 91–113; Zinn, "Loud and Clear."

45. Pseudonym.

46. Critiques of the term "second generation" fall into four main categories. First, the term is imprecise, and has been rendered even more confusing with the introduction of terms such as "1.25" and "1.75" to refer to children who immigrated as small children or as young adults. Second, the term suggests that "foreignness" is a heritable category that is passed from immigrant parents to their children. Third, it flattens the variegations in experiences and legal statuses *within* the category of "second generation." And finally, it severs the connections between children and their families by suggesting that the second generation is more "advanced" in a teleological progression of assimilation or integration into the host country. See Marinaro and Walston, "Italy's 'Second Generations'"; Bjørn Thomassen, "'Second Generation Immigrants' or 'Italians with Immigrant Parents'? Italian and European Perspectives on Immigrants and Their Children," *Bulletin of Italian Politics* 2, no. 1 (2010): 21–44; Stephen Small, *Police and People in London: A Group of Young Black People* (London: Policy Studies Institute, 1983).

47. There were many earlier attempts to reform Italian nationality law before 2011, all unsuccessful. For more information, see Marchetti, "Trees without Roots," 45–67; De Franceschi, *La cittadinanza come luogo di lotta*.

48. Vladimiro Polchi, "'L'Italia sono anch'io': Due leggi per la cittadinanza agli immigrati," *La Repubblica*, June 22, 2011, http://www.repubblica.it/solidarieta/immigrazione/2011/06/22/news/campagna_cittadinanza-18041906/.

49. "Documenti," *L'Italia Sono Anch'io* (blog), accessed July 25, 2018, http://www.litaliasonoanchio.it/index.php?id=522.

50. Annalisa Camilli, "Ius soli, ius sanguinis, ius culturae: Tutto sulla riforma della cittadinanza," *Internazionale*, October 20, 2017, https://www.internazionale.it/notizie/annalisa-camilli/2017/10/20/riforma-cittadinanza-da-sapere.

51. Emanuela Stella, "'E' italiano chi nasce in Italia.' La Kyenge a Venezia per '18 ius soli,'" *La Repubblica*, August 25, 2013, http://www.repubblica.it/solidarieta/immigrazione/2013/08/25/news/italiano_chi_nasce_in_italia_kyenge_presenta_a_venezia_18_ius_soli-65259182/.

52. Annalisa Camilli, "Cos'è lo ius soli e come funziona la cittadinanza in altri paesi europei," *Internazionale*, June 21, 2017, https://www.internazionale.it/notizie/annalisa-camilli/2017/06/21/ius-soli-cittadinanza-italia.

53. Zinn, "Loud and Clear," 379.

54. Lorgia García Peña, "Black in English: Race, Migration, and National Belonging in Postcolonial Italy," *Kalfou* 3, no. 2 (October 31, 2016): 211, https://doi.org/10.15367/kf.v3i2.102.

55. Fred Kuwornu, *18 Ius soli*, documentary, 2012, http://vimeo.com/37011695.

56. Merrill, "In Other Wor(l)ds," 78.

57. Clarissa Clò, "Hip Pop Italian Style: The Postcolonial Imagination of Second-Generation Authors in Italy," in Lombardi-Diop and Romeo, *Postcolonial Italy*, 275–92.

58. Gilroy, *The Black Atlantic*, 17.

59. Keaton, *Muslim Girls*.

60. In 2012, the Northern League's EU parliamentary representative Mario Borghezio went so far as to call Balotelli "a *padano* with dark skin." *Padania* is a term revived by the Northern League in the 1990s to refer to northern Italy. See "Borghezio su Mario: 'Balotelli? E' un padano con la pelle scura," *Il Giorno*, June 30, 2012, https://www.ilgiorno.it/brescia/cronaca/2012/06/30/737145-milano-borghezio-balotelli-padano.shtml.

61. Allan Pred, *Even in Sweden: Racisms, Racialized Spaces, and the Popular Geographical Imagination* (Berkeley: University of California Press, 2000), 79.

62. Stuart Hall, "Conclusion: The Multi-Cultural Question," in *Un/Settled Multiculturalisms: Diasporas, Entanglements, Transruptions*, ed. Barnor Hesse (New York: St. Martin's Press, 2000), 209–41.

63. Stuart Hall, "Race, the Floating Signifier," Media Education Foundation, 1997, https://www.mediaed.org/transcripts/Stuart-Hall-Race-the-Floating-Signifier-Transcript.pdf; Camilla Hawthorne and Pina Piccolo, "'Razza' e 'umano' non sono termini banali," *Frontiere News*, July 26, 2016, http://frontierenews.it/2016/07/razza-e-umano-non-sono-termini-banali/.

64. "Ius soli al Senato, 7mila emendamenti della Lega," *Public Policy*, April 28, 2016, https://www.publicpolicy.it/lega-senato-emendamenti-cittadinanza-58641.html.

65. Andrea Morigi, "Più immigrati uguale più attentati ma se possiamo cacciarli siamo sicuri," *Libero*, accessed March 27, 2018, uguale-piu-attentati-ma-se-possiamo-cacciarli-siamo-sicuri-.html.

66. While the name of this group evokes the *sans-papiers* (without papers) movement in France, there are important differences between these mobilizations: Italiani senza cittadinanza were born and/or raised in Italy, and due to the country's citizenship laws inherit their parents' citizenship and live in Italy with a long-term residency permit; the *sans-papiers* are undocumented workers mobilizing for a regularization of their immigration status and less exploitative labor conditions.

67. Luca Bussotti, "A History of Italian Citizenship Laws during the Era of the Monarchy (1861–1946)," *Advances in Historical Studies* 5, no. 4 (2016): 145, https://doi.org/10.4236/ahs.2016.54014.

68. "Cittadinanza: Sì della Camera allo ius soli. La nuova legge passa al Senato," *La Repubblica*, October 13, 2015, http://www.repubblica.it/politica/2015/10/13/news/legge_cittadinanza_senato-124967907/.

69. Massimo Solani, "Pacciotti: 'L'Italia non può trattare milioni di persone come cittadini di Serie B,'" *Democratica.it* (blog), accessed March 28, 2018, http://test.democratica.info/interviste/pacciotti-italia-immigrazione-legge-cittadinanza/?amp.

70. Gilroy, *Black Atlantic*.

71. Lombardi-Diop and Romeo, *Postcolonial Italy*.

72. Gloria Anzaldúa, *Borderlands* (1987; repr., San Francisco: Aunt Lute Books, 1999).

73. García Peña, "Black in English," 222–23.

74. It is important to note that the "fear of replacement" is a commonly cited concern among white nationalist groups across Europe and the United States, and can be directly linked to French writer Renaud Camus's notion of "the great replacement." See Sergio Rame, "Ius soli, è sostituzione etnica: Subito 800mila nuovi 'italiani,'" *Il Giornale*, June 15, 2017, http://www.ilgiornale.it/news/ius-soli-sostituzione-etnica-subito-800mila-nuovi-italiani-1409527.html; Thomas Chatterton Williams, "The French Origins of 'You

Will Not Replace Us,'" *New Yorker*, November 27, 2017, https://www.newyorker.com /magazine/2017/12/04/the-french-origins-of-you-will-not-replace-us.

75. Monica Rubino, "Fertility Day, Renzi: 'Campagna inguardabile.' Lorenzin: 'Basta polemiche, contano i fatti,'" *La Repubblica*, September 22, 2016, http://www.repubblica .it/politica/2016/09/22/news/fertility_day_al_via_proteste_piazza-148297333/.

76. Associated Press, "Rep. Steve King: U.S. Doesn't Need 'Somebody Else's Babies,'" PBS NewsHour, March 13, 2017, https://www.pbs.org/newshour/politics/rep-steve-king -u-s-doesnt-need-somebody-elses-babies.

77. Istat, "Cittadini non comunitari."

78. Many scholars of Black Europe have noted that the preoccupation among European states with the supposed threat of radical Islam has overshadowed concerns about people of African descent, with the result that "there are less and less resources for Blacks and less attention to them as they are rendered marginal." See Stephen Small, introduction to Hine, Keaton, and Small, *Black Europe and the African Diaspora*, xxxii; Philomena Essed and Kwame Nimako, "Designs and (Co)Incidents: Cultures of Scholarship and Public Policy on Immigrants/Minorities in the Netherlands," *International Journal of Comparative Sociology* 47, no. 3–4 (2006): 281–312, https://doi.org/10.1177/0020715206065784.

79. Generally speaking, Black people in Italy are interpellated primarily as "racial subjects," while Arabs and North Africans are interpellated primarily as "Muslims," thus invisibilizing the presence of Black Muslims in Italy. One notable exception is the Italian-Somali writer Igiaba Scego, who has written extensively about being Muslim. See, for instance, Igiaba Scego, "Non in mio nome," *Internazionale*, January 7, 2015, https://www .internazionale.it/opinione/igiaba-scego/2015/01/07/non-in-mio-nome.

80. Goldberg, "Racial Europeanization." The Muslim presence in what is now Italy dates back to ninth-century Sicily. Today, Islam is the second-most widely practiced religion in Italy after Christianity (including Catholicism); there are almost 1.5 million Muslims in Italy, and almost one-third of Italy's immigrant population is Muslim. Nonetheless, Islam (unlike Catholicism, Judaism, Buddhism, Hinduism, and some other Christian sects) is not formally recognized by the Italian state because it is seen by the government to be incompatible with the principles of the Italian constitution. This means that mosques cannot benefit from the *otto per mille* (0.8 percent) funding for organized religions that is compulsorily drawn from Italians' annual income taxes. While concerns about Blackness and Islam in Italian space are often held separately in public discourse in Italy, the use of Catholicism as a "race-neutral" stand-in for whiteness suggests that Islamophobia and anti-Black racism should actually be analyzed in relation to one another. See Mustafa Hameed, "Lacking Recognition, Italy's Muslims Face an Uncertain Future," *Washington Post*, May 28, 2013, https:// www.washingtonpost.com/national/on-faith/lacking-recognition-italys-muslims-face-an -uncertain-future/2013/05/28/e0d2761c-c7b3-11e2-9cd9-3b9a22a4000a_story.html.

81. Goldberg, "Racial Europeanization," 344.

82. "Ius soli, al Senato manca il numero legale. Assenti tutti i M5s e i centristi. Manca 1/3 dei Dem," *La Repubblica*, December 23, 2017, http://www.repubblica.it/politica/2017 /12/23/news/cittadinanza_al_senato_manca_il_numero_legale_muore_lo_ius_soli -184997182/.

83. Italiani senza Cittadinanza, "Ius soli: #Italiani senza cittadinanza invia una lettera aperta a Mattarella," *Giuridica.net* (blog), December 27, 2017, https://giuridica.net /ius-soli-italiani-senza-cittadinanza-invia-una-lettera-aperta-a-mattarella/.

84. Agamben, "Perché non ho firmato."

85. Giorgio Agamben, *Homo Sacer: Sovereign Power and Bare Life* (Stanford, CA: Stanford University Press, 1998); Giorgio Agamben, *State of Exception* (Chicago: University of Chicago Press, 2008).

86. Agamben, "Perché non ho firmato."

87. Alexander G. Weheliye and Léopold Lambert, "Claiming Humanity: A Black Critique of the Concept of Bare Life," *The Funambulist*, July 28, 2014, https://thefunambulist.net/podcast/alexander-weheliye-claiming-humanity-a-black-critique-of-the-concept-of-bare-life; Alexander G. Weheliye, *Habeas Viscus: Racializing Assemblages, Biopolitics, and Black Feminist Theories of the Human* (Durham, NC: Duke University Press, 2014).

88. Charles T. Lee, "Bare Life, Interstices, and the Third Space of Citizenship," *Women's Studies Quarterly* 38, no. 1/2 (2010): 58.

89. Mezzadra and Neilson, *Border as Method*.

90. Isin and Nielsen, *Acts of Citizenship*.

91. Hannah Arendt, *Imperialism* (New York: Harcourt Brace & World, 1976), 175–76.

92. Ruth Lister, "Inclusive Citizenship: Realizing the Potential," *Citizenship Studies* 11, no. 1 (2007): 52, https://doi.org/10.1080/13621020601099856.

93. Engin Fahri Isin, *Being Political: Genealogies of Citizenship* (Minneapolis: University of Minnesota Press, 2002), 3–4.

94. Sandro Mezzadra, "The Proliferation of Borders and the Right to Escape," *Refugee Watch: A South Asian Journal on Forced Migration* 41 (2013): 11; Ilker Ataç, Kim Rygiel, and Maurice Stierl, "Introduction: The Contentious Politics of Refugee and Migrant Protest and Solidarity Movements: Remaking Citizenship from the Margins," *Citizenship Studies* 20, no. 5 (2016): 533, https://doi.org/10.1080/13621025.2016.1182681.

95. In a sense, it seems that the critical citizenship studies literature effectively tells us that national citizenship *doesn't* matter (because of the multiple, overlapping, and transnational webs of political attachment that characterize our world), or that it *should not* matter (because it is inherently exclusive). Linda Bosniak offers some important reflections on the trend of focusing on "postnational" or "transnational" citizenship, and the need for scholars to continue thinking about citizenship in the context of "national society." See Linda Bosniak, *The Citizen and the Alien: Dilemmas of Contemporary Membership* (Princeton, NJ: Princeton University Press, 2008), 6.

96. Zinn, "Loud and Clear," 382.

97. This bears a resemblance to Benedict Anderson's assertion in *Imagined Communities* that racism and nationalism have distinct ontological bases and thus should not be conflated. Benedict Anderson, *Imagined Communities: Reflections on the Origin and Spread of Nationalism* (New York: Verso, 2006), 148–50.

98. Chandan Reddy, *Freedom with Violence: Race, Sexuality, and the US State* (Durham, NC: Duke University Press, 2011).

99. Goldberg, *Racial State*. Similarly to Cedric Robinson's argument in *Black Marxism* that there is no capitalism that precedes racism, Goldberg suggests that there is no modern state that precedes racism.

100. Goldberg argues that the modern state is "nothing less than a racial state." In this way, he directs attention away from the extreme cases of "racist states" such as Nazi Germany or apartheid South Africa toward the broad realm of processes by which states include and exclude using the category of "race." See Goldberg, *Racial State*, 2, 9, 114.

101. Goldberg, *Racial State*, 9. See also Mehta, "Liberal Strategies of Exclusion"; Talal Asad, "Conscripts of Western Civilization," in *Dialectical Anthropology: Essays in Honor of Stanley Diamond*, ed. Christine Ward Gailey, vol. 1, *Civilization in Crisis: Anthropological Perspectives* (Gainesville: University Press of Florida, 1992), 333–51.

102. Cacho, *Social Death*; Reddy, *Freedom with Violence*.

103. Andall, *Gender, Migration and Domestic Service*.

104. Hans Lucht, *Darkness before Daybreak: African Migrants Living on the Margins in Southern Italy Today* (Berkeley: University of California Press, 2012), 22; A. Sivanan-

dan, "UK Commentary: Racism 1992," *Race & Class* 30, no. 3 (January 1, 1989): 85–90, https://doi.org/10.1177/030639688903000309.

105. Roberto Saviano, "Mai sentito parlare di Jerry Masslo?," *La Repubblica*, August 24, 2014, http://www.repubblica.it/cronaca/2014/08/24/news/saviano_jerry_masslo-94354580/.

106. Jennifer Parmelee, "'Italian Dream' Soured by Racism," *Washington Post*, August 31, 1989, https://www.washingtonpost.com/archive/politics/1989/08/31/italian-dream-soured-by-racism/37f5c1d6-b8fb-4b8e-86af-e6d1b5a4f2a9/.

107. Alessandra Di Maio, "Black Italia: Contemporary Migrant Writers from Africa," in Hine, Keaton, and Small, *Black Europe and the African Diaspora*, 119–44; Merrill, *Alliance of Women*.

108. Jeffrey Cole, *The New Racism in Europe: A Sicilian Ethnography* (Cambridge: Cambridge University Press, 2005).

109. "Jerry Masslo, l'uomo che scoprì il razzismo in Italia," *Stranieri in Italia*, August 25, 2011, https://stranieriinitalia.it/attualita/jerry-masslo-luomo-che-scopri-il-razzismo-in-italia/.

110. Smith attended the demonstration at the invitation of UISP (Unione Italiana Sport Per Tutti—Italian Union of Sport for Everybody). See "Sport e lotta a razzismo: L'Uisp nel nome di Jerry Masslo," UISP Nazionale, accessed October 14, 2020, http://www.uisp.it//nazionale/pagina/sport-e-lotta-a-razzismo-luisp-nel-nome-di-jerry-masslo.

111. "Immigration Policies in Italy," *Struggles in Italy* (blog), July 11, 2012, https://strugglesinitaly.wordpress.com/equality/en-immigration-policies-in-italy/.

112. The Legge Martelli also brought Italy in line with the broader European Union immigration policy framework, in preparation for Italy's ascension to the EU in 1992.

113. "Immigration Policies in Italy."

114. Guido Tintori, "Ius Soli the Italian Way: The Long and Winding Road to Reform the Citizenship Law," *Contemporary Italian Politics* 10, no. 4 (November 27, 2018): 434–50, https://doi.org/10.1080/23248823.2018.1544360.

115. Governo Italiano, Ministero degli Affari Esteri e della Cooperazione Internazionale, "Citizenship," accessed January 21, 2021, https://www.esteri.it/mae/en/servizi/stranieri/cittadinanza_0.html.

116. Giovanna Zincone and Marzia Basili, "Country Report: Italy," EUDO Citizenship Observatory (Florence: European University Institute, 2013), 3.

117. Under the 1992 nationality law, refugees could gain Italian citizenship after five years of residency, and adopted children could gain Italian citizenship after seven years of residency. Jus soli only exists for children born in Italy to stateless parents (*apolidi*), unknown parents, or parents who cannot transmit their citizenship to their children.

118. Donald Carter and Heather Merrill, "Bordering Humanism: Life and Death on the Margins of Europe," *Geopolitics* 12, no. 2 (2007): 248–64, https://doi.org/10.1080/14650040601168867.

119. Kamala Visweswaran, *Un/Common Cultures: Racism and the Rearticulation of Cultural Difference* (Durham, NC: Duke University Press, 2010).

120. Caterina Romeo, "Racial Evaporations: Representing Blackness in African Italian Postcolonial Literature," in Lombardi-Diop and Romeo, *Postcolonial Italy*, 221–36.

121. Alana Lentin, *Racism and Anti-racism in Europe* (London: Pluto Press, 2004); Cristina Lombardi-Diop, "Spotless Italy: Hygiene, Domesticity, and the Ubiquity of Whiteness in Fascist and Postwar Consumer Culture," *California Italian Studies* 2, no. 1 (2011), http://escholarship.org/uc/item/8vt6r0vf; Romeo, "Racial Evaporations."

122. As I will discuss in chapter 3, there has also been a return to an explicit language of "race" among the Italian Far Right in the last several years.

123. Goldberg, "Racial Europeanization"; Frantz Fanon, "Racism and Culture," in *Toward the African Revolution: Political Essays* (1964; repr., New York: Grove Press,

1988); Verena Stolcke, "Talking Culture: New Boundaries, New Rhetorics of Exclusion in Europe," *Current Anthropology* 36, no. 1 (February 1, 1995): 1–24, https://doi.org/10 .1086/204339; Martin Barker, *The New Racism: Conservatives and the Ideology of the Tribe* (Toronto: Junction Books, 1981); Sivanandan, "UK Commentary"; Pierre-André Taguieff, *La force du préjugé: Essai sur le racisme et ses doubles* (Paris: La Découverte, 1988); Eduardo Bonilla-Silva, *Racism without Racists: Color-Blind Racism and the Persistence of Racial Inequality in America* (2003; repr., Lanham, MD: Rowman & Littlefield, 2017).

124. It is important to clarify that this is different from the *biologistic* conflation of race and citizenship seen during Italian colonialism and fascism, when physiognomy was used to mark the boundaries of Italianness.

125. Giovanni Sartori, "L'Italia non è una nazione meticcia. Ecco perché lo ius soli non funziona," *Corriere della Sera*, June 17, 2013, http://www.corriere.it/opinioni/13 _giugno_17/sartori-ius-soli-integrazione-catena-equivoci_686dbf54-d728-11e2-a4df -7eff8733b462.shtml.

126. This will be discussed further in chapter 3.

127. Sartori, "L'Italia non è una nazione meticcia."

128. Tatiana Petrovich Njegosh, "La finizione della razza, la linea del colore e il meticciato," in *Il colore della nazione*, ed. Gaia Giuliani (Milan: Mondadori, 2015), 224.

129. Goldberg, "Racial Europeanization," 338.

130. Rosy D'Elia, "Il Decreto Salvini cambia la cittadinanza: Le conseguenze umane," *Più Culture* (blog), January 16, 2019, https://www.piuculture.it/2019/01/le-conseguenze -umane-il-decreto-salvini-cambia-la-cittadinanza/; Angelo Massaro, "Cittadinanza italiana da 730 giorni a 4 anni, tutte le novità del Decreto Salvini sulle cittadinanze," *Cittadinanza Italiana*, October 2, 2018, https://www.cittadinanza.biz/cittadinanza-italiana -da-730-giorni-a-4-anni-il-testo-definitivo-del-decreto-salvini/.

131. Lee, "Bare Life," 58.

132. Lee, *Ingenious Citizenship*, 13–20.

133. Emilio Giacomo Berrocal, "Building Italian-ness through the Logic of the 'Other in Us' and the 'Self in the Other': An Anti-nationalist Approach to the Italian Debate on a New Citizenship Law," *Bulletin of Italian Politics* 2, no. 1 (2010): 69–90.

2. BLACK ENTREPRENEURS AND THE "(RE)MAKING" OF ITALY

1. This chapter is derived in part from Camilla Hawthorne, "Making Italy: Afro-Italian Entrepreneurs and the Racial Boundaries of Citizenship," *Social & Cultural Geography* (2019): 1–21, https://doi.org/10.1080/14649365.2019.1597151.

2. Candice Whitney, "Breaking Ground for Emerging Designers: Milan's First Afro Pop Shop Milano," *Women Change Africa* (blog), June 14, 2017, http://womenchangeafrica .blogspot.com/2017/06/breaking-ground-for-emerging-designers.html.

3. "FierAfric 2019: Cultura, arte e cibo nella fiera dell'Africa," *Mente Locale* (blog), May 28, 2019, https://www.mentelocale.it/milano/eventi/128404-fierafric-2019-cultura -arte-cibo-fiera-africa.htm.

4. Chimamanda Ngozi Adichie, "The Danger of a Single Story," TEDGlobal2009, https://www.ted.com/talks/chimamanda_adichie_the_danger_of_a_single_story.

5. Achille Mbembe, "Afropolitanism," in *Africa Remix: Contemporary Art of a Continent*, ed. Njami Simon (Johannesburg: Jacana Media, 2007), 26–30; Taiye Selasi, "Bye-Bye Babar," *The LIP*, March 3, 2005, http://thelip.robertsharp.co.uk/?p=76.

6. Arendt, *Imperialism*.

7. Arlene Dávila, *Barrio Dreams: Puerto Ricans, Latinos, and the Neoliberal City* (Berkeley: University of California Press, 2004), 13–14; Elizabeth M. Liew Siew Chin, *Pur-*

chasing Power: Black Kids and American Consumer Culture (Minneapolis: University of Minnesota Press, 2001).

8. For more on the concept of "respectability politics," see Evelyn Brooks Higginbotham, *Righteous Discontent: The Women's Movement in the Black Baptist Church, 1880–1920* (Cambridge, MA: Harvard University Press, 1994).

9. Alessandro Brogi, *Confronting America: The Cold War between the United States and the Communists in France and Italy* (Chapel Hill: University of North Carolina Press, 2011); Nikolaos Papadogiannis, *Militant around the Clock?: Left-Wing Youth Politics, Leisure, and Sexuality in Post-Dictatorship Greece, 1974–1981* (New York: Berghahn Books, 2015); Andrea Pirni, "I giovani italiani, la 'non politica' e nuovi cleavages," *SocietàMutamentoPolitica* 3, no. 5 (2012): 157–71.

10. Andall, *Gender, Migration and Domestic Service*; Rhacel Salazar Parreñas, *The Force of Domesticity: Filipina Migrants and Globalization* (New York: New York University Press, 2008).

11. I thank Heather Merrill for these important insights regarding the relationship between entrepreneurship and labor organizing in Italy.

12. Jim Edwards, "Italy's 'Perma-Recession' Could Trigger a €2 Trillion Financial Crisis That Threatens the Eurozone Itself," *Business Insider*, April 21, 2019, https://www.businessinsider.com/italy-perma-recession-systemic-crisis-threatens-eurozone-2019-4; Roberto di Quirico, "Italy and the Global Economic Crises," *Bulletin of Italian Politics* 2, no. 2 (2010): 3–19.

13. Sartori, "L'Italia non è una nazione meticcia."

14. Henry A. Giroux, "Spectacles of Race and Pedagogies of Denial: Anti-Black Racist Pedagogy under the Reign of Neoliberalism," *Communication Education* 52, no. 3–4 (2003): 191–211, https://doi.org/10.1080/0363452032000156190; David Theo Goldberg, *The Threat of Race: Reflections on Racial Neoliberalism* (Malden, MA: Wiley-Blackwell, 2009); Michael Omi and Howard Winant, *Racial Formation in the United States* (1986; repr., London: Routledge, 2014).

15. Deborah E. Ward, *The White Welfare State: The Racialization of U.S. Welfare Policy* (Ann Arbor: University of Michigan Press, 2009); Michael G. Lacy, "Black Frankenstein and Racial Neoliberalism in Contemporary American Cinema: Reanimating Racial Monsters in Changing Lanes," in *The Routledge Companion to Global Popular Culture*, ed. Toby Miller (London: Routledge, 2014), 233.

16. In the United States, for example, racial neoliberalism has constructed the figure of the Black "welfare queen."

17. Goldberg, *Threat of Race*, 337 (emphasis in the original).

18. Maurizio Ferrera, "The Uncertain Future of the Italian Welfare State," *West European Politics* 20, no. 1 (1997): 231–49, https://doi.org/10.1080/01402389708425183; Ascoli Ugo and Pavolini Emmanuele, *The Italian Welfare State in a European Perspective: A Comparative Analysis* (Bristol, UK: Policy Press, 2016). Ironically, this sparse social assistance and an institutional reliance on the family to provide care is directly linked to the recruitment of foreign workers into Italy beginning as early as the 1960s. As Jacqueline Andall has argued, female domestic workers from countries including Cape Verde, Ethiopia, Eritrea, and the Philippines were systematically hired between the 1960s and 1980s to provide childcare for northern Italian families where both parents worked full time. These migrant workers replaced southern Italian workers, who had previously been migrating to northern Italy to work as live-in domestic laborers until their economic prospects (and the economic development of southern Italy generally) improved. See Andall, *Gender, Migration and Domestic Service*.

19. Vladimiro Polchi, "La Stranieri Spa vale come la Fiat: il Pil degli immigrati in Italia pesa 127 miliardi," *La Repubblica*, October 7, 2016, https://www.repubblica.it/economia

/2016/10/10/news/economia_immigrati_pil-149285846/; Andrea Carli, "Gli immigrati in Italia producono il 9% del Pil, più di Croazia e Ungheria," *Il Sole 24 ORE*, October 18, 2017, 24, https://www.ilsole24ore.com/art/gli-immigrati-italia-producono-9percento-pil-piu-croazia-e-ungheria--AEAYrxqC; Carlo Andrea Finotto, "Immigrati: Il rapporto costi-benefici è positivo per l'Italia. Ecco perché," *Il Sole 24 ORE*, July 4, 2018, https://www.ilsole24ore.com/art/immigrati-rapporto-costi-benefici-e-positivo-l-italia-ecco-perche-AEltRrGF.

20. "Italy MP 'Blacks Up' for Anti-migrant Speech," *Al Jazeera English*, January 17, 2014, http://www.aljazeera.com/news/europe/2014/01/italy-mp-blacks-up-anti-migrant-speech-20141175475595566.html.

21. Vladimiro Polchi, "Migranti, gli otto falsi miti da sfatare," *La Repubblica*, October 13, 2016, http://www.repubblica.it/cronaca/2016/10/13/news/migranti_falsi_miti_bonino-149688642/.

22. Maya Oppenheim, "Samuel L. Jackson and Magic Johnson Mistaken for 'Lazy Migrants' by Italians after Shopping in Tuscany," *Independent* (UK), August 21, 2017, http://www.independent.co.uk/arts-entertainment/films/news/samuel-l-jackson-magic-johnson-lazy-migrants-italy-tuscany-forte-dei-marmi-louis-vuitton-a7905026.html.

23. Mitchell, "Different Diasporas," 549.

24. Sergio Rame, "Migranti, Boldrini al Senato: 'Approvate subito lo ius soli,'" *Il Giornale*, June 16, 2016, http://www.ilgiornale.it/news/politica/boldrini-ringrazia-i-migranti-meticciato-forma-cultura-1272560.html.

25. Michel Foucault, *The Birth of Biopolitics: Lectures at the Collège de France, 1978–1979*, ed. Michel Senellart, trans. Graham Burchell (2004; repr., New York: Palgrave Macmillan, 2010), 147.

26. See Cedric Robinson's arguments about intra-European racialism, which, as early as the feudal period, separated out groups such as the Irish, the Roma, Jews, and Slavs. Robinson, *Black Marxism*, 2005.

27. Stoler, *Carnal Knowledge and Imperial Power*; Anne McClintock, *Imperial Leather: Race, Gender, and Sexuality in the Colonial Contest* (London: Routledge, 2013); Zine Magubane, *Bringing the Empire Home: Race, Class, and Gender in Britain and Colonial South Africa* (Chicago: University of Chicago Press, 2004).

28. Wong, *Race and the Nation*; Welch, *Vital Subjects*.

29. Cesare Lombroso and Guglielmo Ferrero, *Criminal Woman, the Prostitute, and the Normal Woman* (1893; repr., Durham, NC: Duke University Press, 2004); Schneider, *Italy's "Southern Question."*

30. W. E. B. Du Bois, *Black Reconstruction in America, 1860–1880* (1935; repr., New York: The Free Press, 1998); David R. Roediger, *The Wages of Whiteness: Race and the Making of the American Working Class*, rev. ed. (New York: Verso, 1999).

31. Shilliam, *Race and the Undeserving Poor*; Owen Parker, "Book Review: *Race and the Undeserving Poor*," *SPERI* (blog), September 15, 2018, http://speri.dept.shef.ac.uk/2018/09/16/book-review-race-and-the-undeserving-poor/.

32. Merrill, "In Other Wor(l)ds," 82.

33. Gisella Ruccia, "Ius soli, La Russa (FdI): 'Usa bambini come scudi umani e vuol trasformare Italia in sala parto di tutta l'Africa,'" *Il Fatto Quotidiano*, September 28, 2017, http://www.ilfattoquotidiano.it/2017/09/28/ius-soli-la-russa-fdi-usa-bambini-come-scudi-umani-e-vuol-trasformare-italia-in-sala-parto-di-tutta-lafrica/3883483/.

34. Robinson, *Black Marxism*.

35. Stuart Hall, "Introducing NLR," *New Left Review*, I, no. 1 (1960): 1–3.

36. Maria Paola Nanni, ed., "Rapporto immigrazione e imprenditoria 2016: Aggiornamento statistico," Centro Studi e Ricerche IDOS (Rome: IDOS, 2016), https://www

.dossierimmigrazione.it/en/prodotto/rapporto-immigrazione-e-imprenditoria-2016 -aggiornamento-statistico/.

37. Maurizio Ambrosini and Nazareno Panichella, "Immigrazione, occupazione e crisi economica in Italia," *Quaderni di Sociologia*, no. 72 (2016): 115–34, https://doi.org /10.4000/qds.1578.

38. This chapter is deeply indebted to geographer Heather Merrill's research on Black spaces and situated intersectionality in Italy. Her work provides invaluable insight into the multiple ways that Black Italians have transformed Italy into a diasporic node of interconnection.

39. Annalisa Frisina and Camilla Hawthorne, "Italians with Veils and Afros: Gender, Beauty, and the Everyday Anti-racism of the Daughters of Immigrants in Italy," *Journal of Ethnic and Migration Studies* 44, no. 5 (2018): 718–35, https://doi.org/10.1080 /1369183X.2017.1359510.

40. Ayana Byrd and Lori Tharps, *Hair Story: Untangling the Roots of Black Hair in America* (New York: St. Martin's Press, 2014).

41. Brown, *Dropping Anchor, Setting Sail*; Small, *20 Questions and Answers*.

42. See http://www.africansummerschool.org/mission/ for more information.

43. Tiffany M. Gill, "'I Had My Own Business . . . So I Didn't Have to Worry': Beauty Salons, Beauty Culturists and the Politics of African-American Female Entrepreneurship," in *Beauty and Business: Commerce, Gender, and Culture in Modern America*, ed. Philip Scranton (London: Routledge, 2014), 169–94.

44. Maxine Craig, "The Decline and Fall of the Conk; or, How to Read a Process," *Fashion Theory* 1, no. 4 (1997): 399–419, https://doi.org/10.2752/136270497779613657; Tanisha C. Ford, *Liberated Threads: Black Women, Style, and the Global Politics of Soul* (Chapel Hill: University of North Carolina Press, 2015); Tiffany M. Gill, *Beauty Shop Politics: African American Women's Activism in the Beauty Industry* (Champaign: University of Illinois Press, 2010); Robin D. G. Kelley, "Nap Time: Historicizing the Afro," *Fashion Theory* 1, no. 4 (1997): 339–51, https://doi.org/10.2752/136270497779613666; Susannah Walker, "Black Is Profitable: The Commodification of the Afro, 1960–1975," *Enterprise & Society* 1, no. 3 (2000): 536–64.

45. Massimo Coppola, *Nappy Girls*, documentary, 2014, http://video.corriere.it/nappy -girls/5291ec12-4416-11e4-bbc2-282fa2f68a02; Laura Badaracchi, "Lo stile afro di Evelyne è un successo," *Donna Moderna* 28, no. 5 (August 19, 2015); Rosanna Campisi, "Saranno italiani," *Gioia*, October 22, 2015; Marta Dore, "Orgoglio Nappy," *Gioia*, November 28, 2015; Igiaba Scego, "Capelli di libertà," *L'Espresso*, 2016.

46. Annalisa Frisina and Camilla Hawthorne, "Riconoscersi nel successo di Evelyne, lottare nel ricordo di Abba. Un viaggio tra le icone nere dei figli delle migrazioni in Italia," in *A fior di pelle: Bianchezza, nerezza, visualità*, ed. Elisa Bordin and Stefano Bosco (Verona: Ombre Corte, 2017).

47. *Vu cumprà*, derived from "Vuoi comprare?" (Do you want to buy?) is a phrase used to refer to foreign (primarily African, and typically Senegalese) street hawkers in Italy. See Donald Martin Carter, *States of Grace: Senegalese in Italy and the New European Immigration* (Minneapolis: University of Minnesota Press, 1997).

48. In addition to making use of their language skills, Black Italian entrepreneurs have also played an important role in the development of e-commerce and social media content production in Italy. The Internet emerged as an important tool for Black Italian women entrepreneurs because it allows them to save money on material overhead costs and also helps to overcome the geographical dispersion that characterizes the Black presence in Italy. The tech savvy of many young Black Italians is significant considering that Internet penetration rates in Italy have lagged behind other European countries; in fact,

in Italy immigrant communities often surpass "native" Italians in certain digital communication practices. See Viviana Premazzi, "Integrazione online: Nativi e migranti fuori e dentro la rete," FIERI Rapporti Di Ricerca, October 2010, http://fieri.it/wp-content/uploads/2011/03/Lintegrazione-online-nativi-e-migranti-fuori-e-dentro-la-rete.pdf. For more information on the state of the Internet in Italy, see also https://opennet.net/research/profiles/italy.

49. Angela also wrote and self-published a book about natural hair care in 2017. See Angela Haisha Adamou, *Love Is in the Hair, vol. 1, Consigli per avere ricci belli, sani e senza capricci* (independently published, 2017).

50. Barbara Ganz, "L'eleganza della riccia," *Alley Oop* (blog), March 5, 2016, http://www.alleyoop.ilsole24ore.com/2016/03/05/leleganza-della-riccia/; Loretta Grace, "Il disagio di essere una beauty junkie nera in Italia," *Grace on Your Dash* (blog), March 1, 2016, http://www.graceonyourdash.com/in-italia-essere-una-beautyjunkie-nera-e-un-problema/.

51. As Forgacs and Gundle note, the concept of "Made in Italy" also has antecedents in Fascist and postwar Italy. See David Forgacs and Stephen Gundle, *Mass Culture and Italian Society from Fascism to the Cold War* (Bloomington: Indiana University Press, 2007).

52. Fabio Savelli and Arcangelo Rociola, "Ecco dov'è finito il Made in Italy negli anni della Grande Crisi," *Corriere della Sera*, July 27, 2013, http://www.corriere.it/economia/13_luglio_28/ecco-dove-finito-made-in-italy_8f2d99b2-f6df-11e2-9839-a8732bb379b1.shtml; Rachel Sanderson, "The Real Value of Being 'Made in Italy,'" *Financial Times*, January 19, 2011, https://www.ft.com/content/ab98f3b4-2417-11e0-a89a-00144feab49a; "Made in Italy? Not for Much Longer as Artisans and Skills Disappear," *Deutsche Welle*, June 19, 2013, http://www.dw.com/en/made-in-italy-not-for-much-longer-as-artisans-and-skills-disappear/a-16887589; "Italian Manufacturing: A Washout," *Economist*, August 10, 2013, https://www.economist.com/news/business/21583283-years-crisis-have-reinforced-pressure-italys-once-envied-industrial-base-washout. Yanagisako and Lisa Rofel have explored the ways that Italian textile and clothing firms attempt to "transfer the prestige and market value of 'Made in Italy' to 'Designed in Italy'" as they increasingly turn to joint ventures with Chinese entrepreneurs to export manufacturing to China. See, for instance, Sylvia J. Yanagisako, "Transnational Family Capitalism: Producing 'Made in Italy' in China," in *Vital Relations: Modernity and the Persistent Life of Kinship*, ed. Susan McKinnon and Fenella Cannell (Santa Fe, NM: School for Advanced Research Press, 2013), 67.

53. This line of argument is indebted to Marxist feminist critique, and particularly to the work of scholars such as Sylvia Yanagisako and Silvia Federici. This literature has approached the gendered relations of social reproduction as more than the "merely cultural" embellishments atop capitalism's material base, and it also resists the separation between the political economic and the cultural as two distinct (but not equally important) terrains of struggle. See, for instance, Judith Butler, "Merely Cultural," *New Left Review* 1, no. 227 (1998): 33–44; Sylvia Junko Yanagisako, *Producing Culture and Capital: Family Firms in Italy* (Princeton, NJ: Princeton University Press, 2002); Silvia Federici, *Caliban and the Witch* (New York: Autonomedia, 2004); Papavero, "Minori e seconde generazioni"; Donald Martin Carter, "Blackness over Europe: Meditations on Cultural Belonging," in *Africa in Europe: Studies in Transnational Practice in the Long Twentieth Century*, ed. Eve Rosenhaft and Robbie John Macvicar Aitken (Liverpool: Liverpool University Press, 2013), 201–13; Heather Merrill, "Postcolonial Borderlands: Black Life Worlds and Relational Place in Turin, Italy," *ACME: An International Journal for Critical Geographies* 13, no. 2 (2014): 263–94. It is important to note that discussions about the Italian brain drain typically include only white Italians, despite the fact that large numbers of children of immigrants have also left Italy in the wake of the economic cri-

sis, for countries such as the United Kingdom. One exception to this trend can be found in the short documentary series *The Expats*, created by Italian-Haitian Johanne Affricot. Each episode of *The Expats* tells the story of a Black Italian creative professional who has moved abroad in search of greater opportunities. More information on the series is available at http://theexpats.griotmag.com/en/about/; Paolo Balduzzi and Alessandro Rosina, "Giovani talenti che lasciano l'Italia: Fonti, dati e politiche di un fenomeno complesso," *La Rivista delle Politiche Sociali* 3 (2011): 43–59.

54. Mauro Favale, "'Boicotta i negozi stranieri': Il marchio dei razzisti sulle saracinesche di Roma," *La Repubblica*, April 15, 2017, http://roma.repubblica.it/cronaca/2017/04/15/news/_boicotta_i_negozi_stranieri_il_marchio_dei_razzisti_sulle_saracinesche_di_roma-163019709/; Tom Kington, "Anti-immigrant Italians Find a New Foe: Food from Abroad," *Guardian*, November 15, 2009, http://www.theguardian.com/world/2009/nov/15/italys-kebab-war-hots-up; Igiaba Scego, "Igiaba Scego: La cittadinanza italiana ai figli di migranti è una conquista per tutti," *Cosmopolitan*, February 28, 2017, http://www.cosmopolitan.it/lifecoach/a116749/cittadinanza-italiana-ai-figli-di-migranti-igiaba-scego/.

55. Lisa Rofel and Sylvia J. Yanagisako, *Fabricating Transnational Capitalism: A Collaborative Ethnography of Italian-Chinese Global Fashion* (Durham, NC: Duke University Press, 2018); Elizabeth L. Krause, *Tight Knit: Global Families and the Social Life of Fast Fashion* (Chicago: University of Chicago Press, 2018).

56. Igiaba Scego, "Sausages," *Warscapes*, June 1, 2013, http://www.warscapes.com/retrospectives/food/sausages.

57. In one notable example, the young Burkinabe Madi Sakande was celebrated on the national television program *Mi manda Rai Tre* for saving a failing Italian refrigeration company. Like Evelyne Afaawua, Sakande was also the recipient of a MoneyGram Award for entrepreneurship in Italy. See https://www.facebook.com/mimandarai3/videos/10158673134395252/ for more information.

58. Annalisa Frisina and Camilla Hawthorne, "Sulle pratiche estetiche antirazziste delle figlie delle migrazioni," in Giuliani, *Il colore della nazione*, 200–214.

59. As recounted in chapter 1, signs held by members of the Lega Nord during a discussion of citizenship reform in the Italian Senate on July 15, 2017, actually bore the phrase "STOP INVASIONE" (STOP THE INVASION) in bolded, uppercase letters. See "Ius soli, discussione in Senato: È bagarre. Contusa ministra Fedeli e Boldrini dice basta alla violenza in Aula," *La Repubblica*, June 15, 2017, http://www.repubblica.it/politica/2017/06/15/news/ius_soli_discussione_senato-168161564/; Nirmal Puwar, *Space Invaders: Race, Gender and Bodies Out of Place* (Oxford: Berg, 2004).

60. Philomena Essed, *Understanding Everyday Racism: An Interdisciplinary Theory*, vol. 2 (Thousand Oaks, CA: SAGE, 1991).

61. Francesca Ferrario, "Dalla Russia alla Nigeria all'Italia ragionando su ricci e cittadinanza," *Medium* (blog), April 13, 2017, https://medium.com/migrantentrepreneurs-europe/dalla-russia-alla-nigeria-allitalia-ragionando-su-ricci-e-cittadinanza-1bab38f2b65.

62. Jayne O. Ifekwunigwe, "Recasting 'Black Venus' in the 'New' African Diaspora," in *Globalization and Race: Transformations in the Cultural Production of Blackness*, ed. Kamari Maxine Clarke and Deborah A. Thomas (Durham, NC: Duke University Press, 2006), 206–25; Frisina and Hawthorne, "Riconoscersi nel successo di Evelyne"; Puwar, *Space Invaders*.

63. Patricia Ehrkamp, "The Limits of Multicultural Tolerance? Liberal Democracy and Media Portrayals of Muslim Migrant Women in Germany," *Space and Polity* 14, no. 1 (2010): 13–32, https://doi.org/10.1080/13562571003737718; Barbara Yngvesson, "Migrant Bodies and the Materialization of Belonging in Sweden," *Social & Cultural Geography* 16, no. 5 (2015): 536–51, https://doi.org/10.1080/14649365.2015.1009856.

64. Giorgio Napolitano, "Intervento del Presidente Napolitano all'incontro dedicato ai 'nuovi cittadini italiani,'" Presidenza della Repubblica, November 15, 2011, http://presidenti.quirinale.it/elementi/Continua.aspx?tipo=Discorso&key=2302.

65. Igiaba Scego, *La mia casa è dove sono* (Turin: Loescher, 2012); Tailmoun, Valeri, and Tesfaye, *Campioni d'Italia?*

66. James Fallows, "Happy 150th Birthday, Italy!," *Atlantic*, March 17, 2011, https://www.theatlantic.com/international/archive/2011/03/happy-150th-birthday-italy/72591/; Sylvia Poggioli, "A Divided Italy to Mark Unification Anniversary," *NPR*, March 17, 2011, http://www.npr.org/2011/03/17/134602534/a-divided-italy-prepares-for-unification-anniversary.

67. Carter, "Blackness over Europe"; Gioia Panzarell, "Venditori di libri per strada come intermediari culturali della letteratura della migrazione," *El Ghibli* (blog), 2017, http://www.el-ghibli.org/wp-content/uploads/2017/07/I-venditori-di-libri-per-strada-come-intermediari-culturali-della-letteratura-della-migrazione-G.-Panzarella.pdf.

68. Douglas R. Holmes, *Integral Europe: Fast-Capitalism, Multiculturalism, Neofascism* (Princeton, NJ: Princeton University Press, 2010).

69. Goldberg, *Threat of Race*, 337.

70. "Milano, bruciate tre palme in Piazza Duomo," *La Stampa*, February 20, 2017, http://www.lastampa.it/2017/02/19/milano/milano-parzialmente-bruciate-tre-palme-in-piazza-duomo-FUnHqCgV4FHSOKvRKSi7DP/pagina.html.

71. Portelli, "Problem of the Color Blind"; Giuliani, "L'Italiano Negro," 573. For a more detailed description of the palm tree controversy, see Camilla Hawthorne, "L'Italia Meticcia? The Black Mediterranean and the Racial Cartographies of Citizenship," in *The Black Mediterranean: Bodies, Borders, and Citizenship in the Contemporary Migration Crisis*, ed. Gabriele Proglio, Camilla Hawthorne, Ida Danewid, P. Khalil Saucier, Giuseppe Grimaldi, Angelica Pesarini, Timothy Raeymaekers, Giulia Grechi, Vivian Gerrand (London: Palgrave Macmillan, 2021), 169–98.

72. Malkki, "National Geographic."

73. Choate, *Emigrant Nation*.

74. Ilaria Giglioli, "From 'A Frontier Land' to 'A Piece of North Africa in Italy': The Changing Politics of 'Tunisianness' in Mazara del Vallo, Sicily," *International Journal of Urban and Regional Research* 41, no. 5 (September 1, 2017): 749–66, https://doi.org/10.1111/1468-2427.12544.

75. I will discuss the history of claims about Italy's Mediterraneanness in greater detail in chapter 3.

76. Johanne Affricot, "The Vogue Italia Cover with Maty Fall Is Not Just a Cover," *GRIOT* (blog), February 10, 2020, https://griotmag.com/en/italian-beauty-the-vogue-italia-cover-with-maty-fall-is-not-just-a-cover/.

77. Affricot, "Vogue Italia Cover."

77. Giuliani, "L'Italiano Negro"; Ilaria Giglioli, "Producing Sicily as Europe: Migration, Colonialism and the Making of the Mediterranean Border between Italy and Tunisia," *Geopolitics* 22, no. 2 (2017): 407–28, https://doi.org/10.1080/14650045.2016.1233529.

78. Tamara K. Nopper, "The Wages of Non-Blackness: Contemporary Immigrant Rights and Discourses of Character, Productivity, and Value," *InTensions* 5 (Fall/Winter 2011): 1.

79. Rising rates of immigration from Africa and the Caribbean to the United States has brought increased attention to the intersections of Blackness and immigration status in the United States. See, for instance, Fumilayo Showers, "Being Black, Foreign and Woman: African Immigrant Identities in the United States," *Ethnic and Racial Studies* 38, no. 10 (August 9, 2015): 1815–30, https://doi.org/10.1080/01419870.2015.1036763. In addition, the association of "brown-ness" and Latinidad with immigration invisibilizes

the significant presence of Afro-Latinx immigrants in the United States. The Black Alliance for Just Immigration (https://baji.org/) was founded for this reason—to bring Black voices into discussions of immigrants' rights and immigration policy in the United States.

80. According to UNHCR, the five main origin countries for refugees arriving to Italy by sea between January and April 2017 were Nigeria, Bangladesh, Guinea, Côte d'Ivoire, and Gambia. See UNCHR Bureau for Europe, "Desperate Journeys—January to April 2017," June 14, 2017, https://data2.unhcr.org/en/documents/details/57696. See also the report by the MEDMIG research group, Heaven Crawley, Franck Düvell, Katharine Jones, Simon McMahon, and Nando Sigona, "Destination Europe? Understanding the Dynamics and Drivers of Mediterranean Migration in 2015," 2016, http://www.medmig.info/wp-content/uploads/2016/12/research-brief-destination-europe.pdf.

81. "Pascal" is a pseudonym. Antonietta Demurtas, "Italia, capitale straniero," Lettera43, accessed August 8, 2017, http://www.lettera43.it/it/articoli/economia/2011/10/01/italia-capitale-straniero/20484/.

82. "Ambrosian," or ambrosiano, refers to the city of Milan (the term derives from the city's patron saint, Ambrose).

83. "Cittadini stranieri in Italia—2017," Tuttitalia.it, 2017, https://www.tuttitalia.it/statistiche/cittadini-stranieri-2017/.

84. Daniela Uva, "Comunicato stampa: Immigrazione, una nuova chiave di lettura per la città globale. I candidati sindaci chiamati al confronto durante il convegno 'Il Welfare Ambrosiano e i Cittadini Globali,'" press release, May 2, 2016. http://www.globusetlocus.org/agenda/il-welfare-ambrosiano-e-i-cittadini-globali.kl.

85. Jordanna Matlon, "Racial Capitalism and the Crisis of Black Masculinity," American Sociological Review 81, no. 5 (2016): 1014–38, https://doi.org/10.1177/0003122416658294.

86. The recent controversy over a Gucci advertising campaign that attempted to re-create the imagery and style of 1960s soul is but one example of the fraught racial politics of representing Blackness and Black style in Italy. See Reginaldo Cerolini, "Fosco immaginario," La Macchina Sognante, no. 7 (June 19, 2017), http://www.lamacchinasognante.com/fosco-immaginario-reginaldo-cerolini/; R. Eric Thomas, "Gucci's Diversity Drag," New York Times, April 17, 2017, https://www.nytimes.com/2017/04/17/fashion/gucci-black-models-diversity.html. The Benetton apparel company also achieved notoriety in the 1990s for its advertisements linking racial difference to aesthetic consumption. See Les Back and Vibeke Quaade, "Dream Utopias, Nightmare Realities: Imaging Race and Culture within the World of Benetton Advertising," Third Text 7, no. 22 (1993): 65–80, https://doi.org/10.1080/09528829308576402; Henry Giroux, "Consuming Social Change: The 'United Colors of Benetton,'" Cultural Critique 26 (Winter 1993–94): 5–32.

87. Amy Larocca, "The Bodies Artist," The Cut, August 9, 2016, http://www.thecut.com/2016/08/vanessa-beecroft-bodies-artist.html.

88. Robinson, Black Marxism, 2005; Robin D. G. Kelley, "What Did Cedric Robinson Mean by Racial Capitalism?," Boston Review, January 12, 2017, http://bostonreview.net/race/robin-d-g-kelley-what-did-cedric-robinson-mean-racial-capitalism; Donna J. Haraway, Primate Visions: Gender, Race, and Nature in the World of Modern Science (1989; repr., London: Routledge, 2013), 208.

89. Ananya Roy, "Subjects of Risk: Technologies of Gender in the Making of Millennial Modernity," Public Culture 24, no. 1 (66) (January 1, 2012): 131–55, https://doi.org/10.1215/08992363-1498001.

90. Shirley Anne Tate, Black Beauty: Aesthetics, Stylization, Politics (Abingdon, UK: Routledge, 2016), 12.

91. "Immigrants, We Get the Job Done" is a song that was adapted from Lin-Manuel Miranda's hit Broadway musical Hamilton and released as a track on the The Hamilton Mixtape in 2017. "Immigrants" was accompanied by a music video depicting hardworking

immigrants sewing American flags in a garment factory, cleaning, carving meat in a slaughterhouse, picking fruit, and performing various forms of care work. The song was intended to counter the idea that immigrants steal "native" American jobs, by implying that immigrants are performing the kinds of grueling work that American citizens do not want to do. But the song was also criticized by many immigrants' rights activists for glorifying the exploitation of migrant labor, and implying that immigrants should only be tolerated because of the labor they perform.

3. MEDITERRANEANISM, AFRICA, AND THE RACIAL BORDERS OF ITALIANNESS

1. Marilena Umuhoza Delli, *Razzismo all'italiana* (Milan: Arcane Editrice, 2016).

2. Some other recent examples include Scego, *Italiani per vocazione*; Tommy Kuti, *Ci rido sopra: Crescere con la pelle nera nell'Italia di Salvini* (Milan: Rizzoli, 2019); Esperance Hakuzwimana Ripanti, *E poi basta: Manifesto di una donna nera italiana* (Gallarate, Italy: People, 2019); Igiaba Scego, ed., *Future: Il domani narrato dalle voci di oggi* (Florence: Effequ, 2019); Delli, *Razzismo all'italiana*; Loretta Grace, *Skin* (Milan: Mondadori, 2019).

3. The woman's reaction echoes an observation recorded by anthropologist Jeffrey Cole in his book *The New Racism in Europe*, when a Sicilian professor declared, "We can't be racist because we've been emigrants for so long!" (101).

4. Camilla Hawthorne and Pina Piccolo, "'Meticciato' o della problematicità di una parola," *La Macchina Sognante* 5 (2016), http://www.lamacchinasognante.com/meticciato-o-della-problematicita-di-una-parola-camilla-hawthorne-e-pina-piccolo/.

5. Vetri Nathan, "Mimic-Nation, Mimic-Men," in *National Belongings: Hybridity in Italian Colonial and Postcolonial Cultures*, ed. Jacqueline Andall and Derek Duncan (Bern: Peter Lang, 2010), 41–62.

6. "Immigrazione, Kyenge: 'L'Italia è meticcia, lo ius soli sarà figlio del paese nuovo,'" *Il Fatto Quotidiano*, June 10, 2013, http://www.ilfattoquotidiano.it/2013/06/10/immigrazione-kyenge-litalia-e-meticcia-ius-soli-sara-figlio-del-paese-nuovo/621519/.

7. Andall and Duncan, *National Belongings*.

8. Nathan, "Mimic-Nation, Mimic-Men."

9. Igiaba Scego, "Italy Is My Country—But It Must Face Its Racist History," *Guardian*, September 16, 2018, sec. World news, https://www.theguardian.com/world/2018/sep/16/italy-must-face-racist-history.

10. Valerie McGuire, *Italy's Sea: Empire and Nation in the Mediterranean, 1895–1945* (Liverpool: Liverpool University Press, 2020).

11. Michel Foucault, *Discipline and Punish: The Birth of the Prison* (1975; repr., New York: Vintage Books, 2012); Wendy Brown, *Politics Out of History* (Princeton, NJ: Princeton University Press, 2001).

12. Robert Young notes that in the late nineteenth century, the British often characterized themselves as a "mongrel" race produced through the intermixture of many different European types (Celts, Saxons, Normans, Danes, etc.). But what is distinct about Italy is that its supposed racial indeterminacy was a result of "hybridization" not only with Europeans, but with Africans and Asians as well. See Jinthana Haritaworn, *The Biopolitics of Mixing: Thai Multiracialities and Haunted Ascendancies* (London: Routledge, 2012); Robert J. C. Young, *Colonial Desire: Hybridity in Theory, Culture and Race* (London: Routledge, 2005).

13. Haritaworn, *Biopolitics of Mixing*.

14. Iain Chambers, *Mediterranean Crossings: The Politics of an Interrupted Modernity* (Durham, NC: Duke University Press, 2008); Roberto M. Dainotto, *Europe (in The-*

ory) (Durham, NC: Duke University Press, 2007); Karla Mallette, *European Modernity and the Arab Mediterranean: Toward a New Philology and a Counter-Orientalism* (Philadelphia: University of Pennsylvania Press, 2011); Claudio Fogu and Lucia Re, "Italy in the Mediterranean Today: A New Critical Topography," *California Italian Studies* 1, no. 1 (2010), https://escholarship.org/uc/item/6dk918sn.

15. Georg Wilhelm Friedrich Hegel, *The Philosophy of History* (1837; repr., Colonial Press, 1900), 87.

16. Pred, *Even in Sweden.*

17. Camilla Hawthorne, "Black Matters Are Spatial Matters: Black Geographies for the Twenty-First Century," *Geography Compass* 13, no. 11 (2019): 7, https://doi.org/10.1111/gec3.12468.

18. Goldberg, "Racial Europeanization."

19. Haritaworn, *Biopolitics of Mixing,* 15.

20. Angelo Matteo Caglioti, "Race, Statistics and Italian Eugenics: Alfredo Niceforo's Trajectory from Lombroso to Fascism (1876–1960)," *European History Quarterly* 47, no. 3 (2017): 461–89, https://doi.org/10.1177/0265691417707164.

21. In fact, Cesare Lombroso wrote a book titled *Anti-Semitism and the Modern Sciences* (1894), in which he argues against many of the central claims of scientific anti-Semitism.

22. N. Gordon-Chipembere, *Representation and Black Womanhood: The Legacy of Sarah Baartman* (New York: Springer, 2011); Britt Rusert, *Fugitive Science: Empiricism and Freedom in Early African American Culture* (New York: New York University Press, 2017); Sadiah Qureshi, *Peoples on Parade: Exhibitions, Empire, and Anthropology in Nineteenth-Century Britain* (Chicago: University of Chicago Press, 2011); Rachel Holmes, *The Hottentot Venus: The Life and Death of Saartjie Baartman: Born 1789–Buried 2002* (New York: Bloomsbury, 2016); Clifton C. Crais and Pamela Scully, *Sara Baartman and the Hottentot Venus: A Ghost Story and a Biography* (Princeton, NJ: Princeton University Press, 2009); Anne Fausto-Sterling, "Gender, Race, and Nation: The Comparative Anatomy of 'Hottentot' Women in Europe, 1815–17," in *Skin Deep, Spirit Strong: The Black Female Body in American Culture,* ed. Kimberly Wallace-Sanders (Ann Arbor: University of Michigan Press, 2002), 66–98; Katherine McKittrick, "Science Quarrels Sculpture: The Politics of Reading Sarah Baartman," *Mosaic* 43, no. 2 (2010): 113.

23. As Barbara Sòrgoni writes, the body of Sarah Baartman was used by Liberal and Fascist scientists to visualize the racial and gendered boundaries of Italianness. For Lombroso, for instance, Baartman's physiognomy and the presence of similar traits among Italian prostitutes was used to support his arguments about a biological origin of crime. See Barbara Sòrgoni, "'Defending the Race': The Italian Reinvention of the Hottentot Venus during Fascism," *Journal of Modern Italian Studies* 8, no. 3 (2010): 411–24.

24. Small, *20 Questions and Answers,* 8.

25. Antonio Gramsci, *The Southern Question,* trans. Pasquale Verdicchio (Toronto: Guernica Editions, 2005).

26. Schneider, *Italy's "Southern Question."*

27. Fabrizio De Donno, "La Razza Ario-Mediterranea: Ideas of Race and Citizenship in Colonial and Fascist Italy, 1885–1941," *Interventions* 8, no. 3 (2006): 394–412, https://doi.org/10.1080/13698010600955958.

28. Arthur Comte de Gobineau, *The Inequality of Human Races* (New York: G. P. Putnam's Sons, 1915); De Donno, "La Razza Ario-Mediterranea," 396; Gaia Giuliani, *Race, Nation and Gender in Modern Italy: Intersectional Representations in Visual Culture* (London: Palgrave Macmillan, 2018), 36.

29. Mary Gibson, "Biology or Climate? Race and 'Deviance' in Italian Criminology, 1880–1920," in Schneider, *Italy's "Southern Question,"* 100.

30. Shelleen Greene, *Equivocal Subjects: Between Italy and Africa—Constructions of Racial and National Identity in the Italian Cinema* (New York: Bloomsbury, 2012).

31. Mia Fuller, "Italian Colonial Rule," in *Oxford Bibliographies*, May 6, 2016, https://www.oxfordbibliographies.com/view/document/obo-9780199846733/obo-9780199846733-0150.xml.

32. Gibson, "Biology or Climate?," 100.

33. Francesco Cassata, "Between Lombroso and Pareto: The Italian Way to Eugenics," *Building the New Man: Eugenics, Racial Science and Genetics in Twentieth-Century Italy* (Budapest: Central European University Press, 2013), 9–42, http://books.openedition.org/ceup/723; Vito Teti, *La razza maledetta: Origini del pregiudizio antimeridionale* (Rome: Manifestolibri, 2011).

34. Daniel Pick, "The Faces of Anarchy: Lombroso and the Politics of Criminal Science in Post-Unification Italy," *History Workshop Journal* 21, no. 1 (March 20, 1986): 66, https://doi.org/10.1093/hwj/21.1.60; Giuliani and Lombardi-Diop, *Bianco e nero*, 32; Cristina Lombardi-Diop, "Mothering the Nation: An Italian Woman in Colonial Eritrea," in *ItaliAfrica: Bridging Continents and Cultures*, ed. Sante Matteo (Stony Brook, NY: Forum Italicum, 2001), 183.

35. Giuliani, "L'Italiano Negro," 575.

36. Mary Gibson and Nicole Hahn Rafter, "Editors' Introduction," in *Criminal Man* by Cesare Lombroso (Durham, NC: Duke University Press, 2006), 18.

37. Cesare Lombroso, *L'uomo bianco e l'uomo di colore: Letture sull' origine e le varietà delle razze umane* (Padua: F. Sacchetto, 1871), 10. See also Steven Epstein, *Speaking of Slavery: Color, Ethnicity, and Human Bondage in Italy* (Ithaca, NY: Cornell University Press, 2001), 7.

38. Lombroso, *L'uomo bianco e l'uomo di colore*, 222; Nicole Hahn Rafter, *The Criminal Brain: Understanding Biological Theories of Crime* (New York: New York University Press, 2008), 72.

39. As Gibson observes, Lombroso seems to have tentatively resolved this ambiguity by leaving open the possibility for malleability through environment or social intervention in the milieu for some groups (Jews and certain southern Italians, depending on the extent of their intermixture with Aryans), but not others (i.e., Africans). See Gibson, "Biology or Climate?," 105.

40. Caglioti, "Race, Statistics and Italian Eugenics."

41. David Forgacs, *Italy's Margins: Social Exclusion and Nation Formation since 1861* (Cambridge: Cambridge University Press, 2014), 103.

42. Caglioti, "Race, Statistics and Italian Eugenics," 465–66.

43. Silvana Patriarca, *Italianità: La costruzione del carattere nazionale* (Rome: Gius. Laterza & Figli S.p.A., 2014).

44. Giuseppe Sergi, *Origine e diffusione della stirpe mediterranea* (Rome: Società Editrice Dante Alighieri, 1895); Giovanni Cerro, "Giuseppe Sergi: The Portrait of a Positivist Scientist," *Journal of Anthropological Sciences* 95 (2017): 109–36, https://doi.org/10.4436/jass.95007.

45. Here it is important to note that Sergi and his contemporaries used the terms *razza* (race), *ceppo* (stock), and *stirpe* (kinship). Giuliani notes that *stirpe* corresponds to a "composite group of people"; during the early Fascist period, this term was also used in reference to Mediterranean groups whose shared relationships were tied to the Roman Empire. Yet, she and Mary Gibson note, authors rarely distinguished systematically between these terms, and often used them interchangeably. See Giuliani, "L'Italiano Negro," 579; Gibson, "Biology or Climate?"

46. According to a letter written to Cesare Lombroso in 1897, Sergi saw Venice as an example par excellence of the population mixing that constituted the contemporary Med-

iterranean stock. Archivio Storico del Museo di Antropologia Criminale Cesare Lombroso (Torino), Donazione Carrara, CL 248. See also Sergi, *Origine e diffusione*, 31. Lucia Re, "Italians and the Invention of Race: The Poetics and Politics of Difference in the Struggle over Libya, 1890–1913," *California Italian Studies* 1, no. 1 (2010), http://escholarship.org/uc/item/96k3w5kn.

47. Giuseppe Sergi, *Gli Arii in Europa e in Asia: studio etnografico, con figure e carte* (Turin: Fratelli Bocca, 1903), vi, cited in Aaron Gillette, *Racial Theories in Fascist Italy* (London: Routledge, 2003). According to Sergi (and again, unlike Gobineau), the Dark Ages were actually caused by the arrival of "savage," uncivilized Aryan invaders.

48. Ann Hallamore Caesar, *Printed Media in Fin-de-Siecle Italy: Publishers, Writers, and Readers* (London: Routledge, 2017).

49. Pasquale Verdicchio, *Bound by Distance: Rethinking Nationalism through the Italian Diaspora* (Madison, NJ: Fairleigh Dickinson University Press, 1997), 29–30; Giuseppe Sergi, *Arii e italici: Attorno all'Italia preistorica, con figure dimostrative* (Turin: Bocca, 1898); Re, "Italians and the Invention of Race"; Gibson, "Biology or Climate?," 111.

50. Many scholars have grappled with the relationship between the production of racial categories and the production of scientific knowledge—specifically, whether the practices of bracketing, isolation, and simplification that characterize various strands of scientific racism are mere aberrations or are fundamentally inextricable from science. I refer to the practices of Lombroso, Niceforo, and Sergi as "science" rather than "pseudoscience" because the research they conducted was at the time considered to be standard scientific practice. For more on these debates, see Donna J. Haraway, *Modest_Witness@ Second_Millennium.FemaleMan©_Meets_OncoMouse™: Feminism and Technoscience* (London: Routledge, 1997); Naomi Zack, *Philosophy of Science and Race* (London: Routledge, 2014); Evelynn M. Hammonds and Rebecca M. Herzig, *The Nature of Difference: Sciences of Race in the United States from Jefferson to Genomics* (Cambridge, MA: MIT Press, 2009); Stephen Jay Gould, *The Mismeasure of Man*, rev. ed. (New York: W. W. Norton 2006).

51. Stefan Kühl, *For the Betterment of the Race: The Rise and Fall of the International Movement for Eugenics and Racial Hygiene* (New York: Springer, 2013) (originally published in German as *Die Internationale der Rassisten: Aufstieg und Niedergang der internationalen eugenischen Bewegung im 20. Jahrhundert* [Frankfurt: Campus Verlag, 1997]), as cited in Caglioti, "Race, Statistics and Italian Eugenics."

52. Peter D'Agostino, "Craniums, Criminals, and the 'Cursed Race': Italian Anthropology in American Racial Thought, 1861–1924," *Comparative Studies in Society and History* 44, no. 2 (2002): 319–43.

53. Jennifer Guglielmo and Salvatore Salerno, *Are Italians White?: How Race Is Made in America* (London: Routledge, 2012); Cazzato, "Fractured Mediterranean and Imperial Difference."

54. It was not until the late twentieth century that Italian citizenship could be passed through the maternal line of descent. Pesarini, "Blood Is Thicker Than Water"; De Donno, "La Razza Ario-Mediterranea"; Barbara Sòrgoni, *Parole e corpi: Antropologia, discorso giuridico e politiche sessuali interrazziali nella colonia Eritrea, 1890–1941* (Naples: Liguori, 1998).

55. De Donno, "La Razza Ario-Mediterranea."

56. De Donno.

57. I thank my colleague Angelo Matteo Caglioti for suggesting this evocative phrasing.

58. Miguel Mellino, "De-provincializing Italy: Notes on Race, Racialization, and Italy's Coloniality," in Lombardi-Diop and Romeo, *Postcolonial Italy*, 92; Caglioti, "Race, Statistics and Italian Eugenics," 475. See, for instance, Renzo De Felice, *Mussolini il duce*

(Turin: Einaudi, 1996); Renzo De Felice, *Storia degli ebrei italiani sotto il fascismo* (Turin: Einaudi, 2005).

59. Caglioti, "Race, Statistics and Italian Eugenics."

60. Rosetta Giuliani Caponetto, *Fascist Hybridities: Representations of Racial Mixing and Diaspora Cultures under Mussolini* (New York: Springer, 2016).

61. Caglioti, "Race, Statistics and Italian Eugenics," 476.

62. Caglioti, 462; De Donno, "La Razza Ario-Mediterranea," 406; Ruth Ben-Ghiat, *Fascist Modernities: Italy, 1922–1945* (Berkeley: University of California Press, 2001); Welch, *Vital Subjects*.

63. Giuliani, "L'Italiano Negro," 582; Giuliani and Lombardi-Diop, *Bianco e nero*.

64. Nicola Labanca, *La guerra italiana per la Libia: 1911–1931* (Bologna: Il Mulino, 2012); Gabriele Proglio, *Libia 1911–1912: Immaginari coloniali e italianità* (Mondadori Education, 2016).

65. Re, "Italians and the Invention of Race," 5.

66. De Donno, "La Razza Ario-Mediterranea"; Barbara Sòrgoni, "Racist Discourses and Practices in the Italian Empire under Fascism," in *The Politics of Recognizing Difference: Multiculturalism Italian Style*, ed. Ralph Grillo and Jeff Pratt (Aldershot, UK: Ashgate, 2002), 41–57.

67. Gillette, *Racial Theories in Fascist Italy*.

68. Glenda Sluga, *The Problem of Trieste and the Italo-Yugoslav Border: Difference, Identity, and Sovereignty in Twentieth-Century Europe* (Albany: State University of New York Press, 2001), 52.

69. Giuliani, "L'Italiano Negro."

70. De Donno, "La Razza Ario-Mediterranea," 403.

71. De Donno, 403–4. The Italian Fascist regime had a complex relationship with the Catholic Church. The 1929 Lateran Treaty suspended church-state conflict in Italy by recognizing Vatican City as an independent state. In addition, the Catholic Church was supportive of Fascist pronatalist policies in the Italian countryside, and had its own tradition of anti-Semitic racist thought. In the mid-1930s, however, the Catholic Church began to change its stance on Jews and oppose Nazi Germany. See also Caglioti, "Race, Statistics and Italian Eugenics"; Gaia Giuliani, "Gender, Race and the Colonial Archive. Sexualized Exoticism and Gendered Racism in Contemporary Italy," *Italian Studies* 71, no. 4 (2016): 550–67, https://doi.org/10.1080/00751634.2016.1222767.

72. Karen Pinkus, *Bodily Regimes: Italian Advertising under Fascism* (Minneapolis: University of Minnesota Press, 1995), 56.

73. Maria Coletti, "Fantasmi d'Africa, dal muto al sonoro: Facce, facette, e blackface," in *L'Africa in Italia: Per una controstoria postcoloniale del cinema italiano*, ed. Leonardo De Franceschi (Rome: Aracne, 2013), 75–92; Sandra Ponzanesi, "Beyond the Black Venus: Colonial Sexual Politics and Contemporary Visual Practices," in *Italian Colonialism. Legacies and Memories*, ed. Jacqueline Andall and Derek Duncan (Oxford: Peter Lang, 2005), 165–89; Sonia Sabelli, "L'eredità del colonialismo nelle rappresentazioni contemporanee del corpo femminile nero," *Zapruder*, 23 (2010): 106–15; Merrill, *Black Spaces*, 47; Forgacs, *Italy's Margins*, 76.

74. Giuliani, "L'Italiano Negro."

75. Ruth Iyob, "Madamismo and Beyond: The Construction of Eritrean Women," *Nineteenth-Century Contexts* 22, no. 2 (2000): 217–38, https://doi.org/10.1080/089054900 08583509; Sandra Ponzanesi, "The Color of Love: Madamismo and Interracial Relationships in the Italian Colonies," *Research in African Literatures* 43, no. 2 (2012): 155–72, https://doi.org/10.2979/reseafrilite.43.2.155; Giulia Barrera, "Mussolini's Colonial Race Laws and State-Settler Relations in Africa Orientale Italiana (1935–41)," *Journal of Mod-*

ern Italian Studies 8, no. 3 (2003): 425–43, https://doi.org/10.1080/095851703200001
13770.

76. Iyob, "Madamismo and Beyond," 218.

77. De Donno, "La Razza Ario-Mediterranea," 399–400.

78. Roberta Pergher, *Mussolini's Nation-Empire* (Cambridge: Cambridge University Press, 2018); Ruth Ben-Ghiat and Mia Fuller, introduction to *Italian Colonialism*, ed. Ruth Ben-Ghiat and Mia Fuller (Palgrave Macmillan, 2008), 1–12; Mark I. Choate, *Emigrant Nation: The Making of Italy Abroad* (Cambridge, MA: Harvard University Press, 2008).

79. The 1933 law made explicit reference to "race," and race in turn was understood as something that could be scientifically measured in the body. "Mixed-race" children of unknown parentage were forced to undergo a series of physical measurements to determine whether they had sufficiently "Italian" racial features. See Pesarini, "Blood Is Thicker Than Water"; De Donno, "La Razza Ario-Mediterranea"; Sòrgoni, "Racist Discourses and Practices."

80. De Donno, "La Razza Ario-Mediterranea"; Barrera, "Mussolini's Colonial Race Laws"; Pesarini, "Blood Is Thicker Than Water."

81. Pesarini, "Blood Is Thicker Than Water"; Merrill, *Black Spaces.*

82. Under the 1938 Racial Laws, Jewish Italians were stripped of key civil rights including the ability to run for office and pursue higher education.

83. Igiaba Scego, "La vera storia di Faccetta nera," *Internazionale*, August 6, 2015, https://www.internazionale.it/opinione/igiaba-scego/2015/08/06/faccetta-nera-razzismo.

84. The Italian terms *meticcio* and *meticciato* themselves derive from the Spanish *mestizo / mestizaje*, which—as Marisol de la Cadena reminds us—referred to the transgression of religious, class, or cultural boundaries before it signified a person of mixed or "hybrid" racial background. See Marisol de la Cadena, "Are *Mestizos* Hybrids? The Conceptual Politics of Andean Identities," *Journal of Latin American Studies* 37, no. 2 (2005): 259–84, https://doi.org/10.1017/S0022216X05009004; Luigi Romani, "Meticciato, meticcio," *Treccani, l'enciclopedia italiana*, July 19, 2008, http://www.treccani.it/magazine/lingua_italiana/articoli/parole/meticciato.html.

85. Francesco Cassata, *La difesa della razza: Politica, ideologia e immagine del razzismo fascista* (Turin: G. Einaudi, 2008); Pinkus, *Bodily Regimes.*

86. Caglioti, "Race, Statistics and Italian Eugenics."

87. One reason why Marro is less well known is that very few of his notes and records remain today because of his ties to Italian Fascism. In addition, there were fierce debates among the Fascist Aryanists about whether race was a purely biological or spiritual concept, and Marro was ultimately on the losing side of this battle. Marro tended to focus on the spiritual character of race as opposed to physical characteristics. This is likely because Marro saw himself as a critic of the Italian positivist school of racial science. For Marro, physical features did not provide clear evidence of where racial lines began and ended. Marro's critique likely stemmed from the fact that because many Italians shared certain physical traits (such as skin color) with their colonized subjects, physiognomy did not provide a sufficient basis on which Italian superiority or authority could be determined— hence, the turn to "spiritual" qualities. Nonetheless, Marro was also criticized by Landra for his insufficiently "scientific" analysis of race, and it was this "biological" camp that ultimately triumphed. The biological anthropologist Gianluigi Mangiapane, based at the University of Turin, has played a key role in recuperating the documents tied to Marro that remain in the archives of the university's Museum of Anthropology and Ethnography. Many thanks to Dr. Mangiapane for allowing me to browse the collection of Marro's writings at the University of Turin and for sharing his own biographical research on this relatively unknown but nonetheless influential figure in Fascist Italy.

88. Paolo Berruti, Gianluigi Mangiapane, Donatella Minaldi, and Emma Robino Massa, *L'arte della folla nelle collezioni del Museo di Antropologia di Torino* (Turin: Le Nuove Muse, 2010).

89. Giovanni Marro, "Un allarme per il razzismo italiano," *La Vita Italiana* 29, no. 236 (March 1941): 5–17.

90. Gianluigi Mangiapane and Erika Grasso, "Il patrimonio, i non detti e il silenzio: Le storie del MAET," *roots§routes* (blog), May 14, 2019, https://www.roots-routes.org /patrimonio-non-detti-silenzio-le-storie-del-maet-gianluigi-mangiapane-erika-grasso/.

91. Giovanni Marro, *La sala della razza nella rassegna "Torino e l'autarchia"* (Turin: Tipografia Silvestrelli e Cappelletto, 1939).

92. Doreen Massey, *For Space* (Thousand Oaks: SAGE, 2005), 69.

93. De Donno, "La Razza Ario-Mediterranea."

94. The use of *razzisti* (which directly translates as "racist") in this context lies somewhere between Kwame Anthony Appiah's notions of racialism (the idea that inherited characteristics allow us to divide humans into races) and racism (the idea that positive moral characteristics are unevenly distributed across races). See Kwame Anthony Appiah, "Racisms," in *Anatomy of Racism*, ed. David Goldberg (Minneapolis: University of Minnesota Press, 1990), 3–17.

95. My explanatory comments are bracketed.

96. This inconsistency stands as a remnant of the debates among the scientists who helped to write the manifesto under Mussolini's instructions—as Aaron Gillette points out, in earlier drafts the Italians were actually identified as a Mediterranean race. See Aaron Gillette, "The Origins of the 'Manifesto of Racial Scientists,'" *Journal of Modern Italian Studies* 6, no. 3 (2001): 313, https://doi.org/10.1080/13545710110084253.

97. Luca Bussotti, "History of Italian Citizenship Laws," 143; Hom, *Empire's Mobius Strip*.

98. Mia Fuller, *Moderns Abroad: Architecture, Cities and Italian Imperialism* (London: Routledge, 2007). As Mia Fuller has demonstrated, the Fascist state saw *northern Africa* as more closely linked to the Roman Empire and by extension modern Italy, while sub-Saharan Africa (i.e., Eritrea, Ethiopia, and Somalia) was understood as prehistoric, lacking the necessary archaeological footprint necessary to connect it to the great Mediterranean civilizations of antiquity. During the Liberal and early Fascist periods, the Horn of Africa was regarded as "a mythical kingdom" inhabited by a more "noble" (and, at least in the case of Eritrea and Ethiopia, Christian) sub-Saharan African population— an idea tied to Sergi's Euro-Mediterranean race originating in the highlands of the Horn of Africa. The notion of a civilizational divide between North and sub-Saharan Africa persisted into late Fascism, translating into different colonial management and architectural practices applied by Italian administrators to the two regions.

99. Nicola Labanca, *Oltremare: Storia dell'espansione coloniale italiana* (Bologna: Il Mulino, 2007).

100. Mellino, "De-provincializing Italy," 88.

101. Lombardi-Diop, "Spotless Italy."

102. Lombardi-Diop.

103. Visweswaran, *Un/Common Cultures.*

104. UNESCO, "Four Statements on the Race Question" (Paris: UNESCO, 1969), http://refugeestudies.org/UNHCR/UNHCR.%20Four%20Statements%20on%20 the%20Race%20Question.pdf.

105. Goldberg, "Racial Europeanization"; Caterina Romeo, "Racial Evaporations: Representing Blackness in African Italian Postcolonial Literature," in Lombardi-Diop and Romeo, *Postcolonial Italy*, 221.

106. Mellino, "De-provincializing Italy," 92.

107. Lombardi-Diop, "Spotless Italy."

108. Patriarca, *Italianità*; Claudio Fogu, *"Italiani Brava Gente*: The Legacy of Fascist Historical Culture on Italian Politics of Memory," in *The Politics of Memory in Postwar Europe*, ed. Richard Ned Lebow, Wulf Kansteiner, and Claudio Fogu (Durham, NC: Duke University Press, 2006), 147–76.

109. Lombardi-Diop, "Spotless Italy."

110. Silvana Patriarca, "'Gli italiani non sono razzisti': Costruzioni dell'italianità tra gli anni Cinquanta e il 1986," in Giuliani, *Il colore della nazione*, 32–45.

111. Greene, *Equivocal Subjects*; Shelleen Greene, "Buffalo Soldiers on Film: Il soldato afroamericano nel cinema neorealista e postbellico italiano," in De Franceschi, *L'Africa in Italia*, 93–108.

112. Fred Kuwornu, *Blaxploitalian: 100 Years of Blackness in Italian Cinema*, documentary, 2016, https://vimeo.com/488197441.

113. Lombardi-Diop, "Spotless Italy."

114. Kristin Ross, *Fast Cars, Clean Bodies: Decolonization and the Reordering of French Culture* (Cambridge, MA: MIT Press, 1996).

115. Giglioli, "Producing Sicily as Europe."

116. Portelli, "Problem of the Color Blind"; Cristina Lombardi-Diop, "Postracial / Postcolonial Italy," in Lombardi-Diop and Romeo, *Postcolonial Italy*, 175.

117. Merrill, *Alliance of Women*.

118. Rosario Di Raimondo, "Domenica Salvini a Bologna, due giorni ad alta tensione," *La Repubblica*, November 1, 2015, http://bologna.repubblica.it/cronaca/2015/11/02/news /arriva_salvini_due_giorni_ad_alta_tensione-126423194/.

119. Carter and Merrill, "Bordering Humanism."

120. "Perché la razza bianca non esiste secondo la scienza," *La Repubblica*, January 18, 2018, https://www.repubblica.it/scienze/2018/01/18/news/perche_la_razza_bianca_non _esiste_secondo_la_scienza-186782903/.

121. Francesca Gandolfo, *Il Museo Coloniale di Roma (1904–1971): Fra le zebre nel paese dell'olio di ricino* (Rome: Gangemi Editore SpA, 2015).

122. "'Bologna è meticcia': La contestazione non violenta che manda in bestia i Salviner," *Radio Città del Capo* (blog), November 9, 2015, https://www.youtube.com /watch?v=RZKGic0_O_g&ab_channel=RadioCitt%C3%A0delCapo. Frisina and Hawthorne, "Riconoscersi nel successo di Evelyne," 192.

123. Fanpage.it, "Chi sono (davvero) quelli scesi in piazza con Salvini," November 10, 2015, YouTube video, 9:39, https://www.youtube.com/watch?v=snMbCsK3hd8. See timestamp 5:59. I thank Annalisa Frisina for bringing this to my attention.

124. "Manifestazione antirazzista per 'Milano meticcia,' centri sociali e comitati al corteo contro la Lega Nord," *Il Giorno*, October 18, 2014, https://www.ilgiorno.it/milano /cronaca/manifestazione-antirazzista-milano-meticcia-1.315186.

125. "Napoli è meticcia: VIII edizione del Mediterraneo antirazzista," *Comunicare il Sociale* (blog), June 26, 2019, http://www.comunicareilsociale.com/2019/06/26/napoli-e -meticcia-viii-edizione-del-mediterraneo-antirazzista/; "Migranti, a Palermo il Mediterraneo antirazzista: Sport per inclusione sociale," *Il Fatto Quotidiano*, May 10, 2019, https://www.ilfattoquotidiano.it/2019/05/10/migranti-a-palermo-il-mediterraneo -antirazzista-sport-per-inclusione-sociale/5169329/.

126. Associazione per gli Studi Giuridici sull'Immigrazione (ASGI), "Codice di condotta per le ONG coinvolte nel salvataggio di migranti in mare: Il commento dell'ASGI," Melting Pot Europa, July 25, 2017, https://www.meltingpot.org/Codice-di-condotta-per -le-ONG-coinvolte-nel-salvataggio-di.html.

127. Claudio Fogu, "From *Mare Nostrum* to *Mare Aliorum*: Mediterranean Theory and Mediterraneism in Contemporary Italian Thought," *California Italian Studies* 1, no. 1

(2010), https://escholarship.org/uc/item/7vp210p4; Luigi Cazzato, "Mediterranean: Co-loniality, Migration and Decolonial Practices," *Politics: Rivista di Studi Politici* 5, no. 21 (2016), https://doi.org/10.6093/2279-7629/3978.

128. Franco Cassano, *Il pensiero meridiano* (Rome: Gius. Laterza & Figli S.p.A., 2015).

129. Giglioli, "Producing Sicily as Europe."

130. Pierfranco Malizia, *Interculturalismo: Studio sul vivere "individualmente-insieme-con-gli-altri"* (Milan: FrancoAngeli, 2005), 22.

131. See figure 3.5 for a graphical illustration of *meticciato*'s return at the end of the twentieth century.

132. Portelli, "Problem of the Color Blind."

133. "Il paese arcobaleno: Italia ricca di diversità genetica," *Corriere della Sera*, January 20, 2014, http://www.corriere.it/scienze_e_tecnologie/14_gennaio_19/paese-arco baleno-italia-ricca-diversita-genetica-bf158fe4-8119-11e3-a1c3-05b99f5e9b32.shtml; Marco Capocasa, Paolo Anagnostou, Valeria Bachis, Cinzia Battaggia, Stefania Bertoncini, Gianfranco Biondi, Alessio Boattini, et al., "Linguistic, Geographic and Genetic Isolation: A Collaborative Study of Italian Populations," *Journal of Anthropological Sciences* 92 (2014): 201–31, https://download.repubblica.it/pdf/2014/scienze/jass-reports.pdf.

134. Guido Barbujani, *Gli africani siamo noi: Alle origini dell'uomo* (Rome: Laterza, 2016); Daniele Giori, "Razzismo, genetista: 'La razza bianca? Senza immigrazione gli europei avrebbero la pelle scura,'" *Il Fatto Quotidiano*, January 28, 2018, https://www .ilfattoquotidiano.it/2018/01/28/razzismo-genetista-le-razza-bianca-senza-immigrazione -gli-europei-avrebbero-la-pelle-scura/4118255/.

135. Ian Law, *Mediterranean Racisms: Connections and Complexities in the Racialization of the Mediterranean Region* (New York: Springer, 2014).

136. "Manifesto degli scienziati antirazzisti 2008," July 10, 2008, http://www .meltingpot.org/Manifesto-degli-scienziati-antirazzisti-2008.html.

137. Laura Harris, "L'abbandono: Who's Meticcio / Whose Meticcio in the Eritrea-Italy Diaspora?," in Matteo, *ItaliAfrica*, 192–204.

138. Valentina Migliarini, "'Colour-Evasiveness' and Racism without Race: The Disablement of Asylum-Seeking Children at the Edge of Fortress Europe," *Race Ethnicity and Education* 21, no. 4 (July 4, 2018): 438–57, https://doi.org/10.1080/13613324.2017.1417252.

139. The word "race" appears only once in the Italian constitution, in the first section of Article 3: "All citizens have equal social dignity and are equal before the law, without distinction of sex, race, language, religion, political opinion, personal and social conditions." See Maria Teresa Milcia and Gaia Giuliani, "Giochi al buio o parole per dirlo? Riflessioni su razza, razzismo e antirazzismo intorno a un colloquio con Gaia Giuliani," *Voci: Annuale di Scienze Umane* 13 (2016): 171–89.

140. Sante Matteo, "Introduction: African Italy, Bridging Continents and Cultures," in Matteo, *ItaliAfrica*, 5.

141. Giuliani, "L'Italiano Negro."

142. Tatiana Petrovich Njegosh, "Gli italiani sono bianchi? Per una storia culturale della linea del colore in Italia," in *Parlare di razza: La lingua del colore tra Italia e Stati Uniti*, ed. Tatiana Petrovich Njegosh and Anna Scacchi (Verona: Ombre Corte, 2012), 13–45. Quoted in Pesarini, "Blood Is Thicker Than Water."

143. Guglielmo and Salerno, *Are Italians White?*

144. Of course, there has been an African presence in the Italian peninsula for as long as written and archaeological records exist, long before people from the African continent were racialized as "Black."

145. Aimé Césaire, *Discourse on Colonialism* (1950; repr., New York: Monthly Review Press, 2000) (emphasis in the original).

146. Luigi Ripamonti, "Gli italiani non esistono. Siamo un grande mix genetico. Tranne i sardi," *Corriere della Sera*, March 5, 2018, https://www.corriere.it/salute/18_maggio_02/italiani-mix-genetico-tranne-sardi-eab18cda-4e32-11e8-98a3-3b5657755c11.shtml; Italian senza Cittadinanza, "Gli Italiani? Non esistono," Facebook, May 3, 2018, https://www.facebook.com/italianisenzacittadinanza/posts/2075653602716034.

4. TRANSLATION AND THE LIVED GEOGRAPHIES OF THE BLACK MEDITERRANEAN

1. This chapter is adapted from my article, "In Search of Black Italia: Notes on Race, Belonging, and Activism in the Black Mediterranean," *Transition* 123, no. 1 (June 17, 2017): 152–74.

2. Gloria Wekker, *White Innocence: Paradoxes of Colonialism and Race* (Durham, NC: Duke University Press, 2016), 17; Philomena Essed and Isabel Hoving, *Dutch Racism* (Amsterdam: Rodopi, 2014).

3. Simone Browne, *Dark Matters: On the Surveillance of Blackness* (Durham, NC: Duke University Press, 2015).

4. Timothy Raeymaekers, "The Racial Geography of the Black Mediterranean," *Liminal Geographies* (blog), January 21, 2015, http://www.timothyraeymaekers.net/2015/01/the-racial-geography-of-the-black-mediterranean/.

5. Hawthorne and Piccolo, "'Razza' e 'umano.'"

6. United Nations High Commissioner for Refugees (UNCHR), "Italy: UNHCR Update #10," March 16, 2017, https://data2.unhcr.org/en/documents/details/53633.

7. Graham-Harrison, "Migrants from West Africa"; Matina Stevis, Joe Parkinson, and Nichole Sobecki, "Thousands Flee Isolated Eritrea to Escape Life of Conscription and Poverty," *Wall Street Journal*, February 2, 2016, http://www.wsj.com/articles/eritreans-flee-conscription-and-poverty-adding-to-the-migrant-crisis-in-europe-1445391364; Efam Awo Dovi, "Migration: Taking Rickety Boats to Europe," *Africa Renewal*, 2017, http://www.un.org/africarenewal/magazine/special-edition-youth-2017/migration-taking-rickety-boats-europe.

8. Maurice Stierl, "Contestations in Death—the Role of Grief in Migration Struggles," *Citizenship Studies* 20, no. 2 (2016): 173, https://doi.org/10.1080/13621025.2015.1132571.

9. Beatrice Montini, "Fermo, picchiato a sangue e ucciso aveva reagito a insulti razzisti," *Corriere della Sera*, July 6, 2016, http://www.corriere.it/cronache/16_luglio_06/fermo-reagisce-insulti-razzisti-nigeriano-massacrato-coma-irreversibile-e69a92be-4393-11e6-831b-0b63011f1840.shtml.

10. Paolo Gallori and Chiara Nardinocchi, "Fermo, difende la compagna da insulti razzisti. Nigeriano picchiato a morte da ultrà locale," *La Repubblica*, July 6, 2016, http://www.repubblica.it/cronaca/2016/07/06/news/fermo_muore_nigeriano_aggredito_da_ultra_locale-143565559/.

11. "Appello per una Sala di Medicina a Bologna dedicata a Emmanuel Chidi Nnamdi (Italiano e Inglese)," *La Macchina Sognante* (blog), July 12, 2016, http://www.lamacchinasognante.com/appello-per-una-sala-di-medicina-a-bologna-dedicata-a-emmanuel-chidi-namdi/.

12. "Nigerian Man Beaten to Death in Racist Attack," Vatican Radio, July 7, 2016, http://en.radiovaticana.va/news/2016/07/07/nigerian_man_beaten_to_death_in_racist_attack/1242717.

13. I use the phrase "Black body" deliberately in this particular instance to mark the inherent dehumanization of the racializing (or, to borrow Fanonian terminology, epidermalizing) gaze.

14. "Fermo, Matteo Salvini: 'Prego per Emmanuel, non doveva morire. L'immigrazione non porta nulla di buono,'" *L'Huffington Post* (blog), July 7, 2016, http://www.huffington post.it/2016/07/07/salvini-emmanuel_n_10854424.html.

15. I will explore this division further in chapter 5.

16. Fanon, *Black Skin, White Masks*, 89.

17. Portelli, "Problem of the Color Blind," 30; Fanon, *Black Skin, White Masks*, xii.

18. Merrill, *Alliance of Women*, xxi; Kate Hepworth and Olivia Hamilton, "'Let Me Stay Home': Apparetenenza, luogo e giovani di seconda generazione in Italia," *Studi Culturali* 11, no. 3 (2014): 493–509; Gerardo Adinolfi, "Modou e Mor chi erano le vittime," *La Repubblica*, December 13, 2011, http://firenze.repubblica.it/cronaca/2011/12/13/news /modou_e_mor_chi_erano_le_vittime-26561561/.

19. Melissa Coburn, *Race and Narrative in Italian Women's Writing since Unification* (Madison, NJ: Fairleigh Dickinson, 2013); Essed, *Understanding Everyday Racism*.

20. Sheena McKenzie, "Black Lives Matter Protests Spread to Europe," CNN, July 11, 2016, http://www.cnn.com/2016/07/11/europe/black-lives-matter-protests-europe/index .html.

21. "Black Lives Matter in France, Too," editorial, *New York Times*, July 29, 2016, https://www.nytimes.com/2016/07/29/opinion/black-lives-matter-in-france-too.html; James McAuley, "Black Lives Matter Movement Comes to France. But Will It Translate?," *Washington Post*, August 8, 2016, https://www.washingtonpost.com/world/black-lives -matter-movement-comes-to-france-but-will-it-translate/2016/08/07/7606567e-58cd -11e6-8b48-0cb344221131_story.html.

22. Sewell Chan, "Black Lives Matter Activists Stage Protests across Britain," *New York Times*, August 5, 2016, https://www.nytimes.com/2016/08/06/world/europe/black-lives -matter-demonstrations-britain.html.

23. Foucault, *The History of Sexuality*, 135.

24. Marvely Goma Perseverance, "Lettera Aperta Di Marvely Goma Perseverance per Abba Ed Emmanuel," *GRIOT*, accessed July 9, 2016, http://griotmag.com/it/lettera -marvely-goma-perseverance-abba-ed-emmanuel/. See also https://www.facebook.com /MarvelyPerseverance/posts/10207294970394261.

25. Pseudonym.

26. In 2015, ENAR released an influential and widely cited report on Afrophobia in Europe. ENAR Europe, "Racist Murder in Italy Is a Wake-Up Call for a European #Black-LivesMatter," July 7, 2016, http://www.enar-eu.org/Racist-murder-in-Italy-is-a-wake -up-call-for-a-European-BlackLivesMatter.

27. Steven Mazie, "What Does 'No Justice, No Peace' Really Mean?," *Big Think* (blog), December 5, 2014, http://bigthink.com/praxis/what-does-no-justice-no-peace-really -mean; Malik Wanous, "Stay Human: A Diary, a Reminder of Palestine," *Arab Center for Research and Policy Studies* (blog), August 11, 2011, https://www.dohainstitute.org/en /ResearchAndStudies/Pages/Stay_Human_A_diary_a_reminder_of_Palestine.aspx.

28. Facebook post, July 26, 2016.

29. Emphasis added.

30. Bayo Holsey, *Routes of Remembrance: Refashioning the Slave Trade in Ghana* (Chicago: University of Chicago Press, 2008).

31. Stephen Small, *20 Questions and Answers*; Brown, *Dropping Anchor, Setting Sail*, 42.

32. Anna Everett, *Digital Diaspora: A Race for Cyberspace* (Albany: State University of New York Press, 2009); Michelle M. Wright, "Finding a Place in Cyberspace: Black Women, Technology, and Identity," *Frontiers: A Journal of Women Studies* 26, no. 1 (2005): 48–59, https://doi.org/10.1353/fro.2005.0017.

33. Gado Alzouma, "Identities in a 'Fragmegrated' World: Black Cyber-Communities and the French Integration System," *African and Black Diaspora: An International Jour-

nal 1, no. 2 (2008): 201–14, https://doi.org/10.1080/17528630802224130; Krystal Strong and Shaun Ossei-Owusu, "Naija Boy Remix: Afroexploitation and the New Media Creative Economies of Cosmopolitan African Youth," *Journal of African Cultural Studies* 26, no. 2 (2014): 189–205, https://doi.org/10.1080/13696815.2013.861343.

34. Pseudonym.

35. See also García Peña, "Black in English."

36. Brown, *Dropping Anchor, Setting Sail*, 53.

37. Michelle M. Wright, "Postwar Blackness and the World of Europe," *Österreichisches Zeitschrift für Geschichtswissenschaften* 17, no. 2 (2006): 147; Michelle M. Wright, *Physics of Blackness: Beyond the Middle Passage Epistemology* (Minneapolis: University of Minnesota Press, 2015).

38. Campt, *Other Germans*.

39. Darlene Clark Hine, preface to Hine, Keaton, and Small, *Black Europe and the African Diaspora*, xvii–xix; Asad, "Conscripts of Western Civilization"; Scott, *Conscripts of Modernity*; Gloria Wekker, "Another Dream of a Common Language: Imagining Black Europe . . . ," in Hine, Keaton, and Small, *Black Europe and the African Diaspora*, 280.

40. Wright, *Physics of Blackness*; Wright, "Postwar Blackness."

41. Hall, "Cultural Identity and Diaspora," 228.

42. Jacqueline Nassy Brown, "Black Europe and the African Diaspora: A Discourse on Location," in Hine, Keaton, and Small, *Black Europe and the African Diaspora*, 201. See also Brown, *Dropping Anchor, Setting Sail*.

43. Brown, *Dropping Anchor, Setting Sail*, 40–41; Paul Gilroy, *"There Ain't No Black in the Union Jack": The Cultural Politics of Race and Nation* (1987; repr. Chicago: University of Chicago Press, 1991); Gilroy, *The Black Atlantic*. For a related engagement with Gilroy's conceptualization of diaspora, see also Stefan Helmreich, "Kinship, Nation, and Paul Gilroy's Concept of Diaspora," *Diaspora: A Journal of Transnational Studies* 2, no. 2 (1992): 243–49, https://doi.org/10.1353/dsp.1992.0016.

44. Brown, *Dropping Anchor, Setting Sail*, 99.

45. Stephen Small notes that most European countries think of themselves as nonracist, instead "pointing the finger" to other, supposedly "more racist" countries in Europe and beyond: "European nations have always shared strikingly similar intentions, ideologies and practices, with regard to Africa and black people, despite affirming their distinct differences." See Stephen Small, "Theorizing Visibility and Vulnerability in Black Europe and the African Diaspora," *Ethnic and Racial Studies* 41, no. 6 (2018): 1194, https://doi.org/10.1080/01419870.2018.1417619; Small, *20 Questions and Answers*.

46. Cole, *New Racism in Europe*; Merrill, *Alliance of Women*.

47. Alessandro Sallusti, "Il governo inventa l'Italia razzista," *Il Giornale*, July 11, 2016, http://www.ilgiornale.it/news/politica/governo-inventa-litalia-razzista-1282525.html.

48. Ironically, after Italian national unification it was not uncommon for northern Italian commentators to draw comparisons between *southern Italians* and Native Americans. See, for instance, Leopoldo Franchetti's description, quoted in Moe, *View from Vesuvius*, 239. For more on the racial politics of comparison in postunification Italy, see also Wong, *Race and the Nation*.

49. Robinson, *Black Marxism*; Paul Khalil Saucier and Tryon P. Woods, "Ex Aqua: The Mediterranean Basin, Africans on the Move, and the Politics of Policing," *Theoria* 61, no. 141 (2014): 55–75, https://doi.org/10.3167/th.2014.6114104; Bono, *Schiavi*.

50. IRAAS-AAADSColumbiaU, "IRAAS Conversations Lecture w/ Prof. Crystal Fleming," Columbia University, New York, March 15, 2016, YouTube video, 1:17:31, https://www.youtube.com/watch?v=IGFVBgUXytg; Crystal Marie Fleming, *Resurrecting Slavery: Racial Legacies and White Supremacy in France* (Philadelphia: Temple University Press, 2017).

51. Andreas Wimmer and Nina Glick Schiller, "Methodological Nationalism and the Study of Migration," *European Journal of Sociology / Archives Européennes de Sociologie / Europäisches Archiv für Soziologie* 43, no. 2 (2002): 217–40; Manu Goswami, "Rethinking the Modular Nation Form: Toward a Sociohistorical Conception of Nationalism," *Comparative Studies in Society and History* 44, no. 4 (2002): 770–99; Armando Gnisci, *Creoli, meticci, migranti, clandestini e ribelli* (Rome: Meltemi Editore, 1998).

52. "Bologna è meticcia"; "A Milano arriva Innesti, il festival degli 'italiani ibridi,'" Redattore Sociale, June 18, 2016, http://www.redattoresociale.it/Notiziario/Articolo /510774/A-Milano-arriva-Innesti-il-festival-degli-italiani-ibridi.

53. Carter and Merrill, "Bordering Humanism."

54. Mitchell, "Different Diasporas"; Sabine Broeck, "White Fatigue, or, Supplementary Notes on Hybridity," in *Reconstructing Hybridity: Postcolonial Studies in Transition*, ed. Joel Kuortti and Jopi Nyman (Amsterdam: Rodopi, 2007), 43–58.

55. F. James Davis, *Who Is Black?: One Nation's Definition* (University Park: Penn State University Press, 2010); Richard T. Schaefer, "One-Drop Rule," in *Encyclopedia of Race, Ethnicity, and Society* (Thousand Oaks, CA: SAGE, March 20, 2008), 1:998–99.

56. Barrera, "Mussolini's Colonial Race Laws."

57. Robert J. C. Young, "The Italian Postcolonial," in Lombardi-Diop and Romeo, *Postcolonial Italy*, 31–34; Cole, *New Racism in Europe*, 9.

58. Clelia Bartoli, *Razzisti per legge: L'Italia che discrimina* (Rome: Gius. Laterza & Figli, 2012).

59. Sabine Broeck, "The Erotics of African American Endurance, Or: On the Right Side of History?," in *Germans and African Americans*, ed. Larry A. Greene and Anke Ortlepp (Jackson: University Press of Mississippi, 2010), 126–40, https://doi.org/10.14325 /mississippi/9781604737844.003.0008.

60. Gassid Mohamed, "Non uccidete l'umano," *Frontiere News*, July 17, 2016, http:// frontierenews.it/2016/07/non-uccidete-umano-fermo-paura-diverso/. Pina Piccolo and I wrote a response to Gassid Mohamed's article; see Hawthorne and Piccolo, "'Razza' e 'umano.'"

61. Drawing on Jacqueline Nassy Brown (2009, 91–92), here I understand political subjectivity (as opposed to identity) as something that draws on particular constructions of identity in response to a broader set of political conditions.

62. Stuart Hall, "Gramsci's Relevance for the Study of Race and Ethnicity," *Journal of Communication Inquiry* 10, no. 2 (June 1, 1986): 5–27, https://doi.org/10.1177 /019685998601000202; Stuart Hall, "Race, Articulation, and Societies Structured in Dominance," in *Sociological Theories: Race and Colonialism* (Paris: UNESCO, 1980); Hall, "Gramsci's Relevance."

63. Edward W. Said, "Traveling Theory Reconsidered," in *Reflections on Exile and Other Essays* (Cambridge, MA: Harvard University Press, 2000), 436–52; Adam David Morton, "Traveling with Gramsci: The Spatiality of Passive Revolution," in *Gramsci: Space, Nature, Politics*, ed. Michael Ekers, Gillian Hart, Stefan Kipfer, and Alex Loftus (Hoboken, NJ: John Wiley & Sons, 2012), 60.

64. Hall, "Gramsci's Relevance," 8; Pasquale Verdicchio, "The Preclusion of Postcolonial Discourse in Southern Italy," in Allen and Russo, *Revisioning Italy*, 193.

65. Fatima El-Tayeb, *European Others: Queering Ethnicity in Postnational Europe* (Minneapolis: University of Minnesota Press, 2011), xvi.

66. El-Tayeb, xvii.

67. Goldberg, *Threat of Race*, 67.

68. Goldberg, "Racial Europeanization."

69. Goldberg, 335.

70. Goldberg, *Racial State*, 69; Hall, "Gramsci's Relevance," 23.

71. Law, *Mediterranean Racisms*.

72. Law.

73. Alessandra Di Maio, "Mediterraneo nero: Le rotte dei migranti nel millennio globale," in *La citta' cosmopolita*, ed. Giulia de Spuches and Vincenzo Guarrasi (Palermo: Palumbo Editore, 2012), 142–63.

74. This demographic balance is already beginning to shift toward southern Italy with the most recent refugee "emergency" and the insertion of irregular migrants into the informal or "black" economies of southern Italian agriculture and construction. This will be addressed further in the book's conclusion.

75. Saucier and Woods, "Ex Aqua," 64.

76. Christina Sharpe, *In the Wake: On Blackness and Being* (Durham, NC: Duke University Press, 2016).

77. Ida Danewid, "White Innocence in the Black Mediterranean: Hospitality and the Erasure of History," *Third World Quarterly* 38, no. 7 (2017): 1674–89, https://doi.org/10.1080/01436597.2017.1331123.

78. Raeymaekers, "Introduction: Europe's Bleeding Border," 168.

79. Timothy Raeymaekers, "Working the Black Mediterranean," *Liminal Geographies* (blog), January 21, 2015, http://www.timothyraeymaekers.net/2015/01/working-the-black-mediterranean/.

80. Kelley, foreword to Robinson, *Black Marxism*, xiv.

81. Chambers, *Mediterranean Crossings*, 137. See also John Wright, "Cats, Musk, Gold and Slaves: Staples of the Northbound Saharan Trade," *Journal of North African Studies* 16, no. 3 (September 1, 2011): 415–20, https://doi.org/10.1080/13629387.2010.492156.

82. "The Black Mediterranean and the Migrant Crisis," Birmingham City University, Birmingham, UK, November 9, 2016. See also Olivette Otele, *African Europeans: An Untold History* (New York: Basic Books, 2021).

83. Gabriele Proglio, "Is the Mediterranean a White Italian-European Sea? The Multiplication of Borders in the Production of Historical Subjectivity," *Interventions* 20, no. 3 (2018): 6, https://doi.org/10.1080/1369801X.2017.1421025.

84. Hegel, *Philosophy of History*; Sir Halford John Mackinder, *Democratic Ideals and Reality: A Study in the Politics of Reconstruction* (New York: H. Holt, 1919); Fernand Braudel, *The Mediterranean and the Mediterranean World in the Age of Philip II* (1949; repr., Berkeley: University of California Press, 1995).

85. Gabriele Proglio, ed., *Decolonizing the Mediterranean* (Cambridge: Cambridge Scholars, 2016), ix.

86. The title of this section is indebted to Norma Alarcón's 1989 article "Traddutora, Traditora: A Paradigmatic Figure of Chicana Feminism," and to her discussion of linguistic mediation as a potential act of betrayal.

87. Pseudonym.

88. Esther and Marcus are both pseudonyms. *Nuovi italiani* is one of many terms used to describe the children of immigrants who were born and raised in Italy.

89. Brent Hayes Edwards, *The Practice of Diaspora: Literature, Translation, and the Rise of Black Internationalism* (Cambridge, MA: Harvard University Press, 2009), 5.

90. Edwards, *Practice of Diaspora*, 8.

91. Recently, various translators have proposed *nerezza* and *nerità* as possible translations for "Blackness," though neither term has reached widespread circulation in Italy.

92. "La ministra Kyenge si presenta: 'Sono nera, non di colore e lo dico con fierezza,'" *Corriere della Sera*, May 3, 2013, http://www.corriere.it/politica/13_maggio_03/kyenge-nera_5b24eea0-b3db-11e2-a510-97735eec3d7c.shtml.

93. Pseudonym.

94. VèVè A. Clark, "Developing Diaspora Literacy and Marasa Consciousness," *Theatre Survey* 50, no. 1 (May 2009): 11, https://doi.org/10.1017/S0040557409000039.

95. Hine, Keaton, and Small, *Black Europe and the African Diaspora*; Baldwin, *Notes of a Native*; Grada Kilomba, *Plantation Memories: Episodes of Everyday Racism* (Münster: Unrast, 2008).

96. May Ayim, *Blues in Black and White: A Collection of Essays, Poetry, and Conversations* (Trenton: Africa World Press, 2003), 93–94.

97. Merrill, "Postcolonial Borderlands," 279; Carter, "Blackness over Europe," 204.

98. May Opitz, Katharina Oguntoye, and Dagmar Schultz, *Showing Our Colors: Afro-German Women Speak Out* (1986; repr., Amherst: University of Massachusetts Press, 1992); Jennifer Michaels, "The Impact of Audre Lorde's Politics and Poetics on Afro-German Women Writers," *German Studies Review* 29, no. 1 (2006): 21–40.

99. "Neri Italiani—Black Italians" is the name of an Afro-descendant youth organization in Rome.

100. Giuliani, "Gender, Race and the Colonial Archive," 2.

5. REFUGEES AND CITIZENS-IN-WAITING

1. All names in this dialogue are pseudonyms.

2. Doreen Massey, *Space, Place, and Gender* (Minneapolis: University of Minnesota Press, 1994); Merrill, "Postcolonial Borderlands," 267.

3. Scott, *Conscripts of Modernity*.

4. Goldberg, *Racial State*.

5. Scott, *Conscripts of Modernity*; David Scott, *Omens of Adversity: Tragedy, Time, Memory, Justice* (Durham, NC: Duke University Press, 2013); Greg Beckett, "The Politics of Disjuncture, or Freedom from a Caribbean Point of View," *Small Axe: A Caribbean Journal of Criticism* 21, no. 2 (53) (2017): 184–92, https://doi.org/10.1215/07990537-4156906.

6. Bonilla, *Non-Sovereign Futures*, 43.

7. Yarimar Bonilla, "Freedom, Sovereignty, and Other Entanglements," *Small Axe: A Caribbean Journal of Criticism* 21, no. 2 (53) (2017): 206, https://doi.org/10.1215/07990537-4156930.

8. According to Bonilla (2017, 206), maroon political projects are emblematic of strategic entanglement, as they "undertook political projects that were predicated on various forms of coexistence, interdependence, and noninterference—rather than sovereign control." This differs from other readings of maroons, such as those more common in Afro-pessimist theory, which approaches these communities as examples of "Black fugitivity." Afro-pessimist conceptions of fugitivity, I argue, tend to emphasize disengagement as opposed to entanglement. For various perspectives on marronage, refusal, entanglement, and fugitivity, see, for instance, Bonilla, "Freedom, Sovereignty, and Other Entanglements"; Paul Khalil Saucier and Tryon P. Woods, *On Marronage: Ethical Confrontations with Antiblackness* (Trenton, NJ: Africa World Press, 2015); Damien M. Sojoyner, "Another Life Is Possible: Black Fugitivity and Enclosed Places," *Cultural Anthropology* 32, no. 4 (2017): 514–36, https://doi.org/10.14506/ca32.4.04.

9. The complex relationship between Eritreans and Ethiopians in Italy, and particularly the embrace by some of the unifying category *habesha* (a term referring to people from the highlands of Eritrea and Ethiopia, from which the name "Abyssinia" is derived), is beyond the scope of this chapter.

10. Del Boca, "Myths, Suppressions, Denials."

11. Gian-Luca Podesta, "L'emigrazione italiana in Africa orientale," *Annales de Demographie Historique* 113, no. 1 (2007): 7, http://www.ilcornodafrica.it/rds-01emigrazione

.pdf; Gian-Luca Podesta, "Colonists and 'Demographic' Colonists: Family and Society in Italian Africa," *Annales de Demographie Historique* 122, no. 2 (2011): 205–31.

12. Giulia Barrera, "Mussolini's Colonial Race Laws." Note also that various forms of interracial relationships (spanning the spectrum from coercive to voluntary) were also relatively common in the Portuguese colonies, a phenomenon that shaped Gilberto Freyre's notion of Lusotropicalism. Lusotropicalism's emphasis on miscegenation, racial liminality, and Portuguese "southernness" shares many traits with Italian invocations of Mediterraneanism. Iyob, "Madamismo and Beyond."

13. Nicola Labanca, "Colonial Rule, Colonial Repression and War Crimes in the Italian Colonies," *Journal of Modern Italian Studies* 9, no. 3 (2004): 300–313, https://doi.org /10.1080/1354571042000254737; Ponzanesi, "Beyond the Black Venus."

14. Del Boca, "Myths, Suppressions, Denials."

15. Fuller, *Moderns Abroad*.

16. Labanca, "Colonial Rule, Colonial Repression."

17. De Donno, "La Razza Ario-Mediterranea."

18. Del Boca, "Myths, Suppressions, Denials," 18.

19. Del Boca, 18.

20. Alessandro Triulzi, "Displacing the Colonial Event," *Interventions* 8, no. 3 (2006): 434, https://doi.org/10.1080/13698010600956055; Rino Bianchi and Igiaba Scego, *Roma negata: Percorsi postcoloniali nella città* (Rome: Ediesse, 2014); Del Boca, "Myths, Suppressions, Denials"; Ruth Iyob, "The Ethiopian-Eritrean Conflict: Diasporic vs. Hegemonic States in the Horn of Africa, 1991–2000," *Journal of Modern African Studies* 38, no. 4 (2000): 659–82; Paola Tabet, *La pelle giusta* (Turin: Einaudi, 1997).

21. Many of Italy's post–World War II labor needs were filled by internal migrants from southern Italy.

22. At this time, the Eritreans arriving to Italy were recognized as Ethiopian citizens, as Eritrea was federated with Ethiopia by the United Nations in 1952 and subsequently annexed by Ethiopia. From 1941 to 1952, Eritrea was governed by a British military administration. Andall, *Gender, Migration and Domestic Service*.

23. "Cittadini stranieri in Italia—2017," Tuttitalia.it, 2017, https://www.tuttitalia.it /statistiche/cittadini-stranieri-2017/.

24. Angelica Pesarini, "Colour Strategies: Negotiations of Black Mixed Race Women's Identities in Colonial and Postcolonial Italy" (PhD diss., University of Leeds, 2015), http:// etheses.whiterose.ac.uk/10103/; Hannah Giorgis, "Ethiopia and Eritrea's Long History with Lasagna," *Taste* (blog), May 4, 2018, https://www.tastecooking.com/ethiopian -diasporas-long-history-lasagna/; Pesarini, "Blood Is Thicker Than Water."

25. Forgacs, *Italy's Margins*.

26. Nicole Trujillo-Pagán, "A Tale of Four Cities: The Boundaries of Blackness for Ethiopian Immigrants in Washington, DC, Tel Aviv, Rome, and Melbourne," *Social Identities* 25, no. 1 (2019): 58–75, https://doi.org/10.1080/13504630.2017.1418601.

27. Camilla Hawthorne, "Asmarina: Post Colonial Heritages," Doppiozero, May 13, 2016, http://www.doppiozero.com/materiali/why-africa/asmarina-post-colonial-heritages.

28. Victoria Bernal, *Nation as Network: Diaspora, Cyberspace, and Citizenship* (Chicago: University of Chicago Press, 2014).

29. Erin Komada, "Turned Away: The Detrimental Effect of Italy's Public Security Law on Undocumented Children's Right to Education," *Boston University Law Journal* 29 (2011): 451–74.

30. Derek Gregory, *The Colonial Present: Afghanistan. Palestine. Iraq* (Hoboken, NJ: Wiley, 2004). For a discussion of the relationship between Italian decolonization and refugee regimes, see Pamela Ballinger, *The World Refugees Made: Decolonization and the Foundation of Postwar Italy* (Ithaca, NY: Cornell University Press, 2020).

31. Alem Abbai and Marco Luzzi, *S.I.C.: Stranieri in casa*, documentary, 1998, https://www.youtube.com/watch?v=Q0LFHT8q_98&ab_channel=MarcoLuzzi (part 1), https://www.youtube.com/watch?v=mk777lSLRsI&t=1s&ab_channel=MarcoLuzzi (part 2).

32. Louis Althusser, "Ideology and Ideological State Apparatuses (Notes toward an Investigation)," in *Lenin and Philosophy and Other Essays* (New York: Monthly Review Press, 1971).

33. "Europe Gets 8,000 Refugees Daily," BBC News, September 25, 2015, http://www.bbc.com/news/world-europe-34356758.

34. "Everything You Want to Know about Migration across the Mediterranean," *Economist*, April 21, 2015, https://www.economist.com/blogs/economist-explains/2015/05/economist-explains-6.

35. "Mediterranean 'Most Dangerous Sea Crossing in World'—New Report," Amnesty International, June 15, 2015, https://www.amnesty.org.uk/press-releases/mediterranean-most-dangerous-sea-crossing-world-new-report; "Over 3,770 Migrants Have Died Trying to Cross the Mediterranean to Europe in 2015," International Organization for Migration, December 31, 2015, https://www.iom.int/news/over-3770-migrants-have-died-trying-cross-mediterranean-europe-2015.

36. "The Mediterranean's Deadly Migrant Routes," BBC News, April 22, 2015, sec. Europe, https://www.bbc.com/news/world-europe-32387224.

37. Maurice Stierl, "A Fleet of Mediterranean Border Humanitarians," *Antipode* 50, no. 3 (2018): 704–24, https://doi.org/10.1111/anti.12320.

38. According to the United Nations, a person who requests protection while overseas and is then given permission to enter a receiving country is a *refugee*; a person who requests protection after entering the receiving country is an *asylum seeker*.

39. Yermi Brenner, "Far Away, So Close: For Migrants, Reaching Italy Is Only the Start," Al Jazeera English, August 20, 2015, http://america.aljazeera.com/articles/2015/8/20/far-away-so-close-for-migrants-reaching-italy-is-only-the-start.html.

40. For a discussion of the experiences of "transit migrants" in Italy, see Eleanor Paynter, "The Liminal Lives of Europe's Transit Migrants," *Contexts*, June 7, 2018, https://doi.org/10.1177/1536504218776959.

41. Davide Coppo and Vincenzo Latronico, "Didn't Cross the Desert to End Up in a Square," *Cartography* 1, accessed April 24, 2018, https://bycartography.com/en/stories/didnt-cross-the-desert-to-end-up-in-a-square/.

42. Dino Messina, "Le armi chimiche in Etiopia e l'ammissione di Montanelli," *Corriere della Sera*, April 2, 2016, https://www.corriere.it/extra-per-voi/2016/04/02/armi-chimiche-etiopia-l-ammissione-montanelli-54d37986-f8fc-11e5-b97f-6d5a0a6f6065.shtml.

43. In 1969, on the television show *L'ora della verità*, the Italian-Eritrean feminist journalist Elvira Banotti publicly criticized Montanelli for raping a child. See *Quando Montanelli Comprò e Violentò Una Bambina Di 12 Anni*, accessed March 17, 2020, https://www.youtube.com/watch?v=PYgSwluzYxs&ab_channel=zosozeppelin. In 2019, members of the feminist collective Non Una Di Meno poured pink paint onto the statue on Indro Montanelli in the Montanelli Public Gardens to draw attention to his racist-sexist abuse, which remains largely overlooked in hagiographic commemorations of the journalist. See Zad El Bacha, "La vicenda di Montanelli non è solo 'passato': è anche il nostro presente," *Vice* (blog), March 11, 2019, https://www.vice.com/it/article/59x4y3/statua-montanelli-colonialismo; Francesca Coin, "Il riscatto femminista della storia," *Jacobin Italia*, March 13, 2019, https://jacobinitalia.it/il-riscatto-femminista-della-storia/.

44. Nicolò Barattini, "Cambio Passo, quando i cittadini accolgono i migranti," *TWIG Magazine* (blog), April 8, 2016, http://www.thetwigmagazine.com/2016/04/08/cambio-passo/.

45. Mackda Ghebremariam Tesfau' and Giuseppe Grimaldi have conducted in-depth research on community-led refugee resettlement efforts. See, for instance, Grimaldi's work on the mobilizations of second-generation Eritrean youth to assist newly arrived refugees in Porta Venezia: Giuseppe Grimaldi, "The Black Mediterranean: Liminality and the Reconfiguration of Afroeuropeanness," *Open Cultural Studies* 3, no. 1 (2019): 414–27, https://doi.org/10.1515/culture-2019-0035.

46. Merrill, *Black Spaces*.

47. According to Security Set 94/2009, which made undocumented immigration a crime, housing an undocumented immigrant in Italy is punishable by up to three years in prison.

48. Andrea Muehlebach, *The Moral Neoliberal: Welfare and Citizenship in Italy* (Chicago: University of Chicago Press, 2012).

49. Matteo Congregalli, "'Those Who Arrive Here Want to Become Ghosts'—Milan's People Smuggling Trade," VICE News, September 23, 2015, https://news.vice.com/article/those-who-arrive-here-want-to-become-ghosts-milans-people-smuggling-trade.

50. Alan Maglio and Medhin Paolos, *Asmarina: Voices and Images of a Postcolonial Heritage*, documentary, 2015, http://asmarinaproject.com/; Hawthorne, "Asmarina."

51. *Accoglienza* refers to refugee reception and resettlement.

52. In 2014 and again in 2015, hundreds of refugees descended on the Milano Centrale train station hoping to leave Italy for northern Europe; a large number of these refugees were from Syria. For more information, see Alessandra Coppola, "Emergenza profughi, altri 260 siriani in Centrale," *Corriere della Sera*, June 11, 2014, http://milano.corriere.it/notizie/cronaca/14_giugno_11/emergenza-profughi-altri-260-siriani-centrale-fdfbeb5e-f130-11e3-affc-25db802dc057.shtml; Gianni Rosini, "Milano, centinaia di profughi accampati in stazione centrale. Obiettivo: 'Trovare un trafficante per lasciare l'Italia,'" *Il Fatto Quotidiano*, May 10, 2015, http://www.ilfattoquotidiano.it/2015/05/10/milano-centinaia-di-profughi-accampati-in-stazione-centrale-obiettivo-trovare-un-trafficante-per-lasciare-litalia/1670158/.

53. At least some of this can be attributed to the much smaller size of the Eritrean community in Milan—in 2017, there were 1,742 Eritreans (with non-Italian citizenship) living in the city, compared to 35,884 from Egypt and 7,861 from Morocco alone. For additional information on the composition of Milan's immigrant communities, see "Cittadini stranieri Milano 2017," Tuttitalia.it, 2021, https://www.tuttitalia.it/lombardia/18-milano/statistiche/cittadini-stranieri-2017/.

54. Mahmood Mamdani, "Good Muslim, Bad Muslim: A Political Perspective on Culture and Terrorism," *American Anthropologist* 104, no. 3 (2002): 766–75.

55. "Viminale: 'Sbarchi calati dell'80% nel 2018,'" *Stranieri in Italia*, January 1, 2019, https://stranieriinitalia.it/attualita/attualita-sp-754/viminale-sbarchi-calati-dell-80-nel-2018/; Raja Abdulrahim, "Libyan Coast Guard Returns Europe-Bound Migrants to War Zone," *Wall Street Journal*, December 7, 2019, sec. World, https://www.wsj.com/articles/libyan-coast-guard-returns-europe-bound-migrants-to-war-zone-11575723601.

56. Olivia C. Harrison, "Transcolonial Cartographies: Kateb Yacine and Mohamed Rouabhi Stage Palestine in France-Algeria," in *The Postcolonial World*, ed. Jyotsna G. Singh and David D. Kim (Abingdon, UK: Routledge, 2017), 244; Olivia C. Harrison, *Transcolonial Maghreb: Imagining Palestine in the Era of Decolonization* (Palo Alto, CA: Stanford University Press, 2015).

57. Stuart Hall, *Familiar Stranger: A Life between Two Islands* (Durham, NC: Duke University Press, 2017).

58. Bonilla, *Non-Sovereign Futures*, xiii.

59. For a related discussion of engagement with the state and the "uncomfortable and problematic position of 'being at home with the law,'" see Jennifer C. Nash, *Black*

Feminism Reimagined: After Intersectionality (Durham, NC: Duke University Press, 2018), 122.

60. Maurice Stierl has also critiqued the "academic exercise of romantic abstraction" in some accounts of migrant resistance. See Maurice Stierl, *Migrant Resistance in Contemporary Europe* (London: Routledge, 2018).

61. Stuart Hall, as referenced in Angela Davis, *Freedom Is a Constant Struggle: Ferguson, Palestine, and the Foundations of a Movement*, ed. Frank Barat (Chicago: Haymarket Books, 2016), 144–45.

62. Gilmore, *Golden Gulag*, 191.

63. "Italy Shooting: Mein Kampf Found in Home of Suspect," *Guardian*, February 4, 2018, http://www.theguardian.com/world/2018/feb/04/macerata-shooting-mein-kampf -found-in-home-of-suspect-italy-luca-traini.

64. Pietro Castelli Gattinara and Francis O'Connor, "An Italian Neo-Fascist Shot 6 Immigrants. So Why Won't Italy's Political Parties Condemn Xenophobia?," *Washington Post*, February 9, 2018, https://www.washingtonpost.com/news/monkey-cage/wp/2018/02/09/an -italian-neo-fascist-shot-6-migrants-how-does-this-play-into-the-upcoming-elections/.

65. Ylenia Gostoli, "Protests and Questions over Killing of Senegal Migrant Idy Diene," Al Jazeera English, March 8, 2018, https://www.aljazeera.com/news/2018/03 /protests-questions-killing-senegal-migrant-idy-diene-180308130543754.html.

66. A video of the demonstration can be found online: Abrham Fa, "Manifestazione per Idy a Firenze, parenti e tutta la comunita di stranieri," Facebook, March 10, 2018, https://www.facebook.com/abrham.fa/videos/1722563141120963/.

67. Scott, *Conscripts of Modernity*, 4. Glen Coulthard, for instance, has argued that anti-essentialist critiques of the liberal politics of recognition must first consider the ongoing power of the (settler colonial) state to adjudicate claims for recognition. See chapter 3 of Glen Sean Coulthard, *Red Skin, White Masks: Rejecting the Colonial Politics of Recognition* (Minneapolis: University of Minnesota Press, 2014).

68. See, for instance, Angela Y. Davis and Elizabeth Martínez, "Coalition Building among People of Color," *Inscriptions* 7, accessed March 17, 2020, https://culturalstudies .ucsc.edu/inscriptions/volume-7/angela-y-davis-elizabeth-martinez/; Keeanga-Yamahtta Taylor, *How We Get Free: Black Feminism and the Combahee River Collective* (Chicago: Haymarket Books, 2017); Bernice Johnson Reagon, "Coalition Politics: Turning the Century," in *Home Girls: A Black Feminist Anthology*, ed. Barbara Smith (New York: Kitchen Table: Women of Color Press, 1983), 356–68.

69. W. E. B. Du Bois, *Dusk of Dawn: An Essay toward an Autobiography of a Race Concept* (1940; repr., New Brunswick, NJ: Transaction Publishers, 2011), 639.

70. Du Bois, 640.

71. Hawthorne, "Asmarina."

72. Merrill, *Black Spaces*; Maurice Stierl, "Of Migrant Slaves and Underground Railroads - Movement, Containment, Freedom," *American Behavioral Scientist* 64, no. 4 (2020), https://doi.org/10.1177/0002764219883006. 10.1177/.

CONCLUSION

1. Note for the epigraph: *Brigante* refers to the history of brigandage or banditry (*brigantaggio*) in southern Italy during the latter half of the nineteenth century. *Brigantaggio* has been explained both as a response to massive wealth inequality after the unification of Italy, as well as a form of popular revolt against unification.

2. Jon Henley and Antonio Voce, "Italian Elections 2018—Full Results," *Guardian*, March 5, 2018, http://www.theguardian.com/world/ng-interactive/2018/mar/05/italian -elections-2018-full-results-renzi-berlusconi.

3. In the 2018 elections, the party formerly known as the Lega Nord (Northern League) dropped the "Nord" from its name in a bid to court voters from southern Italy.

4. "Why the Populists Won," *Economist*, March 8, 2018, https://www.economist.com /europe/2018/03/08/why-the-populists-won.

5. Istat, "Indicatori demografici," November 30, 2017, http://www.istat.it.

6. Istat, "I dati del censimento 2011," May 3, 2018, https://www.istat.it/it/immigrati /tutti-i-dati/dati-del-censimento.

7. Yvan Sagnet and Leonardo Palmisano, *Ghetto Italia: I braccianti stranieri tra caporalato e sfruttamento* (Rome: Fandango Libri, 2015). See also Timothy Raeymaekers, "On the Politics of Claiming Peripheral Space," *Tracce Urbane: Rivista Italiana Transdisciplinare di Studi Urbani* 3, no. 5 (July 2, 2019), https://doi.org/10.13133/2532-6562_3 .5.14557; Lucht, *Darkness before Daybreak*.

8. Andrea Scotto, "Una riflessione sui recenti fatti avvenuti a Castel Volturno," *Huffington Post* (blog), July 21, 2014, https://www.huffingtonpost.it/arturo-scotto/riflessione -fatti-castel-volturno_b_5604142.html.

9. All names in this section, except for Mary, are pseudonyms.

10. Moya Bailey, "New Terms of Resistance: A Response to Zenzele Isoke," *Souls* 15, no. 4 (2013): 341, https://doi.org/10.1080/10999949.2014.884451.

11. ANSA, "Caporalato: 180,000 'Vulnerable' Workers in Italian Agriculture," *InfoMigrants*, October 20, 2020, sec. News, https://www.infomigrants.net/en/post/28014 /caporalato-180-000-vulnerable-workers-in-italian-agriculture.

12. *Terroni* is a derogative term used to refer to people from southern Italy—it literally translates as "people of the dirt."

13. "I Terroni Uniti le cantano a Salvini: 30 artisti contro il razzismo in 'Gente do sud,'" Adnkornos, March 10, 2017, http://www.adnkronos.com/intrattenimento/spettacolo/2017 /03/10/terroni-uniti-cantano-salvini-artisti-contro-razzismo-gente-sud-video_7UMw VCNWfkud5OeNFy7r2J.html?refresh_ce.

14. "Gente do sud," Antiwar Songs, 2017, https://www.antiwarsongs.org/canzone.php ?id=55448&lang=it.

15. "Motherland ▷ Vhelade," *GRIOT* (blog), June 26, 2017, https://griotmag.com/en /motherland-%e2%96%b7-vhelade/.

16. Hall, "Gramsci's Relevance," 416, https://doi.org/10.1177/019685998601000202; John Berger, "How to Live with Stones," in Ekers et al., *Gramsci*, 6–11, https://doi.org/10 .1002/9781118295588.part2.

17. Pred, *Even in Sweden*, 125.

18. The first paragraphs of this section are adapted from Hawthorne, "In Search of Black Italia."

19. McKittrick, "On Plantations," 947 (emphasis added).

20. Scott, *Conscripts of Modernity*.

21. Césaire, *Discourse on Colonialism*. Quoted in David Scott, "The Re-enchantment of Humanism: An Interview with Sylvia Wynter," *Small Axe: A Caribbean Journal of Criticism* 8 (2000): 119–207.

22. El-Tayeb, *European Others*, xix.

23. El-Tayeb, xviii.

24. Dipesh Chakrabarty, *Provincializing Europe: Postcolonial Thought and Historical Difference* (Princeton, NJ: Princeton University Press, 2000).

25. Joshua Jelly-Schapiro, *Island People: The Caribbean and the World* (New York: Knopf Doubleday, 2016).

26. C. L. R. James, *The Black Jacobins: Toussaint L'Ouverture and the San Domingo Revolution* (1938; repr., New York: Penguin Books Limited, 2001), 392.

27. Gilroy, *Black Atlantic*.

28. For a longer discussion of Glissant's analysis of the Mediterranean, see Franck Collin and Michelle Zerba, "La dialectique méditerranée-caraïbe d'Édouard Glissant," in *Édouard Glissant: l'éclat et l'obscur*, ed. Dominique Aurélia, Alexandre Leupin, and Jean-Pierre Sainton, 237–60 (Martinique: Presses universitaires des Antilles, 2020); Édouard Glissant, *Poetics of Relation* (1990; repr., Ann Arbor: University of Michigan Press, 1997), 33.

29. Eve Kosofsky Sedgwick, *Touching Feeling: Affect, Pedagogy, Performativity* (Durham, NC: Duke University Press, 2003), 123; Maurice Stierl, "A Sea of Struggle—Activist Border Interventions in the Mediterranean Sea," *Citizenship Studies* 20, no. 5 (July 3, 2016): 561–78, https://doi.org/10.1080/13621025.2016.1182683; Proglio, "Is the Mediterranean a White Italian-European Sea?"; Di Maio, "Black Italia."

30. Glissant, *Poetics of Relation*, 49.

31. J. Michael Dash, introduction to *Caribbean Discourse: Selected Essays*, by Édouard Glissant (Charlottesville: University of Virginia Press, 1989), xli. These insights are also a useful rejoinder to a faddish "hype of hybridity," which uncritically celebrates examples of in-betweenness without considering the conditions of possibility that make hybridity possible (including histories of racial theorization and scientific racism), or the ways that some forms of hybridity are actually quite compatible with global processes of capital accumulation. Indeed, as Robert Young has suggested, "hybridity" itself can only appear as a problem or conceptual framework when it is already assumed that there are pre-existing and bounded racial or cultural groups (otherwise, "hybridity" as such would not merit a name; it would be merely another relational state of being). The same could be said for the "invention" of the Mediterranean as a scientific object of inquiry by nineteenth-century European scholars—precisely because of the ontological challenges it posed to regionally bounded studies of history and environment. See Young, *Colonial Desire*.

32. Cecilia Butini, "There's No End in Sight for Matteo Salvini's War on Migrants," *Foreign Policy* (blog), August 21, 2019, https://foreignpolicy.com/2019/08/21/theres-no-end-in-sight-for-matteo-salvinis-war-on-migrants-league-liga-open-arms-rescue-ships-mediteranean-libya/; Elizabeth Schumacher, "Italy: Salvini Is Out, but Migrants Still Endure His Policies," *Deutsche Welle*, September 1, 2019, https://www.dw.com/en/italy-salvini-is-out-but-migrants-still-endure-his-policies/a-50229057; Antonio Mitrotti, "Il rovesciamento di prospettiva sulla misura di revoca della cittadinanza nel 'dibattuto' Decreto sicurezza 'Salvini,'" Osservatorio Costituzionale 1–2/2019, Associazione Italiana dei Constituzionali, April 12, 2019, https://www.osservatorioaic.it/images/rivista/pdf/2019_1-2_04_Mitrotti.pdf.

33. Jason Horowitz, "Italy's Government Collapses, Turning Chaos into Crisis," *New York Times*, August 20, 2019, https://www.nytimes.com/2019/08/20/world/europe/italy-pm-giuseppe-conte-resign.html.

CODA

1. Scego, *Future*.

2. "Le statistiche coronavirus in Italia," Statistiche nel Coronavirus del Mundo, 2020, https://statistichecoronavirus.it/coronavirus-italia/.

3. ISMU, "I tassi di affezione da Covid-19 tra le nazionalità straniere in Italia," *Fondazione ISMU* (blog), May 13, 2020, https://www.ismu.org/i-tassi-di-affezione-da-covid-19-tra-le-nazionalita-straniere-in-italia/.

4. "La diffusione del contagio nei centri d'accoglienza," *Vita*, November 5, 2020, http://www.vita.it/it/article/2020/11/05/la-diffusione-del-contagio-nei-centri-daccoglienza/157248/; Alessandro Puglia, "Quei migranti invisibili sulle navi quarantena," *Vita*, October 7, 2020, http://www.vita.it/it/article/2020/10/07/quei-migranti-invisibili-sulle-navi-quarantena/156901/.

5. "A State-by-State Look at 15 Months of Coronavirus in Prisons," Marshall Project, July 1, 2021, https://www.themarshallproject.org/2020/05/01/a-state-by-state-look-at -coronavirus-in-prisons.

6. Lorenzo D'Agostino, "'Cynical': Critics Slam Italy's Amnesty for Undocumented Migrants," Al Jazeera English, May 30, 2020, https://www.aljazeera.com/news/2020/5/30 /cynical-critics-slam-italys-amnesty-for-undocumented-migrants.

7. Brandi Summers, Camilla Hawthorne, and Theresa Hice Fromille, "Black Geographies of Quarantine: A Dialogue with Brandi Summers, Camilla Hawthorne, and Theresa Hice Fromille," *UCHRI Foundry*, November 2020, https://uchri.org/foundry/black -geographies-of-quarantine-a-dialogue-with-brandi-summers-camilla-hawthorne -and-theresa-hice-fromille/.

8. "Coronavirus, quando la paura del contagio serve solo a mascherare il razzismo," *La Stampa*, February 2, 2020, https://www.lastampa.it/cronaca/2020/02/02/news/coronavirus -da-casapound-ai-campi-di-calcio-il-razzismo-e-di-casa-in-italia-1.38415778; Elisa Anzolin and Angelo Amante, "First Italian Dies of Coronavirus as Outbreak Flares in North," Reuters, February 21, 2020, https://www.reuters.com/article/us-china-health-italy-idUSK BN20F0UI.

9. As of May 2020, the national average infection rate was 2.1 cases per 1,000 residents. See ISMU, "I tassi di affezione da Covid-19."

10. "Sardine a Napoli, dopo il flop Santori espelle il leader napoletano e lui attacca: 'Non sono democratici,'" *Il Mattino*, February 19, 2020, https://www.ilmattino.it/napoli /politica/sardine_napoli_espulso_mattia_santori_ultime_notizie-5061777.html; "Sardine, a Scampia il primo flop: Un centinaio i presenti. 'Comunicazione sbagliata, forse percepiti come un corpo estraneo,'" *Il Fatto Quotidiano*, February 6, 2020, sec. Politica, https://www.ilfattoquotidiano.it/2020/02/06/sardine-a-scampia-il-primo-flop-un-cen tinaio-i-presenti-comunicazione-sbagliata-forse-percepiti-come-un-corpo-estraneo /5698452/.

11. Antonio Di Costanzo, "Napoli, i migranti in protesta: 'Siamo le sardine nere,'" *La Repubblica*, December 7, 2019, https://napoli.repubblica.it/cronaca/2019/12/07/news/napoli _i_migranti_in_protesta_siamo_le_sardine_nere_-242797344/; ANSA, "'Black Sardines' Debut in Naples as Migrants Protest," *InfoMigrants*, December 10, 2019, sec. News, https:// www.infomigrants.net/en/post/21431/black-sardines-debut-in-naples-as-migrants-protest; Movimento Migranti e Rifugiati Napoli, "Sardine Nere, Sardine Napoletane, 6000 Sardine," Facebook, February 20, 2020, https://www.facebook.com/MovimentoMigrantieRifugiati Napoli/photos/a.101987851298376/136010641229430/?type=3.

12. "Milano per George Floyd: Migliaia di manifestanti in piazza contro il razzismo," *La Repubblica*, June 7, 2020, https://milano.repubblica.it/cronaca/2020/06/07/news/george _floyd_razzismo_milano_manifestazione_black_lives_matter-258654957/.

13. Anthony Julian Tamburri, "Public Monuments and Indro Montanelli: A Case of Misdirected Reverence?," *La Voce di New York* (blog), June 24, 2020, https://www .lavocedinewyork.com/en/news/2020/06/24/public-monuments-and-indro-montanelli -a-case-of-misdirected-reverence/.

14. Asale Angel-Ajani, "Domestic Enemies and Carceral Circles: African Women and Criminalization in Italy," in *Global Lockdown: Race, Gender, and the Prison-Industrial Complex*, ed. Julia Sudbury (London: Routledge, 2014), 3–18; Asale Angel-Ajani, *Strange Trade: The Story of Two Women Who Risked Everything in the International Drug Trade* (Berkeley: Seal Press, 2010).

15. Kimberlé Williams Crenshaw, "The Unmattering of Black Lives," *New Republic*, May 21, 2020, https://newrepublic.com/article/157769/unmattering-black-lives.

16. Angelica Pesarini and Camilla Hawthorne, "Black Lives Matter anche da noi?," *Jacobin Italia*, September 24, 2020, https://jacobinitalia.it/black-lives-matter-anche-da da

-noi/. See also Camilla Hawthorne and Angelica Pesarini, "Making Black Lives Matter in Italy: A Transnational Dialogue," *Public Books*, December 11, 2020, https://www.publicbooks.org/making-black-lives-matter-in-italy-a-transnational-dialogue/.

17. Along these lines, some activists in Europe have used the language of abolition to call for the abolition of Frontex, the European Union border agency. See Maurice Stierl, "Black Lives Are Being Lost in the Mediterranean—but the World Remains Silent," *The Conversation*, July 8, 2020, http://theconversation.com/black-lives-are-being-lost-in-the-mediterranean-but-the-world-remains-silent-141822.

18. Rachel Kushner, "Is Prison Necessary? Ruth Wilson Gilmore Might Change Your Mind," *New York Times*, April 17, 2019, https://www.nytimes.com/2019/04/17/magazine/prison-abolition-ruth-wilson-gilmore.html.

METHODOLOGICAL APPENDIX

1. On the subject of document analysis, see Annelise Riles, ed., *Documents: Artifacts of Modern Knowledge* (Ann Arbor: University of Michigan Press, 2006).

2. Audra Simpson, *Mohawk Interruptus: Political Life across the Borders of Settler States* (Durham, NC: Duke University Press, 2014); Savannah Shange, "Black Girl Ordinary: Flesh, Carcerality, and the Refusal of Ethnography," *Transforming Anthropology* 27, no. 1 (2019): 3–21, https://doi.org/10.1111/traa.12143.

3. For a thorough account of anti-Black surveillance and profiling in the context of airport security, see Browne, *Dark Matters*.

4. Brown, *Dropping Anchor, Setting Sail*, 2005; Campt, *Other Germans*.

5. Campt, *Other Germans*, 183.

6. Ashanté M. Reese, *Black Food Geographies: Race, Self-Reliance, and Food Access in Washington* (Chapel Hill: University of North Carolina Press, 2019), 16.

7. Steven Gregory, *The Devil behind the Mirror: Globalization and Politics in the Dominican Republic* (Oakland: University of California Press, 2006), 12.

Bibliography

Abbai, Alem, and Marco Luzzi. *S.I.C.: Stranieri in casa*. Documentary. 1998. https://www
.youtube.com/watch?v=Q0LFHT8q_98&ab_channel=MarcoLuzzi (part 1), https://
www.youtube.com/watch?v=mk777lSLRsI&t=1s&ab_channel=MarcoLuzzi
(part 2).

Abdulrahim, Raja. "Libyan Coast Guard Returns Europe-Bound Migrants to War Zone."
Wall Street Journal, December 7, 2019, sec. World. https://www.wsj.com/articles
/libyan-coast-guard-returns-europe-bound-migrants-to-war-zone-11575
723601.

Acquisto della cittadinanza. Pub. L. No. Legge n. 91 del 1992. (1992). https://www.senato
.it/japp/bgt/showdoc/17/DOSSIER/941909/index.html?part=dossier_dossier1
-sezione_sezione11-h1_h14.

Adamou, Angela Haisha. *Love Is in the Hair*. Vol. 1, *Consigli per avere ricci belli, sani e
senza capricci*. Independently published, 2017.

Adichie, Chimamanda Ngozi. "The Danger of a Single Story." TEDGlobal2009. https://
www.ted.com/talks/chimamanda_adichie_the_danger_of_a_single_story.

Adinolfi, Gerardo. "Modou e Mor chi erano le vittime." *La Repubblica*, December 13,
2011. http://firenze.repubblica.it/cronaca/2011/12/13/news/modou_e_mor_chi
_erano_le_vittime-26561561/.

Adnkornos. "I Terroni Uniti le cantano a Salvini: 30 artisti contro il razzismo in 'Gente
do sud.'" March 10, 2017. http://www.adnkronos.com/intrattenimento/spettacolo
/2017/03/10/terroni-uniti-cantano-salvini-artisti-contro-razzismo-gente-sud
-video_7UMwVCNWfkud5OeNFy7r2J.html?refresh_ce.

Affricot, Johanne. "The Vogue Italia Cover with Maty Fall Is Not Just a Cover." *GRIOT*
(blog), February 10, 2020. https://griotmag.com/en/italian-beauty-the-vogue-italia
-cover-with-maty-fall-is-not-just-a-cover/.

Agamben, Giorgio. *Homo Sacer: Sovereign Power and Bare Life*. Stanford, CA: Stanford
University Press, 1998.

——. "Perché non ho firmato l'appello sullo ius soli." *Quodlibet*, October 18, 2017. https://
www.quodlibet.it/giorgio-agamben-perch-on-ho-firmato-l-appello-sullo-ius
-soli.

——. *State of Exception*. Chicago: University of Chicago Press, 2008.

Agnew, John. "The Myth of Backward Italy in Modern Europe." In *Revisioning Italy: National Identity and Global Culture*, edited by Beverly Allen and Mary J. Russo,
23–42. Minneapolis: University of Minnesota Press, 1997.

Alarcón, Norma. "Traddutora, Traditora: A Paradigmatic Figure of Chicana Feminism."
Cultural Critique, no. 13 (1989): 57–87. https://doi-org.oca.ucsc.edu/10.2307/135
4269.

Alexander, M. Jacqui. *Pedagogies of Crossing: Meditations on Feminism, Sexual Politics,
Memory, and the Sacred*. Durham, NC: Duke University Press, 2005.

Al Jazeera English. "Italy MP 'Blacks Up' for Anti-migrant Speech." January 17, 2014.
http://www.aljazeera.com/news/europe/2014/01/italy-mp-blacks-up-anti
-migrant-speech-2014117547559566.html.

Althusser, Louis. "Ideology and Ideological State Apparatuses (Notes toward an Investigation)." *Lenin and Philosophy and Other Essays*. New York: Monthly Review Press, 1971.

Alzouma, Gado. "Identities in a 'Fragmegrated' World: Black Cyber-Communities and the French Integration System." *African and Black Diaspora: An International Journal* 1, no. 2 (2008): 201–14. https://doi.org/10.1080/17528630802224130.

Ambrosetti, Elena, and Eralba Cela. "Demography of Race and Ethnicity in Italy." In *The International Handbook of the Demography of Race and Ethnicity*, edited by Rogelio Saenz, Nestor Rodriguez, and David Embrick, 457–82. International Handbooks of Population 4. London: Springer, 2015.

Ambrosini, Maurizio, and Nazareno Panichella. "Immigrazione, occupazione e crisi economica in Italia." *Quaderni di Sociologia*, no. 72 (2016): 115–34. https://doi.org/10.4000/qds.1578.

Amnesty International. "Mediterranean 'Most Dangerous Sea Crossing in World'—New Report." June 15, 2015. https://www.amnesty.org.uk/press-releases/mediterranean-most-dangerous-sea-crossing-world-new-report.

Andall, Jacqueline. *Gender, Migration and Domestic Service: The Politics of Black Women in Italy*. Aldershot, UK: Ashgate, 2000.

——. "Second-Generation Attitude? African-Italians in Milan." *Journal of Ethnic and Migration Studies* 28, no. 3 (2002): 389–407. https://doi.org/10.1080/13691830220146518.

Andall, Jacqueline, and Derek Duncan. *National Belongings: Hybridity in Italian Colonial and Postcolonial Cultures*. Bern: Peter Lang, 2010.

Anderson, Benedict. *Imagined Communities: Reflections on the Origin and Spread of Nationalism*. Rev. ed. New York: Verso, 2006.

Angel-Ajani, Asale. "Domestic Enemies and Carceral Circles: African Women and Criminalization in Italy." In *Global Lockdown: Race, Gender, and the Prison-Industrial Complex*, edited by Julia Sudbury, 3–18. London: Routledge, 2014.

——. "Italy's Racial Cauldron: Immigration, Criminalization and the Cultural Politics of Race." *Cultural Dynamics* 12, no. 3 (2000): 331–52. https://doi.org/10.1177/092137400001200304.

——. *Strange Trade: The Story of Two Women Who Risked Everything in the International Drug Trade*. Berkeley, CA: Seal Press, 2010.

ANSA. "'Black Sardines' Debut in Naples as Migrants Protest." *InfoMigrants*, December 10, 2019, sec. News. https://www.infomigrants.net/en/post/21431/black-sardines-debut-in-naples-as-migrants-protest.

——. "Caporalato: 180,000 'Vulnerable' Workers in Italian Agriculture." *InfoMigrants*, October 20, 2020, sec. News. https://www.infomigrants.net/en/post/28014/caporalato-180-000-vulnerable-workers-in-italian-agriculture.

Antiwar Songs. "Gente do sud." 2017. https://www.antiwarsongs.org/canzone.php?id=55448&lang=it.

Anzaldúa, Gloria. *Borderlands*. 1987. Reprint, San Francisco: Aunt Lute Books, 1999.

Anzolin, Elisa, and Angelo Amante. "First Italian Dies of Coronavirus as Outbreak Flares in North." *Reuters*, February 21, 2020. https://www.reuters.com/article/us-china-health-italy-idUSKBN20F0UI.

Appiah, Kwame Anthony. "Racisms." In *Anatomy of Racism*, edited by David Goldberg, 3–17. Minneapolis: University of Minnesota Press, 1990.

Arendt, Hannah. *Imperialism*. New York: Harcourt Brace & World, 1976.

Asad, Talal. "Conscripts of Western Civilization." In *Dialectical Anthropology: Essays in Honor of Stanley Diamond*, vol. 1, *Civilization in Crisis: Anthropological Perspectives*, edited by Christine Ward Gailey, 333–51. Gainesville: University Press of Florida, 1992.

——. "What Do Human Rights Do? An Anthropological Enquiry." *Theory & Event* 4, no. 4 (January 1, 2000). https://muse.jhu.edu/article/32601.

ASGI (Associazione per gli Studi Giuridici sull'Immigrazione). "Codice di condotta per le ONG coinvolte nel salvataggio di migranti in mare: Il commento dell'ASGI." Melting Pot Europa, July 25, 2017. https://www.meltingpot.org/Codice-di-con dotta-per-le-ONG-coinvolte-nel-salvataggio-di.html.

Associated Press. "Italy Shooting: Mein Kampf Found in Home of Suspect." *Guardian*, February 4, 2018. http://www.theguardian.com/world/2018/feb/04/macerata -shooting-mein-kampf-found-in-home-of-suspect-italy-luca-traini.

——. "Rep. Steve King: U.S. Doesn't Need 'Somebody Else's Babies.'" PBS NewsHour, March 13, 2017. https://www.pbs.org/newshour/politics/rep-steve-king-u-s-doesnt -need-somebody-elses-babies.

Associazione Il Razzismo è una Brutta Storia. "Chimamanda Ngozi Adichie—Afroitalini e cittadinanza." November 18, 2019. http://www.razzismobruttastoria.net/2019/11 /18/chimamanda-ngozi-adichie-a-bookcity-milano-2019-afroitaliani-e-citta dinanza/.

Ataç, Ilker, Kim Rygiel, and Maurice Stierl. "Introduction: The Contentious Politics of Refugee and Migrant Protest and Solidarity Movements: Remaking Citizenship from the Margins." *Citizenship Studies* 20, no. 5 (2016): 527–44. https://doi.org/10 .1080/13621025.2016.1182681.

Ayim, May. *Blues in Black and White: A Collection of Essays, Poetry, and Conversations.* Trenton: Africa World Press, 2003.

Bacchetta, Paola, Tina Campt, Inderpal Grewal, Caren Kaplan, Minoo Moallem, and Jennifer Terry. "Transnational Feminist Practices against War." *Meridians* 2, no. 2 (2002): 302–8.

Bacha, Zad El. "La vicenda di Montanelli non è solo 'passato': È anche il nostro presente." *Vice* (blog), March 11, 2019. https://www.vice.com/it/article/59x4y3/statua-monta nelli-colonialismo.

Back, Les, and Vibeke Quaade. "Dream Utopias, Nightmare Realities: Imaging Race and Culture within the World of Benetton Advertising." *Third Text* 7, no. 22 (1993): 65–80. https://doi.org/10.1080/09528829308576402.

Badaracchi, Laura. "Lo stile afro di Evelyne è un successo." *Donna Moderna* 28, no. 5 (August 19, 2015).

Bailey, Moya. "New Terms of Resistance: A Response to Zenzele Isoke." *Souls* 15, no. 4 (2013): 341–43. https://doi.org/10.1080/10999949.2014.884451.

Balduzzi, Paolo, and Alessandro Rosina. "Giovani talenti che lasciano l'Italia: Fonti, dati e politiche di un fenomeno complesso." *La Rivista delle Politiche Sociali* 3 (2011): 43–59.

Baldwin, James. *Notes of a Native Son.* 1955. Reprint, Boston: Beacon Press, 1984.

Balibar, Etienne, and Immanuel Maurice Wallerstein. *Race, Nation, Class: Ambiguous Identities.* New York: Verso Books, 1991.

Ballinger, Pamela. *The World Refugees Made: Decolonization and the Foundation of Post-war Italy.* Ithaca, NY: Cornell University Press, 2020.

Barattini, Nicolò. "Cambio Passo, quando i cittadini accolgono i migranti." *TWIG Magazine* (blog), April 8, 2016. http://www.thetwigmagazine.com/2016/04/08/cambio-passo/.

Barbujani, Guido. *Gli africani siamo noi: Alle origini dell'uomo.* Rome: Laterza, 2016.

Barker, Martin. *The New Racism: Conservatives and the Ideology of the Tribe.* Toronto: Junction Books, 1981.

Barrera, Giulia. "Mussolini's Colonial Race Laws and State-Settler Relations in Africa Orientale Italiana (1935–41)." *Journal of Modern Italian Studies* 8, no. 3 (2003): 425–43. https://doi.org/10.1080/09585170320000113770.

Bartoli, Clelia. *Razzisti per legge: L'Italia che discrimina*. Rome: Gius. Laterza & Figli, 2012.
BBC News. "Europe Gets 8,000 Refugees Daily." September 25, 2015. http://www.bbc .com/news/world-europe-34356758.
——. "The Mediterranean's Deadly Migrant Routes." April 22, 2015, sec. Europe. https:// www.bbc.com/news/world-europe-32387224.
Beckett, Greg. "The Politics of Disjuncture, or Freedom from a Caribbean Point of View." *Small Axe: A Caribbean Journal of Criticism* 21, no. 2 (53) (2017): 184–92. https:// doi.org/10.1215/07990537-4156906.
Ben-Ghiat, Ruth. *Fascist Modernities: Italy, 1922–1945*. Berkeley: University of California Press, 2001.
Ben-Ghiat, Ruth, and Mia Fuller. Introduction to *Italian Colonialism*, edited by Ruth Ben-Ghiat and Mia Fuller, 1–12. London: Palgrave Macmillan, 2008.
Berger, John. "How to Live with Stones." In *Gramsci: Space, Nature, Politics*, edited by Michael Ekers, Gillian Hart, Stefan Kipfer, and Alex Loftus, 6–11. Hoboken, NJ: John Wiley & Sons, 2012. https://doi.org/10.1002/9781118295588.part2.
Bernal, Victoria. *Nation as Network: Diaspora, Cyberspace, and Citizenship*. Chicago: University of Chicago Press, 2014.
Berrocal, Emilio Giacomo. "Building Italian-ness through the Logic of the 'Other in Us' and the 'Self in the Other': An Anti-nationalist Approach to the Italian Debate on a New Citizenship Law." *Bulletin of Italian Politics* 2, no. 1 (2010): 69–90.
Berruti, Paolo, Gianluigi Mangiapane, Donatella Minaldi, and Emma Robino Massa. *L'arte della folla nelle collezioni del Museo di Antropologia di Torino*. Turin: Le Nuove Muse, 2010.
Bianchi, Rino, and Igiaba Scego. *Roma negata: Percorsi postcoloniali nella città*. Rome: Ediesse, 2014.
Bitjoka, Otto. *Talea: Il merito mette radici*. Segrate, Italy: Grafiche Moretti, 2010.
Bloemraad, Irene. *Becoming a Citizen: Incorporating Immigrants and Refugees in the United States and Canada*. Berkeley: University of California Press, 2006.
Bloemraad, Irene, Anna Korteweg, and Gökçe Yurdakul. "Citizenship and Immigration: Multiculturalism, Assimilation, and Challenges to the Nation-State." *Annual Review of Sociology* 34, no. 1 (2008): 153–79. https://doi.org/10.1146/annurev.soc.34 .040507.134608.
Bonifazi, Corrado, Frank Heins, Salvatore Strozza, and Mattia Vitiello. "Italy: The Italian Transition from an Emigration to Immigration Country." IDEA working paper no. 5. Brussels: European Commission, 2009. https://www.researchgate.net /publication/267773953_Italy_The_Italian_transition_from_an_emigration_to _immigration_country.
Bonilla, Yarimar. "Freedom, Sovereignty, and Other Entanglements." *Small Axe: A Caribbean Journal of Criticism* 21, no. 2 (53) (2017): 201–8. https://doi.org/10.1215 /07990537-4156930.
——. *Non-Sovereign Futures: French Caribbean Politics in the Wake of Disenchantment*. Chicago: University of Chicago Press, 2015.
Bonilla-Silva, Eduardo. *Racism without Racists: Color-Blind Racism and the Persistence of Racial Inequality in America*. 2003. Reprint, Lanham, MD: Rowman & Littlefield, 2017.
Bono, Salvatore. *Schiavi: Una storia mediterranea (XV--XIX secolo)*. Bologna: Il Mulino, 2016.
Bosniak, Linda. *The Citizen and the Alien: Dilemmas of Contemporary Membership*. Princeton, NJ: Princeton University Press, 2008.
Braudel, Fernand. *The Mediterranean and the Mediterranean World in the Age of Philip II*. 1949. Reprint, Berkeley: University of California Press, 1995.

Brenner, Yermi. "Far Away, So Close: For Migrants, Reaching Italy Is Only the Start." Al Jazeera English, August 20, 2015. http://america.aljazeera.com/articles/2015/8/20 /far-away-so-close-for-migrants-reaching-italy-is-only-the-start.html.

Broeck, Sabine. "The Erotics of African American Endurance, Or: On the Right Side of History?" In *Germans and African Americans*, edited by Larry A. Greene and Anke Ortlepp, 126–40. Jackson: University Press of Mississippi, 2010. https://doi .org/10.14325/mississippi/9781604737844.003.0008.

——. "White Fatigue, or, Supplementary Notes on Hybridity." In *Reconstructing Hybridity: Postcolonial Studies in Transition*, edited by Joel Kuortti and Jopi Nyman, 43–58. Amsterdam: Rodopi, 2007.

Brogi, Alessandro. *Confronting America: The Cold War between the United States and the Communists in France and Italy*. Chapel Hill: University of North Carolina Press, 2011.

Brown, Jacqueline Nassy. "Black Europe and the African Diaspora: A Discourse on Location." In *Black Europe and the African Diaspora*, edited by Darlene Clark Hine, Trica Danielle Keaton, and Stephen Small, 201–11. Urbana: University of Illinois Press, 2009.

——. *Dropping Anchor, Setting Sail: Geographies of Race in Black Liverpool*. Princeton, NJ: Princeton University Press, 2005.

Brown, Wendy. *Politics Out of History*. Princeton, NJ: Princeton University Press, 2001.

Browne, Simone. *Dark Matters: On the Surveillance of Blackness*. Durham, NC: Duke University Press, 2015.

Brubaker, Rogers. *Citizenship and Nationhood in France and Germany*. Cambridge, MA: Harvard University Press, 2009.

Burtenshaw, Rónán. "Raceocracy: An Interview with Dr. Barnor Hesse—Part 1." *Irish Left Review* (blog), October 24, 2012. http://www.irishleftreview.org/2012/10/24/rac eocracy/.

Bussotti, Luca. "A History of Italian Citizenship Laws during the Era of the Monarchy (1861–1946)." *Advances in Historical Studies* 5, no. 4 (2016): 143–67. https://doi.org /10.4236/ahs.2016.54014.

Butini, Cecilia. "There's No End in Sight for Matteo Salvini's War on Migrants." *Foreign Policy* (blog), August 21, 2019. https://foreignpolicy.com/2019/08/21/theres-no-end -in-sight-for-matteo-salvinis-war-on-migrants-league-liga-open-arms-rescue -ships-mediterranean-libya/.

Butler, Judith. "Merely Cultural." *New Left Review* 1, no. 227 (1998): 33–44.

Byrd, Ayana, and Lori Tharps. *Hair Story: Untangling the Roots of Black Hair in America*. New York: St. Martin's Press, 2014.

Cacho, Lisa Marie. *Social Death: Racialized Rightlessness and the Criminalization of the Unprotected*. New York: New York University Press, 2012.

Caesar, Ann Hallamore. *Printed Media in Fin-de-Siecle Italy: Publishers, Writers, and Readers*. London: Routledge, 2017.

Caglioti, Angelo Matteo. "Race, Statistics and Italian Eugenics: Alfredo Niceforo's Trajectory from Lombroso to Fascism (1876–1960)." *European History Quarterly* 47, no. 3 (2017): 461–89. https://doi.org/10.1177/0265691417707164.

Camilli, Annalisa. "Cos'è lo ius soli e come funziona la cittadinanza in altri paesi europei." *Internazionale*, June 21, 2017. https://www.internazionale.it/notizie/annalisa -camilli/2017/06/21/ius-soli-cittadinanza-italia.

——. "Ius soli, ius sanguinis, ius culturae: Tutto sulla riforma della cittadinanza." *Internazionale*, October 20, 2017. https://www.internazionale.it/notizie/annalisa-camilli /2017/10/20/riforma-cittadinanza-da-sapere.

Campisi, Rosanna. "Saranno italiani." *Gioia*, October 22, 2015.

Campt, Tina Marie. *Other Germans: Black Germans and the Politics of Race, Gender, and Memory in the Third Reich*. Ann Arbor: University of Michigan Press, 2005.

Capocasa, Marco, Paolo Anagnostou, Valeria Bachis, Cinzia Battaggia, Stefania Bertoncini, Gianfranco Biondi, Alessio Boattini, et al. "Linguistic, Geographic and Genetic Isolation: A Collaborative Study of Italian Populations." *Journal of Anthropological Sciences* 92 (2014): 201–31. https://download.repubblica.it/pdf /2014/scienze/jass-reports.pdf.

Caponetto, Rosetta Giuliani. *Fascist Hybridities: Representations of Racial Mixing and Diaspora Cultures under Mussolini*. New York: Springer, 2016.

Carli, Andrea. "Gli immigrati in Italia producono il 9% del Pil, più di Croazia e Ungheria." *Il Sole 24 ORE*, October 18, 2017. https://www.ilsole24ore.com/art/gli-immigrati -italia-producono-9percento-pil-piu-croazia-e-ungheria--AEAYrxqC.

Carling, Jørgen. "Refugees Are Also Migrants. All Migrants Matter." *Border Criminologies* (blog), September 16, 2015. https://www.law.ox.ac.uk/research-subject-groups /centre-criminology/centreborder-criminologies/blog/2015/09/refugees-are-also.

Cartaldo, Claudio. "Immigrata veste col Tricolore: Denunciata per vilipendio." *Il Giornale*, June 11, 2017. http://www.ilgiornale.it/news/cronache/immigrata-veste-col -tricolore-denunciata-vilipendio-1408137.html.

Carter, Donald Martin. "Blackness over Europe: Meditations on Cultural Belonging." In *Africa in Europe: Studies in Transnational Practice in the Long Twentieth Century*, edited by Eve Rosenhaft and Robbie John Macvicar Aitken, 201–13. Liverpool: Liverpool University Press, 2013.

——. *States of Grace: Senegalese in Italy and the New European Immigration*. Minneapolis: University of Minnesota Press, 1997.

Carter, Donald, and Heather Merrill. "Bordering Humanism: Life and Death on the Margins of Europe." *Geopolitics* 12, no. 2 (2007): 248–64. https://doi.org/10.1080 /14650040601168867.

Cassano, Franco. *Il pensiero meridiano*. Rome: Gius. Laterza & Figli, 2015.

Cassata, Francesco. "Between Lombroso and Pareto: The Italian Way to Eugenics." In *Building the New Man: Eugenics, Racial Science and Genetics in Twentieth-Century Italy*, 9–42. Budapest: Central European University Press, 2013. http://books .openedition.org/ceup/723.

——. *La difesa della razza: Politica, ideologia e immagine del razzismo fascista*. Turin: G. Einaudi, 2008.

Castles, Stephen, and Alastair Davidson. *Citizenship and Migration: Globalization and the Politics of Belonging*. London: Routledge, 2020.

Cazzato, Luigi Carmine. "Fractured Mediterranean and Imperial Difference: Mediterraneanism, Meridionism, and John Ruskin." *Journal of Mediterranean Studies* 26, no. 1 (2017): 69–78.

——. "Mediterranean: Coloniality, Migration and Decolonial Practices." *Politics: Rivista di Studi Politici* 5, no. 21 (2016). https://doi.org/10.6093/2279-7629/3978.

Cerolini, Reginaldo. "Fosco immaginario." *La Macchina Sognante*, no. 7 (June 19, 2017). http://www.lamacchinasognante.com/fosco-immaginario-reginaldo-cerolini/.

Cerro, Giovanni. "Giuseppe Sergi: The Portrait of a Positivist Scientist." *Journal of Anthropological Sciences* 95 (2017): 109–36. https://doi.org/10.4436/jass.95007.

Césaire, Aimé. *Discourse on Colonialism*. 1950. Reprint, New York: Monthly Review Press, 2000.

Chakrabarty, Dipesh. *Provincializing Europe: Postcolonial Thought and Historical Difference*. Princeton, NJ: Princeton University Press, 2000.

Chambers, Iain. *Mediterranean Crossings: The Politics of an Interrupted Modernity*. Durham, NC: Duke University Press, 2008.

Chan, Sewell. "Black Lives Matter Activists Stage Protests across Britain." *New York Times*, August 5, 2016. https://www.nytimes.com/2016/08/06/world/europe/black-lives-matter-demonstrations-britain.html.

Chin, Elizabeth M. Liew Siew. *Purchasing Power: Black Kids and American Consumer Culture*. Minneapolis: University of Minnesota Press, 2001.

Choate, Mark I. *Emigrant Nation: The Making of Italy Abroad*. Cambridge, MA: Harvard University Press, 2008.

Clark, VèVè A. "Developing Diaspora Literacy and Marasa Consciousness." *Theatre Survey* 50, no. 1 (May 2009): 9–18. https://doi.org/10.1017/S0040557409000039.

Clò, Clarissa. "Hip Pop Italian Style: The Postcolonial Imagination of Second-Generation Authors in Italy." In *Postcolonial Italy: Challenging National Homogeneity*, edited by Cristina Lombardi-Diop and Caterina Romeo, 275–92. New York: Palgrave Macmillan, 2012.

Coburn, Melissa. *Race and Narrative in Italian Women's Writing since Unification*. Madison, NJ: Fairleigh Dickinson University Press, 2013.

Coin, Francesca. "Il riscatto femminista della storia." *Jacobin Italia*, March 13, 2019. https://jacobinitalia.it/il-riscatto-femminista-della-storia/.

Cole, Jeffrey. *The New Racism in Europe: A Sicilian Ethnography*. Cambridge: Cambridge University Press, 2005.

Cole, Teju. "Migrants Are Welcome." *Verso* (blog), September 7, 2015. https://www.versobooks.com/blogs/2226-teju-cole-migrants-are-welcome.

Coletti, Maria. "Fantasmi d'Africa, dal muto al sonoro. Facce, facette, e blackface." In *L'Africa in Italia: Per una controstoria postcoloniale del cinema italiano*, edited by Leonardo De Franceschi, 75–92. Rome: Aracne, 2013.

Collin, Franck, and Michelle Zerba. "La dialectique méditerranée-caraïbe d'Édouard Glissant." In *Édouard Glissant: l'éclat et l'obscur*, edited by Dominique Aurélia, Alexandre Leupin, and Jean-Pierre Sainton, 237–260 (Martinique: Presses universitaires des Antilles, 2020).

Collins, Patricia Hill. "It's All in the Family: Intersections of Gender, Race, and Nation." *Hypatia* 13, no. 3 (1998): 62–82.

Colombo, Enzo, Luisa Leonini, and Paola Rebughini. "Different but Not Stranger: Everyday Collective Identifications among Adolescent Children of Immigrants in Italy." *Journal of Ethnic and Migration Studies* 35, no. 1 (2009): 37–59. https://doi.org/10.1080/13691830802489101.

Comunicare il Sociale. "Napoli è meticcia: VIII edizione del Mediterraneo Antirazzista," June 26, 2019. http://www.comunicareilsociale.com/2019/06/26/napoli-e-meticcia-viii-edizione-del-mediterraneo-antirazzista/.

Congregalli, Matteo. "'Those Who Arrive Here Want to Become Ghosts'—Milan's People Smuggling Trade." *VICE News*, September 23, 2015. https://news.vice.com/article/those-who-arrive-here-want-to-become-ghosts-milans-people-smuggling-trade.

Coppo, Davide, and Vincenzo Latronico. "Didn't Cross the Desert to End Up in a Square." *Cartography*, no. 1. Accessed April 24, 2018. https://bycartography.com/en/stories/didnt-cross-the-desert-to-end-up-in-a-square/.

Coppola, Alessandra. "Emergenza profughi, altri 260 siriani in Centrale." *Corriere della Sera*, June 11, 2014. http://milano.corriere.it/notizie/cronaca/14_giugno_11/emergenza-profughi-altri-260-siriani-centrale-fdfbeb5e-f130-11e3-affc-25db802dc057.shtml.

Coppola, Massimo. *Nappy Girls*. Documentary, 2014. http://video.corriere.it/nappy-girls/5291ec12-4416-11e4-bbc2-282fa2f68a02.

Cordasco, Francesco. "Bollettino Dell'Emigrazione (1902–1927): A Guide to the Chronicles of Italian Mass Emigration." In *The Columbus People: Perspectives in Italian Immi-

gration to the Americas and Australia, edited by Lydio F. Tomasi, Piero Gastaldo, and Thomas Row, 499–509. Staten Island, NY: Center for Migration Studies, 1994.

Corriere della Sera. "Il paese arcobaleno: Italia ricca di diversità genetica." January 20, 2014. http://www.corriere.it/scienze_e_tecnologie/14_gennaio_19/paese-arcobaleno -italia-ricca-diversita-genetica-bf158fe4-8119-11e3-a1c3-05b99f5e9b32.shtml.

——. "La ministra Kyenge si presenta: 'Sono nera, non di colore e lo dico con fierezza.'" May 3, 2013. http://www.corriere.it/politica/13_maggio_03/kyenge-nera_5b24eea0 -b3db-11e2-a510-97735eec3d7c.shtml.

Coulthard, Glen Sean. *Red Skin, White Masks: Rejecting the Colonial Politics of Recognition.* Minneapolis: University of Minnesota Press, 2014.

Cox, Aimee Meredith. *Shapeshifters: Black Girls and the Choreography of Citizenship.* Durham, NC: Duke University Press, 2015.

Craig, Maxine. "The Decline and Fall of the Conk; or, How to Read a Process." *Fashion Theory* 1, no. 4 (1997): 399–419. https://doi.org/10.2752/136270497779613657.

Crais, Clifton C., and Pamela Scully. *Sara Baartman and the Hottentot Venus: A Ghost Story and a Biography.* Princeton, NJ: Princeton University Press, 2009.

Crawley, Heaven, Franck Düvell, Katharine Jones, Simon McMahon, and Nando Sigona. "Destination Europe? Understanding the Dynamics and Drivers of Mediterranean Migration in 2015." 2016. http://www.medmig.info/wp-content/uploads/2016/12 /research-brief-destination-europe.pdf.

Crenshaw, Kimberlé Williams. "The Unmattering of Black Lives." *New Republic*, May 21, 2020. https://newrepublic.com/article/157769/unmattering-black-lives.

Cumming-Bruce, Nick. "Number of People Fleeing Conflict Is Highest since World War II, U.N. Says." *New York Times*, June 19, 2019. https://www.nytimes.com/2019/06 /19/world/refugees-record-un.html.

D'Agostino, Lorenzo. "'Cynical': Critics Slam Italy's Amnesty for Undocumented Migrants." Al Jazeera English, May 30, 2020. https://www.aljazeera.com/news/2020 /5/30/cynical-critics-slam-italys-amnesty-for-undocumented-migrants.

D'Agostino, Peter. "Craniums, Criminals, and the 'Cursed Race': Italian Anthropology in American Racial Thought, 1861–1924." *Comparative Studies in Society and History* 44, no. 2 (2002): 319–43.

Dainotto, Roberto M. *Europe (in Theory).* Durham, NC: Duke University Press, 2007.

Dal Lago, Enrico. *William Lloyd Garrison and Giuseppe Mazzini: Abolition, Democracy, and Radical Reform.* Baton Rouge: Louisiana State University Press, 2013.

Danewid, Ida. "White Innocence in the Black Mediterranean: Hospitality and the Erasure of History." *Third World Quarterly* 38, no. 7 (2017): 1674–89. https://doi.org /10.1080/01436597.2017.1331123.

Dash, J. Michael. Introduction to *Caribbean Discourse: Selected Essays*, by Édouard Glissant, xi–xliv. Charlottesville: University of Virginia Press, 1989.

Dávila, Arlene. *Barrio Dreams: Puerto Ricans, Latinos, and the Neoliberal City.* Berkeley: University of California Press, 2004.

Davis, Angela. *Freedom Is a Constant Struggle: Ferguson, Palestine, and the Foundations of a Movement.* Edited by Frank Barat. Chicago: Haymarket Books, 2016.

Davis, Angela Y., and Elizabeth Martínez. "Coalition Building among People of Color." *Inscriptions* 7. Accessed March 17, 2020. https://culturalstudies.ucsc.edu/inscriptions /volume-7/angela-y-davis-elizabeth-martinez/.

Davis, F. James. *Who Is Black?: One Nation's Definition.* University Park: Penn State University Press, 2010.

Davis, Muriam Haleh, and Thomas Serres. *North Africa and the Making of Europe: Governance, Institutions and Culture.* London: Bloomsbury, 2018.

Davis, Robert. *Christian Slaves, Muslim Masters: White Slavery in the Mediterranean, The Barbary Coast, and Italy, 1500–1800.* London: Palgrave Macmillan UK, 2003.

De Donno, Fabrizio. "La Razza Ario-Mediterranea: Ideas of Race and Citizenship in Colonial and Fascist Italy, 1885–1941." *Interventions* 8, no. 3 (2006): 394–412. https://doi.org/10.1080/13698010600955958.

De Felice, Renzo. *Mussolini il duce.* Turin: Einaudi, 1996.

——. *Storia degli ebrei italiani sotto il fascismo.* Turin: Einaudi, 2005.

De Franceschi, Leonardo. *La cittadinanza come luogo di lotta: Le seconde generazioni in Italia fra cinema e serialità.* Rome: Arcane Editrice, 2018.

De la Cadena, Marisol. "Are *Mestizos* Hybrids? The Conceptual Politics of Andean Identities." *Journal of Latin American Studies* 37, no. 2 (2005): 259–84. https://doi.org/10.1017/S0022216X05009004.

Del Boca, Angelo. "The Myths, Suppressions, Denials, and Defaults of Italian Colonialism." In *A Place in the Sun: Africa in Italian Colonial Culture from Post-Unification to the Present*, edited by Patrizia Palumbo, 17–36. Berkeley: University of California Press, 2003.

D'Elia, Rosy. "Il Decreto Salvini cambia la cittadinanza: Le conseguenze umane." *Più Culture* (blog), January 16, 2019. https://www.piuculture.it/2019/01/le-conseguenze-umane-il-decreto-salvini-cambia-la-cittadinanza/.

Delli, Marilena Umuhoza. *Razzismo all'italiana.* Milan: Arcane Editrice, 2016.

Demurtas, Antonietta. "Italia, capitale straniero." *Lettera43*, October 1, 2011.

Deutsche Welle. "Made in Italy? Not for Much Longer as Artisans and Skills Disappear." June 19, 2013. http://www.dw.com/en/made-in-italy-not-for-much-longer-as-artisans-and-skills-disappear/a-16887589.

Di Costanzo, Antonio. "Napoli, i migranti in protesta: 'Siamo le sardine nere.'" *La Repubblica*, December 7, 2019. https://napoli.repubblica.it/cronaca/2019/12/07/news/napoli_i_migranti_in_protesta_siamo_le_sardine_nere_-242797344/.

Di Maio, Alessandra. "Black Italia: Contemporary Migrant Writers from Africa." In *Black Europe and the African Diaspora*, edited by Darlene Clark Hine, Trica Danielle Keaton, and Stephen Small, 119–44. Urbana: University of Illinois Press, 2009.

——. "Mediterraneo nero: Le rotte dei migranti nel millennio globale." In *La citta' cosmopolita*, edited by Giulia de Spuches and Vincenzo Guarrasi, 142–63. Palermo: Palumbo Editore, 2012.

Di Meo, Alessandro. *Tientsin, la concessione italiana: Storia delle relazioni tra Italia e Cina (1866–1947).* Rome: Ginevra Bentivoglio EditoriA, 2015.

Di Raimondo, Rosario. "Domenica Salvini a Bologna, due giorni ad alta tensione." *La Repubblica*, November 1, 2015. http://bologna.repubblica.it/cronaca/2015/11/02/news/arriva_salvini_due_giorni_ad_alta_tensione-126423194/.

Donati, Sabina. *A Political History of National Citizenship and Identity in Italy, 1861–1950.* Palo Alto, CA: Stanford University Press, 2013.

Dore, Marta. "Orgoglio Nappy." *Gioia*, November 28, 2015.

Dovi, Efam Awo. "Migration: Taking Rickety Boats to Europe." *Africa Renewal*, 2017. http://www.un.org/africarenewal/magazine/special-edition-youth-2017/migration-taking-rickety-boats-europe.

Du Bois, W. E. B. *Black Reconstruction in America, 1860–1880.* 1935. Reprint, New York: The Free Press, 1998.

——. *Dusk of Dawn: An Essay toward an Autobiography of a Race Concept.* 1940. Reprint, New Brunswick, NJ: Transaction Publishers, 2011.

——. *The Souls of Black Folk*. 1903. Reprint, Oxford: Oxford University Press, 2007.

Economist. "Everything You Want to Know about Migration across the Mediterranean." April 21, 2015. https://www.economist.com/blogs/economist-explains/2015/05 /economist-explains-6.

——. "Italian Manufacturing: A Washout." August 10, 2013. https://www.economist.com /news/business/21583283-years-crisis-have-reinforced-pressure-italys-once -envied-industrial-base-washout.

——. "Why the Populists Won." March 8, 2018. https://www.economist.com/europe/2018 /03/08/why-the-populists-won.

Edwards, Brent Hayes. *The Practice of Diaspora: Literature, Translation, and the Rise of Black Internationalism*. Cambridge, MA: Harvard University Press, 2009.

Edwards, Jim. "Italy's 'Perma-Recession' Could Trigger a €2 Trillion Financial Crisis That Threatens the Eurozone Itself." *Business Insider*, April 21, 2019. https://www .businessinsider.com/italy-perma-recession-systemic-crisis-threatens-eurozone -2019-4.

Ehrkamp, Patricia. "The Limits of Multicultural Tolerance? Liberal Democracy and Media Portrayals of Muslim Migrant Women in Germany." *Space and Polity* 14, no. 1 (2010): 13–32. https://doi.org/10.1080/13562571003737718.

El-Tayeb, Fatima. *European Others: Queering Ethnicity in Postnational Europe*. Minneapolis: University of Minnesota Press, 2011.

ENAR Europe. "Racist Murder in Italy Is a Wake-Up Call for a European #BlackLives-Matter," July 7, 2016. http://www.enar-eu.org/Racist-murder-in-Italy-is-a-wake-up -call-for-a-European-BlackLivesMatter.

Epstein, Steven. *Speaking of Slavery: Color, Ethnicity, and Human Bondage in Italy*. Ithaca, NY: Cornell University Press, 2001.

Essed, Philomena. *Understanding Everyday Racism: An Interdisciplinary Theory*. Vol. 2. Thousand Oaks, CA: SAGE, 1991.

Essed, Philomena, and Isabel Hoving. *Dutch Racism*. Amsterdam: Rodopi, 2014.

Essed, Philomena, and Kwame Nimako. "Designs and (Co)Incidents: Cultures of Scholarship and Public Policy on Immigrants/Minorities in the Netherlands." *International Journal of Comparative Sociology* 47, no. 3–4 (2006): 281–312. https://doi .org/10.1177/0020715206065784.

Council of Europe. European Convention on Nationality. European Treaty Series no. 166. Strasbourg, November 6, 1997. https://rm.coe.int/168007f2c8.

Evans, Margaret. "Europe Tut-Tuts While African Migrants Die on Its Doorstep." CBC, November 18, 2013. https://www.cbc.ca/news/world/europe-tut-tuts-while-african -migrants-die-on-its-doorstep-1.2425050.

Everett, Anna. *Digital Diaspora: A Race for Cyberspace*. Albany: State University of New York Press, 2009.

Fa, Abrham. "Manifestazione per Idy a Firenze, parenti e tutta la comunita di stranieri." Facebook, March 10, 2018. https://www.facebook.com/abrham.fa/videos/17225631 41120963/.

Fallows, James. "Happy 150th Birthday, Italy!" *Atlantic*, March 17, 2011. https://www .theatlantic.com/international/archive/2011/03/happy-150th-birthday-italy /72591/.

Fanon, Frantz. *Black Skin, White Masks*. 1952. Reprint, New York: Grove Press, 2008.

——. "Racism and Culture." In *Toward the African Revolution: Political Essays*. 1964. Reprint, New York: Grove Press, 1988.

——. *The Wretched of the Earth*. 1963. Reprint, New York: Grove Press, 2007.

Fanpage.it. "Chi sono (davvero) quelli scesi in piazza con Salvini." November 10, 2015. YouTube video, 9:39. https://www.youtube.com/watch?v=snMbCsK3hd8.

Fargues, Philippe. "Four Decades of Cross-Mediterranean Undocumented Migration to Europe: A Review of the Evidence." Geneva: International Organization for Migration, 2017.

Fausto-Sterling, Anne. "Gender, Race, and Nation: The Comparative Anatomy of 'Hottentot' Women in Europe, 1815–17." In *Skin Deep, Spirit Strong: The Black Female Body in American Culture*, edited by Kimberly Wallace-Sanders, 66–98. Ann Arbor: University of Michigan Press, 2002.

Favale, Mauro. "'Boicotta i negozi stranieri,' Il marchio dei razzisti sulle saracinesche di Roma." *La Repubblica*, April 15, 2017. http://roma.repubblica.it/cronaca/2017/04/15/news/_boicotta_i_negozi_stranieri_il_marchio_dei_razzisti_sulle_saracinesche_di_roma-163019709/.

Federici, Silvia. *Caliban and the Witch*. New York: Autonomedia, 2004.

Ferrario, Francesca. "Dalla Russia alla Nigeria all'Italia ragionando su ricci e cittadinanza." *Medium* (blog), April 13, 2017. https://medium.com/migrantentrepreneurs-europe/dalla-russia-alla-nigeria-allitalia-ragionando-su-ricci-e-cittadinanza-1bab38f2b65.

Ferrera, Maurizio. "The Uncertain Future of the Italian Welfare State." *West European Politics* 20, no. 1 (1997): 231–49. https://doi.org/10.1080/01402389708425183.

Finotto, Carlo Andrea. "Immigrati: Il rapporto costi-benefici è positivo per l'Italia. Ecco perché." *Il Sole 24 ORE*, July 4, 2018. https://www.ilsole24ore.com/art/immigrati-rapporto-costi-benefici-e-positivo-l-italia-ecco-perche-AEltRrGF.

Fiore, Teresa. "The Emigrant Post-'Colonia' in Contemporary Immigrant Italy." In *Postcolonial Italy: Challenging National Homogeneity*, edited by Cristina Lombardi-Diop and Caterina Romeo, 71–82. New York: Palgrave Macmillan, 2012.

Fleming, Crystal Marie. *Resurrecting Slavery: Racial Legacies and White Supremacy in France*. Philadelphia: Temple University Press, 2017.

Fogu, Claudio. "From *Mare Nostrum* to *Mare Aliorum*: Mediterranean Theory and Mediterraneism in Contemporary Italian Thought." *California Italian Studies* 1, no. 1 (2010). https://escholarship.org/uc/item/7vp210p4.

——. "*Italiani Brava Gente*: The Legacy of Fascist Historical Culture on Italian Politics of Memory." In *The Politics of Memory in Postwar Europe*, edited by Richard Ned Lebow, Wulf Kansteiner, and Claudio Fogu, 147–76. Durham, NC: Duke University Press, 2006.

Fogu, Claudio, and Lucia Re. "Italy in the Mediterranean Today: A New Critical Topography." *California Italian Studies* 1, no. 1 (2010). https://escholarship.org/uc/item/6dk918sn.

Ford, Tanisha C. *Liberated Threads: Black Women, Style, and the Global Politics of Soul*. Chapel Hill: University of North Carolina Press, 2015.

Forgacs, David. *Italy's Margins: Social Exclusion and Nation Formation since 1861*. Cambridge: Cambridge University Press, 2014.

Forgacs, David, and Stephen Gundle. *Mass Culture and Italian Society from Fascism to the Cold War*. Bloomington: Indiana University Press, 2007.

Foucault, Michel. *The Birth of Biopolitics: Lectures at the Collège de France, 1978–1979*. Edited by Michel Senellart. Translated by Graham Burchell. 2004. Reprint, New York: Palgrave Macmillan, 2010.

——. *Discipline and Punish: The Birth of the Prison*. 1975. Reprint, New York: Vintage Books, 2012.

——. *The History of Sexuality*. Vol. 1, *An Introduction*. Translated by Robert Hurley. 1984. Reprint, New York: Vintage, 1990.

——. "The Subject and Power." *Critical Inquiry* 8, no. 4 (1982): 777–95.

Franchetti, Leopoldo, and Sidney Sonnino. *La Sicilia nel 1876*. Florence: Tip. di G. Barbèra, 1877.

Frisina, Annalisa. *Giovani musulmani d'Italia*. Rome: Carocci, 2007.

Frisina, Annalisa, and Camilla Hawthorne. "Italians with Veils and Afros: Gender, Beauty, and the Everyday Anti-racism of the Daughters of Immigrants in Italy." *Journal of Ethnic and Migration Studies* 44, no. 5 (2018): 718–35. https://doi.org/10.1080/1369183X.2017.1359510.

——. "Riconoscersi nel successo di Evelyne, lottare nel ricordo di Abba. Un viaggio tra le icone nere dei figli delle migrazioni in Italia." In *A fior di pelle: Bianchezza, nerezza, visualità*, edited by Elisa Bordin and Stefano Bosco. Verona: Ombre Corte, 2017.

——. "Sulle pratiche estetiche antirazziste delle figlie delle migrazioni." In *Il colore della nazione*, edited by Gaia Giuliani, 200–214. Milan: Mondadori, 2015.

Fuller, Mia. "Italian Colonial Rule." In *Oxford Bibliographies*, May 6, 2016. https://www.oxfordbibliographies.com/view/document/obo-9780199846733/obo-9780199846733-0150.xml.

——. *Moderns Abroad: Architecture, Cities and Italian Imperialism*. London: Routledge, 2007.

Gabaccia, Donna R. *Italy's Many Diasporas*. London: Routledge, 2013.

Gallori, Paolo, and Chiara Nardinocchi. "Fermo, difende la compagna da insulti razzisti. Nigeriano picchiato a morte da ultrà locale." *La Repubblica*, July 6, 2016. http://www.repubblica.it/cronaca/2016/07/06/news/fermo_muore_nigeriano_aggredito_da_ultra_locale-143565559/.

Gandolfo, Francesca. *Il Museo Coloniale di Roma (1904–1971): Fra le zebre nel paese dell'olio di ricino*. Rome: Gangemi Editore, 2015.

Ganz, Barbara. "L'eleganza della riccia." *Alley Oop* (blog), March 5, 2016. http://www.alleyoop.ilsole24ore.com/2016/03/05/leleganza-della-riccia/.

García Peña, Lorgia. "Black in English: Race, Migration, and National Belonging in Postcolonial Italy." *Kalfou* 3, no. 2 (October 31, 2016). https://doi.org/10.15367/kf.v3i2.102.

Gattinara, Pietro Castelli, and Francis O'Connor. "An Italian Neo-Fascist Shot 6 Immigrants. So Why Won't Italy's Political Parties Condemn Xenophobia?" *Washington Post*, February 9, 2018. https://www.washingtonpost.com/news/monkey-cage/wp/2018/02/09/an-italian-neo-fascist-shot-6-migrants-how-does-this-play-into-the-upcoming-elections/.

Gibson, Mary. "Biology or Climate? Race and 'Deviance' in Italian Criminology, 1880–1920." In *Italy's "Southern Question": Orientalism in One Country*, edited by Jane Schneider, 99–116. Oxford: Berg, 1998.

Gibson, Mary, and Nicole Hahn Rafter. "Editors' Introduction." In *Criminal Man* by Cesare Lombroso, 1–36. Durham, NC: Duke University Press, 2006.

Giglioli, Ilaria. "From 'A Frontier Land' to 'A Piece of North Africa in Italy': The Changing Politics of 'Tunisianness' in Mazara del Vallo, Sicily." *International Journal of Urban and Regional Research* 41, no. 5 (September 1, 2017): 749–66. https://doi.org/10.1111/1468-2427.12544.

——. "Producing Sicily as Europe: Migration, Colonialism and the Making of the Mediterranean Border between Italy and Tunisia." *Geopolitics* 22, no. 2 (2017): 407–28. https://doi.org/10.1080/14650045.2016.1233529.

Gill, Tiffany M. *Beauty Shop Politics: African American Women's Activism in the Beauty Industry*. Champaign: University of Illinois Press, 2010.

——. "'I Had My Own Business . . . So I Didn't Have to Worry': Beauty Salons, Beauty Culturists and the Politics of African-American Female Entrepreneurship." In *Beauty and Business: Commerce, Gender, and Culture in Modern America*, edited by Philip Scranton, 169–94. London: Routledge, 2014.

Gillette, Aaron. "The Origins of the 'Manifesto of Racial Scientists.'" *Journal of Modern Italian Studies* 6, no. 3 (2001): 305–23. https://doi.org/10.1080/13545710110084253.
——. *Racial Theories in Fascist Italy.* London: Routledge, 2003.
Gilmore, Ruth Wilson. "Fatal Couplings of Power and Difference: Notes on Racism and Geography." *Professional Geographer* 54, no. 1 (2002): 15–24. https://doi.org/10.1111/0033-0124.00310.
——. *Golden Gulag: Prisons, Surplus, Crisis, and Opposition in Globalizing California.* Berkeley: University of California Press, 2007.
Gilroy, Paul. *"There Ain't No Black in the Union Jack": The Cultural Politics of Race and Nation.* 1987. Reprint, Chicago: University of Chicago Press, 1991.
——. *The Black Atlantic: Modernity and Double Consciousness.* Cambridge, MA: Harvard University Press. 1993.
Giordano, Cristiana. *Migrants in Translation: Caring and the Logics of Difference in Contemporary Italy.* Berkeley: University of California Press, 2014.
——. "Practices of Translation and the Making of Migrant Subjectivities in Contemporary Italy." *American Ethnologist* 35, no. 4 (2008): 588–606. https://doi.org/10.1111/j.1548-1425.2008.00100.x.
Giorgis, Hannah. "Ethiopia and Eritrea's Long History with Lasagna." *Taste* (blog), May 4, 2018. https://www.tastecooking.com/ethiopian-diasporas-long-history-lasagna/.
Giori, Daniele. "Razzismo, genetista: 'La razza bianca? Senza immigrazione gli europei avrebbero la pelle scura.'" *Il Fatto Quotidiano*, January 28, 2018. https://www.ilfattoquotidiano.it/2018/01/28/razzismo-genetista-le-razza-bianca-senza-immigrazione-gli-europei-avrebbero-la-pelle-scura/4118255/.
Giovani Musulmani d'Italia GMI. Facebook. Accessed March 19, 2020. https://www.facebook.com/GiovaniMusulmanidItaliaGMI/.
Giroux, Henry. "Consuming Social Change: The 'United Colors of Benetton.'" *Cultural Critique* 26 (Winter 1993–94): 5–32.
——. "Spectacles of Race and Pedagogies of Denial: Anti-Black Racist Pedagogy under the Reign of Neoliberalism." *Communication Education* 52, no. 3–4 (2003): 191–211. https://doi.org/10.1080/0363452032000156190.
Giuliani, Gaia. "Gender, Race and the Colonial Archive: Sexualized Exoticism and Gendered Racism in Contemporary Italy." *Italian Studies* 71, no. 4 (2016): 550–67. https://doi.org/10.1080/00751634.2016.1222767.
——. "L'Italiano Negro: The Politics of Colour in Early Twentieth-Century Italy." *Interventions* 16, no. 4 (2014): 572–87. https://doi.org/10.1080/1369801X.2013.851828.
——. *Race, Nation and Gender in Modern Italy: Intersectional Representations in Visual Culture.* London: Palgrave Macmillan, 2018.
Giuliani, Gaia, and Cristina Lombardi-Diop. *Bianco e nero: Storia dell'identità razziale degli italiani.* Milan: Mondadori Education, 2013.
Glenn, Evelyn Nakano. *Unequal Freedom.* Cambridge, MA: Harvard University Press, 2002.
Glissant, Édouard. *Poetics of Relation.* 1990. Reprint, Ann Arbor: University of Michigan Press, 1997.
Gnisci, Armando. *Creoli, meticci, migranti, clandestini e ribelli.* Rome: Meltemi Editore, 1998.
Gobineau, Arthur Comte de. *The Inequality of Human Races.* New York: G. P. Putnam's Sons, 1915.
Goldberg, David Theo. "Racial Europeanization." *Ethnic and Racial Studies* 29, no. 2 (2006): 331–64. https://doi.org/10.1080/01419870500465611.
——. *The Racial State.* Malden, MA: Blackwell, 2002.

——. *The Threat of Race: Reflections on Racial Neoliberalism*. Malden, MA: Wiley-Blackwell, 2009.

Gonzales, Roberto G., and Nando Sigona. "Mapping the Soft Borders of Citizenship: An Introduction." In *Within and Beyond Citizenship: Borders, Membership and Belonging*, edited by Nando Sigona and Roberto G. Gonzales, 1–14. London: Routledge, 2017.

Gordon-Chipembere, N. *Representation and Black Womanhood: The Legacy of Sarah Baartman*. New York: Springer, 2011.

Gostoli, Ylenia. "Protests and Questions over Killing of Senegal Migrant Idy Diene." Al Jazeera English, March 8, 2018. https://www.aljazeera.com/news/2018/03/protests-questions-killing-senegal-migrant-idy-diene-180308130543754.html.

Goswami, Manu. "Rethinking the Modular Nation Form: Toward a Sociohistorical Conception of Nationalism." *Comparative Studies in Society and History* 44, no. 4 (2002): 770–99.

Gould, Stephen Jay. *The Mismeasure of Man*. Rev. ed. New York: W. W. Norton, 2006.

Governo Italiano. Ministero degli Affari Esteri e della Cooperazione Iternazionale. "Citizenship." Accessed January 21, 2021. https://www.esteri.it/mae/en/servizi/stranieri/cittadinanza_0.html.

Grace, Loretta. "Il disagio di essere una beauty junkie nera in Italia." *Grace on Your Dash* (blog), March 1, 2016. http://www.graceonyourdash.com/in-italia-essere-una-beautyjunkie-nera-e-un-problema/.

——. *Skin*. Milan: Mondadori, 2019.

Graham-Harrison, Emma. "Migrants from West Africa Being 'Sold in Libyan Slave Markets.'" *Guardian*, April 10, 2017. https://www.theguardian.com/world/2017/apr/10/libya-public-slave-auctions-un-migration.

Gramsci, Antonio. *Quaderni dal carcere*. Turin: Einaudi, 2001.

——. *Selections from the Prison Notebooks*. Edited by Quintin Hoare and Geoffrey Nowell Smith. New York: International Publishers, 1971.

——. *The Southern Question*. Translated by Pasquale Verdicchio. Toronto: Guernica Editions, 2005.

Greene, Shelleen. "Buffalo Soldiers on Film: Il soldato afroamericano nel cinema neorealista e postbellico italiano." In *L'Africa in Italia: Per una controstoria postcoloniale del cinema italiano*, edited by Leonardo De Franceschi, 93–108. Rome: Aracne, 2013.

——. *Equivocal Subjects: Between Italy and Africa—Constructions of Racial and National Identity in the Italian Cinema*. New York: Bloomsbury, 2012.

Gregory, Derek. *The Colonial Present: Afghanistan. Palestine. Iraq*. Hoboken, NJ: Wiley, 2004.

Gregory, Steven. *The Devil behind the Mirror: Globalization and Politics in the Dominican Republic*. Berkeley: University of California Press, 2006.

Grewal, Inderpal. *Saving the Security State: Exceptional Citizens in Twenty-First-Century America*. Durham, NC: Duke University Press, 2017.

Grignetti, Francesco. "'Immigrazione diffusa,' la risposta italiana alle banlieue." *La Stampa*, May 2, 2016. http://www.lastampa.it/2016/05/02/esteri/immigrazione-diffusa-la-risposta-italiana-alle-banlieue-8p5OH0i0xLdTcN0uFaWuPM/pagina.html.

Grimaldi, Giuseppe. "The Black Mediterranean: Liminality and the Reconfiguration of Afroeuropeanness." *Open Cultural Studies* 3, no. 1 (2019): 414–27. https://doi.org/10.1515/culture-2019-0035.

GRIOT (blog). "Motherland ▷ Vhelade." June 26, 2017. https://griotmag.com/en/motherland-%e2%96%b7-vhelade-afrosarda/.

Guglielmo, Jennifer, and Salvatore Salerno. *Are Italians White?: How Race Is Made in America*. London: Routledge, 2012.

Hagan, Ampson. "Algeria's Black Fear." *Africa Is a Country* (blog), August 2017. https://africasacountry.com/2017/08/algerias-black-fear/.

Hall, Stuart. "Conclusion: The Multi-Cultural Question." In *Un/Settled Multiculturalisms: Diasporas, Entanglements, Transruptions*, edited by Barnor Hesse, 209–41. New York: St. Martin's Press, 2000.

———. "Cultural Identity and Diaspora." In *Colonial Discourse and Post-Colonial Theory: A Reader*, 227–37. London: Harvester Wheatsheaf, 1994.

———. *Familiar Stranger: A Life between Two Islands*. Durham, NC: Duke University Press, 2017.

———. "Gramsci's Relevance for the Study of Race and Ethnicity." *Journal of Communication Inquiry* 10, no. 2 (June 1, 1986): 5–27. https://doi.org/10.1177/0196859986010 00202.

———. "Introducing NLR." *New Left Review*, I, no. 1 (1960): 1–3.

———. "Race, Articulation, and Societies Structured in Dominance." In *Sociological Theories: Race and Colonialism*. Paris: UNESCO, 1980.

———. "Race, the Floating Signifier." Media Education Foundation, 1997. https://www.mediaed.org/transcripts/Stuart-Hall-Race-the-Floating-Signifier-Transcript.pdf.

Hameed, Mustafa. "Lacking Recognition, Italy's Muslims Face an Uncertain Future." *Washington Post*, May 28, 2013. https://www.washingtonpost.com/national/on -faith/lacking-recognition-italys-muslims-face-an-uncertain-future/2013/05/28 /e0d2761c-c7b3-11e2-9cd9-3b9a22a4000a_story.html.

Hammonds, Evelynn M., and Rebecca M. Herzig. *The Nature of Difference: Sciences of Race in the United States from Jefferson to Genomics*. Cambridge, MA: MIT Press, 2009.

Hansen, Peo, and Stefan Jonsson. *Eurafrica: An Untold Story*. London: Bloomsbury Academic, 2014.

Haraway, Donna J. *Modest_Witness@Second_Millennium.FemaleMan©_Meets_Onco-Mouse™: Feminism and Technoscience*. London: Routledge, 1997.

———. *Primate Visions: Gender, Race, and Nature in the World of Modern Science*. 1989. Reprint, London: Routledge, 2013.

Haritaworn, Jinthana. *The Biopolitics of Mixing: Thai Multiracialities and Haunted Ascendancies*. London: Routledge, 2012.

Harris, Laura. "L'abbandono: Who's Meticcio / Whose Meticcio in the Eritrea-Italy Diaspora?" In *ItaliAfrica: Bridging Continents and Cultures*, edited by Sante Matteo, 192–204. Stony Brook, NY: Forum Italicum, 2001.

Harrison, Olivia C. "Transcolonial Cartographies: Kateb Yacine and Mohamed Rouabhi Stage Palestine in France-Algeria." In *The Postcolonial World*, edited by Jyotsna G. Singh and David D. Kim, 243–59. Abingdon, UK: Routledge, 2017.

———. *Transcolonial Maghreb: Imagining Palestine in the Era of Decolonization*. Palo Alto, CA: Stanford University Press, 2015.

Hawthorne, Camilla. "Asmarina: Post Colonial Heritages." Doppiozero, May 13, 2016. http://www.doppiozero.com/materiali/why-africa/asmarina-post-colonial -heritages.

———. "Black Matters Are Spatial Matters: Black Geographies for the Twenty-First Century." *Geography Compass* 13, no. 11 (2019): 13:e12468. https://doi.org/10.1111 /gec3.12468.

———. "Dangerous Networks: Internet Regulations as Racial Border Control in Italy." In *DigitalSTS: A Handbook and Fieldguide*, edited by Janet Vertesi and David Ribes, 178–97. Princeton, NJ: Princeton University Press, 2019.

——. "In Search of Black Italia: Notes on Race, Belonging, and Activism in the Black Mediterranean." *Transition* 123, no. 1 (June 17, 2017): 152–74.

——. "L'Italia Meticcia? The Black Mediterranean and the Racial Cartographies of Citizenship." In *The Black Mediterranean: Bodies, Borders, and Citizenship in the Contemporary Migration Crisis*, edited by Gabriele Proglio, Angelica Pesarini, Camilla Hawthorne, and Timothy Raeymaekers, 169–98. London: Palgrave Macmillan, 2021.

——. "Making Italy: Afro-Italian Entrepreneurs and the Racial Boundaries of Citizenship." *Social & Cultural Geography* (2019): 1–21. https://doi.org/10.1080/14649365 .2019.1597151.

Hawthorne, Camilla, and Angelica Pesarini. "Making Black Lives Matter in Italy: A Transnational Dialogue." *Public Books*, December 11, 2020. https://www.publicbooks.org /making-black-lives-matter-in-italy-a-transnational-dialogue/.

Hawthorne, Camilla, and Pina Piccolo. "'Meticciato' o della problematicità di una parola." *La Macchina Sognante* 5 (2016). http://www.lamacchinasognante.com/meticciato-o -della-problematicita-di-una-parola-camilla-hawthorne-e-pina-piccolo/.

——. "'Razza' e 'umano' non sono termini banali." *Frontiere News*, July 26, 2016. http:// frontierenews.it/2016/07/razza-e-umano-non-sono-termini-banali/.

Hegel, Georg Wilhelm Friedrich. *The Philosophy of History*. 1837. Reprint, Colonial Press, 1900.

Helmreich, Stefan. "Kinship, Nation, and Paul Gilroy's Concept of Diaspora." *Diaspora: A Journal of Transnational Studies* 2, no. 2 (1992): 243–49. https://doi.org/10.1353 /dsp.1992.0016.

Henley, Jon, and Antonio Voce. "Italian Elections 2018—Full Results." *Guardian*, March 5, 2018. http://www.theguardian.com/world/ng-interactive/2018/mar/05 /italian-elections-2018-full-results-renzi-berlusconi.

Henry, Paget. *Caliban's Reason: Introducing Afro-Caribbean Philosophy*. London: Routledge, 2002.

Hepworth, Kate, and Olivia Hamilton. "'Let Me Stay Home': Apparetenenza, luogo e giovani i seconda generazione in Italia." *Studi Culturali* 11, no. 3 (2014): 493–509.

Herzfeld, Michael. "Practical Mediterraneanism: Excuses for Everything, from Epistemology to Eating." In *Rethinking the Mediterranean*, edited by William V. Harris, 45–63. Oxford: Oxford University Press, 2005.

Hesse, Barnor. "Afterword: Europe's Undecidability." In *Black Europe and the African Diaspora*, edited by Darlene Clark Hine, Trica Danielle Keaton, and Stephen Small, 291–304. Urbana: University of Illinois Press, 2009.

Higginbotham, Evelyn Brooks. *Righteous Discontent: The Women's Movement in the Black Baptist Church, 1880–1920*. Cambridge, MA: Harvard University Press, 1994.

Hine, Darlene Clark. Preface to *Black Europe and the African Diaspora*, edited by Darlene Clark Hine, Trica Danielle Keaton, and Stephen Small, xvii–xix. Urbana: University of Illinois Press, 2009.

Hine, Darlene Clark, Trica Danielle Keaton, and Stephen Small. *Black Europe and the African Diaspora*. Urbana: University of Illinois Press, 2009.

Holmes, Douglas R. *Integral Europe: Fast-Capitalism, Multiculturalism, Neofascism*. Princeton, NJ: Princeton University Press, 2010.

Holmes, Rachel. *The Hottentot Venus: The Life and Death of Saartjie Baartman: Born 1789–Buried 2002*. New York: Bloomsbury, 2016.

Holsey, Bayo. *Routes of Remembrance: Refashioning the Slave Trade in Ghana*. Chicago: University of Chicago Press, 2008.

Holston, James. "Insurgent Citizenship in an Era of Global Urban Peripheries." *City & Society* 21, no. 2 (2009): 245–67. https://doi.org/10.1111/j.1548-744X.2009.01024.x.

Hom, Stephanie Malia. *Empire's Mobius Strip: Historical Echoes in Italy's Crisis of Migration and Detention.* Ithaca, NY: Cornell University Press, 2019.

hooks, bell. *Feminist Theory: From Margin to Center.* London: Pluto Press, 2000.

Horowitz, Jason. "Italy's Government Collapses, Turning Chaos into Crisis." *New York Times,* August 20, 2019, sec. World. https://www.nytimes.com/2019/08/20/world /europe/italy-pm-giuseppe-conte-resign.html.

Howard, Marc Morje. *The Politics of Citizenship in Europe.* Cambridge: Cambridge University Press, 2009.

Ifekwunigwe, Jayne O. "Recasting 'Black Venus' in the 'New' African Diaspora." In *Globalization and Race: Transformations in the Cultural Production of Blackness,* edited by Kamari Maxine Clarke and Deborah A. Thomas, 206–25. Durham, NC: Duke University Press, 2006.

Il Fatto Quotidiano. "Immigrazione, Kyenge: 'L'Italia è meticcia, lo ius soli sarà figlio del paese nuovo.'" June 10, 2013. http://www.ilfattoquotidiano.it/2013/06/10/immi grazione-kyenge-litalia-e-meticcia-ius-soli-sara-figlio-del-paese-nuovo/621519/.

——. "Migranti, a Palermo il Mediterraneo antirazzista: Sport per inclusione sociale." May 10, 2019. https://www.ilfattoquotidiano.it/2019/05/10/migranti-a-palermo-il -mediterraneo-antirazzista-sport-per-inclusione-sociale/5169329/.

——. "Sardine, a Scampia il primo flop: Un centinaio i presenti. 'Comunicazione sbagliata, forse percepiti come un corpo estraneo.'" February 6, 2020, sec. Politica. https://www.ilfattoquotidiano.it/2020/02/06/sardine-a-scampia-il-primo-flop -un-centinaio-i-presenti-comunicazione-sbagliata-forse-percepiti-come-un -corpo-estraneo/5698452/.

Il Giorno. "Borghezio su Mario: 'Balotelli? E' un padano con la pelle scura.'" June 30, 2012. https://www.ilgiorno.it/brescia/cronaca/2012/06/30/737145-milano-borghezio -balotelli-padano.shtml.

——. "Manifestazione antirazzista per 'Milano meticcia,' centri sociali e comitati al corteo contro la Lega Nord." October 18, 2014. https://www.ilgiorno.it/milano/cronaca /manifestazione-antirazzista-milano-meticcia-1.315186.

Il Mattino. "Sardine a Napoli, dopo il flop Santori espelle il leader napoletano e lui attacca: 'Non sono democratici.'" February 19, 2020. https://www.ilmattino.it/napoli /politica/sardine_napoli_espulso_mattia_santori_ultime_notizie-5061777.html.

Imarisha, Walidah, and Adrienne Maree Brown. *Octavia's Brood: Science Fiction Stories from Social Justice Movements.* Oakland, CA: AK Press, 2015.

International Organization for Migration. "Key Migration Terms." January 14, 2015. https://www.iom.int/key-migration-terms.

——. "Over 3,770 Migrants Have Died Trying to Cross the Mediterranean to Europe in 2015." December 31, 2015. https://www.iom.int/news/over-3770-migrants-have -died-trying-cross-mediterranean-europe-2015.

IRAAS-AAADSColumbiaU. "IRAAS Conversations Lecture w/ Prof. Crystal Fleming." Columbia University, New York, March 15, 2016. YouTube video, 1:17:31. https:// www.youtube.com/watch?v=IGFVBgUXytg,

Isin, Engin F. *Being Political: Genealogies of Citizenship.* Minneapolis: University of Minnesota Press, 2002.

——. "Engaging, Being, Political." *Political Geography* 24 (2005): 373–87.

Isin, Engin F., and Greg M. Nielsen. *Acts of Citizenship.* London: Zed Books, 2013.

ISMU. "I tassi di affezione da Covid-19 tra le nazionalità straniere in Italia." *Fondazione ISMU* (blog), May 13, 2020. https://www.ismu.org/i-tassi-di-affezione-da-covid-19 -tra-le-nazionalita-straniere-in-italia/.

Istat. "Cittadini non comunitari: Presenza, nuovi ingressi e acquisizioni di cittadinanza." Press release, October 30, 2016. https://www.istat.it/it/archivio/223598.

——. "I dati del censimento 2011." May 3, 2018. https://www.istat.it/it/immigrati/tutti-i -dati/dati-del-censimento.

——. "Indicatori demografici." November 30, 2017. https://www.istat.it/it/archivio /208951.

Italiani senza Cittadinanza. "Gli Italiani? Non esistono." Facebook, May 3, 2018. https:// www.facebook.com/italianisenzacittadinanza/posts/2075653602716034.

——. "Ius soli: #Italiani senza cittadinanza invia una lettera aperta a Mattarella." *Giuridica.net* (blog), December 27, 2017. https://giuridica.net/ius-soli-italiani-senza -cittadinanza-invia-una-lettera-aperta-a-mattarella/.

Iyob, Ruth. "Madamismo and Beyond: The Construction of Eritrean Women." *Nineteenth-Century Contexts* 22, no. 2 (2000): 217–38. https://doi.org/10.1080 /08905490008583509.

——. "The Ethiopian–Eritrean Conflict: Diasporic vs. Hegemonic States in the Horn of Africa, 1991–2000." *Journal of Modern African Studies* 38, no. 4 (2000): 659–82.

Jamaica Global Online. "Unwelcomed Immigrants, Birther Lies, Windrush Atrocity and Trumpism: Orlando Patterson on Blacks in America and Britain," July 18, 2019. https://www.jamaicaglobalonline.com/unwelcomed-immigrants-birther-lies -windrush-atrocity-and-trumpism-orlando-patterson-on-blacks-in-america-and -britain/.

James, C.L.R. *The Black Jacobins: Toussaint L'Ouverture and the San Domingo Revolution.* 1938. Reprint, New York: Penguin Books, 2001.

Jelly-Schapiro, Joshua. *Island People: The Caribbean and the World.* New York: Knopf Doubleday, 2016.

Jones, Martha S. *Birthright Citizens: A History of Race and Rights in Antebellum America.* Cambridge: Cambridge University Press, 2018.

Joppke, Christian. *Immigration and the Nation-State: The United States, Germany, and Great Britain.* Oxford: Oxford University Press, 1999.

Joseph-Gabriel, Annette K. *Reimagining Liberation: How Black Women Transformed Citizenship in the French Empire.* Champaign: University of Illinois Press, 2019.

Kaplan, Caren. *Aerial Aftermaths: Wartime from Above.* Durham, NC: Duke University Press, 2017.

Karni, Annie, and Sheryl Gay Stolberg. "Trump Offers Temporary Protections for 'Dreamers' in Exchange for Wall Funding." *New York Times,* January 19, 2019. https://www .nytimes.com/2019/01/19/us/politics/trump-proposal-daca-wall.html.

Keaton, Trica Danielle. *Muslim Girls and the Other France: Race, Identity Politics, and Social Exclusion.* Bloomington: Indiana University Press, 2006.

Kelley, Robin D. G. Foreword to *Black Marxism: The Making of the Black Radical Tradition,* by Cedric J. Robinson, xi–xxvi. 1983. Reprint, Chapel Hill: University of North Carolina Press, 2005.

——. "Nap Time: Historicizing the Afro." *Fashion Theory* 1, no. 4 (1997): 339–51. https:// doi.org/10.2752/136270497779613666.

——. "What Did Cedric Robinson Mean by Racial Capitalism?" *Boston Review,* January 12, 2017. http://bostonreview.net/race/robin-d-g-kelley-what-did-cedric-robinson-mean -racial-capitalism.

Kilomba, Grada. *Plantation Memories: Episodes of Everyday Racism.* Münster: Unrast, 2008.

Kington, Tom. "Anti-immigrant Italians Find a New Foe: Food from Abroad." *Guardian,* November 15, 2009. http://www.theguardian.com/world/2009/nov/15/italys -kebab-war-hots-up.

Komada, Erin. "Turned Away: The Detrimental Effect of Italy's Public Security Law on Undocumented Children's Right to Education." *Boston University Law Journal* 29 (2011): 451–74.

Koopmans, Ruud, Paul Statham, Marco Giugni, and Florence Passy. *Contested Citizenship: Immigration and Cultural Diversity in Europe*. Minneapolis: University of Minnesota Press, 2005.

Krause, Elizabeth L. *Tight Knit: Global Families and the Social Life of Fast Fashion*. Chicago: University of Chicago Press, 2018.

Kühl, Stefan. *Die Internationale der Rassisten: Aufstieg und Niedergang der internationalen eugenischen Bewegung im 20. Jahrhundert*. Frankfurt: Campus Verlag, 1997.

——. *For the Betterment of the Race: The Rise and Fall of the International Movement for Eugenics and Racial Hygiene*. New York: Springer, 2013.

Kushner, Rachel. "Is Prison Necessary? Ruth Wilson Gilmore Might Change Your Mind (Published 2019)." *New York Times*, April 17, 2019, sec. Magazine. https://www.nytimes.com/2019/04/17/magazine/prison-abolition-ruth-wilson-gilmore.html.

Kuti, Tommy. *Ci rido sopra: Crescere con la pelle nera nell'Italia di Salvini*. Milan: Rizzoli, 2019.

Kuwornu, Fred. *Blaxploitalian: 100 Years of Blackness in Italian Cinema*. Documentary, 2016. https://vimeo.com/488197441.

——. *18 Ius Soli*. Documentary, 2012. http://vimeo.com/37011695.ch1n55.

Labanca, Nicola. "Colonial Rule, Colonial Repression and War Crimes in the Italian Colonies." *Journal of Modern Italian Studies* 9, no. 3 (2004): 300–313. https://doi.org/10.1080/1354571042000254737.

——. *La guerra italiana per la Libia: 1911–1931*. Bologna: Il Mulino, 2012.

——. *Oltremare: Storia dell'espansione coloniale italiana*. Bologna: Il Mulino, 2007.

Lacy, Michael G. "Black Frankenstein and Racial Neoliberalism in Contemporary American Cinema: Reanimating Racial Monsters in Changing Lanes." In *The Routledge Companion to Global Popular Culture*, edited by Toby Miller, 229–43. London: Routledge, 2014.

La Macchina Sognante. "Appello per una Sala di Medicina a Bologna dedicata a Emmanuel Chidi Nnamdi (italiano e inglese)." July 12, 2016. http://www.lamacchinasognante.com/appello-per-una-sala-di-medicina-a-bologna-dedicata-a-emmanuel-chidi-namdi/.

La Repubblica. "Cittadinanza: Sì della Camera allo ius soli. La nuova legge passa al Senato." October 13, 2015. http://www.repubblica.it/politica/2015/10/13/news/legge_cittadinanza_senato-124967907/.

——. "Ius soli, al Senato manca il numero legale. Assenti tutti i M5s e i centristi. Manca 1/3 dei Dem." December 23, 2017. http://www.repubblica.it/politica/2017/12/23/news/cittadinanza_al_senato_manca_il_numero_legale_muore_lo_ius_soli-184997182/.

——. "Ius soli, discussione in Senato: È bagarre. Contusa ministra Fedeli e Boldrini dice basta alla violenza in Aula." *La Repubblica*, June 15, 2017. http://www.repubblica.it/politica/2017/06/15/news/ius_soli_discussione_senato-168161564/.

——. "Milano per George Floyd: Migliaia di manifestanti in piazza contro il razzismo." June 7, 2020. https://milano.repubblica.it/cronaca/2020/06/07/news/george_floyd_razzismo_milano_manifestazione_black_lives_matter-258654957/.

——. "Perché la razza bianca non esiste secondo la scienza." January 18, 2018. https://www.repubblica.it/scienze/2018/01/18/news/perche_la_razza_bianca_non_esiste_secondo_la_scienza-186782903/.

Larocca, Amy. "The Bodies Artist." *The Cut*, August 9, 2016. http://www.thecut.com/2016/08/vanessa-beecroft-bodies-artist.html.

La Stampa. "Coronavirus, quando la paura del contagio serve solo a mascherare il razzismo." February 2, 2020. https://www.lastampa.it/cronaca/2020/02/02/news/coronavirus -da-casapound-ai-campi-di-calcio-il-razzismo-e-di-casa-in-italia-1.38415778.

——. "Milano, bruciate tre palme in Piazza Duomo." February 20, 2017. http://www .lastampa.it/2017/02/19/milano/milano-parzialmente-bruciate-tre-palme-in -piazza-duomo-FUnHqCgV4FHSOKvRKSi7DP/pagina.html.

Law, Ian. *Mediterranean Racisms: Connections and Complexities in the Racialization of the Mediterranean Region.* New York: Springer, 2014.

Lee, Charles T. "Bare Life, Interstices, and the Third Space of Citizenship." *Women's Studies Quarterly* 38, no. 1/2 (2010): 57–81.

——. *Ingenious Citizenship: Recrafting Democracy for Social Change.* Durham, NC: Duke University Press, 2016.

Lentin, Alana. *Racism and Anti-racism in Europe.* London: Pluto Press, 2004.

L'Huffington Post (blog). "Fermo, Matteo Salvini: 'Prego per Emmanuel, non doveva morire. L'immigrazione non porta nulla di buono,'" July 7, 2016. http://www .huffingtonpost.it/2016/07/07/salvini-emmanuel_n_10854424.html.

Lister, Ruth. "Inclusive Citizenship: Realizing the Potential." *Citizenship Studies* 11, no. 1 (2007): 49–61. https://doi.org/10.1080/13621020601099856.

L'Italia Sono Anch'io (blog). "Documenti." Accessed July 25, 2018. http://www .litaliasonoanchio.it/index.php?id=522.

Lombardi-Diop, Cristina. "Mothering the Nation: An Italian Woman in Colonial Eritrea." In *ItaliAfrica: Bridging Continents and Cultures,* edited by Sante Matteo. Stony Brook, NY: Forum Italicum, 2001.

——. "Postracial / Postcolonial Italy." In *Postcolonial Italy: Challenging National Homogeneity,* edited by Cristina Lombardi-Diop and Caterina Romeo, 175–87. New York: Palgrave Macmillan, 2012.

——. "Spotless Italy: Hygiene, Domesticity, and the Ubiquity of Whiteness in Fascist and Postwar Consumer Culture." *California Italian Studies* 2, no. 1 (2011). http:// escholarship.org/uc/item/8vt6r0vf.

Lombardi-Diop, Cristina, and Caterina Romeo. "Introduction: Paradigms of Postcoloniality in Contemporary Italy." In *Postcolonial Italy: Challenging National Homogeneity,* edited by Cristina Lombardi-Diop and Caterina Romeo, 1–30. New York: Palgrave Macmillan, 2012.

——, eds. *Postcolonial Italy: Challenging National Homogeneity.* New York: Palgrave Macmillan, 2012.

Lombroso, Cesare. *L'uomo bianco e l'uomo di colore: Letture sull' origine e le varietà delle razze umane.* Padua: F. Sacchetto, 1871.

Lombroso, Cesare, and Guglielmo Ferrero. *Criminal Woman, the Prostitute, and the Normal Woman.* 1893. Reprint, Durham, NC: Duke University Press, 2004.

Lorde, Audre. *Sister Outsider: Essays and Speeches.* 1984. Reprint, New York: Penguin, 2020.

Losurdo, Domenico. *Liberalism: A Counter-History.* London: Verso Books, 2014.

Lucht, Hans. *Darkness before Daybreak: African Migrants Living on the Margins in Southern Italy Today.* Berkeley: University of California Press, 2012.

Lyons, Patrick. "Trump Wants to Abolish Birthright Citizenship. Can He Do That?" *New York Times,* August 22, 2019. https://www.nytimes.com/2019/08/22/us/birthright -citizenship-14th-amendment-trump.html.

Mackinder, Sir Halford John. *Democratic Ideals and Reality: A Study in the Politics of Reconstruction.* New York: H. Holt, 1919.

Maglio, Alan, and Medhin Paolos. *Asmarina: Voices and Images of a Postcolonial Heritage.* Documentary, 2015. http://asmarinaproject.com/.

Magubane, Zine. *Bringing the Empire Home: Race, Class, and Gender in Britain and Colonial South Africa*. Chicago: University of Chicago Press, 2004.

Malizia, Pierfranco. *Interculturalismo: Studio sul vivere "individualmente-insieme-con-gli-altri."* Milan: FrancoAngeli, 2005.

Malkki, Liisa. "National Geographic: The Rooting of Peoples and the Territorialization of National Identity among Scholars and Refugees." *Cultural Anthropology* 7, no. 1 (1992): 24–44.

Mallette, Karla. *European Modernity and the Arab Mediterranean: Toward a New Philology and a Counter-Orientalism*. Philadelphia: University of Pennsylvania Press, 2011.

Mamdani, Mahmood. "Good Muslim, Bad Muslim: A Political Perspective on Culture and Terrorism." *American Anthropologist* 104, no. 3 (2002): 766–75.

Mangiapane, Gianluigi, and Erika Grasso. "Il patrimonio, i non detti e il silenzio: Le storie del MAET." *roots§routes* (blog), May 14, 2019. https://www.roots-routes.org /patrimonio-non-detti-silenzio-le-storie-del-maet-gianluigi-mangiapane-erika -grasso/.

Marboah, Theophilus (@Theoimani). "Perché la storia del nero americano è unica anche in questo . . ." Instagram Story, November 27, 2019.

Marchetti, Chiara. "'Trees without Roots': The Reform of Citizenship Challenged by the Children of Immigrants in Italy." *Bulletin of Italian Politics* 2, no. 1 (2010): 45–67.

Marchetti, Sabrina. *Black Girls: Migrant Domestic Workers and Colonial Legacies*. Leiden: Brill, 2014.

Marinaro, Isabella Clough, and James Walston. "Italy's 'Second Generations': The Sons and Daughters of Migrants." *Bulletin of Italian Politics* 2, no. 1 (2010): 5–19.

Marro, Giovanni. *La sala della razza nella rassegna "Torino e l'autarchia."* Turin: Tipografia Silvestrelli e Cappelletto, 1939.

——. "Un allarme per il razzismo italiano." *La Vita Italiana* 29, no. 236 (March 1941): 5–17.

Marshall, T. H. *Citizenship and Social Class*. 1950. Reprint, London: Pluto Press, 1987.

Marshall Project. "A State-by-State Look at 15 Months of Coronavirus in Prisons." July 1, 2021. https://www.themarshallproject.org/2020/05/01/a-state-by-state-look-at -coronavirus-in-prisons.

Massaro, Angelo. "Cittadinanza italiana da 730 giorni a 4 anni, tutte le novità del Decreto Salvini sulle cittadinanze." *Cittadinanza Italiana*, October 2, 2018. https:// www.cittadinanza.biz/cittadinanza-italiana-da-730-giorni-a-4-anni-il-testo -definitivo-del-decreto-salvini/.

Massey, Doreen. *For Space*. Thousand Oaks, CA: SAGE, 2005.

——. *Space, Place, and Gender*. Minneapolis: University of Minnesota Press, 1994.

Matlon, Jordanna. "Racial Capitalism and the Crisis of Black Masculinity." *American Sociological Review* 81, no. 5 (2016): 1014–38. https://doi.org/10.1177/0003122416658294.

Matteo, Sante. "Introduction: African Italy, Bridging Continents and Cultures." In *ItaliAfrica: Bridging Continents and Cultures*, edited by Sante Matteo, 1–20. Stony Brook, NY: Forum Italicum, 2001.

Mayer, Larry. "Italian Earthquakes: A Legacy of the Past and a Preview of the Future." In *ItaliAfrica: Bridging Continents and Cultures*, edited by Sante Matteo, 23–37. Stony Brook, NY: Forum Italicum, 2001.

Mazie, Steven. "What Does 'No Justice, No Peace' Really Mean?" *Big Think* (blog), December 5, 2014. http://bigthink.com/praxis/what-does-no-justice-no-peace-really-mean.

Mazzini, Giuseppe. "Intorno alla questione dei negri in America." In *Scritti editi ed inediti di Giuseppe Mazzini*, 27:163–65. Imola, Italy: Cooperativa Tipografico-Editrice P. Galeati, 1940.

Mbembe, Achille. "Afropolitanism." In *Africa Remix: Contemporary Art of a Continent*, edited by Njami Simon, 26–30. Johannesburg: Jacana Media, 2007.

McAuley, James. "Black Lives Matter Movement Comes to France. But Will It Translate?" *Washington Post*, August 8, 2016. https://www.washingtonpost.com/world/black-lives-matter-movement-comes-to-france-but-will-it-translate/2016/08/07/7606567e-58cd-11e6-8b48-0cb344221131_story.html.

McClintock, Anne. *Imperial Leather: Race, Gender, and Sexuality in the Colonial Contest.* London: Routledge, 2013.

McGuire, Valerie. *Italy's Sea: Empire and Nation in the Mediterranean, 1895–1945.* Liverpool: Liverpool University Press, 2020.

McKenzie, Sheena. "Black Lives Matter Protests Spread to Europe." CNN, July 11, 2016. http://www.cnn.com/2016/07/11/europe/black-lives-matter-protests-europe/index.html.

McKittrick, Katherine. "Commentary: Worn Out." *Southeastern Geographer* 57, no. 1 (2017): 96–100. https://doi.org/10.1353/sgo.2017.0008.

——. *Demonic Grounds: Black Women and the Cartographies of Struggle.* Minneapolis: University of Minnesota Press, 2006.

——. "On Plantations, Prisons, and a Black Sense of Place." *Social & Cultural Geography* 12, no. 8 (2011): 947–63. https://doi.org/10.1080/14649365.2011.624280.

——. "Science Quarrels Sculpture: The Politics of Reading Sarah Baartman." *Mosaic* 43, no. 2 (2010): 113.

McKittrick, Katherine, and Clyde Woods, eds. "No One Knows the Mysteries at the Bottom of the Ocean." In *Black Geographies and the Politics of Place*, 1–13. Boston: South End Press, 2007.

Mehta, Uday S. "Liberal Strategies of Exclusion." *Politics & Society* 18, no. 4 (1990): 427–54. https://doi.org/10.1177/003232929001800402.

Mellino, Miguel. "De-provincializing Italy: Notes on Race, Racialization, and Italy's Coloniality." In *Postcolonial Italy: Challenging National Homogeneity*, edited by Cristina Lombardi-Diop and Caterina Romeo, 83–99. New York: Palgrave Macmillan, 2012.

Melotti, Umberto. "Immigration and Security in Europe: A Look at the Italian Case." In *The Frontiers of Europe: A Transatlantic Problem?*, edited by Federiga M. Bindi and Irina Angelescu, 107–26. Washington, DC: Brookings Institution Press, 2011.

Mente Locale. "FierAfric 2019: Cultura, arte e cibo nella fiera dell'Africa," May 28, 2019. https://www.mentelocale.it/milano/eventi/128404-fierafric-2019-cultura-arte-cibo-fiera-africa.htm.

Meret, Susi, Elisabetta Della Corte, and Maria Sangiuliano. "The Racist Attacks against Cécile Kyenge and the Enduring Myth of the 'Nice' Italian." *OpenDemocracy* (blog), August 28, 2013. http://www.opendemocracy.net/can-europe-make-it/susi-meret-elisabetta-della-corte-maria-sangiuliano/racist-attacks-against-c%C3%A9cile.

Merrill, Heather. *An Alliance of Women: Immigration and the Politics of Race.* Minneapolis: University of Minnesota Press, 2006.

——. *Black Spaces: African Diaspora in Italy.* London: Routledge, 2018. https://doi.org/10.4324/9781351000758.

——. "In Other Wor(l)ds: Situated Intersectionality in Italy." In *Spaces of Danger: Culture and Power in the Everyday*, edited by Heather Merrill and Lisa M. Hoffman, 77–100. Athens: University of Georgia Press, 2015.

——. "Postcolonial Borderlands: Black Life Worlds and Relational Place in Turin, Italy." *ACME: An International Journal for Critical Geographies* 13, no. 2 (2014): 263–94.

Merrill, Heather, and Donald Martin Carter. "Inside and Outside Italian Political Culture: Immigrants and Diasporic Politics in Turin." *GeoJournal* 58, no. 2/3 (2002): 167–75.

Messina, Dino. "Le armi chimiche in Etiopia e l'ammissione di Montanelli." *Corriere della Sera*, April 2, 2016. https://www.corriere.it/extra-per-voi/2016/04/02/armi-chimiche-etiopia-l-ammissione-montanelli-54d37986-f8fc-11e5-b97f-6d5a0a6f6065.shtml.

Mezzadra, Sandro. "The Proliferation of Borders and the Right to Escape." *Refugee Watch: A South Asian Journal on Forced Migration* 41 (2013): 1–14.

Mezzadra, Sandro, and Brett Neilson. *Border as Method, or, the Multiplication of Labor.* Durham, NC: Duke University Press, 2013.

Michaels, Jennifer. "The Impact of Audre Lorde's Politics and Poetics on Afro-German Women Writers." *German Studies Review* 29, no. 1 (2006): 21–40.

Migliarini, Valentina. "'Colour-Evasiveness' and Racism without Race: The Disablement of Asylum-Seeking Children at the Edge of Fortress Europe." *Race Ethnicity and Education* 21, no. 4 (July 4, 2018): 438–57. https://doi.org/10.1080/13613324.2017.1417252.

Milcia, Maria Teresa, and Gaia Giuliani. "Giochi al buio o parole per dirlo? Riflessioni su razza, razzismo e antirazzismo intorno a un colloquio con Gaia Giuliani." *Voci: Annuale di Scienze Umane* 13 (2016): 171–89.

Miller, Zeke, Jill Colvin, and Jonathan Lemire. "Trump Digs in on Racist Tweets: 'Many People Agree with Me.'" Associated Press, July 16, 2019. https://apnews.com/9924c846abf84cfeabb76e6045190b42.

Mills, Charles W. *The Racial Contract.* 1997. Reprint, Ithaca, NY: Cornell University Press, 2014.

Mitchell, Katharyne. "Different Diasporas and the Hype of Hybridity." *Environment and Planning D: Society and Space* 15, no. 5 (1997): 533–53. https://doi.org/10.1068/d150533.

Mitrotti, Antonio. "Il rovesciamento di prospettiva sulla misura di revoca della cittadinanza nel 'dibattuto' Decreto Sicurezza 'Salvini.'" Osservatorio Costituzionale 1–2/2019. Rome: Associazione Italiana dei Constituzionali, April 12, 2019. https://www.osservatorioaic.it/images/rivista/pdf/2019_1-2_04_Mitrotti.pdf.

ModenaToday. "Cittadinanza italiana, boom di richieste e tempi di attesa interminabili." February 18, 2016. http://www.modenatoday.it/cronaca/numeri-richieste-attese-cittadinanza-italiana-modena.2015.html.

Moe, Nelson J. *The View from Vesuvius: Italian Culture and the Southern Question.* Berkeley: University of California Press, 2002.

Mohamed, Gassid. "Non uccidete l'umano." *Frontiere News*, July 17, 2016. http://frontierenews.it/2016/07/non-uccidete-umano-fermo-paura-diverso/.

Montini, Beatrice. "Fermo, picchiato a sangue e ucciso aveva reagito a insulti razzisti." *Corriere della Sera*, July 6, 2016. http://www.corriere.it/cronache/16_luglio_06/fermo-reagisce-insulti-razzisti-nigeriano-massacrato-coma-irreversibile-e69a92be-4393-11e6-831b-0b63011f1840.shtml.

Morigi, Andrea. "Più immigrati uguale più attentati ma se possiamo cacciarli siamo sicuri." *Libero*, July 25, 2016.

Morton, Adam David. "Traveling with Gramsci: The Spatiality of Passive Revolution." In *Gramsci: Space, Nature, Politics*, edited by Michael Ekers, Gillian Hart, Stefan Kipfer, and Alex Loftus, 47–64. Hoboken, NJ: John Wiley & Sons, 2012.

Movimento Migranti e Rifugiati Napoli. "Sardine Nere, Sardine Napoletane, 6000 Sardine." Facebook, February 20, 2020. https://www.facebook.com/MovimentoMigrantieRifugiatiNapoli/photos/a.101987851298376/136010641229430/?type=3.

Muehlebach, Andrea. *The Moral Neoliberal: Welfare and Citizenship in Italy.* Chicago: University of Chicago Press, 2012.

Nadotti, Cristina. "Crescono gli studenti non cittadini italiani: Il 61% è nato in Italia." *La Repubblica*, March 29, 2018. http://www.repubblica.it/scuola/2018/03/29/news

/crescono_gli_studenti_non_cittadini_italiani_il_61_e_nato_in_italia-19252
4586/.

Nanni, Maria Paola, ed. "Rapporto immigrazione e imprenditoria 2016: Aggiornamento statistico." Centro Studi e Ricerche IDOS. Rome: IDOS, 2016. https://www .dossierimmigrazione.it/en/prodotto/rapporto-immigrazione-e-imprenditoria -2016-aggiornamento-statistico/.

Napolitano, Giorgio. "Intervento del Presidente Napolitano all'incontro dedicato ai 'nuovi cittadini italiani.'" Presidenza della Repubblica, November 15, 2011. http:// presidenti.quirinale.it/elementi/Continua.aspx?tipo=Discorso&key=2302.

Nash, Jennifer C. *Black Feminism Reimagined: After Intersectionality*. Durham, NC: Duke University Press, 2018.

Nathan, Vetri. "Mimic-Nation, Mimic-Men." In *National Belongings: Hybridity in Italian Colonial and Postcolonial Cultures*, edited by Jacqueline Andall and Derek Duncan, 41–62. Bern: Peter Lang, 2010.

New York Times. "Black Lives Matter in France, Too." Editorial. July 29, 2016. https:// www.nytimes.com/2016/07/29/opinion/black-lives-matter-in-france-too.html.

Nimako, Kwame, and Stephen Small. "Theorizing Black Europe and African Diaspora: Implications for Citizenship, Nativism, and Xenophobia." In *Black Europe and the African Diaspora*, edited by Stephen Small, Trica Danielle Keaton, and Stephen Small, 212–37. Urbana: University of Illinois Press, 2009.

99posseofficial. "Terroni Uniti—Gente do Sud." March 10, 2017. YouTube video, 7:40. https://www.youtube.com/watch?v=TVKGGyoUlRo.

Njegosh, Tatiana Petrovich. "Gli italiani sono bianchi? Per una storia culturale della linea del colore in Italia." In *Parlare di razza: La lingua del colore tra Italia e Stati Uniti*, edited by Tatiana Petrovich Njegosh and Anna Scacchi, 13–45. Verona: Ombre Corte, 2012.

——. "La finizione della razza, la linea del colore e il meticciato." In *Il colore della nazione*, edited by Gaia Giuliani, 213–27. Milan: Mondadori, 2015.

Nopper, Tamara K. "The Wages of Non-Blackness: Contemporary Immigrant Rights and Discourses of Character, Productivity, and Value." *InTensions* 5 (Fall / Winter 2011): 1–25.

Nwabuzo, Ojeaku. "Afrophobia in Europe." ENAR Shadow Report 2014–2015 (European Network against Racism, 2015). https://www.enar-eu.org/IMG/pdf/shadowreport _afrophobia_final_with_corrections.pdf.

Occhetta, Francesco. "La Cittadinanza in Italia." *La Civiltà Cattolica* 4, no. 3919 (October 5, 2013): 14–24.

Omi, Michael, and Howard Winant. *Racial Formation in the United States*. 1986. Reprint, London: Routledge, 2014.

Opitz, May, Katharina Oguntoye, and Dagmar Schultz. *Showing Our Colors: Afro-German Women Speak Out*. 1986. Reprint, Amherst: University of Massachusetts Press, 1992.

Oppenheim, Maya. "Samuel L Jackson and Magic Johnson Mistaken for 'Lazy Migrants' by Italians after Shopping in Tuscany." *Independent* (UK), August 21, 2017. http:// www.independent.co.uk/arts-entertainment/films/news/samuel-l-jackson -magic-johnson-lazy-migrants-italy-tuscany-forte-dei-marmi-louis-vuitton -a7905026.html.

Otele, Olivette. *African Europeans: An Untold History*. New York: Basic Books, 2021.

Panzarell, Gioia. "Venditori di libri per strada come intermediari culturali della letteratura della migrazione." *El Ghibli* (blog), 2017. http://www.el-ghibli.org/wp-content /uploads/2017/07/I-venditori-di-libri-per-strada-come-intermediari-culturali -della-letteratura-della-migrazione-G.-Panzarella.pdf.

Paolo, Paolo di. "Mirandola, quella ragazza nera vestita con il tricolore." *La Repubblica*, June 9, 2017. https://bologna.repubblica.it/cronaca/2017/06/09/news/mirandola _ragazza_tricolore-167693538/.

Papadogiannis, Nikolaos. *Militant around the Clock?: Left-Wing Youth Politics, Leisure, and Sexuality in Post-Dictatorship Greece, 1974–1981.* New York: Berghahn Books, 2015.

Papadopoulos, Dimitris, and Vassilis S. Tsianos. "After Citizenship: Autonomy of Migration, Organisational Ontology and Mobile Commons." *Citizenship Studies* 17, no. 2 (April 1, 2013): 178–96. https://doi.org/10.1080/13621025.2013.780736.

Papavero, Giorgia. "Minori e seconde generazioni." Milan: Fondazione ISMU, 2015.

Parker, Owen. "Book Review: *Race and the Undeserving Poor*." *SPERI* (blog), September 15, 2018. http://speri.dept.shef.ac.uk/2018/09/16/book-review-race-and-the -undeserving-poor/.

Parmelee, Jennifer. "'Italian Dream' Soured by Racism." *Washington Post*, August 31, 1989. https://www.washingtonpost.com/archive/politics/1989/08/31/italian-dream -soured-by-racism/37f5c1d6-b8fb-4b8e-86af-e6d1b5a4f2a9/.

Parreñas, Rhacel Salazar. *The Force of Domesticity: Filipina Migrants and Globalization.* New York: New York University Press, 2008.

Patriarca, Silvana. "'Gli italiani non sono razzisti': Costruzioni dell'italianità tra gli anni Cinquanta e il 1986." In *Il colore della nazione*, edited by Gaia Giuliani, 32–45. Milan: Mondadori Education, 2015.

——. *Italianità: La costruzione del carattere nazionale.* Rome: Gius. Laterza & Figli, 2014.

Patterson, Orlando. *Slavery and Social Death: A Comparative Study.* Cambridge, MA: Harvard University Press, 2018.

Paynter, Eleanor. "The Liminal Lives of Europe's Transit Migrants:" *Contexts*, June 7, 2018. https://doi.org/10.1177/1536504218776959.

Pergher, Roberta. *Mussolini's Nation-Empire.* Cambridge: Cambridge University Press, 2018.

Perseverance, Marvely Goma. "Lettera aperta di Marvely Goma Perseverance per Abba Ed Emmanuel." *GRIOT*, accessed July 9, 2016. http://griotmag.com/it/lettera -marvely-goma-perseverance-abba-ed-emmanuel/.

Pesarini, Angelica. "'Blood Is Thicker Than Water': The Materialization of the Racial Body in Fascist East Africa." *Zapruder World: An International Journal for the History of Social Conflict* 4 (2017). http://zapruderworld.org/journal/past-volumes /volume-4/blood-is-thicker-than-water-the-materialization-of-the-racial-body -in-fascist-east-africa/.

——. "Colour Strategies: Negotiations of Black Mixed Race Women's Identities in Colonial and Postcolonial Italy." PhD diss., University of Leeds, 2015. http://etheses .whiterose.ac.uk/10103/.

Pesarini, Angelica, and Camilla Hawthorne. "Black Lives Matter anche da noi?" *Jacobin Italia*, September 24, 2020. https://jacobinitalia.it/black-lives-matter-anche-da -noi/.

Pesarini, Angelica, and Guido Tintori. "Mixed Identities in Italy: A Country in Denial." In *The Palgrave International Handbook of Mixed Racial and Ethnic Classification*, edited by Zarine L. Rocha and Peter J. Aspinall, 349–65. Cham: Springer International,2020. https://doi.org/10.1007/978-3-030-22874-3_19.

Pick, Daniel. "The Faces of Anarchy: Lombroso and the Politics of Criminal Science in Post-Unification Italy." *History Workshop Journal* 21, no. 1 (March 20, 1986): 60–86. https://doi.org/10.1093/hwj/21.1.60.

Pinkus, Karen. *Bodily Regimes: Italian Advertising under Fascism.* Minneapolis: University of Minnesota Press, 1995.

Pinto, Jovita dos Santos, Noémi Michel, Patricia Purtschert, Paola Bacchetta, and Vanessa Naef. "Baldwin's Transatlantic Reverberations: Between 'Stranger in the Village' and *I Am Not Your Negro*." *James Baldwin Review* 6 (2020): 176–98.

Pirni, Andrea. "I giovani italiani, la 'non politica' e nuovi cleavages." *SocietàMutamentoPolitica* 3, no. 5 (2012): 157–71.

Podesta, Gian-Luca. "Colonists and 'Demographic' Colonists: Family and Society in Italian Africa." *Annales de Demographie Historique* 122, no. 2 (2011): 205–31.

——. "L'emigrazione italiana in Africa orientale." *Annales de Demographie Historique* 113, no. 1 (2007): 59–84. http://www.ilcornodafrica.it/rds-01emigrazione.pdf.

Poggioli, Sylvia. "A Divided Italy to Mark Unification Anniversary." *NPR*, March 17, 2011. http://www.npr.org/2011/03/17/134602534/a-divided-italy-prepares-for-unification-anniversary.

Pojmann, Wendy A. *Immigrant Women and Feminism in Italy*. Aldershot, UK: Ashgate, 2006.

Polchi, Vladimiro. "'L'Italia sono anch'io': Due leggi per la cittadinanza agli immigrati." *La Repubblica*, June 22, 2011. http://www.repubblica.it/solidarieta/immigrazione /2011/06/22/news/campagna_cittadinanza-18041906/.

——. "La Stranieri Spa vale come la Fiat: Il Pil degli immigrati in Italia pesa 127 miliardi." *La Repubblica*, October 7, 2016. https://www.repubblica.it/economia/2016 /10/10/news/economia_immigrati_pil-149285846/.

——. "Migranti, gli otto falsi miti da sfatare." *La Repubblica*, October 13, 2016. http://www .repubblica.it/cronaca/2016/10/13/news/migranti_falsi_miti_bonino-149688642/.

Ponzanesi, Sandra. "Beyond the Black Venus: Colonial Sexual Politics and Contemporary Visual Practices." In *Italian Colonialism: Legacies and Memories*, edited by Jacqueline Andall and Derek Duncan, 165–89. Oxford: Peter Lang, 2005.

——. "The Color of Love: Madamismo and Interracial Relationships in the Italian Colonies." *Research in African Literatures* 43, no. 2 (2012): 155–72. https://doi.org/10 .2979/reseafrilite.43.2.155.

Pop, Valentina. "Italy Grants Citizenship to Lampedusa Dead." *EUobserver*, October 7, 2013. https://euobserver.com/justice/121681.

Portelli, Alessandro. "The Problem of the Color Blind: Notes on the Discourse of Race in Italy." In *Crossroutes—The Meaning of Race for the 21st Century*, edited by Paola Boi and Sabine Broeck, 29–39. Hamburg: LIT, 2003.

Pred, Allan. *Even in Sweden: Racisms, Racialized Spaces, and the Popular Geographical Imagination*. Berkeley: University of California Press, 2000.

Premazzi, Viviana. "Integrazione online: Nativi e migranti fuori e dentro la rete." FIERI Rapporti di Ricerca, October 2010. http://fieri.it/wp-content/uploads/2011/03 /Lintegrazione-online-nativi-e-migranti-fuori-e-dentro-la-rete.pdf.

Progetto Melting Pot Europa. "La concessione e l'accertamento della cittadinanza italiana." September 13, 2009. http://www.meltingpot.org/La-concessione-e-l-accertamento -della-cittadinanza-italiana.html.

——. "Manifesto degli scienziati antirazzisti 2008." July 10, 2008. http://www.meltingpot .org/Manifesto-degli-scienziati-antirazzisti-2008.html.

Proglio, Gabriele, ed. *Decolonizing the Mediterranean*. Cambridge: Cambridge Scholars, 2016.

——. "Is the Mediterranean a White Italian-European Sea? The Multiplication of Borders in the Production of Historical Subjectivity." *Interventions* 20, no. 3 (2018): 1–22. https://doi.org/10.1080/1369801X.2017.1421025.

——. *Libia 1911–1912: Immaginari coloniali e italianità*. Mondadori Education, 2016.

Puar, Jasbir K. *Terrorist Assemblages: Homonationalism in Queer Times*. Durham, NC: Duke University Press, 2007.

Public Policy. "Ius soli al Senato, 7mila emendamenti della Lega." April 28, 2016. https:// www.publicpolicy.it/lega-senato-emendamenti-cittadinanza-58641.html.

Puglia, Alessandro. "Quei migranti invisibili sulle navi quarantena." *Vita*, October 7, 2020. http://www.vita.it/it/article/2020/10/07/quei-migranti-invisibili-sulle-navi -quarantena/156901/.

Puwar, Nirmal. *Space Invaders: Race, Gender and Bodies out of Place.* Oxford: Berg, 2004.

Quirico, Roberto di. "Italy and the Global Economic Crises." *Bulletin of Italian Politics* 2, no. 2 (2010): 3–19.

Qureshi, Sadiah. *Peoples on Parade: Exhibitions, Empire, and Anthropology in Nineteenth-Century Britain.* Chicago: University of Chicago Press, 2011.

Radio Città del Capo. "'Bologna è meticcia': La contestazione non violenta che manda in bestia i Salviner," November 9, 2015. https://www.youtube.com/watch?v=RZKGic0 _O_g&ab_channel=RadioCitt%C3%A0delCapo.

Raeymaekers, Timothy. "Introduction: Europe's Bleeding Border and the Mediterranean as a Relational Space." *ACME: An International Journal for Critical Geographies* 13, no. 2 (2014): 163–72.

———. "On the Politics of Claiming Peripheral Space." *Tracce Urbane: Rivista Italiana Transdisciplinare di Studi Urbani* 3, no. 5 (July 2, 2019). https://doi.org/10.13133 /2532-6562_3.5.14557.

———. "The Racial Geography of the Black Mediterranean." *Liminal Geographies* (blog), January 21, 2015. http://www.timothyraeymaekers.net/2015/01/the-racial -geography-of-the-black-mediterranean/.

———. "Working the Black Mediterranean." *Liminal Geographies* (blog), January 21, 2015. http://www.timothyraeymaekers.net/2015/01/working-the-black-mediterra nean/.

Rafter, Nicole Hahn. *The Criminal Brain: Understanding Biological Theories of Crime.* New York: New York University Press, 2008.

Rame, Sergio. "Ius soli, è sostituzione etnica: Subito 800mila nuovi 'italiani.'" *Il Giornale*, June 15, 2017. http://www.ilgiornale.it/news/ius-soli-sostituzione-etnica -subito-800mila-nuovi-italiani-1409527.html.

———. "Migranti, Boldrini al Senato: 'Approvate subito lo ius soli.'" *Il Giornale*, June 16, 2016. http://www.ilgiornale.it/news/politica/boldrini-ringrazia-i-migranti-meticciato -forma-cultura-1272560.html.

Rankine, Claudia. *Citizen: An American Lyric.* Minneapolis, MN: Graywolf Press, 2014.

Re, Lucia. "Italians and the Invention of Race: The Poetics and Politics of Difference in the Struggle over Libya, 1890–1913." *California Italian Studies* 1, no. 1 (2010). http://escholarship.org/uc/item/96k3w5kn.

Reagon, Bernice Johnson. "Coalition Politics: Turning the Century." In *Home Girls: A Black Feminist Anthology*, edited by Barbara Smith, 356–68. New York: Kitchen Table: Women of Color Press, 1983.

Redattore Sociale. "A Milano arriva Innesti, il festival degli 'italiani ibridi.'" June 18, 2016. http://www.redattoresociale.it/Notiziario/Articolo/510774/A-Milano-arriva -Innesti-il-festival-degli-italiani-ibridi.

Reddy, Chandan. *Freedom with Violence: Race, Sexuality, and the US State.* Durham, NC: Duke University Press, 2011.

Reese, Ashanté M. *Black Food Geographies: Race, Self-Reliance, and Food Access in Washington.* Chapel Hill: University of North Carolina Press, 2019.

Reuters. "Italy Revokes Lease for Site of Bannon's Right-Wing Academy." June 1, 2019. https://www.reuters.com/article/us-italy-monastery-bannon-idUSKCN1T235I.

Riles, Annelise, ed. *Documents: Artifacts of Modern Knowledge.* Ann Arbor: University of Michigan Press, 2006.

Ripamonti, Luigi. "Gli italiani non esistono. Siamo un grande mix genetico. Tranne i sardi." *Corriere della Sera*, March 5, 2018. https://www.corriere.it/salute/18_maggio _02/italiani-mix-genetico-tranne-sardi-eab18cda-4e32-11e8-98a3-3b5657755c11 .shtml.

Ripanti, Esperance Hakuzwimana. *E poi basta: Manifesto di una donna nera italiana.* Gallarate, Italy: People, 2019.

Robinson, Cedric J. *Black Marxism: The Making of the Black Radical Tradition.* 1983. Reprint, Chapel Hill: University of North Carolina Press, 2005.

Rocco, Raymond A. *Transforming Citizenship: Democracy, Membership, and Belonging in Latino Communities.* East Lansing: Michigan State University Press, 2014.

Roediger, David R. *The Wages of Whiteness: Race and the Making of the American Working Class.* Rev. ed. New York: Verso, 1999.

Rofel, Lisa, and Sylvia J. Yanagisako. *Fabricating Transnational Capitalism: A Collaborative Ethnography of Italian-Chinese Global Fashion.* Durham, NC: Duke University Press, 2018.

Romani, Luigi. "Meticciato, meticcio." *Treccani, l'enciclopedia italiana.* July 19, 2008. http://www.treccani.it/magazine/lingua_italiana/articoli/parole/meticciato .html.

Romeo, Caterina. "Racial Evaporations: Representing Blackness in African Italian Postcolonial Literature." In *Postcolonial Italy: Challenging National Homogeneity*, edited by Cristina Lombardi-Diop and Caterina Romeo, 221–36. New York: Palgrave Macmillan, 2012.

Rosini, Gianni. "Milano, centinaia di profughi accampati in stazione centrale. Obiettivo: 'Trovare un trafficante per lasciare l'Italia.'" *Il Fatto Quotidiano*, May 10, 2015. http://www.ilfattoquotidiano.it/2015/05/10/milano-centinaia-di-profughi -accampati-in-stazione-centrale-obiettivo-trovare-un-trafficante-per-lasciare -litalia/1670158/.

Ross, Kristin. *Fast Cars, Clean Bodies: Decolonization and the Reordering of French Culture.* Cambridge, MA: The MIT Press, 1996.

Roy, Ananya. "Subjects of Risk: Technologies of Gender in the Making of Millennial Modernity." *Public Culture* 24, no. 1 (66) (January 1, 2012): 131–55. https://doi.org/10 .1215/08992363-1498001.

Rubino, Monica. "Fertility Day, Renzi: 'Campagna inguardabile.' Lorenzin: 'Basta polemiche, contano i fatti.'" *La Repubblica*, September 22, 2016. http://www.repubblica.it /politica/2016/09/22/news/fertility_day_al_via_proteste_piazza-148297333/.

Ruccia, Gisella. "Ius soli, la Russa (FdI): 'Usa bambini come scudi umani e vuol trasformare Italia in sala parto di tutta l'Africa.'" *Il Fatto Quotidiano*, September 28, 2017. http://www.ilfattoquotidiano.it/2017/09/28/ius-soli-la-russa-fdi-usa-bambini -come-scudi-umani-e-vuol-trasformare-italia-in-sala-parto-di-tutta-lafrica /3883483/.

Rusert, Britt. *Fugitive Science: Empiricism and Freedom in Early African American Culture.* New York: New York University Press, 2017.

Sabelli, Sonia. "L'eredità del colonialismo nelle rappresentazioni contemporanee del corpo femminile nero." *Zapruder* 23 (2010): 106–15.

Sagnet, Yvan, and Leonardo Palmisano. *Ghetto Italia: I braccianti stranieri tra caporalato e sfruttamento.* Rome: Fandango Libri, 2015.

Said, Edward W. "Traveling Theory Reconsidered." In *Reflections on Exile and Other Essays*, 436–52. Cambridge, MA: Harvard University Press, 2000.

Salaita, Steven. *Inter/Nationalism: Decolonizing Native America and Palestine.* Minneapolis: University of Minnesota Press, 2016.

Sallusti, Alessandro. "Il governo inventa l'Italia razzista." *Il Giornale*, July 11, 2016. http://www.ilgiornale.it/news/politica/governo-inventa-litalia-razzista-1282525.html.

Sanderson, Rachel. "The Real Value of Being 'Made in Italy.'" *Financial Times*, January 19, 2011. https://www.ft.com/content/ab98f3b4-2417-11e0-a89a-00144feab49a.

Sartori, Giovanni. "L'Italia non è una nazione meticcia. Ecco perché lo ius soli non funziona." *Corriere della Sera*, June 17, 2013. http://www.corriere.it/opinioni/13_giugno_17/sartori-ius-soli-integrazione-catena-equivoci_686dbf54-d728-11e2-a4df-7eff8733b462.shtml.

Saucier, Paul Khalil, and Tryon P. Woods. "Ex Aqua: The Mediterranean Basin, Africans on the Move, and the Politics of Policing." *Theoria* 61, no. 141 (2014): 55–75. https://doi.org/10.3167/th.2014.6114104.

——. *On Marronage: Ethical Confrontations with Antiblackness*. Trenton, NJ: Africa World Press, 2015.

Savelli, Fabio, and Arcangelo Rociola. "Ecco dov'è finito il Made in Italy negli anni della Grande Crisi." *Corriere della Sera*, July 27, 2013. http://www.corriere.it/economia/13_luglio_28/ecco-dove-finito-made-in-italy_8f2d99b2-f6df-11e2-9839-a8732bb379b1.shtml.

Saviano, Roberto. "Mai sentito parlare di Jerry Masslo?" *La Repubblica*, August 24, 2014. http://www.repubblica.it/cronaca/2014/08/24/news/saviano_jerry_masslo-94354580/.

Sceats, Sonya. "Opinion: Theresa May's Legacy Is the Hostile Environment—How Can She Evoke Nicholas Winton in Her Resignation Speech?" *Independent* (UK), May 25, 2019. https://www.independent.co.uk/voices/theresa-may-resigns-hostile-environment-nicholas-winton-immigration-windrush-scandal-a8929966.html.

Scego, Igiaba. "Capelli di libertà." *L'Espresso*, 2016.

——, ed. *Future: Il domani narrato dalle voci di oggi*. Florence: Effequ, 2019.

——. "Igiaba Scego: La cittadinanza italiana ai figli di migranti è una conquista per tutti." *Cosmopolitan*, February 28, 2017. http://www.cosmopolitan.it/lifecoach/a116749/cittadinanza-italiana-ai-figli-di-migranti-igiaba-scego/.

——, ed. *Italiani per vocazione*. Fiesole, Italy: Cadmo, 2005.

——. "Italy Is My Country—but It Must Face Its Racist History." *Guardian*, September 16, 2018, sec. World news. https://www.theguardian.com/world/2018/sep/16/italy-must-face-racist-history.

——. *La mia casa è dove sono*. Turin: Loescher, 2012.

——. "La vera storia di Faccetta nera." *Internazionale*, August 6, 2015. https://www.internazionale.it/opinione/igiaba-scego/2015/08/06/faccetta-nera-razzismo.

——. "Non in mio nome." *Internazionale*, January 7, 2015. https://www.internazionale.it/opinione/igiaba-scego/2015/01/07/non-in-mio-nome.

——. "Sausages." *Warscapes*, June 1, 2013. http://www.warscapes.com/retrospectives/food/sausages.

Schaefer, Richard T. "One-Drop Rule." In *Encyclopedia of Race, Ethnicity, and Society*, 1:998–99. Thousand Oaks, CA: SAGE, 2008.

Schneider, Jane. "The Dynamics of Neo-Orientalism in Italy (1848–1995)." In *Italy's "Southern Question": Orientalism in One Country*, edited by Jane Schneider, 1–23. New York: Bloomsbury Academic, 1998.

——, ed. *Italy's "Southern Question": Orientalism in One Country*. New York: Bloomsbury Academic, 1998.

Schumacher, Elizabeth. "Italy: Salvini Is Out, but Migrants Still Endure His Policies." *Deutsche Welle*, September 1, 2019. https://www.dw.com/en/italy-salvini-is-out-but-migrants-still-endure-his-policies/a-50229057.

Scott, David. *Conscripts of Modernity: The Tragedy of Colonial Enlightenment*. Durham, NC: Duke University Press, 2004.

———. *Omens of Adversity: Tragedy, Time, Memory, Justice*. Durham, NC: Duke University Press, 2013.

———. "The Re-enchantment of Humanism: An Interview with Sylvia Wynter." *Small Axe: A Caribbean Journal of Criticism* 8 (2000): 119–207.

Scotto, Andrea. "Una riflessione sui recenti fatti avvenuti a Castel Volturno." *Huffington Post* (blog), July 21, 2014. https://www.huffingtonpost.it/arturo-scotto/riflessione -fatti-castel-volturno_b_5604142.html.

Sedgwick, Eve Kosofsky. *Touching Feeling: Affect, Pedagogy, Performativity*. Durham, NC: Duke University Press, 2003.

Selasi, Taiye. "Bye-Bye Babar." *The LIP*, March 3, 2005. http://thelip.robertsharp.co.uk/ ?p=76.

———. "When We Speak of Nationality, What Do We Mean?" *New York Times*, December 4, 2014. https://www.nytimes.com/2014/12/04/opinion/taiye-selasi-when-we -speak-of-nationality-what-do-we-mean.html.

Sergi, Giuseppe. *Arii e italici: Attorno all'Italia preistorica, con figure dimostrative*. Turin: Bocca, 1898.

———. *Gli Arii in Europa e in Asia: Studio etnografico, con figure e carte*. Turin: Fratelli Bocca, 1903.

———. *Origine e diffusione della stirpe mediterranea*. Rome: Società Editrice Dante Alighieri, 1895.

Shange, Savannah. "Black Girl Ordinary: Flesh, Carcerality, and the Refusal of Ethnography." *Transforming Anthropology* 27, no. 1 (2019): 3–21. https://doi.org/10.1111 /traa.12143.

Sharpe, Christina. *In the Wake: On Blackness and Being*. Durham, NC: Duke University Press, 2016.

Shilliam, Robbie. *Race and the Undeserving Poor: From Abolition to Brexit*. Newcastle upon Tyne, UK: Agenda, 2018.

Showers, Fumilayo. "Being Black, Foreign and Woman: African Immigrant Identities in the United States." *Ethnic and Racial Studies* 38, no. 10 (August 9, 2015): 1815– 30. https://doi.org/10.1080/01419870.2015.1036763.

Simpson, Audra. *Mohawk Interruptus: Political Life across the Borders of Settler States*. Durham, NC: Duke University Press, 2014.

Sivanandan, A. "UK Commentary: Racism 1992." *Race & Class* 30, no. 3 (January 1, 1989): 85–90. https://doi.org/10.1177/030639688903000309.

Sluga, Glenda. *The Problem of Trieste and the Italo-Yugoslav Border: Difference, Identity, and Sovereignty in Twentieth-Century Europe*. Albany: State University of New York Press, 2001.

Small, Stephen. Introduction to *Black Europe and the African Diaspora*, edited by Darlene Clark Hine, Trica Danielle Keaton, and Stephen Small, xxiii–xxxviii. Urbana: University of Illinois Press, 2009.

———. *Police and People in London: A Group of Young Black People*. London: Policy Studies Institute, 1983.

———. "Theorizing Visibility and Vulnerability in Black Europe and the African Diaspora." *Ethnic and Racial Studies* 41, no. 6 (2018): 1182–97. https://doi.org/10.1080/01419870 .2018.1417619.

———. *20 Questions and Answers on Black Europe*. Amsterdam: Amrit Publishers, 2018.

Small, Stephen, and Rebecca C. King-O'Riain. "Global Mixed Race: An Introduction." In *Global Mixed Race*, edited by Rebecca Chiyoko King-O'Riain, Stephen Small, and Minelle Mahtani, vii–xxii. New York: New York University Press, 2014.

Smythe, S. A. "The Black Mediterranean and the Politics of the Imagination." *Middle East Report* 286 (Spring 2018). https://merip.org/2018/10/the-black-mediterranean -and-the-politics-of-the-imagination/.

Sojoyner, Damien M. "Another Life Is Possible: Black Fugitivity and Enclosed Places." *Cultural Anthropology* 32, no. 4 (2017): 514–36. https://doi.org/10.14506/ca32.4.04.

Solani, Massimo. "Pacciotti: 'L'Italia non può trattare milioni di persone come cittadini Di Serie B.'" *Democratica.It* (blog), October 14, 2016.

Sòrgoni, Barbara. "'Defending the Race': The Italian Reinvention of the Hottentot Venus during Fascism." *Journal of Modern Italian Studies* 8, no. 3 (2010): 411–24.

——. *Parole e corpi: Antropologia, discorso giuridico e politiche sessuali interrazziali nella colonia Eritrea, 1890–1941.* Naples: Liguori, 1998.

——. "Racist Discourses and Practices in the Italian Empire under Fascism." In *The Politics of Recognizing Difference: Multiculturalism Italian Style*, edited by Ralph Grillo and Jeff Pratt, 41–57. Aldershot, UK: Ashgate, 2002.

Spady, Sam. "Reflections on Late Identity: In Conversation with Melanie J. Newton, Nirmala Erevelles, Kim TallBear, Rinaldo Walcott, and Dean Itsuji Saranillio." *Critical Ethnic Studies* 3, no. 1 (2017): 90–115. https://doi.org/10.5749/jcritethnstud.3 .1.0090.

Statistiche Coronavirus. "Le statistiche del coronavirus in Italia," 2020. https:// statistichecoronavirus.it/coronavirus-italia/.

Stella, Emanuela. "'E' italiano chi nasce in Italia.' La Kyenge a Venezia per '18 ius soli.'" *La Repubblica*, August 25, 2013. http://www.repubblica.it/solidarieta/immigrazione /2013/08/25/news/italiano_chi_nasce_in_italia_kyenge_presenta_a_venezia_18 _ius_soli-65259182/.

Stevis, Matina, Joe Parkinson, and Nichole Sobecki. "Thousands Flee Isolated Eritrea to Escape Life of Conscription and Poverty." *Wall Street Journal*, February 2, 2016. http://www.wsj.com/articles/eritreans-flee-conscription-and-poverty-adding-to -the-migrant-crisis-in-europe-1445391364.

Stierl, Maurice. "Black Lives Are Being Lost in the Mediterranean—but the World Remains Silent." *The Conversation*, July 8, 2020. http://theconversation.com/black -lives-are-being-lost-in-the-mediterranean-but-the-world-remains-silent-14 1822.

——. "Contestations in Death—the Role of Grief in Migration Struggles." *Citizenship Studies* 20, no. 2 (2016): 173–91. https://doi.org/10.1080/13621025.2015.1132571.

——. "A Fleet of Mediterranean Border Humanitarians." *Antipode* 50, no. 3 (2018): 704– 24. https://doi.org/10.1111/anti.12320.

——. *Migrant Resistance in Contemporary Europe.* London: Routledge, 2018.

——. "Of Migrant Slaves and Underground Railroads—Movement, Containment, Freedom." *American Behavioral Scientist* 64, no. 4 (2020), https://doi.org/10.1177 /0002764219883006. 10.1177/.

——. "A Sea of Struggle—Activist Border Interventions in the Mediterranean Sea." *Citizenship Studies* 20, no. 5 (July 3, 2016): 561–78. https://doi.org/10.1080/13621025 .2016.1182683.

Stolcke, Verena. "Talking Culture: New Boundaries, New Rhetorics of Exclusion in Europe." *Current Anthropology* 36, no. 1 (February 1, 1995): 1–24. https://doi.org/10 .1086/204339.

Stoler, Ann Laura. *Carnal Knowledge and Imperial Power: Race and the Intimate in Colonial Rule.* Berkeley: University of California Press, 2002.

Stranieri in Italia. "Jerry Masslo, l'uomo che scoprì il razzismo in Italia." August 25, 2011. https://stranieriinitalia.it/attualita/jerry-masslo-luomo-che-scopri-il-razzismo -in-italia/.

——. "Viminale: 'Sbarchi calati dell'80% nel 2018.'" January 1, 2019. https://stranieriinitalia
    .it/attualita/attualita-sp-754/viminale-sbarchi-calati-dell-80-nel-2018/.
Strong, Krystal, and Shaun Ossei-Owusu. "Naija Boy Remix: Afroexploitation and the New
    Media Creative Economies of Cosmopolitan African Youth." *Journal of African Cul-
    tural Studies* 26, no. 2 (2014): 189–205. https://doi.org/10.1080/13696815.2013.861343.
Struggles in Italy. "Immigration Policies in Italy," July 11, 2012. https://strugglesinitaly
    .wordpress.com/equality/en-immigration-policies-in-italy/.
Summers, Brandi, Camilla Hawthorne, and Theresa Hice Fromille. "Black Geographies
    of Quarantine: A Dialogue with Brandi Summers, Camilla Hawthorne, and The-
    resa Hice Fromille." *UCHRI Foundry*, November 2020. https://uchri.org/foundry
    /black-geographies-of-quarantine-a-dialogue-with-brandi-summers-camilla
    -hawthorne-and-theresa-hice-fromille/.
Summers, Brandi Thompson. *Black in Place: The Spatial Aesthetics of Race in a Post-
    Chocolate City.* Chapel Hill: University of North Carolina Press Books, 2019.
Tabet, Paola. *La pelle giusta.* Turin: Einaudi, 1997.
Taguieff, Pierre-André. *La force du préjugé: Essai sur le racisme et ses doubles.* Paris: La
    Découverte, 1988.
Tailmoun, Mohamed Abdalla, Mauro Valeri, and Isaac Tesfaye. *Campioni d'Italia? Le
    seconde generazioni e lo sport.* Rome: Sinnos, 2014.
TallBear, Kim. *Native American DNA: Tribal Belonging and the False Promise of Genetic
    Science.* Minneapolis: University of Minnesota Press, 2013.
Tamburri, Anthony Julian. "Public Monuments and Indro Montanelli: A Case of Mis-
    directed Reverence?," *La Voce di New York* (blog), June 24, 2020. https://www
    .lavocedinewyork.com/en/news/2020/06/24/public-monuments-and-indro
    -montanelli-a-case-of-misdirected-reverence/.
Tate, Shirley Anne. *Black Beauty: Aesthetics, Stylization, Politics.* Abingdon, UK: Rout-
    ledge, 2016.
Taylor, Adam. "Why Italian Governments So Often End in Collapse." *Washington Post*,
    August 20, 2019. https://www.washingtonpost.com/world/2019/08/20/why-italian
    -governments-so-often-end-collapse/.
Taylor, Keeanga-Yamahtta. *How We Get Free: Black Feminism and the Combahee River
    Collective.* Chicago: Haymarket Books, 2017.
Tazzioli, Martina. "Spy, Track and Archive: The Temporality of Visibility in Eurosur and
    Jora." *Security Dialogue* 49, no. 4 (August 1, 2018): 272–88. https://doi.org/10.1177
    /0967010618769812.
Teti, Vito. *La razza maledetta: Origini del pregiudizio antimeridionale.* Rome: Manifes-
    tolibri, 2011.
Thomas, R. Eric. "Gucci's Diversity Drag." *New York Times*, April 17, 2017. https://www
    .nytimes.com/2017/04/17/fashion/gucci-black-models-diversity.html.
Thomassen, Bjørn. "'Second Generation Immigrants' or 'Italians with Immigrant Par-
    ents'? Italian and European Perspectives on Immigrants and Their Children." *Bul-
    letin of Italian Politics* 2, no. 1 (2010): 21–44.
Ticktin, Miriam Iris. *Casualties of Care: Immigration and the Politics of Humanitarian-
    ism in France.* Berkeley: University of California Press, 2011.
Tintori, Guido. "Ius Soli the Italian Way: The Long and Winding Road to Reform the
    Citizenship Law." *Contemporary Italian Politics* 10, no. 4 (November 27, 2018):
    434–50. https://doi.org/10.1080/23248823.2018.1544360.
——. "Naturalisation Procedures for Immigrants in Italy." European University Insti-
    tute. Florence: EUDO Citizenship Observatory, February 2013.
Triulzi, Alessandro. "Displacing the Colonial Event." *Interventions* 8, no. 3 (2006): 430–
    43. https://doi.org/10.1080/13698010600956055.

Trouillot, Michel-Rolph. "North Atlantic Universals: Analytical Fictions, 1492–1945." *The South Atlantic Quarterly* 101, no. 4 (2002): 839–58.

Trujillo-Pagán, Nicole. "A Tale of Four Cities: The Boundaries of Blackness for Ethiopian Immigrants in Washington, DC, Tel Aviv, Rome, and Melbourne." *Social Identities* 25, no. 1 (2019): 58–75. https://doi.org/10.1080/13504630.2017.1418601.

Tuttitalia.it. "Cittadini stranieri in Italia—2019." 2020. https://www.tuttitalia.it/statistiche /cittadini-stranieri-2019/.

Ugo, Ascoli, and Pavolini Emmanuele. *The Italian Welfare State in a European Perspective: A Comparative Analysis*. Bristol, UK: Policy Press, 2016.

United Nations High Commissioner for Refugees (UNCHR). "Italy: UNHCR Update #10." March 16, 2017. https://data2.unhcr.org/en/documents/details/53633.

——. "Mediterranean Situation." Operational Data Portal: Refugee Situations, 2020. https://data2.unhcr.org/en/situations/mediterranean.

UNCHR Bureau for Europe. "Desperate Journeys—January to April 2017." June 14, 2017. https://data2.unhcr.org/en/documents/details/57696.

UNESCO. "Four Statements on the Race Question." Paris: UNESCO, 1969. http:// refugeestudies.org/UNHCR/UNHCR.%20Four%20Statements%20on%20 the%20Race%20Question.pdf.

UISP Nazionale. "Sport e lotta a razzismo: L'Uisp nel nome di Jerry Masslo." Accessed October 14, 2020. http://www.uisp.it//nazionale/pagina/sport-e-lotta-a-razzismo -luisp-nel-nome-di-jerry-masslo.

Uva, Daniela. "Comunicato stampa: Immigrazione, una nuova chiave di lettura per la città globale. I candidati sindaci chiamati al confronto durante il convegno 'Il Welfare Ambrosiano e i Cittadini Globali.'" Press release, May 2, 2016. http://www .globusetlocus.org/agenda/il-welfare-ambrosiano-e-i-cittadini-globali.kl.

Vatican Radio. "Nigerian Man Beaten to Death in Racist Attack." July 7, 2016. http://en .radiovaticana.va/news/2016/07/07/nigerian_man_beaten_to_death_in_racist _attack/1242717.

Verdicchio, Pasquale. *Bound by Distance: Rethinking Nationalism through the Italian Diaspora*. Madison, NJ: Fairleigh Dickinson University Press, 1997.

——. "The Preclusion of Postcolonial Discourse in Southern Italy." In *Revisioning Italy: National Identity and Global Culture*, edited by Beverly Allen and Mary J. Russo, 191–212. Minneapolis: University of Minnesota Press, 1997.

Virdee, Satnam. "The Second Sight of Racialised Outsiders in the Imperialist Core." *Third World Quarterly* 38, no. 11 (November 2, 2017): 2396–410. https://doi.org/10.1080 /01436597.2017.1328274.

Virdee, Satnam, and Brendan McGeever. "Racism, Crisis, Brexit." *Ethnic and Racial Studies* 41, no. 10 (August 9, 2018): 1802–19. https://doi.org/10.1080/01419870.2017.1361544.

Visweswaran, Kamala. *Un/Common Cultures: Racism and the Rearticulation of Cultural Difference*. Durham, NC: Duke University Press, 2010.

Vita. "La diffusione del contagio nei centri d'accoglienza." November 5, 2020. http://www .vita.it/it/article/2020/11/05/la-diffusione-del-contagio-nei-centri-daccoglienza /157248/.

Walker, Susannah. "Black Is Profitable: The Commodification of the Afro, 1960–1975." *Enterprise & Society* 1, no. 3 (2000): 536–64.

Wanous, Malik. "Stay Human: A Diary, a Reminder of Palestine." *Arab Center for Research and Policy Studies* (blog), August 11, 2011. https://www.dohainstitute.org /en/ResearchAndStudies/Pages/Stay_Human_A_diary_a_reminder_of_Palest ine.aspx.

Ward, Deborah E. *The White Welfare State: The Racialization of U.S. Welfare Policy*. Ann Arbor: University of Michigan Press, 2009.

Weheliye, Alexander G. *Habeas Viscus: Racializing Assemblages, Biopolitics, and Black Feminist Theories of the Human*. Durham, NC: Duke University Press, 2014.

Weheliye, Alexander G., and Léopold Lambert. "Claiming Humanity: A Black Critique of the Concept of Bare Life." *The Funambulist*, July 28, 2014. https://thefunambulist .net/podcast/alexander-weheliye-claiming-humanity-a-black-critique-of-the -concept-of-bare-life.

Weil, Patrick. "Access to Citizenship: A Comparison of Twenty-Five Nationality Laws." In *Citizenship Today: Global Perspectives and Practices*, edited by T. Alexander Aleinikoff and Douglas Klusmeyer, 17–35. Washington, DC: Carnegie Endowment for International Peace, 2001.

Wekker, Gloria. "Another Dream of a Common Language: Imagining Black Europe. . . ." In *Black Europe and the African Diaspora*, edited by Darlene Clark Hine, Trica Danielle Keaton, and Stephen Small, 277–90. Urbana: University of Illinois Press, 2009.

——. *White Innocence: Paradoxes of Colonialism and Race*. Durham, NC: Duke University Press, 2016.

Welch, Rhiannon Noel. *Vital Subjects: Race and Biopolitics in Italy, 1860–1920*. Oxford: Oxford University Press, 2016.

Whitney, Candice. "Breaking Ground for Emerging Designers: Milan's First Afro Pop Shop Milano." *Women Change Africa* (blog), June 14, 2017. http://womenchangeafrica .blogspot.com/2017/06/breaking-ground-for-emerging-designers.html.

——. "Race, Culture and Colonial Legacy in Today's Italian Citizenship Struggles." *Kheiro Magazine*, June 20, 2017. https://kheiromag.com/race-culture-and-colonial-legacy -in-todays-italian-citizenship-struggles-27b6d9f9649f.

Williams, Thomas Chatterton. "The French Origins of 'You Will Not Replace Us.'" *New Yorker*, November 27, 2017. https://www.newyorker.com/magazine/2017/12/04/the -french-origins-of-you-will-not-replace-us.

Wimmer, Andreas, and Nina Glick Schiller. "Methodological Nationalism and the Study of Migration." *European Journal of Sociology / Archives Européennes de Sociologie / Europäisches Archiv für Soziologie* 43, no. 2 (2002): 217–40.

Winichakul, Thongchai. *Siam Mapped: A History of the Geo-Body of a Nation*. Honolulu: University of Hawai'i Press, 1997.

Wong, Aliza. *Race and the Nation in Liberal Italy, 1861–1911: Meridionalism, Empire, and Diaspora*. London: Palgrave Macmillan, 2006.

Wright, John. "Cats, Musk, Gold and Slaves: Staples of the Northbound Saharan Trade." *The Journal of North African Studies* 16, no. 3 (September 1, 2011): 415–20. https:// doi.org/10.1080/13629387.2010.492156.

Wright, Michelle M. "Finding a Place in Cyberspace: Black Women, Technology, and Identity." *Frontiers: A Journal of Women Studies* 26, no. 1 (2005): 48–59. https:// doi.org/10.1353/fro.2005.0017.

——. *Physics of Blackness: Beyond the Middle Passage Epistemology*. Minneapolis: University of Minnesota Press, 2015.

——. "Postwar Blackness and the World of Europe." *Österreichisches Zeitschrift für Geschichtswissenschaften* 17, no. 2 (2006): 139–48.

Yanagisako, Sylvia Junko. *Producing Culture and Capital: Family Firms in Italy*. Princeton, NJ: Princeton University Press, 2002.

——. "Transnational Family Capitalism: Producing 'Made in Italy' in China." In *Vital Relations: Modernity and the Persistent Life of Kinship*, edited by Susan McKinnon and Fenella Cannell, 63–84. Santa Fe, NM: School for Advanced Research Press, 2013.

Yngvesson, Barbara. "Migrant Bodies and the Materialization of Belonging in Sweden." *Social & Cultural Geography* 16, no. 5 (2015): 536–51. https://doi.org/10.1080/14649365.2015.1009856.

Young, Robert J. C. *Colonial Desire: Hybridity in Theory, Culture and Race.* London: Routledge, 2005.

——. "The Italian Postcolonial." In *Postcolonial Italy: Challenging National Homogeneity,* edited by Cristina Lombardi-Diop and Caterina Romeo, 31–34. New York: Palgrave Macmillan, 2012.

Yuval-Davis, Nira. *Gender and Nation.* 1997. Reprint, London: SAGE, 1997.

Zack, Naomi. *Philosophy of Science and Race.* London: Routledge, 2014.

Zhang, Gaoheng. *Migration and the Media: Debating Chinese Migration to Italy, 1992–2012.* Toronto: University of Toronto Press, 2019.

Zimmerman, Arely M. "Contesting Citizenship from Below: Central Americans and the Struggle for Inclusion." *Latino Studies* 13, no. 1 (March 1, 2015): 28–43. https://doi.org/10.1057/lst.2014.71.

Zincone, Giovanna, and Marzia Basili. "Country Report: Italy." EUDO Citizenship Observatory. Florence: European University Institute, 2013.

Zinn, Dorothy Louise. "Italy's Second Generations and the Expression of Identity through Electronic Media." *Bulletin of Italian Politics* 2, no. 1 (2010): 91–113.

——. "'Loud and Clear': The G2 Second Generations Network in Italy." *Journal of Modern Italian Studies* 16, no. 3 (2011): 373–85. https://doi.org/10.1080/1354571X.2011.565640.

Index

Page references in *italics* refer to illustrative material.

Printed in the USA
CPSIA information can be obtained
at www.ICGtesting.com
CBHW032352030824
12677CB00006B/217

9 781501 762291